Phonics and Reading

3

Teacher's Guide

Author/Editor:
Rachelle Wiersma, M.A.

Managing Editor:
Alan Christopherson, M.S.

Graphic Designer:
Rob Haan

Copy Editors:
Laura Messner
Pamela Ufen
Anita Lanning

Illustrator:
Anthony Kuhlmann

 AOP   804 N. 2nd Ave. E • Rock Rapids, IA 51246-1759
800-622-3070 • www.aop.com

Printed in the United States of America

ISBN 978-0-7403-2549-6

Phonics and Reading 3

Teacher's Guide

Contents

Introduction

Introduction

Horizons Phonics and Reading Grade 3 is another addition to the exciting and innovative Horizons curriculum line. Like the other Horizons materials, there are 160 lessons and 16 tests contained in the two student workbooks. An extensive Teacher's Guide provides plenty of tips and teaching strategies. A reduced student page is included in the Teacher's Guide, along with the instructions and information the teacher will need for the lesson.

The phonics and reading program has three major components: **The Student Workbooks**, **The Readers**, and **The Teacher's Guide**. The three components work together to help the student develop skills in phonics, spelling, and reading.

Curriculum Overview

Horizons Phonics and Reading Grade 3 is a complete, explicit, phonetically based word recognition and reading program. There is a strong emphasis placed on decoding and fluency skills. Students learn to identify the name and sounds of letters and phonemes through picture association and spelling/phonics rules. Dolch sight words are incorporated so that fluency spans the subject areas. Much emphasis is placed on the following: fluency, decoding, spelling, auditory skills, vocabulary development, alphabetizing, rhyming, diacritical marks, syllabication, accents, compound words, affixes, contractions.

There are several activities associated with each skill. The teacher can choose to expand on the skill by utilizing the accumulation of words for each segment. Skill presentation in *Horizons Phonics and Reading Grade 3* follows a three-step process: initial presentation, review a few lessons later, reinforcement of the skill through a sequentially developing vocabulary which allows previous concepts to be utilized in the practice of new. After every tenth lesson, the student is tested to evaluate his or her mastery for the skills presented.

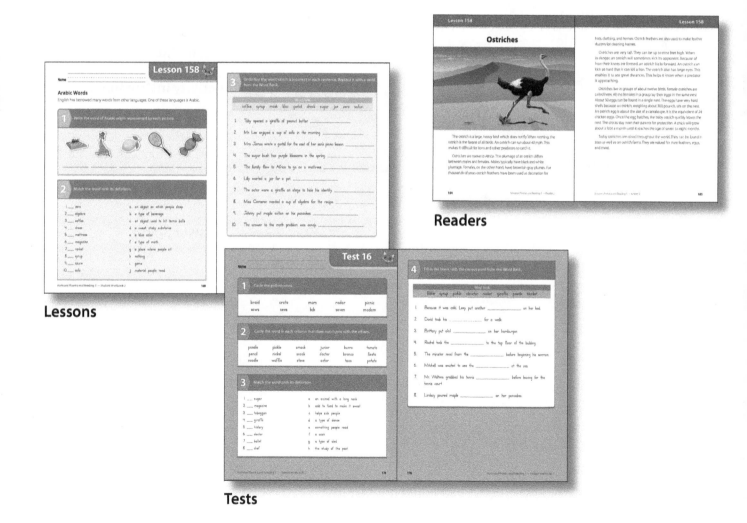

Readers

Lessons

Tests

The Student Workbooks

The *Horizons Phonics and Reading Grade 3 Workbooks* are divided into Student Workbook 1 and Student Workbook 2. Workbook 1 contains Lessons 1-80 along with a test after every ten lessons. Workbook 2 contains Lessons 81-160 along with a test after every ten lessons. The workbook sheets reinforce the material presented in the teacher's edition. The student should not be asked to complete the activity sheet until the material for it is presented.

The student workbooks have perforated pages so the lesson sheets can be removed from the book for the student. Removing the pages is essential to promoting good penmanship. It will be impossible for the student to write neatly on the pages if they are only folded back on the binding of the book. After the lesson pages have been completed, they can be punched and stored in a 3-ring binder. Completed lessons can be used for drill, review, and preparation for the test.

Name Blank
Lesson Title

Perforated Edges

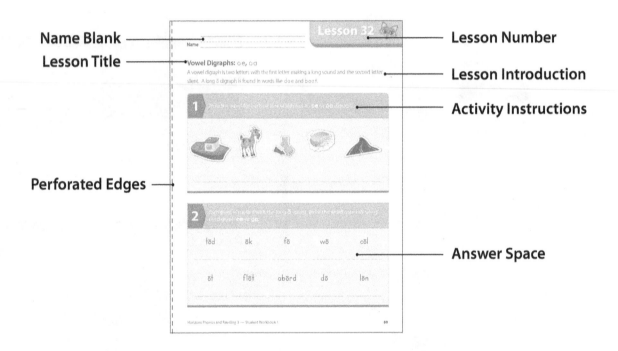

Lesson Number
Lesson Introduction
Activity Instructions

Answer Space

The Readers

The Horizons Phonics and Reading Grade 3 Readers serve as a companion to the workbooks. Like the workbooks, they are divided into two books. *Reader 1, The Frog Prince* contains stories, poems and readings which correspond with the first 80 lessons. *Reader 2, Puss and Boots* contains selections which correspond with the second 80 lessons. Selections may correspond with one or more lessons. The tenth lesson in a unit has a selection which is meant to be read for enjoyment. No discussion questions or detailed lesson ideas will be given for this selection.

Selections were chosen which appeal to a variety of interests. Some students may appreciate the factual essays while others the poetry. Still others may enjoy the humorous stories. Selections were chosen which also fit the Grade 3 reading level and the phonics skills which are taught. Additional attention was paid to the quality of selections chosen. Many pieces included are considered great pieces of children' literature. It is important for children to interact with and appreciate classic literature. Some of the authors students will encounter include Rudyard Kipling, the brothers Grimm, and Beatrix Potter. Selections were also chosen which spoke of the faith of men and women who followed Christ. In this way, readers can learn more about what it means to be a Christian. Others provide the student information about people who made historical contributions.

Additionally the student will be introduced to a variety of literary genres. The student will be asked to read selections of poetry, fiction, and non-fiction. Non-fiction selections in each unit will give the student insights into animals and people.

Some reading selections will serve as introductions to others. Before reading the selection *Rikki-Tikki-Tavi* the student will learn about the animals which are featured in the story. The student will discover the characteristics of both a mongoose and king cobra.

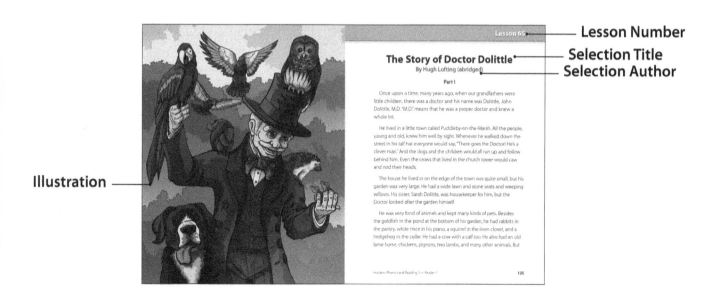

Illustration

Lesson Number

Selection Title

Selection Author

The Teacher's Guide

The Horizons Phonics and Reading Grade 3 Teacher's Guide is the third component of the program. The guide provides instructions on how to present each of the 160 lessons. Typically one lesson should be taught each day of the school year. Prepare for each day by carefully reviewing the material provided in the *Teacher's Guide*. The **Lesson Number** enables you to quickly reference and find the materials that are provided in the different components of the curriculum. The **Lesson Title** highlights the general topic or topics that will be covered in the lesson. The **Overview** is a summary of the concepts and activities that will be covered in the lesson. The **Materials and Supplies** is a list of what will be needed for the lesson. Get these items assembled before starting class with the students. The **Teaching Tips** are classroom teaching procedures that give special instructions for reviewing previous lessons and each activity of the current lesson. Take your time in going over these procedures. Thoroughly think through what you will say and do so that you have a plan in your mind before teaching the lesson to the student. The **Answer Keys** are reduced student pages with answers. These pages allow you to have both the **Teacher Notes** and the **Student Pages** in front of you as you teach the lesson. The **Reading** section has both some general tips for the reading time and some comprehension and discussion questions for each selection.

The student is to complete the activities after you have gone over the instructions, discussed the pictures, and reviewed the words. Allow sufficient time for the student to do each activity before going on to the next. Compliment and encourage the student as he/she works. The material in this guide has been written in the sense of a singular student. We are fully aware that this material will be used both for an individual student and for classrooms with many students. This choice has streamlined the writing in this text.

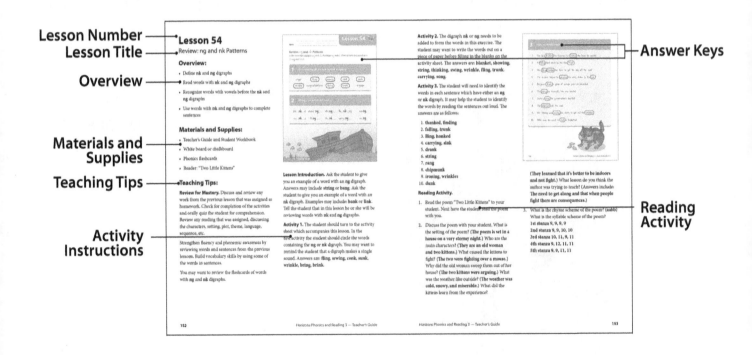

Homework

All lessons are presented in a two-page format. Work that is not completed during the scheduled class and seatwork time can be assigned as homework. Some of the lessons might be difficult to complete during the scheduled class time. These activities can be completed during seatwork time or sent home as homework. If the lesson sheet is sent home every day for the parent to review, he/she will get into the habit of checking for incomplete work that needs to be finished at home. Not all of the activities can be done independently, but some can be started during the class time and completed later.

The Daily Schedule

5	minutes	Review homework and previous lesson(s)
3-5	minutes	Drill difficult words, phonics, and spelling rules
15-20	minutes	Review the instructions for each activity and give the student time to complete them.
1-2	minutes	Review the rules and concepts taught in the lesson
15-20	minutes	Read and discuss the story, poem, and/or essay for the lesson

Lesson List

This section of the Teacher's Guide lists the individual lessons, the primary topics that will be covered, and the reading selections. At a glance it tells where one is, where one has been, and where on is going. A concise summary of this information is given in the Horizons Phonics and Reading 3 Scope and Sequence.

Phonics and Spelling Rules

This section of the Teacher's Guide lists the phonics and spelling rules that are presented in an ongoing basis through the lessons. Make a set of flashcards for these rules that can be used for instruction and review. Each rule has been given a name for identification. The name and a shortened version for the rule can be placed on the flashcard with a few example words. The rules involve not only pronunciation but also spelling and can be used to enhance the spelling program used for the student.

Horizons Phonics and Reading 3 Lesson List

Lesson 1
Short Vowel Sounds: ă, ĕ, ĭ, ŏ, and ŭ
The Howler Monkey

Lesson 2
Long Vowel Sounds: ā, ē, ī, ō, and ū
The Howler Monkey

Lesson 3
Long and Short Vowel Sounds: ā,
ē, ī, ō, ū, ă, ĕ, ĭ, ŏ, and ŭ
Sir Edmund Hillary

Lesson 4
Short Vowel ă and Syllables
Sir Edmund Hillary

Lesson 5
Short Vowel ĕ and Syllables
Sir Edmund Hillary

Lesson 6
Short Vowel ĭ and Pronunciation Markings
Slow and Steady

Lesson 7
Short Vowel ŏ and Pronunciation Markings
Slow and Steady

Lesson 8
Short Vowel ŭ and Pronunciation Markings
Slow and Steady

Lesson 9
Y as a vowel
Slow and Steady

Lesson 10
Review
The Tale of Peter Rabbit

Test 1
Lessons 1-10

Lesson 11
Initial Consonant Blends: br, cr, dr, fr, gr, pr, tr
The Ant and the Grasshopper

Lesson 12
Initial Consonant Blends: bl, cl, fl, gl, pl, sl
The Ant and the Grasshopper

Lesson 13
Initial Consonant Blends: tw, sc,
sk, sm, sn, sp, st, sw
John Newton, Amazing Grace

Lesson 14
Triple Consonant Blends: spl, scr, spr, str
John Newton, Amazing Grace

Lesson 15
Final Consonant Blends: nt, ct, ft, pt, lt
John Newton, Amazing Grace

Lesson 16
Final Consonant Blends: lk, lf, lp, lm, mp, nd
John Newton, Amazing Grace

Lesson 17
Initial and Final Consonant Blends
The Pink River Dolphin

Lesson 18
Consonant Digraphs: ch, th, ph, wh, sh, gh
The Pink River Dolphin

Lesson 19
Consonant Digraphs: gn, wr, tch, ck
The Pink River Dolphin

Lesson 20
Review
The Princess Who Slept On A Pea

Test 2
Lessons 11-20

Lesson 21
Vowel Digraphs: ai, ay
The Frog Prince: Part I

Lesson 22
Vowel Digraphs: ei, ie
The Frog Prince: Part II

Lesson 23
Vowel Digraphs: ee, ea, ey
The Frog Prince

Lesson 24
Vowel Diphthongs: ew, ow
Jackie Robinson

Lesson 25
Vowel Diphthongs: oi, oy, ou
Jackie Robinson

Lesson 26
Wild Colt Endings: old, ild, olt, ost, ind, oll
The Star-Nosed Mole

Lesson 27
Schwa Sound
The Star-Nosed Mole

Lesson 28
Final schwa Sound followed by l, r
My Shadow

Lesson 29
Long Vowels a and i spelled eigh and igh
My Shadow

Lesson 30
Review
The Search for a Good Child

Test 3
Lessons 21-30

Lesson 31
Vowel Diphthongs: au, oo
The Happy Prince: Part I

Lesson 32
Vowel Digraphs: oe, oa
The Happy Prince: Part II

Lesson 33
Review: Vowel Diphthongs and Digraphs
The Happy Prince

Lesson 34
Soft and Hard c sounds
The Alpaca

Lesson 35
Soft and Hard g sounds
The Wind and the Sun

Lesson 36
Endings: age and dge
How the Leaves Came Down

Lesson 37
Sounds of s: /s/, /z/, /zh/
How the Leaves Came Down

Lesson 38
Spelling /k/: c, k, ck, ch
Mother Teresa

Lesson 39
Words with qu
Mother Teresa

Lesson 40
Review
Casey at the Bat

Test 4
Lessons 31-40

Horizons Phonics and Reading 3
Scope and Sequence

Lessons 1-30

- Short and Long Vowel Sounds: ă, ĕ, ĭ, ŏ, ŭ, ā, ē, ī, ō, ū
- Pronunciation Markings
- Y as a vowel
- Consonant Blends: br, cr, dr, fr, gr, pr, tr, bl, cl, fl, gl, pl, sl
- Consonant Blends: tw, sc, sk, sm, sn, sp, st, sw
- Triple Consonant Blends: spl, scr, spr, str
- Final Consonant Blends: nt, ct, ft, pt, lt, lk, lf, lp, lm, mp, nd
- Consonant Digraphs: ch, th, ph, wh, sh, gh, gn, wr, tch, ck
- Vowel Digraphs: ai, ay, ei, ie, ee, ea, ey
- Vowel Diphthongs: ew, ow, oi, oy, ou
- Wild Colt Endings: old, ild, olt, ost, ind, oll
- Schwa Sound
- Final Schwa Sound followed by l, r
- Long Vowels a and i spelled eigh and igh

Lessons 31-60

- Vowel Diphthongs: au, oo
- Vowel Digraphs: oe, oa
- Soft and Hard c sounds
- Soft and Hard g sounds
- Endings: age, dge
- Sounds of s: /s/, /z/, /zh/
- Spelling /k/: c, k, ck, ch
- Words with qu
- R-controlled vowels: ar, ir, er, or, ur, are, air, ear, eer
- Final e: a_e, e_e, i_e, o_e, u_e
- Patterns with ng: ang, eng, ing, ong, ung
- Patterns with nk: ank, enk, ink, onk, unk
- Regular Plurals: adding s, es
- Irregular Plurals: f-v, y-i, no change and great change

Lessons 61- 90

- Rhyming Words: Regular Spelling
- Rhyming Words: Irregular Spelling
- Antonyms
- Synonyms
- Homonyms
- Homographs
- Analogies: parts of a whole, size/degree, category/type, synonyms/antonyms, function/use, grammar
- Contractions with not, would, will, am, had, have, has, is, are, did, could
- Triple Consonant Blends: tch, nch, rch, nth, rth, mpt
- Spelling Adjacent Clusters: rk, rm, rn, rt
- Silent Letters: mb, bt, rh, kn, mn, nge, pse, mpse, nce, ture
- Consonant le syllables: ble, dle, fle, ple, sle, tle, zle, gle, cle, ckle, kle

Lessons 91-120

- CVC Pattern
- CVCe Pattern
- CV and VCC Patterns
- CV/CVC or CVC/VC Patterns
- V/V Pattern
- CVC/CVC Patterns
- CVC/CVC/CVC and CVC/CVC/VC Patterns
- CVC/V/CVC and VC/CVC/CVCC Patterns
- Spelling Words Ending in eer and ation
- Regular Past Tense Verbs
- Irregular Past Tense Verbs
- Root words: ject, duc, duct, tract, spect, scribe, pose, pel, port
- Prefixes: un, re, pre, in, im, il, ir, co, com, con, ex, non, dis, mid, semi, uni, bi, tri, multi, ab, ad, de, over, super, sub, mis, pro, under
- Prefix Combinations

Lessons 121-160

- Suffixes: y, ly, er, ous, ness, ful, able, ment, ance, ion, ist, ish, en, ern, ism, ive, less, dom, hood, teen, ship, like, age
- Combining Prefixes and Suffixes
- Words with Double Consonants: bb, dd, ff, ll, mm, nn, pp, rr, ss, tt, zz
- Double Consonant Endings: ll, dd, ff, ss
- Regular Comparisons: er, est
- Irregular Comparisons
- Inflected Endings: ed, ing, s, es
- Compound Words
- Hyphenated and Open Compound Words
- Clipped Words
- Articles: a/an
- Commonly Confused Words
- Palindromes
- French Words
- Dutch Words
- Greek Words
- German Words
- Latin Words
- Spanish Words
- Arabic Words
- Native American Words

Phonics and Spelling Rules

The 1-1-1 Rule:

Words of one syllable (hop), having one vowel followed by one consonant, need another final consonant (hop + ped) before adding endings that begin with a vowel. This rule does not apply to words with x since x has two sounds /ks/.

Affix Syllable Rule:

The first step in dividing a word into syllables is to check the word for prefixes or suffixes. Prefix/Root/Suffix. When a word has an affix, it is divided between the root and the affix as in mud'/dy and rob'/ber.

Alphabetical Order Rule:

To put a group of words in ABC order, first read all the words. Next, look at the first letter of each word. If the first letters are the same, you should look at the second letter. If those are both the same, go to the third letter, and so on. Finally, put the words in ABC order.

Analogy:

Analogies are comparisons of two word pairs created to show how the pairs relate to one another. They come in many different types. These include synonyms, antonyms, similar, opposite, function, and grammar.

Antonym Rule:

An antonym is a word that means the opposite of another, as in hot – cold.

Articles:

The words a and an are articles. Use the article a before words which make a consonant sound. Use the article an before words which make vowel sounds.

Change f to v Rule:

When a word ends in f or fe, change the f to a v and add es to make the word plural as in leaf/leaves, elf/elves, and wife/wives.

Some nouns ending in f or fe do not change their endings to -ves to make the word plural as in cliff/cliffs and safe/safes.

Some nouns ending in f or fe may or may not change their endings to -ves to make the word plural as in dwarf/dwarfs/dwarves.

Change y to i Rule:

When -er or -est is added to a root word ending in y after a consonant, change the y to i before adding the suffix as in pretty/prettier/prettiest and busy/busier/busiest.

Commonly Confused Words:

Some words are confusing because they sound like other words. Their meanings and spellings are different. Examples include the words desert and dessert.

Comparative Suffix -er Rule:

The suffix -er is used to compare two things as in "His pig is fatter than mine" (comparing two things).

Comparative Suffix -est Rule:

The suffix -est is used to compare more than two things as in "His pigs are the fattest of all" (comparing more than two things).

Compound Words:

When two words are joined together to form one word, the new word is called a compound word. Examples include the words toothbrush, eyelash, and cupcake.

Consonant Blend Rule:

A consonant blend consists of two or more consonants sounded together in such a way that each letter is heard. Their sounds blend together, but each sound is heard as in green, frog, tree, drip, bride.

> chr rule: In words the consonant blend chr- has the sound kr: Chris, chrome

> sch rule: In some words the consonant blend sch- has the sound sk as in school or scheme.

Compound Word Syllable Rule:

A compound word is a word made from two or more words joined together to make one word. The words that make up a compound word are spelled completely and keep their usual spelling as in cowboy, everybody, spaceman, sidewalk, and bedroom. Most compound words are accented on the first word.

Consonant Digraph Rule:

A consonant digraph is two consonants that stay together to make their special sound.

> ch rule: Consonant digraph ch can be used at the beginning or end of a word as in chin, such, sandwich.

> ck rule: In consonant digraph ck, the k is pronounced and the c is silent as in dock and peck.

> gm rule: In consonant digraph gm, the g is silent and the m is pronounced as in diaphragm.

> lm rule: In consonant digraph lm, the l is silent and the m is pronounced as in calm.

> kn rule: In consonant digraph kn, the k is silent and n is pronounced as in knife and knot.

> mb rule: In consonant digraph mb, the b is silent and the m is pronounced as in lamb.

> mn rule: In consonant digraph mn, the n is silent and the m is pronounced as in column.

> ng rule: In consonant digraph ng, the ng makes a blend of the ng sound as in sing and rung.

> ps rule: The s sound is spelled ps as in psalm and psychology.

> sc rule: In the sc consonant digraph before e, i, or y, the c is silent and the s is pronounced as in scene and science.

> sh rule: Consonant digraph sh can be used at the beginning or end of a word as in shed and hash.

sw rule: The s sound is spelled sw as in sword and answer.

tch rule: Consonant digraph tch makes the sound you hear in watch and itch. Use ch at the beginning of a word or after a consonant. Use tch at the end of a word after a short vowel.

th rule: Consonant digraph th can be used at the beginning, middle, or end of a word as in thank, this, athlete, brother, path, and soothe. To determine if th is soft or hard, place three fingers over your throat and say the word. If you feel vibrations when pronouncing the th, then the th is hard.

wh rule: The h sound is spelled wh as in whole and who.

wr rule: In consonant digraph wr, the w is silent and the r is pronounced as in wrong and write.

Consonant Doubling Rule:

When two consonants are the same in the middle of a word, they are called double medial consonants. To divide the word into syllables, break the word between the double consonants. Double consonant letters do not normally follow long vowels and do not follow non-simple vowels. A double consonant is pronounced singly.

Letters that double: b c d f g l m n p r s t v z

Letters that do not double: h j k q w x y

If a word with a short vowel sound ends in a single consonant, usually double the consonant before adding a suffix that begins with a vowel as in tag/tagged/tagging, run/running, and dig/digging.

Contraction Rule:

A contraction is a word that is made from two words.

am rule: In the contraction formed with the word am, the a is removed and replaced with an apostrophe (') as in I + am = I'm.

are rule: In contractions formed with the word are, the a is removed and replaced with an apostrophe (') as in you + are = you're and they + are = they're.

have, has, and had rule: In contractions formed with the word have, has, and had, the ha is removed and replaced with an apostrophe (') as in I + have = I've, he + has = he's, and I + had = I'd.

is rule: In contractions formed with the word is, the i is removed and replaced with an apostrophe (') as in he + is = he's and she + is = she's.

not rule: In contractions formed with the word not, an apostrophe (') is used in place of the letters that are left out as in cannot = can't and could + not = couldn't.

shall rule: In contractions formed with the word shall, the sha is removed and replaced with an apostrophe (') as in he + shall = he'll and she + shall = she'll.

us rule: In contractions formed with the word us, the u is removed and replaced with an apostrophe (') as in let + us = let's.

will rule: In contractions formed with the word will, an apostrophe (') is used in place of the letters that are left out as in we + will = we'll and I + will = I'll.

would rule: In contractions formed with the word would, the woul is removed and replaced with an apostrophe (') as in she + would = she'd.

CVopen Rule:

An open, accented vowel is long; code it with a macron. A macron is a line (ˉ) placed over the long vowel. Examples of words following this rule: no, me, so, we, go, and hi.

Dge and ge Spelling Rule:

Words that end with the sound of /j/ are spelled with -dge or -ge. Use the letters -dge after short vowels as in bridge, fudge, and badge. Use -ge after anything else as in cage, lounge, and page.

Digraph:

A digraph is a two letter combination which makes a single sound.

du Rule: When d is followed by u in some words, it has the sound of j as in education.

ex Rule: The digraph ex has several sounds: ek as in excel and excite, ek-s as in extra and extend, ek-z as in exact and exist, and eks as in exhale and exchange.

gu Rule: When the letter g is followed by u, the g makes a hard sound and the u is silent as in guard and guest. The u is not considered a vowel here.

qu Rule: The letters qu make the /kw/ sound that you hear in queen and quick. The letters qu always appear together.

Diphthong Rule:

A diphthong is two vowel sounds that come together so fast that they are considered one syllable. Examples: ew, oi and oy, ou and ow.

ew rule: The diphthong ew makes the sound you hear in new and chew. Diphthongs are coded with an arc under the letters.

oi & oy rule: The diphthongs oi and oy make the sounds you hear in coin and boy. Diphthongs are coded with an arc under the letters.

ou & ow rule: The diphthongs ou and ow make the sounds you hear in out and how. Diphthongs are coded with an arc under the letters.

Doubling Rule:

When -er or -est is added to some root words that end with one vowel and one consonant, the final consonant is doubled before adding the suffix as in glad/gladder/gladdest.

Drop e Rule:

When the ending -er or -est is added to words ending in final e, the final e is dropped as in fine/finer/finest and brave/braver/bravest. Drop the e before adding a suffix that begins with a vowel such as -ing or -ed as in bake/baking/baked and slice/slicing/sliced.

Drop e Suffix Rule:

A word that ends in e usually drops the e when adding a suffix beginning with a vowel as in move/movable, force/forcible, and rise/risen.

Final Consonant Blends Rule:

The ending consonant blends mp, nk nc, nd, and rd work together to make the sounds you hear in camp, bank, zinc, send, and bird. The ending consonant blends sk, sp, and ng work together to make the sounds you hear in dusk, wasp, and ring.

> dge Rule: The phonogram dge may be used only after a single vowel that says its short sound as in badge, edge, bridge, lodge, budge.

> l Rule: The ending consonant blends lb, ld, lf, lk, lm, and lp work together to make the sounds you hear in bulb, held, golf, silk, film, and gulp.

> ng Rule: The /ng/ is a sound that you make in your throat. When you see an ng in a word, you do not say the /n/ sound and the /g/ sound separately. The sound is made at the back of your throat.

> t Rule: The ending consonant blends ct, ft, lt, nt, pt, rt, st, and xt work together to make the sounds you hear in fact, left, belt, cent, kept, dirt, best, and next.

Final Consonant Doubling Rule: (Twin Consonant Endings Rule)

The letters f, l, s, and z are usually doubled in a one-syllable word that has one vowel followed by only one consonant sound as in muff, stuff, ball, hill, class, kiss, buzz, and fizz. Twin consonants in words are usually treated as a single letter.

Final e Rule:

When a syllable ends in a silent e, the silent e is a signal that the vowel in front of it is long as in make, Pete, kite, rope, and use.

Final k Rule:

In a one-syllable, short vowel word ending with the /k/ sound, the letters ck are used for correct spelling as in duck and rock.

Final le Syllable Rule:

When you have a word that has the old-style spelling in which the -le sounds like -el, divide before the consonant before the -le. For example: a/ble, fum/ble, rub/ble, mum/ble, and thi/stle. The only exceptions to this are ckle words like tick/le.

Final Long Vowel Digraph ie Rule:

The long e vowel digraph ie says long e at the end of a word as in movie.

> i Before e Except After c Rule: When the sound is long e, write ie except after c. When the sound is other than long e, usually write ei. There are always exceptions as in either, seize, and sheik.

> ey Rule: Sometimes ey at the end of a word can make the long e sound as in key.

> ie Rule: The long i vowel digraph ie says long i at the end of a word as in pie and tie.

Final s Rule:

Sometimes s at the end of a word has the sound of /z/ as in was and has.

Final Stable Syllable Rule:

A Final Stable Syllable is a syllable that occurs at the end of a word frequently enough to be considered stable. The final stable syllable is coded first with a bracket (code the e silent) and then code the first syllable of the word. [ble table, [cle uncle, [dle candle, [fle ruffle, [gle goggle, [kle tinkle, [ple staple, [sle hassle, [tle battle, [zle puzzle.

Final Trigraph tch Rule:

Three letters that come together to make one vowel or consonant sound are called trigraphs. They are underlined and some letters are marked silent. The trigraph tch makes the /ch/ sound at the end of a word and comes after a short vowel as in catch and stretch. Mark the t silent.

Final x Rule:

When x comes at the end of a word, it usually is pronounced /ks/ as in box and fox.

Final y Rule:

Sometimes y can make the long e or i sound. The y is usually at the end of the word when it makes the long e or i sound as in bunny and fly.

Hard c or g Rule:

When c or g is followed by a, u, or o, or a consonant, it makes the hard sound.

Homograph Rule:

Homographs are words that are spelled the same, although perhaps pronounced differently as in read/read. Example: We can read the book that we read yesterday.

Homophone or Homonym Rule:

Homophones or homonyms are words that sound the same but have different spellings and different meanings, as in beet/beat, weak/week, and knows/nose.

Initial Consonant Blends

Two consonants can blend together at the beginning of a word to make the sounds you hear in blip, frog, swim, and stem.

with l Rule: The beginning consonant blends bl, cl, fl, gl, pl, and sl work together to make the sounds you hear in blip, clef, flat, glob, plus, and slim.

with r Rule: The beginning consonant blends br, tr, fr, pr, dr, cr, and gr work together to make the sounds you hear in bread, trip, frog, pride, drip, crab, and grim.

with s Rule: The beginning consonant blends sc, sl, sm, sn, sp, st, and sw work together to make the sounds you hear in scum, slop, smog, snob, spit, stem, and swim.

with w Rule: The beginning consonant blends dw, gw, sw, and tw work together to make the sounds you hear in dwelt, Gwen, swing, and twin.

Initial Consonant Digraph rh Rule:
In consonant digraph rh at the beginning of a word, the h is silent and r is pronounced as in rhino and rhyme.

Initial k Rule:
There are two ways to spell the /k/ sound at the beginning of a word.

Spell the /k/ sound with k if the sound comes before e, i, or y as in key, king, and Kyle.

Spell the /k/ sound with a c if the sound comes before a, o, u, or any consonant as in call, come, curb, and cross.

Initial Short Vowel Rule:
The vowels a, e, i, o, and u usually say the short sound when followed by a consonant before the end of a syllable as in at, end, in, odd, and up.

Initial x Rule:
When x comes at the beginning of a word, it often makes the /z/ sound as in xylophone. Very few English words begin with the letter x.

Irregular Plurals Rule:
Some plurals are irregular and no rule can be made for them. Some add letters as in child and children. Some change internal letters as in tooth/teeth.

Some plurals are irregular and no rule can be made for them. Some do not change as in sheep/sheep, moose/moose, deer/deer.

Letter u Rule:
The letter u can have either the long oo or the short oo sound as in tune, ruby, pull, and put.

Long i as igh Rule:
Usually when i is followed by gh , the i is long and the gh is silent. Examples: light and night.

Long Vowel Digraph Rule:

A vowel digraph is two letters with the first letter making a long sound and the second letter being silent. We call this "The first one does the talking, the second keeps on walking." Examples: ee/sheep, ay/may, ai/paint.

> Long Vowel e Digraph Rule: Long e vowel digraphs are ee (sheep, see), ea (leaf, meat), ey (key, money), ie (shield, field), and ei (receipt).

> Long Vowel ei, ey, and ea Digraphs Rule: The vowel digraphs ei, ey, and ea make the long a sound you hear in vein, they, and great.

> Long Vowel Digraph eigh Rule: The vowel combination eigh makes the long a sound you hear in weigh.

> Long Vowel ew, ue, and ui Digraph Rule: The vowel digraphs ew, ue, and ui form a single long u vowel sound as in statue, tissue, blew, threw, suit, and juice.

> Long Vowel ou, ue, and ui Rule: The vowel digraphs ou, ue, and ui form a single long oo sound as in soup, group, statue, tissue, suit, and juice.

Long Vowel Open Syllable Rule:

Vowels a, e, o, and u usually say their names/long sounds at the end of a syllable (navy, me, open, music). These are referred to as open syllables.

Long Vowel Spelling Rule:

Note these common spelling patterns: the spelling a_e is always split as in gate; i_e, o_e, and u_e are very often split as in fine, tone, cute; and ee is rarely split as in feet.

Long Vowel u Rule:

In some words u has the long yoo sound as in unit and music.

Ough as Long oo Rule:

In some words the long oo sound is spelled ough as in through.

Oul as Short oo Rule:

In some words the short oo sound is spelled oul as in should.

Palindrome:

Palindromes are words that are spelled the same forward and backward. An example would be the word did.

Plural Possessive Nouns Rule:

Place an apostrophe after plural nouns ending in s to show possession as in boys/boys' and students/students'. If the plural noun does not end in s, add an apostrophe and s to show possession as in children/children's and men/men's.

Plurals with -es Rule:

If a word ends in -s, -sh, -ch, -x, or -z, the plural is made by adding -es and has the /iz/ sound.

If a words ends in a consonant followed by -o, the plural is formed by adding -es and has the /z/ sound.

Plurals with -s Rule:

The plural form of most nouns is made by adding -s to the end of a word.

If a words ends in a vowel followed by -y, the plural is formed by adding -s. The plurals of most nouns ending with -f, -fe, or -ff are formed by adding -s.

If a word ends in a vowel followed by -o, the plural is formed by adding -s and has the /z/ sound.

Plurals with y Rule:

Words (nouns) ending in y preceded by a vowel keep the y and add -s to form the plural as in boy/boys, monkey/monkeys, and turkey/turkeys.

When a word ends in y after a consonant, usually change the y to an i before adding -es as in bunny/bunnies, city/cities, try/tries, and carry/carries.

Prefix:

A prefix is a word element which can be placed in front of a word to change its meaning. A prefix is always a separate syllable in a word as in re-, un-, dis-, pre-, mis-, and non-.

dis- Rule: The prefix dis- usually means not, no, the opposite, as in dishonest and disrepair.

non- Rule:The prefix non- usually means not, no, other than, as in nonfat and nonfrozen.

mis- Rule: The prefix mis- usually means bad, badly, wrong, lack, as in misadd and miscolor.

pre- Rule: The prefix pre- usually means before, in front of, as in prebake and prescreen.

re- Rule: The prefix re- usually means to do again as in redo and repack.

un- Rule: The prefix un- usually means not, the opposite, as in unstrung, undress, and unlock.

R-Controlled Vowel Rule:

When a vowel is followed by an r in the same syllable, that vowel is R-controlled. It is neither long nor short. In an R-controlled vowel, an r after the vowel makes the vowel sound different from a short or long sound. Examples: st<u>ar</u>, shi<u>rt</u>, t<u>er</u>m, b<u>or</u>n, b<u>ur</u>n.

/air/ Rule: In an R-controlled vowel, an r after the vowel makes the vowel sound different from a short or long sound—spelled ar as in vary, spelled are as in care, spelled air as in stair, spelled eir as in their, spelled ear as in bear, spelled ere as in there.

ar Rule: ar is R-controlled in start, far, and market.

ear Rule: ear is R-controlled in heard, learn, and earnest;

/er/ Rule: R-controlled er, ir, and ur often sound the same /er/. Examples: term, sir, fir, fur.

/er/ Rule: In an R-controlled vowel, an r after the vowel makes the vowel sound different from a short or long sound—spelled eer as in deer and peer, spelled ere as in here and sincere, spelled ear as in hear and ear, and spelled ier as in fierce.

/or/ Rule: In an R-controlled vowel, an r after the vowel makes the vowel sound different from a short or long sound—spelled wor as in worn, spelled war as in wart, spelled ore as in snore, spelled oar as in soar, spelled our as in four, spelled oor as in door.

our Rule: When the vowel pair ou is controlled by a final r at the end of a root, the resulting our, can say /er/ as in journey, flourish, and courage.

wor Rule: The phonogram or may say /er/ when it follows w (work, worm, worthy).

yr Rule: yr is R-controlled in myrrh, myrtle, and martyr.

Rhyme Rule:

Words that rhyme have the same ending sound as in ball/hall and otter/bitter.

Root Word Rule:

A root word is a word to which a suffix or prefix can be added to make a new word.

Schwa Rule:

The schwa is the vowel sound in many lightly pronounced unaccented syllables in words of more than one syllable. The vowels a, i, o, u, and e can stand for the schwa sound. It is sometimes signified by the pronunciation "uh" or symbolized by an upside-down rotated e as in fattər. It is the most common vowel sound in the English language. In a strong syllable the vowel is strong, and in a weak syllable the vowel is weak and makes the schwa sound. In many words -er at the end of a word or syllable makes the schwa sound.

Short Vowel Digraph

Vowel digraphs are two vowels put together in a word that make a long or short sound or have a special sound all their own.

ai Rule: In some words with the ai vowel digraph, the a is silent and the i makes the short sound as in captain.

ea Rule: The vowel digraph ea can stand for the short e sound as in head and bread.

ui Rule: In some words with the ui vowel digraph, the u is silent and the i makes the short sound as in guilt and build.

Short u Spelling Rule:

Short u can be spelled o as in mother, son, and of. Short u can be spelled o_e as in none and some. Short u can be spelled ou as in couple and young. Short u can be spelled oo as in blood and flood.

Short Vowel Rule:

When a word has only one vowel between two consonants, the vowel usually says its short sound as in cat, pet, pin, cod, and cup.

Silent Consonants Rule:

Consonants that are not heard are called silent consonants as in wrap, edge, knit, kitchen, lamb, and sigh. When two consonants are the same in the middle of a word, they are called double medial consonants. A double consonant is pronounced singly as in rabbit and daddy.

Silent Letter Digraphs Rule:

We call the b, g, k, h, and p in the digraphs bt, gn, kn, hn, pn, pt, and gh "ghost letters" to help us remember they used to make a sound but now are silent.

In consonant digraph bt, the b is silent and the t is pronounced as in doubt and subtle.

In consonant digraph gn, the g is silent and the n is pronounced as in sign and align.

In consonant digraph kn, the k is silent and n is pronounced as in know and knob.

In consonant digraph hn, the h is silent and n is pronounced as in John.

In consonant digraph pn, the p is silent and n is pronounced as in pneumonia.

In consonant digraph pt, the p is silent and the t is pronounced as in ptarmigan.

Consonant digraph gh can be silent as in right and nigh.

Silent Vowel Before l Rule:

Vowels before l in unaccented syllables are scarcely heard. Sometimes the vowel sound is dropped altogether, leaving only the sound of l as in fatal, sandal, and mantel.

Singular Possessive Nouns Rule:

Nouns that show ownership or possession are called possessive nouns. Place an apostrophe (') and an s after a singular noun to show possession as in girl/girl's and cat/cat's.

Spellings of the /k/ Sound Rule:

If a word ends in sound of /k/ and has a short vowel just before the /k/ sound, we use ck as in back, stack, and rack.

If the vowel is long before the /k/, we use ke as in make and trike.

If there is a vowel and then a sound before the /k/ sound, we use k alone. It does not matter is the vowel is long or short as in dark and bask.

If there are two vowels before the /k/, we use k as in seek and soak.

Some words with two or more syllables end in the /k/ sound that is spelled with a c as in music and picnic.

Spellings of the /sh/ Sound Rule:

When followed by a vowel in the same syllable, ci, si, and ti often have the sound of sh as in nation, action, special, precious, and mission.

The letters s or ss before u say sh as in sure, tissue, and pleasure.

Spellings of the /z/ Sound Rule:

In some words the sound of /z/ is spelled s or se as in his, has, nose, and noise.

Suffix Rule:

A suffix is an ending that is added to a word to make a new word. When a word ends in a single or a double consonant, the spelling does not usually need to be changed when adding the suffixes -y, -en, or -able/-ible as in frost/frosty, straight/straighten, wear/wearable, and deduct/deductible.

When a word ends with a single consonant that follows a single vowel, the final consonant is usually doubled before the suffix -y is added as in fun/funny and fog/foggy. A suffix is added to the end of a root words to make a new word. A suffix is a syllable if it contains a vowel sound as in -er, -est, -able/ible, -ful, -y, -en, -ness, -less, -ly, -es, -ing, -ed, and -s. Exceptions are the stable syllables.

> -ed Rule: In some words, including all verbs ending in a vowel or voiced consonant, the ending -ed has the sound of d. When -ed is added to a word, it means that something has happened in the past. In some words the ending -ed has the sound of t. The ending -ed has the sound of ed after t and d. In some words, including all verbs ending in a vowel or voiced consonant, the ending -ed has the sound of d.

> -ing Rule: When you add -ing, it means that something is happening now. If a words ends in a consonant followed by -y, keep the y when adding the suffix -ing.

> -er Rule: The suffix -er sometimes means "a person who" or "something that." Example: someone who works is a worker. A person who sings is a singer.

> -ing Rule: When you add -ing, it means something is happening now as in talking and rolling.

> -less or -ness Rule: Usually when the suffixes -less or -ness are added, the spelling of the base word does not change as in fearless and fullness.

> -ly or -ful Rule: Usually when the suffixes -ly or -ful are added, the spelling of the base word does not change as in pain/painful and quick/quickly.

Soft c or g Rule:

When c or g is followed by e, i, or y, it makes the soft sound as in the word city or giraffe

Spellings of the /f/ Sound Rule:

These consonant digraphs can make the f sound: ph as in phonics and graph; gh as in cough and trough; and lf as in calf and half.

Syllable Rule:

A syllable is a pronounceable part of a word.

Synonym Rule:

A synonym is a word having the same or nearly the same meaning as another word, as in big/large, small/little, and closes/shuts.

Triple Consonant Blends Rule:

nce makes the /ns/ sound that you hear in pounce and bounce.

nse makes the /ns/ sound that you hear in sense and dense.

lse makes the /ls/ sound that you hear in false and repulse.

lve makes the /lv/ sound that you hear in twelve and solve.

nge makes the /nj/ sound that you hear in range and plunge.

rch makes the sound that you hear in porch and church.

nch makes the sound that you hear in bench and inch.

rth makes the sound that you hear in worth and earth.

nth makes the sound that you hear in month and ninth.

mpt makes the sound that you hear in prompt and attempt.

lch makes the sound that you hear in squelch and mulch.

scr makes the skr sound that you hear in scream and describe.

spl makes the sound that you hear in splash and splotch.

spr makes the sound that you hear in sprint and spray.

thr makes the sound that you hear in thrash and through.

shr makes the sound that you hear in shrink and shriek.

squ makes the skw sound that you hear in squish and squall.

str makes the sound that you hear in stress and stray.

Vowel ô Spelled al Rule:

The vowel a followed by the letter l often has neither a long nor a short sound but has an ô or aw sound as in small, walnut, salt, and talk.

Vowel ô Spelled au or aw Rule:

Vowel digraphs are two vowels put together in a word that make a long or short sound or have a special sound all their own. The vowel digraphs au and aw stand for the ô or aw sound as in saw, lawn, faucet, and auto.

Vowel ô Spelled o Rule:

In some words the letter o is neither long nor short but has an ô or aw sound. Compare the short o sound in cot, top, Tom, and pod to the ô sound in dog, hog, on, and off.

Vowel ô Spelled ough Rule:

The digraph ough is a very special combination of letters and can be very confusing, so we just have to learn it. It helps to really look at the words and remember the ough combination. It can spell the sound of ô or /aw/ as in bought and thought.

Vowel ô Spelled augh Rule:

The digraph augh can spell the sound of ô or /aw/ as in taught and caught.

Vowel ô Spelled wa or qua Rule:

When the letter a comes after the letters w or qu, it often makes ô or aw sound as in wash and squash.

v_e Rule:

A vowel followed by a consonant and a "sneaky e" is long; code the vowel with a macron (‾) and cross out the "sneaky e." Examples: name, hope, these, like, rule.

VCVopen Syllable Rule:

When a single consonant comes between two vowels or vowel sounds, it is usually divided before the consonant if the first vowel is long. Long vowels at the end of syllables as in ma'/ker and pi'/lot.

VCV Syllable Rule:

VCV means a word has two vowels, so it has two syllables. In the first syllable, the vowel can make a long sound as in ra'/ven, mo'/tor, and pa'/per; a short sound as in riv'/er or de/cide'; or a schwa sound as in a/go', a/way', and po/lite'.

VCCV Syllable Rule:

When a word contains more than one vowel, it could follow the VCCV (vowel-consonant-consonant-vowel) pattern. The first step is to mark the vowels by writing a v under each vowel. Then mark the consonants by writing a c under them. Next, divide the word into syllables by drawing a line between the two consonants. Code the vowels and decide which syllable receives the accent ('). Divide between two consonants unless the consonants form a digraph and are sounded together. VCCV as in hap'/py and chil'/dren.

VCCVCCV Syllable Rule:

VCCVCCV means the word has three vowels, so it has three syllables. The syllable lines go between each pair of consonants, then code each syllable as in dif'/fer/ent', sim'/i/lar', and wil'/der/ness'.

Vowel Diphthong ow Rule:

The vowel diphthong ow can make two sounds: ow as in cow or ow as in snow.

Vowel Digraph Rule:

Vowel digraphs are two vowels put together in a word that make a long or short sound or have a special sound all their own.

> oo Rule: The vowel digraph oo can stand for the vowel sound heard in book or in pool.

> ou Rule: The vowel digraph ou can make the long o sound; ough can make the long o sound.

Vowel Syllable Rule:

Each syllable in a word has a vowel as in focus (fo/cus) and velvet (vel/vet).

V/V Syllable Rule:

Divide between two vowels when they are sounded separately. V/V as in di'/et and cru'/el.

Words from Other Languages:

English has borrowed many words from other languages including French, Dutch, and Greek.

Wild Colt Rule:

Wild Colt words contain either the vowels o or i followed by two consonants as in wild, colt, kind, find, and both.

Lesson Plans

Lesson 1

Short Vowel Sounds: ă, ĕ, ĭ, ŏ, and ŭ

Overview

- Define a short vowel
- Recognize the breve (˘) as a symbol for the short vowel sound
- Read words with short vowel sounds
- Identify words with short vowel sounds

Materials and Supplies

- Teacher's Guide and Student Workbook
- White board or chart paper
- Phonics flashcards
- Reader: "The Howler Monkey"

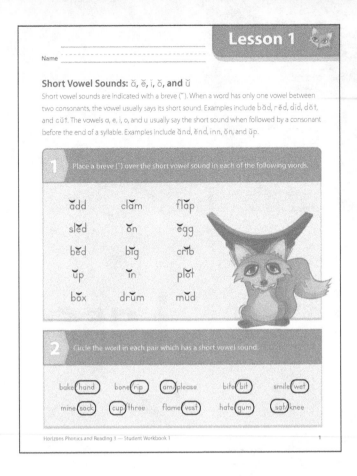

Teaching Tips

Lesson Introduction. Introduce short vowel sounds to the student. Tell the student that short vowel sounds are indicated with a breve (˘). When a word has only one vowel between two consonants, the vowel usually says its short sound. The vowels **a, e, i, o,** and **u** usually say the short sound when followed by a consonant before the end of a syllable. Have the student repeat the sounds of the short vowels **ă, ĕ, ĭ, ŏ,** and **ŭ** with you. You may want to create flashcards with the short vowel sound on one side and a sample word on the other. Use these flashcards to review.

Ask the student to brainstorm a list of words with short vowel sounds. Write these words on the board. This will give the student the opportunity to think of words that he/she may not be able to spell but know. If the student is having trouble thinking of words, the following list may help him/her begin: **track, wreck, pit, log,** and **run.**

Activity 1. Turn to the Student Workbook. Read through the definition at the top of the page. Have the student sound out each word in the first activity emphasizing the short vowel sound. Direct the student to place the breve over the short vowel sound: **ădd, clăm, flăp, slĕd, ŏn, ĕgg, bĕd, bĭg, crĭb, ŭp, ĭn, plŏt, bŏx, drŭm, mŭd.**

Activity 2. Continue with the second activity on the sheet. Do the first problem together. Have the student identify the short vowel sound. The student should circle the words with short vowel sounds: **hand, rip, am, bit, wet, sock, cup, vest, gum, sat.**

Activity 3. The final activity asks the student to fill in the blanks with words with the short vowel sound. As a bonus activity, you could ask the student to identify other words in the sentence that have a short vowel sound. The fill in the blank answers are: **band**, **red**, **crib**, **dog**, **hill**, **cup**, **men**, **sing**.

Reading Activity.

1. Ask the student to read the selection "The Howler Monkey." After he/she has read the selection, discuss the physical characteristics of these monkeys. What do they look like? (**They have black, brown, or red fur. Their faces are bearded.**) How large are they? (**Their bodies are three feet long and their tails add another three feet.**) How much do they weigh? (**They weigh 15 to 22 pounds.**) Continue by asking the student how the monkey received its name. (**The howling sound of the monkeys gave them the name "howler" monkeys.**) Is the story fiction, a made up story, or nonfiction, a true story or one that contains facts about something? (**The selection is nonfiction and gives information about the howler monkey.**) Remind the student that the lesson was about words with short vowel sounds. Ask the student to find five words with short vowel sounds in the selection. (Some examples include: **monkeys, about, another, pick, black, red**.)

2. As an added activity, have the student draw a picture of a howler monkey.

3 Fill in the blank with a word with a short vowel sound.

Word Bank

men   crib   cup   dog   band   red   hill   sing

1. Maggie played the flute in the ___band___.

2. Klay had a ___red___ bike.

3. The infant slept in a ___crib___.

4. The ___dog___ barked when he saw a squirrel.

5. Jack and Jill climbed up a ___hill___.

6. Mrs. Gray drank a ___cup___ of coffee.

7. The ___men___ helped push the car out of the snowbank.

8. Daisy liked to ___sing___ in church.

2   Horizons Phonics and Reading 3 — Student Workbook 1

Lesson 2

Long Vowel Sounds: ā, ē, ī, ō, and ū

Overview

- Define a short vowel

- Identify the macron (ˉ) which identifies the long vowel sound

- Read words with long vowel sounds

- Recognize words with long vowel sound

Materials and Supplies

- Teacher's Guide and Student Workbook

- White board or chart paper

- Phonics flashcards

- Reader: "The Howler Monkey"

Teaching Tips

Review for Mastery. Discuss and review any work from the previous lesson that was assigned as homework. Check for completion of the activities and orally quiz the student for comprehension. Review any reading that was assigned, discussing the characters, setting, plot, theme, language, sequence, etc.

Strengthen fluency and phonemic awareness by reviewing words and sentences from the previous lesson. Build vocabulary skills by using some of the words in sentences.

Lesson Introduction. Introduce long vowel sounds to the student. Tell the student that long vowel sounds are indicated with a macron (ˉ). When a syllable ends in a silent **e**, the silent **e** is a signal that the vowel in front of it is long. Vowels **a, e, i, o**, and **u** usually say their names and have long vowel sounds at the end of a syllable. Have

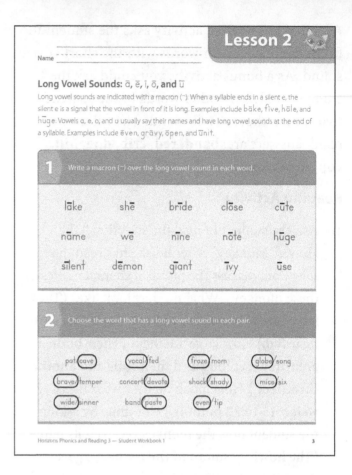

the student repeat the sounds of the long vowel sounds **ā, ē, ī, ō,** and **ū** after you. You may want to create flashcards with the long vowel sound on one side and a sample word on the other. Use these flashcards to review.

Ask the student to brainstorm a list of words with long vowel sounds. Write these words on the board. This will give the student the opportunity to think of words that he/she may not be able to spell but know. If the student is having trouble thinking of words, the following list may help him/her begin: **bake, eject, ice, hopeful**, and **huge**.

Activity 1. Turn to the Student Workbook. Read through the definition at the top of the page. For the first activity, the student should pronounce each word emphasizing the long vowel sounds. Have the student put a macron over the long vowel sound: **lāke, shē, brīde, clōse cūte, nāme wē, nīne, nōte, hūge, sīlent, dēmon, gīant, īvy, ūse.**

Activity 2. In the next activity the student will be asked to identify which word in a pair of words has a long vowel sound. Again, saying the words aloud may help the student recognize which words have long vowel sounds: **cave, vocal, froze, globe, brave, devote, shady, mice, wide, paste, even.**

Activity 3. The final activity asks the student to use words with long vowel sounds to complete the sentences: **cave, hole, kite, icy, lazy, skate, date, bake.**

Reading Activity.

1. Ask the student to reread or review the selection "The Howler Monkey." With the student discuss the habitat of the monkeys. How are the monkeys well-suited for their habitat? (**The monkeys live in the tops of forests. Their loud voices help them protect their territory. Their long tails help them move through the treetops.**) What predators do the monkeys face? (**Harpy eagles and humans.**) While the student and teacher may not go into the forest and cut down trees, what can a person living a distance away do to protect the environment of the the howler monkey? (Answers include: **Only using the resources that we really need and not those that we want. Recycling the goods we use is another way to protect environments both near and far.**) Can the student do things to protect the environment in which he/she lives? (Answers include: **taking care of possessions, not littering, recycling.**) In this lesson, the student studied long vowel sounds. Ask the student to identify five words with long vowel sounds. (Some examples include: **monkeys, use, entire, names, be.**)

2. As an added activity, find a recording on the internet of the sound a howler monkey makes.

Lesson 3

Long and Short Vowel Sounds: ā, ē, ī, ō, ū, ă, ĕ, ĭ, ŏ, and ŭ

Overview

- Identify long and short vowel sounds
- Determine which words have long or short vowel sounds
- Read words with long and short vowel sounds

Materials and Supplies

- Teacher's Guide and Student Workbook
- White board or chart paper
- Phonics flashcards
- Reader: "Sir Edmund Hillary"

Teaching Tips

Review for Mastery. Discuss and review any work from the previous lesson that was assigned as homework. Check for completion of the activities and orally quiz the student for comprehension. Review any reading that was assigned, discussing the characters, setting, plot, theme, language, sequence, etc.

Strengthen fluency and phonemic awareness by reviewing words and sentences from the previous lessons. Build vocabulary skills by using some of the words in sentences.

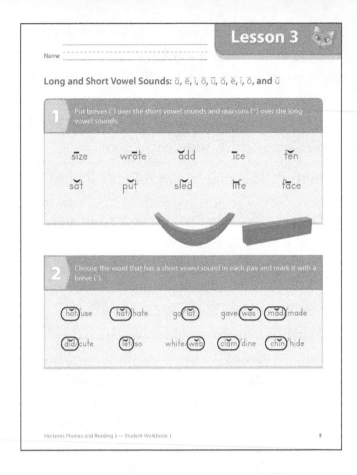

Lesson Introduction. Review words with long and short vowel sounds. Have the student brainstorm words with long and short vowel sounds. You may want to use words where the letter **e** is added and the vowel becomes long. Examples include: **bat – bate, sit – site, can – cane**. If you made flashcards, use them to review.

Activity 1. The student should turn to the first activity and identify which words have long and short vowel sounds. The student should place a breve or macron over the long or short vowel sounds: **sīze, wrōte, ădd, īce, tĕn, săt, pŭt, slĕd, līfe, fāce**.

Activity 2. The second activity asks the student to identify the word with the short vowel sound in each pair: **hŏt, hăt, lŏt, wăs, măd, dĭd, lĕt, wĕb, clăm, chĭn**.

Activity 3. The next activity asks the student to make words with either the long or short vowel sounds by adding or deleting letters. You may want to complete the first one together as a class. Answers for the first set are: **pine, hope, site, ride, tone, tube.** For the second set the answers are: **rob, tot, plan, dim, rat, bid.**

Activity 4. Read the Bible verses together with your student. Have the student find two words with long vowel sounds. Answers include: **lean, own, ways, he, make, straight.** Additionally, you could also have students find words in the passage with short vowel sounds.

Reading Activity.

1. The student should read the first four paragraphs of "Sir Edmund Hillary" which focus on Mt. Everest.

2. After the student has completed the reading, discuss the following questions. How tall is Mt. Everest? **(It is 29,028 feet.)** Where is the mountain located? **(It is located in the Himalaya Mountains between Nepal and China.)** What challenges do climbers of Mt. Everest face? **(The climb itself is dangerous. The climbers also face dangers from the weather and lack of oxygen.)** Why do climbers stay at the Tengboche monastery? **(Their stay allows them to acclimate to the climate and lack of oxygen.)** What happens when people do not receive enough oxygen? **(Their bodies need to work harder to function. Their brains do not think as clearly with a lack of oxygen.)** How long does it take to climb and descend Mt. Everest? **(It takes seven weeks to climb and three days to descend.)** This is a story about a real person. It tells a story about someone's life. What do we call this kind of a story? **(Biography.)** Ask the student to locate three words with long vowel

sounds and three words with short vowel sounds from the selection. (Answers include: **rises, China, make, tallest, in, China.**)

3. As an added activity, have the student look at a map and locate Mt. Everest. Discuss the challenges he/she would face getting from his/her home to the Mt. Everest site.

Lesson 4

Short Vowel ă and Syllables

Overview:

- Review short vowel sounds

- Identify words with the short **ă** vowel sound

- Recognize the short **ă** vowel sounds

- Divide words into syllables

Materials and Supplies:

- Teacher's Guide and Student Workbook

- White board or chart paper

- Phonics flashcards

- Reader: "Sir Edmund Hillary"

Teaching Tips:

Review for Mastery. Discuss and review any work from the previous lesson that was assigned as homework. Check for completion of the activities and orally quiz the student for comprehension. Review any reading that was assigned, discussing the characters, setting, plot, theme, language, sequence, etc.

Strengthen fluency and phonemic awareness by reviewing words and sentences from the previous lessons. Build vocabulary skills by using some of the words in sentences.

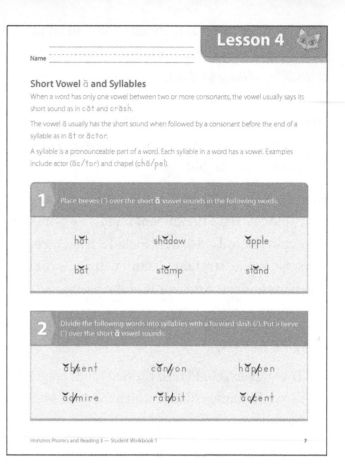

Lesson Introduction.

Lesson Introduction. Introduce the short **ă** vowel sound and syllables to the student. When a word has only one vowel between two or more consonants, the vowel **ă** usually says its short sound as in **căt** and **crăsh**. The vowel **ă** usually has the short sound when followed by a consonant before the end of a syllable as in **ăt** or **ăctor**. A syllable is a pronounceable part of a word. Each syllable in a word has a vowel.

Ask the student to brainstorm a list of words with two syllables. On the board, write the word so the two syllables are separated. Examples include: **print/er, kit/ten, Bi/ble, pa/per**.

Activity 1. Turn to the Student Workbook. Read through the definitions at the top of the page. The first activity asks the student to review short **ă** vowel sounds. Answers are: **hăt, shădow, ăpple, băt, stămp, stănd.**

Activity 2. In the second activity, the student will be asked to divide words into syllables. The student will also need to put a breve over any short vowel sounds. Answers are: **ăb/sent, căn/yon, hăp/pen, ăd/mire, răb/bit, ăc/cent.**

Activity 3. The next section asks the student to identify words with a short **ă** vowel sound. The answers are: **glad, tax, flash, man, handle.**

Activity 4. Finally, have the student find letters with the short **ă** vowel sound in the word search. **See image for answers.**

Reading Activity.

1. Ask the student to read the rest of "Sir Edmund Hillary."

2. After the student has completed the selection, discuss Hillary's early life. **(He was born in New Zealand, worked as a beekeeper, and served in the Air Force.)** Who was Tenzing Norgay? **(He was a Sherpa mountaineer and guide who assisted Hillary on his climb. He was from India and Nepal.)** When did Norgay and Hillary reach the top of Mt. Everest? **(They reached the top on May 29, 1953.)**

3. Have the student find three words in the selection that have the short **ă** sound. **(monastery, was, camp)**

4. As an added activity, have the student write a newspaper article that may have appeared after Hillary and Norgay reached the top of Mt. Everest.

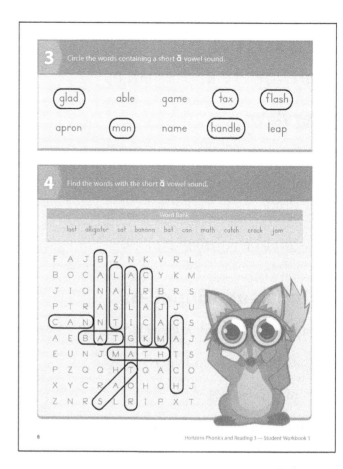

Lesson 5

Short Vowel ĕ and Syllables

Overview:

- Review short vowel sounds
- Identify words with the short **ĕ** vowel sound
- Recognize the short **ĕ** vowel sounds
- Divide words into syllables

Materials and Supplies:

- Teacher's Guide and Student Workbook
- White board or chart paper
- Phonics flashcards
- Reader: "Sir Edmund Hillary"

Teaching Tips:

Review for Mastery. Discuss and review any work from the previous lesson that was assigned as homework. Check for completion of the activities and orally quiz the student for comprehension. Review any reading that was assigned, discussing the characters, setting, plot, theme, language, sequence, etc.

Strengthen fluency and phonemic awareness by reviewing words and sentences from the previous lessons. Build vocabulary skills by using some of the words in sentences.

Lesson Introduction. Introduce the short **ĕ** vowel sound and syllables to the student. When a word has only one vowel between two or more consonants, the vowel **ĕ** usually says its short sound as in **lĕt** and **mĕsh**. The vowel **ĕ** usually has the short sound when followed by a consonant before the end of a syllable as in **ĕnd** or **ĕnter**. A syllable is a pronounceable part of a word. Each syllable in a word has a vowel.

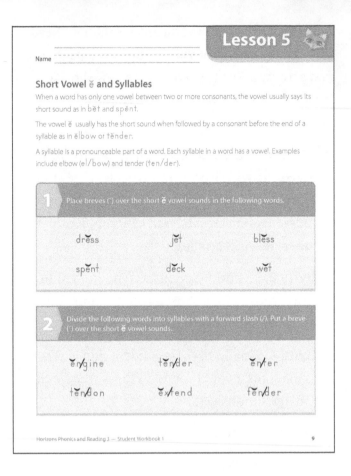

Ask the student to brainstorm a list of words with two syllables. On the board, write the word so the two syllables are separated. Examples include: **en/ter, pa/per, dri/ver, book/let, sum/mer**.

Activity 1. The student should turn to the activity sheet. In the first activity the student needs to place a breve over the short **ĕ** vowel sound in the words. The answers are: **drĕss, jĕt, blĕss, spĕnt, dĕck, wĕt**.

Activity 2. Ask the student to divide each word into two syllables. Once that is completed, the student should put a breve over the short **ĕ** vowel sounds. Answers are: **ĕn/gine, tĕn/der, ĕn/ter, tĕn/don, ĕx/tend, fĕn/der**.

Activity 3. Have the student read the words in the activity. The student should overemphasize the pronunciation of each word. Words containing a short ĕ vowel sound should be circled. Words which should be circled are: **best, ten, beg, fresh, vest**.

Activity 4. Finally, the student should use words with short ĕ vowel sounds to fill in the blank of each sentence. Answers are: **shells, wet, fresh, bell, deck, spent**.

Reading Activity.

1. Ask the student to return to the selection "Sir Edmund Hillary." The student should reread the entire selection. What honor did Hillary receive for climbing Mt. Everest? **(He was honored by the Queen of England and became known as Sir Edmund Hillary.)** How did Sir Edmund Hillary care for the people who lived in the region of Mt. Everest? **(He provided schools for their children. He cleaned up the environment surrounding the mountain.)** Why do you think people continue to want to climb to the top of Mt. Everest? (Answers may include: **Because it's a challenge. It's something that only a few people have done.)** Ask the student to locate three words that contain the short ĕ sound. **(spent, left, them)**

2. Read with your students Psalm 95:1-7 (NIV):

   "Come, let us sing for joy to the LORD;
   let us shout aloud to the Rock of our salvation.

   Let us come before him with thanksgiving
   and extol him with music and song.

   For the LORD is the great God,
   the great King above all gods.

   In his hand are the depths of the earth,
   and the mountain peaks belong to him.

   The sea is his, for he made it,
   and his hands formed the dry land.

   Come, let us bow down in worship,
   let us kneel before the LORD our Maker;

   for he is our God
   and we are the people of his pasture,
   the flock under his care."

3. Discuss the images in the Psalm with your student. Remind the student that God created Mt. Everest long before Sir Edmund Hillary and Tenzing Norgay reached the summit. The mountains and everything in the earth were created by God and belong to Him. You may want to have your student memorize a portion of this Psalm.

3 — Circle the words containing a short ĕ vowel sound.

best   beat   bee   ten   lime

beg   fresh   free   east   vest

4 — Fill in the blank with the correct word with the short ĕ vowel sound.

Word Bank
spent   wet   deck   bell   shells   fresh

1. Sally found _____ **shells** _____ on the seashore.
2. Mrs. Henry hung up the _____ **wet** _____ clothes on the clothesline.
3. Angela enjoyed eating _____ **fresh** _____ fruit.
4. At the sound of the _____ **bell** _____ the students returned to class.
5. Mr. Johnson built a _____ **deck** _____ on the back of his house.
6. James _____ **spent** _____ one dollar on an ice cream cone.

10   Horizons Phonics and Reading 3 — Student Workbook 1

Lesson 6

Short Vowel ĭ and Pronunciation Markings

Overview:

- Review short vowel sounds
- Recall words with the short ĭ vowel sound
- Recognize the short ĭ vowel sounds
- Identify dictionary pronunciation markings

Materials and Supplies:

- Teacher's Guide and Student Workbook
- White board or chart paper
- Phonics flashcards
- Reader: "Slow and Steady"

Teaching Tips:

Review for Mastery. Discuss and review any work from the previous lesson that was assigned as homework. Check for completion of the activities and orally quiz the student for comprehension. Review any reading that was assigned, discussing the characters, setting, plot, theme, language, sequence, etc.

Strengthen fluency and phonemic awareness by reviewing words and sentences from the previous lessons. Build vocabulary skills by using some of the words in sentences.

Lesson Introduction. Introduce the short ĭ vowel sound and syllables to the student. When a word has only one vowel between two or more consonants, the vowel ĭ usually says its short sound as in **bĭt** and **bĭg**. The vowel ĭ usually has the short sound when followed by a consonant before the end of a syllable as in **ĭnvite** or **lĭterature**.

Dictionaries use pronunciation keys or symbols to help the reader pronounce words. The breve and macron, which the student has used in these lessons, are two examples of pronunciation symbols.

Activity 1. Introduce the short vowel ĭ sound to the student. Have the student say the words in Activity 1. After saying the words, ask the student to place a breve over the short ĭ vowel sound. Answers are: **dĭd, lĭt, sĭnk, whĭch, pĭg, mĭnt**.

Activity 2. The second activity asks the student to review dividing words into syllables. Instruct the student to divide each word into two syllables. The student should put a breve over the short ĭ vowel sounds in the words. Answers are: **dĭs/tant, dĭn/ner, wĭt/ness, ĭn/sect, ĭm/press, ĭn/ject**.

Activity 3. The student will be asked to look more carefully at how the breve symbol is used to identify all short vowel sounds in words. The student should put the breve over the short vowel sounds in the activity: **căt, fĭt, mŏp tŭx, lĕt, tŭg.**

Activity 4. The student will be asked to look more carefully at how the macron symbol is used to identify all long vowel sounds in words. The student should put a macron over all long vowel sounds in the activity: **dāy, bē, hīde, hōme, hūge, hī.**

Activity 5. The final activity has the student choose the word in each pair with the short ĭ vowel sound. The answers are: **limp, stitch, spin, fling, chip, gift.**

Reading Activity.

1. Before reading "Slow and Steady," write the word "fable" on the board. Ask the student if he/she knows what a fable is.

2. Explain that a fable is a story that provides a moral or lesson to the reader. The characters in a fable are often talking animals. Can animals really talk? **(No.)** Why do you think that writers use animals to tell the story? **(Answers will vary.)**

3. Explain that the next story students will read is a fable.

4. After the student has read the selection, ask him/her to state the moral or lesson. (The moral is: **slow and steady wins the race.**) Ask the student what that moral means in the story. **(The turtle kept going, but even though he was slow, he won because he didn't stop.)** How can the moral be applied to everyday life? (Answers may include: **Sometimes people want to do things quickly but then they are not done well. Other times people don't think they can do something but by continually moving forward they can accomplish their goals.**)

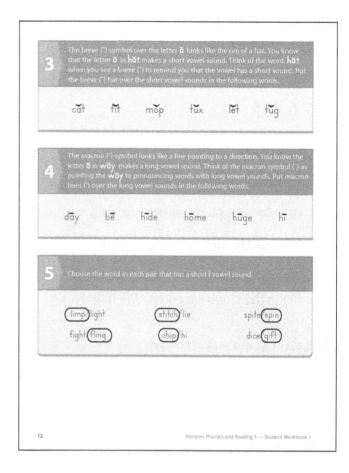

Lesson 7

Short Vowel ŏ and Pronunciation Markings

Overview:

- Review short vowel sounds

- Recall words with the short ŏ vowel sound

- Recognize the short ŏ vowel sounds

- Understand how accent marks are used to indicate the emphasized syllable in a word

Materials and Supplies:

- Teacher's Guide and Student Workbook

- White board or chart paper

- Phonics flashcards

- Reader: "Slow and Steady"

Teaching Tips:

Review for Mastery. Discuss and review any work from the previous lesson that was assigned as homework. Check for completion of the activities and orally quiz the student for comprehension. Review any reading that was assigned, discussing the characters, setting, plot, theme, language, sequence, etc.

Strengthen fluency and phonemic awareness by reviewing words and sentences from the previous lessons. Build vocabulary skills by using some of the words in sentences.

Lesson Introduction. Introduce the short ŏ vowel sound and syllables to the student. When a word has only one vowel between two or more consonants, the vowel ŏ usually says its short sound as in **dŏg** and **lŏst**. The vowel ŏ usually has the short sound when followed by a consonant before the end of a syllable as in **ŏnto** or **cŏttŏn**.

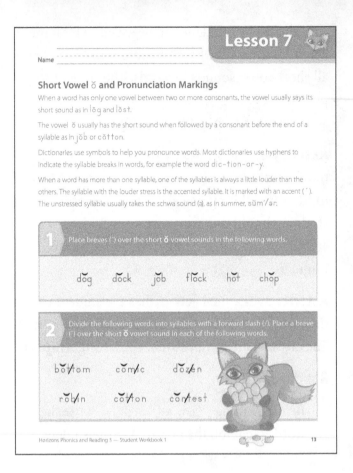

Dictionaries use pronunciation keys or symbols to help the reader pronounce words. The hyphen or forward slash is used to indicate where one syllable ends and another begins. An accent mark is used to indicate which syllable of a word is emphasized. Write the following words on the board: **angry**, **happy**, and **joyful**. First divide the words into syllables and then have the student determine the syllable which should be accented: **an'/gry**, **hap'/py**, **de/lay'**.

Accent Rules:

When a word has more than one syllable, one of the syllables is always a little louder than the others. The syllable with the louder stress is the accented syllable. The unstressed syllable usually takes the schwa (ə) sound.

It may seem that the placement of accents in words is often random or accidental, but these are some rules that usually work.

1. **Accents are often on the first syllable. Examples: ba'/sic, pro'/gram.**

2. **In words that have suffixes or prefixes, the accent is usually on the main root word. Examples: box'/es, un/tie'.**

3. **If de-, re-, ex-, in-, po-, pro-, or a- is the first syllable in a word, it is usually not accented. Examples: de/lay', ex/plore'.**

Activity 1. Ask the student to read each word in the first activity. The student should listen carefully for the short ŏ vowel sound. A breve should be placed over each short ŏ vowel sound. Answers are: **dŏg, dŏck, jŏb, flŏck, hŏt, chŏp**.

Activity 2. Direct the student in dividing each of the words into syllables. Again, a breve should be placed over the short ŏ vowel sound. The answers are: **bŏt/tom, cŏm/ic, dŏz/en, rŏb/in, cŏt/ton, cŏn/test.**

Activity 3. Introduce the student to accent marks. Explain how accent marks are used to indicate which part of a word is emphasized. Ask the student to look back over the second activity. The student should read each word, initially putting the accent on the first syllable and then the second. Help the student to recognize how the sound of a word changes depending on which syllable is accented. The student should first divide the words into syllables. Afterward, the accent is placed on the appropriate syllable of each word. Answers are: **o'/pen, car'/ry, ap'/ple, a/go', mag'/net, be/yond'.**

Activity 4. The final activity asks the student to fill in the blanks with words with the short vowel sound. As a bonus activity, you could ask the student to identify other words in the sentences that have a short vowel sound. The fill in the blank answers are: **dog, fog, dock, cross, song, flock**.

Reading Activity.

1. Have the student return to the selection "Slow and Steady." Ask the student to describe the two main characters in the selection, Quick and Abner. **(Quick was a rabbit who wanted to do everything quickly and didn't pay**

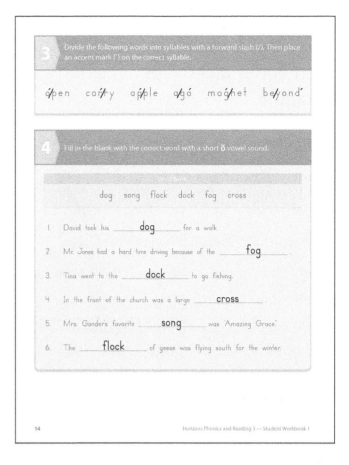

attention to the needs of others. Abner was a turtle who was willing to help others solve their problems. He didn't worry about whether or not he would win. He wanted to do his best.)

2. Ask the student to describe the conflict or problem of the story. (Answers include: **The forest animals wanted to sleep or rest in the morning and the rabbit's morning runs disturbed them.**) Explain that stories contain conflicts. This creates interest in the story.

3. Have the student look for words which describe Quick's morning run. (Answers include: **jumped, curved, ducked, quickly.**) If you were to describe someone running fast, what words could you use? (Answers include: **speedy, rapid, dash, hurry**).

Lesson 8

Short Vowel ŭ and Pronunciation Markings

Overview:

- Review short vowel sounds

- Recall words with the short **ŭ** vowel sound

- Recognize the short **ŭ** vowel sounds

- Use a forward slash to indicate syllable breaks in words

- Understand how accent marks are used to indicate the emphasized syllable in a word

Materials and Supplies:

- Teacher's Guide and Student Workbook

- White board or chart paper

- Phonics flashcards

- Reader: "Slow and Steady"

Teaching Tips:

Review for Mastery. Discuss and review any work from the previous lesson that was assigned as homework. Check for completion of the activities and orally quiz the student for comprehension. Review any reading that was assigned, discussing the characters, setting, plot, theme, language, sequence, etc.

Strengthen fluency and phonemic awareness by reviewing words and sentences from the previous lessons. Build vocabulary skills by using some of the words in sentences.

Lesson Introduction. Introduce the short **ŭ** vowel sound and syllables to the student. When a word has only one vowel between two or more consonants, the vowel **ŭ** usually says its short sound as in **dŭg** and **trŭst**. The vowel **ŭ** usually has the

short sound when followed by a consonant before the end of a syllable as in **ŭnto** or **bŭtton**.

Dictionaries use pronunciation keys or symbols to help the reader pronounce words. The hyphen or forward slash is used to indicate where one syllable ends and another begins. An accent mark is used to indicate which syllable of a word is emphasized. Write the word **present** on the board. Notice how the meaning of the word changes if the accent is placed on the first or second syllable.

Activity 1. The student should read the words and then place breves over the short **ŭ** vowel sounds. Answers are: **cŭb, dŭck, mŭd, rŭg, bŭnk, brŭsh**.

Activity 2. Ask the student to divide each word into two syllables. Once the words have been divided into syllables, the student should determine which vowels have a short sound. Answers are: **sŭd/den, ŭn/less, cŭs/tom, sŭb/ject, ŭn/til, ŭp/set**.

Activity 3. In the third activity, the words are to be divided into syllables. An accent mark should be placed over the stressed syllable. Answers include: **ba'/by, cot'/ton, al/though', wis'/dom, a/bout', win'/dow.**

Activity 4. For the final activity, the student will complete a crossword puzzle with the words with the short **ŭ** vowel sound. Answers are:

Across:	Down:
2. **mud**	1. **dump**
4. **cut**	3. **duck**
6. **cub**	5. **truck**
8. **pumpkin**	7. **bun**

Reading Activity.

1. Ask the student to return to the selection "Slow and Steady." Tell the student that each letter in the alphabet appears in the story at least once.

2. Have the student make a list of some of the words containing all the letters in the alphabet. Some words are:

A   Abner, rabbit

B   branches, rabbit

C   chance, branches

D   deer, sound

E   excitedly, well

F   forest, fast

G   gathered, sprang

H   he, they

I   instead, quick

J   jumped, enjoyed

K   quick, ducked

L   loose, turtle

M   might, named

N   name, action

O   other, action

P   planned, sprang

Q   quick, quickly

R   rabbit, cross

S   slowly, forest

T   trail, action

U   run, under

V   curved, every, deserved

W   won, tweet

X   extra, excitedly

Y   everything, steady, eyes

Z   zooming

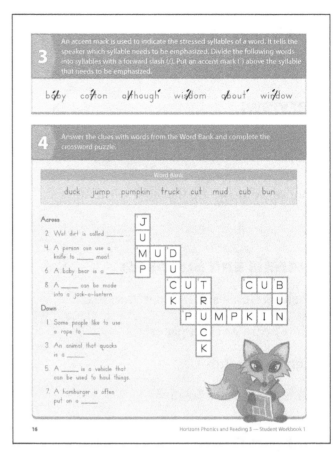

Lesson 9

Y as a Vowel

Overview:

- Identify the sound **y** makes when it is used as a vowel
- Choose words where the letter **y** is used as a vowel

Materials and Supplies:

- Teacher's Guide and Student Workbook
- White board or chart paper
- Phonics flashcards
- Reader: "Slow and Steady"

Teaching Tips:

Review for Mastery. Discuss and review any work from the previous lesson that was assigned as homework. Check for completion of the activities and orally quiz the student for comprehension. Review any reading that was assigned, discussing the characters, setting, plot, theme, language, sequence, etc.

Strengthen fluency and phonemic awareness by reviewing words and sentences from the previous lessons. Build vocabulary skills by using some of the words in sentences.

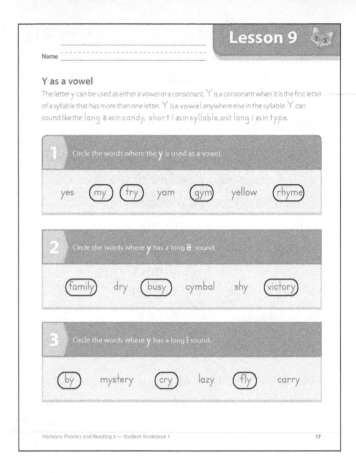

Lesson Introduction. Tell students that the letter **y** can be used as both a vowel and a consonant. Explain that when the letter **y** is used as a vowel it has the long ē or ī sound as in **holy** and **shy**. The letter **y** can have the short ĭ sound as in **myth**, **hymn**, **symbol**, and **typical**.

Ask the student to brainstorm a list of words with the letter **y** used as a vowel. Write these words on the board. This will give the student the opportunity to think of words that he/she may not be able to spell but know. If the student is having trouble thinking of words, the following list may help him/her begin: **baby, hairy, sly, cry, system, rhythm**.

Activity 1. Turn to the Student Workbook. Read through the definition at the top of the page. Direct the student in the first activity where he/she will be asked to identify words where the letter **y** is used as a vowel: **my**, **try**, **gym**, **rhyme**.

Activity 2. In the next activity the student will be asked to circle words where the letter **y** has the long ē vowel sound: **family**, **busy**, **victory**.

Activity 3. The student will continue by identifying words where the letter **y** has a long ī sound: **by**, **cry**, **fly**.

Activity 4. In the final activity, the student will identify pictures of words with the letter **y** used as a vowel. **See image.** Answers are: **cry**, **cymbal**, **fly**, **fry**, **sky**, **spy**.

Reading Activity. Have the student complete one final activity focusing on the selection "Slow and Steady." Ask the student to complete one of the following options:

1. First, the student could write a fable of his/her own based on a moral or lesson he/she has learned. Some morals or lessons may include: *a kind word turns away anger*, *happiness is contagious*, *look before you leap*, or *be prepared*.

2. A second option is for the student to draw a scene from the story "Slow and Steady."

3. A final option is to have the student write a story in which he/she uses every letter of the alphabet.

Lesson 10

Review

Overview:

- Identify short vowel sounds in words
- Divide words into syllables
- Choose the correct syllable in a word to emphasize
- Correctly use the breve and macron signs
- Recognize words using **y** as a consonant or vowel sound

Materials and Supplies:

- Teacher's Guide and Student Workbook
- White board or chart paper
- Phonics flashcards
- Reader: "The Tale of Peter Rabbit"

Teaching Tips:

Review for Mastery. Discuss and review any work from the previous lesson that was assigned as homework. Check for completion of the activities and orally quiz the student for comprehension. Review any reading that was assigned, discussing the characters, setting, plot, theme, language, sequence, etc.

Strengthen fluency and phonemic awareness by reviewing words and sentences from the previous lessons. Build vocabulary skills by using some of the words in sentences. You may want to use the flashcards you created to review.

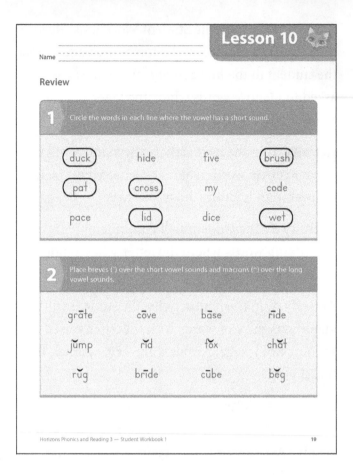

Activity 1. The student should turn to the workbook and complete the first review activity. In this activity the student will circle words which have short vowel sounds. Answers are: **duck, brush, pat, cross, lid, wet**.

Activity 2. Look at the second activity. Ask the student to identify the long or short vowel sound in each word. The student should put breves over words with short vowel sound and macrons over words with long vowel sounds. Answers: **grāte, cōve, bāse, rīde, jŭmp, rĭd, fŏx, chăt, rŭg, brīde, cūbe, bĕg**.

Activity 3. In the next activity the student will be asked to divide words into syllables and put accent marks over the emphasized syllable: **bas'/ket, u/pon' a/gree', pa'/per, sum'/mer, pen'/cil**.

Activity 4. The student will continue the review by identifying words with the letter **y** used as a consonant or a vowel. Answers are: **yellow, yell, yes**.

Reading Activity. Turn to "The Tale of Peter Rabbit" in the Reader. The student should read the selection for his/her personal enjoyment. Have the student look up words for which they do not know the meaning, such as the word "sieve."

*sieve – a device for separating lumps from powdered material, straining liquids, grading particles, etc. consisting of a container with a mesh or perforated bottom through which the material is shaken or poured

— a utensil having many small meshed or perforated openings, used to strain solids from liquids, to separate fine particles of loose matter from coarser ones, etc.

Test 1

Lessons 1-10

Overview:

- Identify words with short vowel sounds

- Recognize words with long vowel sounds

- Divide words into syllables

- Identify dictionary pronunciation markings

- Understand how accent marks are used to indicate the emphasized syllable in a word

- Recall the letter **y** is used as a vowel

Materials and Supplies:

- Student Test

Teaching Tips:

Review for Mastery. Discuss and review any work from the previous lesson that was assigned as homework. Check for completion of the activities and orally quiz the student for comprehension. Review any reading that was assigned.

Lesson Introduction. This lesson tests the material the student learned in the unit. Before the test you may want to ask the student if he/she has any final questions. There may be questions from the review the student will want to go over again. Remind the student that the final test follows a similar format as the review.

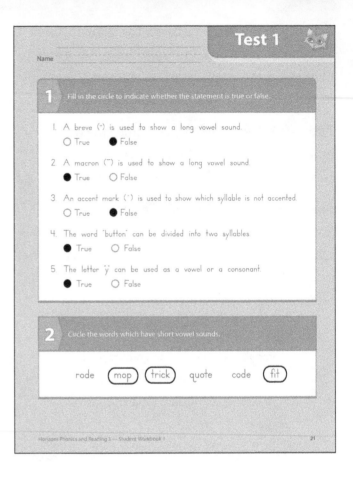

Activity 1. The first section asks the student to remember the dictionary symbols and themes of the unit. The answers to the true/false questions are:

1. **false**
2. **true**
3. **false**
4. **true**
5. **true**

Activity 2. The student will next be tested on words which have short vowel sounds. The student will circle the words which have short vowel sounds. The answers are: **mop, trick, fit.**

Activity 3. In the next activity the student will be tested on the use of **y** as a vowel. The student will be asked to circle the words where **y** is used as a vowel. The answers are: **by, symbol, fly**.

Activity 4. The following activity asks the student to separate the words into syllables. The answers are: **hap/py, wel/come, pa/per, can/dy, pup/py, pil/low**.

Activity 5. The final section of the test has the student divide the words into syllables and put the accent mark on the syllable that receives the accent. The answers to the activity are: **tab'/let, af'/ter, a/ bout', ta'/ble, be/gin', slen'/der.**

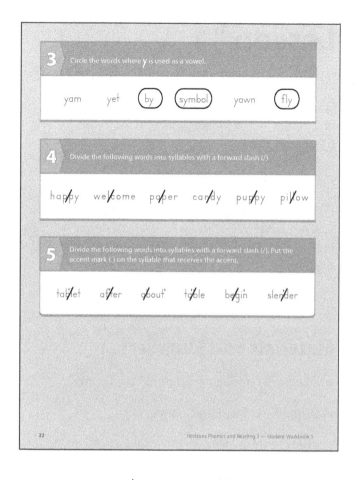

Lesson 11

Initial Consonant Blends: br, cr, dr, fr, gr, pr, tr

Overview:

- Define a consonant blend
- Read words with initial consonant blends
- Match words with initial consonant blends to the pictures
- Add consonant blends to create words

Materials and Supplies:

- Teacher's Guide and Student Workbook
- White board or chart paper
- Phonics flashcards
- Reader: "The Ant and the Grasshopper"

Teaching Tips:

Lesson Introduction. Introduce consonant blends to the student. Tell the student that a consonant blend consists of two or more consonants sounded together in such a way that each letter is heard. In this lesson the student will focus on blends formed with a consonant plus **r**. Have the student repeat the sounds of the consonant blends **br, cr, dr, fr, gr, pr,** and **tr** after you.

You may want to create flashcards with the blend on one side and a sample word on the other. Use these flashcards to review.

Ask the student to brainstorm a list of words beginning with the consonant blends **br, cr, dr, fr, gr, pr,** and **tr**. Write these words on the board. This will give the student the opportunity to think of words that he/she may not be able to spell but know. If the student is having trouble thinking of words,

the following list may help him/her begin: **breakfast, cram, dream, frisbee, grateful, praise,** and **traffic**.

Activity 1. Turn to the Student Workbook. Read through the definition at the top of the page. Have the student identify and spell the names of the consonant blends pictured on the sheet. You may want to identify each, emphasizing the blend before the student writes the word. The pictures are: **dress, broom, frame, crawl, drum, brush tree, grass, price, track, grapes, present.**

Activity 2. Continue with the second activity on the sheet. Do the first one together. Have the student try different blends before the ending. The student should write the correct blend on the blanks. Words are: **broom/groom, tree/free, grin, drive, from, prize, crayon, bread/dread.**

Activity 3. The final activity asks the student to add blends to the beginning of words as well. In this activity, however, more than one word may be formed by combining the blends and the endings.

Words: (Answers may vary.)

ace	**brace, grace, trace**
ip	**drip, grip, trip**
ape	**drape, grape**
ay	**bray, fray, gray, pray, tray**
ag	**brag, crag, drag**
ash	**brash, crash, trash**

Reading Activity.

1. Turn to "The Ant and the Grasshopper" in the Reader.

2. Ask the student to compare and contrast the ant and the grasshopper. (**The ant was busy working and preparing for winter. The grasshopper was enjoying the day and relaxing. During the winter, the ant was well-fed and happy while the grasshopper was hungry and miserable.**) What kind of a story is this? (**Fable.**) What are the characteristics of a fable? (**The animals talk. There is a moral.**)

3. Have the student find five words in the story that are consonant **r** blends. (Answers include: **bright, grasshopper, grass, traveled, bringing, trying, prepare.**)

---

2 Add the consonant blends br, cr, dr, fr, gr, pr, and tr to make the following into words.

gr
br_oom   fr_tree   _grin   _drive

_from   pr_ize   cr_ayon   br_ead
dr

---

3 Add the consonant blends br, cr, dr, fr, gr, pr, and tr to the following. See how many words you can make. The first one is done for you.

ade	_grade_	trade			
ace	brace	grace	trace		
ip	drip	grip	trip		
ape	drape	grape			
ay	bray	fray	gray	pray	tray
ag	brag	crag	drag		
ash	brash	crash	trash		

24   Horizons Phonics and Reading 3 — Student Workbook 1

Lesson 12

Initial Consonant Blends: bl, cl, fl, gl, pl, sl

Overview:

- Define a consonant blend
- Read words with initial consonant blends
- Create words using consonant blends
- Identify words with consonant plus l blends

Materials and Supplies:

- Teacher's Guide and Student Workbook
- White board or chart paper
- Phonics flashcards
- Reader: "The Ant and the Grasshopper"

Teaching Tips:

Review for Mastery. Discuss and review any work from the previous lesson that was assigned as homework. Check for completion of the activities and orally quiz the student for comprehension. Review any reading that was assigned, discussing the characters, setting, plot, theme, language, sequence, etc.

Strengthen fluency and phonemic awareness by reviewing words and sentences from the previous lessons. Build vocabulary skills by using some of the words in sentences.

Lesson Introduction. Introduce consonant blends to the student. Tell the student that a consonant blend consists of two or more consonants sounded together in such a way that each letter is heard. In this lesson the student will focus on blends formed with a consonant plus l. Have the student repeat the sounds of the

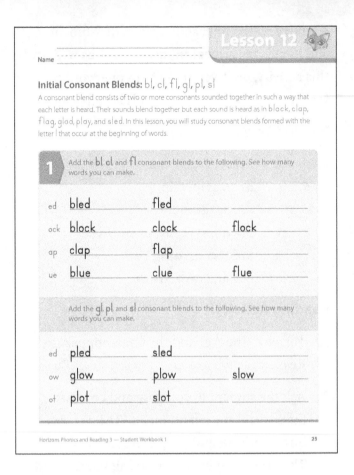

Initial Consonant Blends: bl, cl, fl, gl, pl, sl

A consonant blend consists of two or more consonants sounded together in such a way that each letter is heard. Their sounds blend together but each sound is heard as in black, clap, flag, glad, play, and sled. In this lesson, you will study consonant blends formed with the letter l that occur at the beginning of words.

1 Add the bl, cl, and fl consonant blends to the following. See how many words you can make.

ed	bled	fled	
ock	block	clock	flock
ap	clap	flap	
ue	blue	clue	flue

Add the gl, pl, and sl consonant blends to the following. See how many words you can make.

ed	pled	sled	
ow	glow	plow	slow
ot	plot	slot	

consonant blends after you: **bl, cl, fl, gl, pl,** and **sl.** You may want to create flashcards with the blend on one side and a sample word on the other. Use these flashcards to review.

Ask the student to brainstorm a list of words beginning with the consonant blends **bl, cl, fl, gl, pl,** and **sl.** Write these words on the board. This will give the student the opportunity to think of words that he/she may not be able to spell but know. If the student is having trouble thinking of words, the following list may help him/her begin: **blessed, class, flashlight, glad, plus,** and **slurp.**

Activity 1. Turn to the Student Workbook. Read through the definition at the top of the page. For the first activity, the student will be asked to form words using the consonant blends. The words the student writes may vary based on his/her understanding of words. Go over possible responses together as a class.

Words: (Answers may vary.)

ed	**bled, fled**
ock	**block, clock, flock**
ap	**clap, flap**
ue	**blue, clue, flue**

Words: (Answers may vary.)

ed	**pled, sled**
ow	**glow, plow, slow**
ot	**plot, slot**

Activity 2. In the next activity the student will be asked to use consonant blends in the context of sentences. After the student has completed the activity, go over the correct answers.

Sentences:

1. A **black** dog **played** fetch with the boy.
2. Madison **cleaned** the broken **glass** with a broom.
3. Mrs. Thomas was **glad** to receive a vase of fresh **flowers**.
4. People walked **slowly** on the **slick** sidewalk.
5. Brandon put his **clean clothes** in his **closet**.

Activity 3. The final activity asks the student to identify which words are consonant blends and which ones are not. Just because a word starts with a consonant blend doesn't mean that it is a real word!

Words:

black	clean	bloom	~~clome~~	bleed
glad	slam	sleep	glass	~~slen~~
flag	plus	~~plam~~	flip	plot
~~blad~~	clap	flood	plan	glow

Reading Activity.

1. Have the student summarize the story of "The Ant and the Grasshopper."

2. Tell the student that this story is one of "Aesop's Fables." Explain that Aesop's fables end with a moral or a lesson.

2 Fill in the blanks in the sentences with the consonant blends bl, cl, fl, gl, pl, or sl.

1. A _b_lack dog _p_layed fetch with the boy.
2. Madison _cl_eaned the broken _gl_ass with a broom.
3. Mrs. Thomas was _gl_ad to receive a vase of fresh _fl_owers.
4. People walked _sl_owly on the _sl_ick sidewalk.
5. Brandon put his _cl_ean _cl_othes in his _cl_oset.

3 Put an X over the word in each line which is not a word formed with a bl, cl, fl, gl, pl, or sl consonant blend.

black	clean	bloom	~~clome~~	bleed
glad	slam	sleep	glass	~~slen~~
flag	plus	~~plam~~	flip	plot
~~blad~~	clap	flood	plan	glow

26   Horizons Phonics and Reading 3 — Student Workbook 1

3. Ask the student what the moral or lesson is in this fable. (The last line of the fable is the moral: **It is best to prepare for the needs of future days.**)

4. Discuss how that moral can be applied to the student's life. (Areas in which it could be applied include: **homework, cleaning a room, or saving money.**)

5. The student should turn to "The Ant and the Grasshopper" in the Reader.

6. Have the student identify one word in the story that has the consonant plus **l** blend. (Answers include: **replied, plenty.**)

Lesson 13

Initial Consonant Blends: tw, sc, sk, sm, sn, sp, st, sw

Overview:

- Define a consonant blend
- Read words with initial consonant blends
- Categorize words with consonant blends
- Form words with consonant blends

Materials and Supplies:

- Teacher's Guide and Student Workbook
- White board or chart paper
- Phonics flashcards
- Reader: "John Newton" and "Amazing Grace"

Teaching Tips:

Review for Mastery. Discuss and review any work from the previous lesson that was assigned as homework. Check for completion of the activities and orally quiz the student for comprehension. Review any reading that was assigned, discussing the characters, setting, plot, theme, language, sequence, etc.

Strengthen fluency and phonemic awareness by reviewing words and sentences from the previous lessons. Build vocabulary skills by using some of the words in sentences.

Lesson Introduction. Introduce consonant blends to the student. Tell the student that a consonant blend consists of two or more consonants sounded together in such a way that each letter is heard. In this lesson the student will focus on blends formed with the letters **t** and **s** at the beginning of words. Have the student repeat the sounds of the consonant blends after you: **tw, sc, sk, sm, sn, sp, st,** and **sw.**

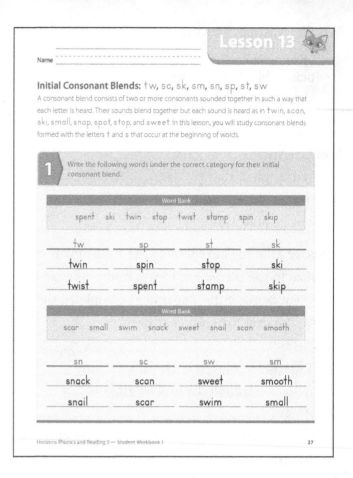

You may want to create flashcards with the blend on one side and a sample word on the other. Use these flashcards to review.

Ask the student to brainstorm a list of words beginning with the consonant blends **tw, sc, sk, sm, sn, sp, st,** and **sw.** Write these words on the board. This will give the student the opportunity to think of words that he/she may not be able to spell but know. If the student is having trouble thinking of words, the following list may help him/her begin: **twist, scale, ski, smile, snail, spot, stop,** and **sweet.**

Activity 1. Turn to the Student Workbook. Read through the definition at the top of the page. Have the student categorize the words with consonant blends in the correct category.

Words:

tw	sp	st	sk
twin	spin	stop	ski
twist	spent	stamp	skip

sn	sc	sw	sm
snack	scan	sweet	smooth
snail	scar	swim	small

Activity 2. Have the student create words using consonant blends. A student's understanding of words may impact the words he/she identifies.

Words: (Answers may vary.)

eet	**tweet**
ap	**snap**
ile	**smile**
ore	**snore, store**
ing	**sting**

Activity 3. Have the student create words using consonant blends. A student's understanding of words may impact the words he/she identifies.

Words: (Answers may vary.)

an	**swan, scan, span**
eep	**sweep**
end	**spend**
irt	**skirt**
y	**spy, sky**

Activity 4. The student should complete the worksheet by finding consonant blend words in the word search. **See image for answers.**

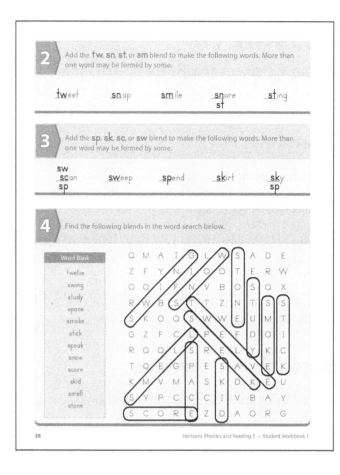

Reading Activity.

1. Turn to the selection "John Newton." Instruct the student to read the selection. Also read the words to the song, "Amazing Grace."

2. After reading, ask the student what John Newton's life was like before he turned to Christ. (**He sinned against God and worked on slave ships.**) What event made John Newton turn to God? (**During a storm he was afraid of death and called out to God.**) What was John Newton's life like after he began to follow Christ? (**He studied the Scripture and became a minister. He prepared excellent sermons that touched people's hearts.**)

3. Find five words with consonant blends **tw, sc, sk, sm, sn, sp, st,** and **sw** in the selection. (Answers include: **twas, Scripture, storm, studying, study, stating, instead, sweet, snares, snow**).

Lesson 14

Triple Consonant Blends: spl, scr, spr, str

Overview:

- Define a triple consonant blend
- Read words with triple consonant blends
- Match triple consonant blends to letters to form words
- Use triple consonant blend words to complete sentences

Materials and Supplies:

- Teacher's Guide and Student Workbook
- White board or chart paper
- Phonics flashcards
- Reader: "John Newton" and "Amazing Grace"

Teaching Tips:

Review for Mastery. Discuss and review any work from the previous lesson that was assigned as homework. Check for completion of the activities and orally quiz the student for comprehension. Review any reading that was assigned, discussing the characters, setting, plot, theme, language, sequence, etc.

Strengthen fluency and phonemic awareness by reviewing words and sentences from the previous lessons. Build vocabulary skills by using some of the words in sentences.

Lesson Introduction. Introduce triple consonant blends to the student. Tell the student that triple consonant blends consist of three consonants sounded together in such a way that each letter is heard. Have the student repeat the sounds of the consonant blends after you: **spl**, **scr**, **spr**, and **str**.

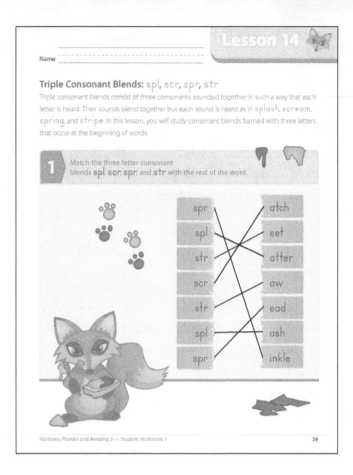

You may want to create flashcards with the blend on one side and a sample word on the other. Use these flashcards to review.

Ask the student to brainstorm a list of words with the consonant blends **spl**, **scr**, **spr**, and **str**. Write these words on the board. This will give the student the opportunity to think of words that he/she may not be able to spell but know. If the student is having trouble thinking of words, the following list may help him/her begin: **splash**, **scrap**, **sprint**, and **stream**.

Activity 1. Turn to the Student Workbook. Read through the definition at the top of the page. Match the three letter consonant blends with the given letters to form words. Words: **sprinkle**, **splatter**, **street**, **scratch**, **straw**, **splash**, **spread**.

Activity 2. Ask the student to form words using three letter consonant blends. The words may vary based on a student's knowledge of words.

ing	**spring, string**
eam	**scream, stream**
it	**split**
een	**spleen, screen**
ain	**sprain, strain**

Activity 3. Have the student use three letter consonant blend words to complete the sentences. Answers: **stream, scribble, strap, stripe, scrub, spread, splash, spring.**

Reading Activity.

1. Return to the selection "John Newton." Ask the student to reread the words to the song "Amazing Grace."

2. Explain that the song was written as a poem with rhymes.

3. Have the student identify which words rhyme at the end of lines. (**The first and third and second and fourth lines rhyme.**)

4. Ask the student to read some of the rhyming words. Ask the student what words in the poem remind him/her of how John Newton came to be a Christian while he was on the ship during the storm. (Answers may include: **He was a wretch, he was lost but found, and safe at home.**)

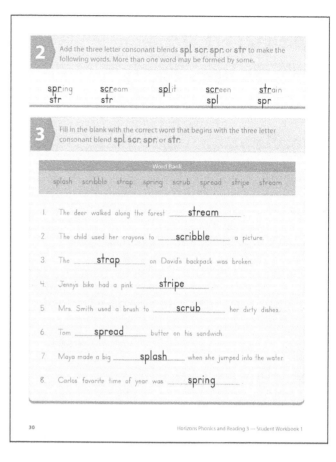

Lesson 15

Final Consonant Blends: nt, ct, ft, pt, lt

Overview:

- Define a consonant blend
- Read words with final consonant blends
- Form words using final consonant blends
- Identify the sounds of final consonant blends
- Complete sentences with words having final consonant blends

Materials and Supplies:

- Teacher's Guide and Student Workbook
- White board or chart paper
- Phonics flashcards
- Reader: "John Newton" and "Amazing Grace"

Teaching Tips:

Review for Mastery. Discuss and review any work from the previous lesson that was assigned as homework. Check for completion of the activities and orally quiz the student for comprehension. Review any reading that was assigned, discussing the characters, setting, plot, theme, language, sequence, etc.

Strengthen fluency and phonemic awareness by reviewing words and sentences from the previous lessons. Build vocabulary skills by using some of the words in sentences.

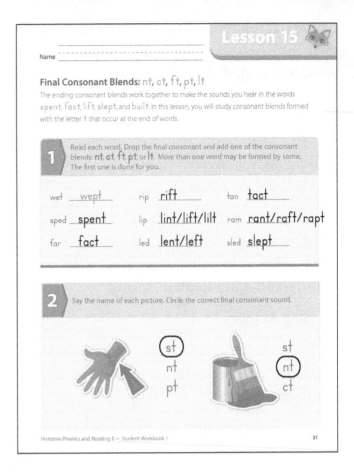

Lesson Introduction. Introduce final consonant blends to the student. Tell the student that final consonant blends consist of two consonants sounded together in such a way that each letter is heard. Have the student repeat the sounds of the consonant blends after you: **nt**, **ct**, **ft**, **pt**, and **lt**.

You may want to create flashcards with the blend on one side and a sample word on the other. Use these flashcards to review.

Ask the student to brainstorm a list of words with the consonant blends **nt**, **ct**, **ft**, **pt**, and **lt**. Write these words on the board. This will give the student the opportunity to think of words that he/she may not be able to spell but know. If the student is having trouble thinking of words, the following list may help him/her begin: **count**, **fact**, **left**, **slept**, and **built**.

Activity 1. Turn to the Student Workbook. Read through the definition at the top of the page. Direct the student in the first activity where students form words using final consonant blends. Answers:

rip	**rift**
tan	**tact**
sped	**spent**
lip	**lint/lift/lilt**
ram	**rant/raft/rapt**
far	**fact**
led	**lent/left**
sled	**slept**

Activity 2. Direct the student to the next activity where he/she will be asked to identify and write words with final two letter consonant blends. Answers: **wrist, paint, crust, plant, left.**

Activity 3. The final activity on the sheet asks the student to identify the word which best completes each sentence. As an added activity, ask the student to make a sentence using the word which wasn't correct. Answers:

1. Carson wanted his parents to **adopt** a dog for his birthday.

2. Mr. Owens painted his **front** door blue.

3. Alice used a broom when she **swept** the sidewalk.

4. James walked **past** the library on his way home.

5. The garden **pest** ate holes in the lettuce.

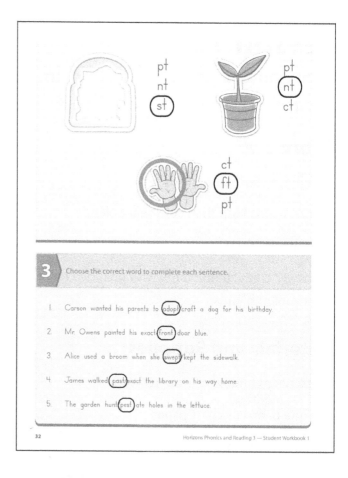

Reading Activity.

1. Have the student focus on the words in "Amazing Grace." Together discuss the themes of the various verses. Take the time to define words which may be unfamiliar to the student.

2. Encourage the student to see how John Newton focused on his sinfulness and the new life he received through Christ.

3. Discuss why the student thinks the song "Amazing Grace" is a favorite hymn of so many people. (Answers may include: **The reminder that despite our sins God still cares for us.**)

Lesson 16

Final Consonant Blends: lk, lf, lp, lm, mp, nd

Overview:

- Define a consonant blend
- Read words with final consonant blends
- Create words with final consonant blends
- Answer clues about words with final two letter consonant blends

Materials and Supplies:

- Teacher's Guide and Student Workbook
- White board or chart paper
- Phonics flashcards
- Reader: "John Newton" and "Amazing Grace"

Teaching Tips:

Review for Mastery. Discuss and review any work from the previous lesson that was assigned as homework. Check for completion of the activities and orally quiz the student for comprehension. Review any reading that was assigned, discussing the characters, setting, plot, theme, language, sequence, etc.

Strengthen fluency and phonemic awareness by reviewing words and sentences from the previous lessons. Build vocabulary skills by using some of the words in sentences.

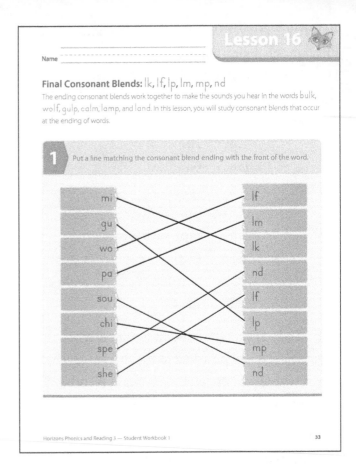

Lesson Introduction. Introduce final consonant blends to the student. Tell the student that final consonant blends consist of two consonants sounded together in such a way that each letter is heard. Have the student repeat the sounds of the consonant blends after you: **lk**, **lf**, **lp**, **lm**, **mp**, and **nd**.

You may want to create flashcards with the blend on one side and a sample word on the other. Use these flashcards to review.

Ask the student to brainstorm a list of words with the consonant blends **lk**, **lf**, **lp**, **lm**, **mp**, and **nd**. Write these words on the board. This will give the student the opportunity to think of words that he/she may not be able to spell but know. If the student is having trouble thinking of words, the following list may help him/her begin: **bulk**, **half**, **help**, **balm**, **lamp**, **brand**.

Activity 1. Turn to the Student Workbook. Read through the definition at the top of the page. Direct the student in the first activity where students form words using final consonant blends. Have the student complete the activity where he/she matches the beginning of a word with an ending consonant blend. Answers: **milk, gulp, wolf, palm, sound, chimp, spend, shelf.**

Activity 2. The student should complete the next activity where words are formed with final two letter consonant blends. Answers may vary:

sta	**stalk, stand, stamp**
ca	**calf, calm, camp**
hu	**hulk, hump**
ye	**yelp**
wa	**walk, wand**

Activity 3. This lesson concludes with a crossword puzzle. The student should answer the clues to form the words that complete the crossword. You will want to go over the correct answers with the student.

Across:	Down:
3. **round**	1. **ground**
5. **walk**	2. **yolk**
7. **help**	4. **lamp**
9. **front**	6. **shelf**
10. **calm**	8. **stamp**

Reading Activity.

1. This will be the final lesson on the selections "John Newton" and "Amazing Grace." Begin by asking the student what he/she can learn from the life of John Newton. (Answers may include: **God wants all people to love him. God can use all kinds of people to serve him.**)

2. Ask the student to find three words in the selection which end with the final consonant blend **nd.** (Answers include: **England, and, sound, found, blind.**)

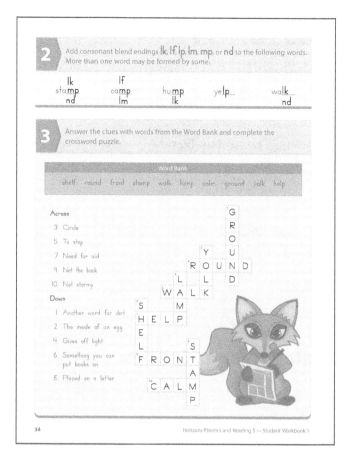

Lesson 17

Initial and Final Consonant Blends

Overview:

- Define a consonant blend

- Read words with initial and final consonant blends

- Create words having initial and final consonant blends

- Identify words with initial and final consonant blends

Materials and Supplies:

- Teacher's Guide and Student Workbook

- White board or chart paper

- Phonics flashcards

- Reader: "The Pink River Dolphin"

Teaching Tips:

Review for Mastery. Discuss and review any work from the previous lesson that was assigned as homework. Check for completion of the activities and orally quiz the student for comprehension. Review any reading that was assigned, discussing the characters, setting, plot, theme, language, sequence, etc.

Strengthen fluency and phonemic awareness by reviewing words and sentences from the previous lessons. Build vocabulary skills by using some of the words in sentences.

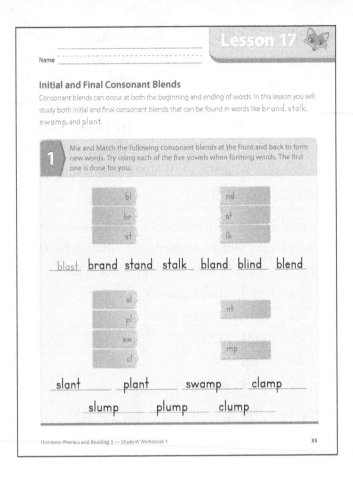

Lesson Introduction. Review initial and final consonant blends with the student. Together brainstorm initial consonant blends such as **bl**, **st**, and **fl**. Brainstorm final consonant blends like **nd**, **lk**, and **st** as well.

You may want to use the flashcards you created to review.

Ask the student to brainstorm a list of words with initial and final consonant blends. Write these words on the board. This will give the student the opportunity to think of words that he/she may not be able to spell but know. If the student is having trouble thinking of words, the following list may help him/her begin: **smash**, **plant**, **slash**, and **twist**.

Activity 1. Turn to the Student Workbook. Direct the student in the first activity where the student mixes and matches initial and final consonant blends to form words. You may want to do a word together before the student continues alone. Answers: **blast, brand, stand, stalk, bland, blend, blind, slant, slump, plump, clump, plant, swamp, clamp**.

Activity 2. In the next activity, the student will be asked to identify words that have both initial and final consonant blends. Emphasize that the words need to have both initial and final consonant blends. Go over the correct answers with the student. Answers: **stamp, strand, clamp, tract, front, ground, blunt, draft**.

Activity 3. For the final activity, the student will read a Bible passage and locate words with initial and final consonant blends. Answers: **perfect, statutes, trustworthy**.

Reading Activity.

1. The student should turn in the Reader to the selection "The Pink River Dolphin."

2. Before reading the selection, ask the student what he/she knows about dolphins. (Answers may include: **They are friendly animals, they do tricks, and they live in the ocean.**)

3. When reading, the student should look for how the dolphins described in this selection are similar or different than what he/she thought a dolphin was like. (**The student may be surprised to learn that dolphins can be pink and not live in the ocean.**) Is this story fiction, make believe or nonfiction, a true story or one that contains facts? (**Nonfiction.**)

4. Ask the student to locate five words that have either initial or final consonant blends. (Words may include: **pink, known, swim, flowing, long, friendly, playful, hump, from, smaller.**)

2 Circle the words that have a consonant blend at the beginning and the end.

wolf	stamp	strand	broom
clamp	tract	sweet	stream
front	ground	colt	flower
blunt	calm	draft	blew

3 Underline all of the words in the following Bible passage that have a consonant blend at the front, back, or both.

The law of the LORD is perfect,

reviving the soul.

The statutes of the LORD are trustworthy,

making wise the simple.

— Psalm 19:7 (NIV)

36   Horizons Phonics and Reading 3 — Student Workbook 1

Lesson 18

Consonant Digraphs: ch, th, ph, wh, sh, gh

Overview:

- Define a consonant digraph
- Read words with consonant digraphs
- Add consonant digraphs to the beginning, middle, and end of words
- Identify words with beginning, middle, and end consonant digraphs

Materials and Supplies:

- Teacher's Guide and Student Workbook
- White board or chart paper
- Phonics flashcards
- Reader: "The Pink River Dolphin"

Teaching Tips:

Review for Mastery. Discuss and review any work from the previous lesson that was assigned as homework. Check for completion of the activities and orally quiz the student for comprehension. Review any reading that was assigned, discussing the characters, setting, plot, theme, language, sequence, etc.

Strengthen fluency and phonemic awareness by reviewing words and sentences from the previous lessons. Build vocabulary skills by using some of the words in sentences.

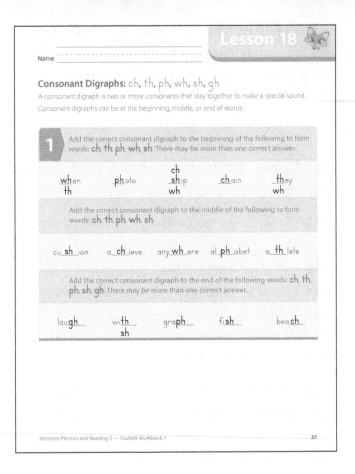

Lesson Introduction. Introduce consonant digraphs to the student. A consonant digraph is two or more consonants that stay together to make a special sound. Consonant digraphs can be at the beginning, middle, or end of words. Have the student repeat the sounds of the consonant digraphs after you: **ch, th, ph, wh, sh, gh.**

You may want to create flashcards with the digraph on one side and a sample word on the other. Use these flashcards to review.

Ask the student to brainstorm a list of words with the consonant digraphs **ch, th, ph, wh, sh, gh.** Write these words on the board. This will give the student the opportunity to think of words that he/she may not be able to spell but know. If the student is having trouble thinking of words, the following list may help him/her begin: **sandwich, thanksgiving, dolphin, where, dishwasher,** and **laughter.**

Activity 1. Turn to the Student Workbook. Read through the definition at the top of the page. Direct the student in the first activity where the student places consonant digraphs at the beginning of words. The student will continue to add consonant digraphs to the middle and end of words as well. Answers:

- **when/then, photo, ship/whip/chip, chain, they/whey**
- **cushion, achieve, anywhere, alphabet, athlete**
- **laugh, with/wish, graph, fish, beach**

Activity 2. The final activity asks the student to place the words in the correct column depending on whether the consonant digraph is at the beginning, middle, or end. Answers:

Beginning	Middle	End
chin	together	enough
their	dolphin	graph
phone	fashion	crush
where		
crush		

Reading Activity.

1. Turn to the selection "The Pink River Dolphin" in the Reader.

2. Ask the student to list three facts about this type of dolphin. (Answers include: **They live in South America, they live in fresh water, and their necks can move from side to side.**) What makes these dolphins different from other dolphins? (Differences include: **color, lack of a dorsal fin, living in fresh water, and a neck that moves from side to side.**)

3. Have the student identify words with consonant digraphs. (Words include: **dolphin, other, fresh, fish, they, south, their, this, these, fishing, changes, where.**)

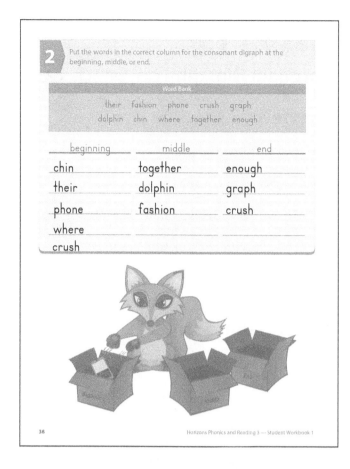

Lesson 19

Consonant Digraphs: gn, wr, tch, ck

Overview:

- Define a consonant digraph
- Read words with consonant digraphs
- Identify words with consonant digraphs
- Form words with consonant digraphs
- Correctly spell words with consonant digraphs

Materials and Supplies:

- Teacher's Guide and Student Workbook
- White board or chart paper
- Phonics flashcards
- Reader: "The Pink River Dolphin"

Teaching Tips:

Review for Mastery. Discuss and review any work from the previous lesson that was assigned as homework. Check for completion of the activities and orally quiz the student for comprehension. Review any reading that was assigned, discussing the characters, setting, plot, theme, language, sequence, etc.

Strengthen fluency and phonemic awareness by reviewing words and sentences from the previous lessons. Build vocabulary skills by using some of the words in sentences.

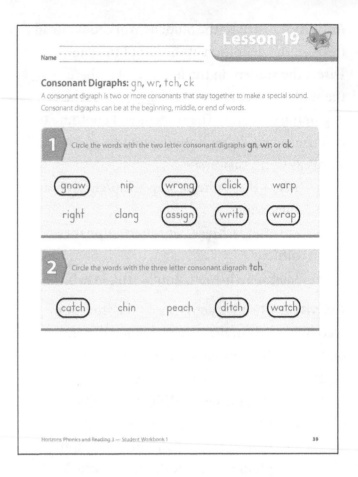

Lesson Introduction. Review consonant digraphs with the student. Have the student repeat the sounds of the consonant digraphs after you: **gn**, **wr**, **tch**, and **ck**.

You may want to create flashcards with the digraph on one side and a sample word on the other. Use these flashcards to review.

Ask the student to brainstorm a list of words with the consonant digraphs **gn**, **wr**, **tch**, **ck**. Write these words on the board. This will give the student the opportunity to think of words that he/she may not be able to spell but know. If the student is having trouble thinking of words, the following list may help him/her begin: **gnaw**, **wrench**, **hatch**, and **check**.

Activity 1. Turn to the Student Workbook. Read through the definition at the top of the page. Direct the student in the first activity where he/she will be asked to identify words with consonant digraphs. Answers: **gnaw**, **wrong**, **click**, **assign**, **write**, **wrap**.

Activity 2. The second activity asks the student to circle the words with three letter consonant digraphs. Answers: **catch**, **ditch**, **watch**.

Activity 3. In the next activity the student will be asked to add consonant digraphs to form words. Go over the answers with the student. Answers: **catch**, **design**, **write**, **watch**, **lock**, **stretch**, **gnaw**, **rack**, **wrong**, **back**.

Activity 4. The final activity asks the student to identify words with consonant digraphs which are spelled correctly. Answers: **wrap**, **catch**, **track**, **gnat**, **rack**, **stretch**, **design**, **write**.

Reading Activity.

1. This will be the final time studying the reading "The Pink River Dolphin." Discuss what challenges the pink river dolphin faces. (**The biggest danger the dolphins face comes from humans.**) What challenges do people bring to the dolphins? (**They are endangering their habitat. They also have boats and fishing equipment which harm the dolphin.**)

2. Ask the student what he/she thinks can be done to protect the dolphin. (Answers may include: **Limits on boating and fishing. They also can make sure the river and the surrounding woods are not overdeveloped.**) Why do you think people should protect animals like the pink river dolphin? (**Help the student to see that God created these animals. God gave people the job of caring for His creation.**)

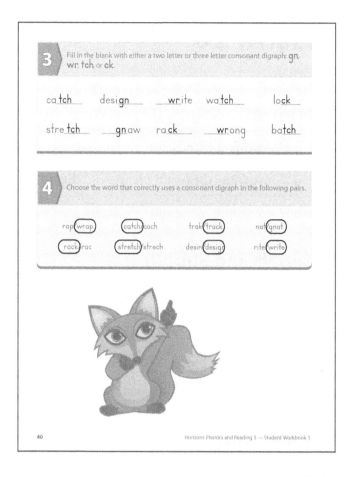

ca<u>tch</u>   desi<u>gn</u>   <u>wr</u>ite   wa<u>tch</u>   lock

stre<u>tch</u>   <u>gn</u>aw   ra<u>ck</u>   <u>wr</u>ong   ba<u>tch</u>

4   Choose the word that correctly uses a consonant digraph in the following pairs.

rap (wrap)   (catch)/cach   trak (track)   nat (gnat)

(rack)/rac   (stretch)/strech   desin (design)   rite (write)

40   Horizons Phonics and Reading 3 — Student Workbook 1

Lesson 20
Review

Overview:

- Define consonant blends and digraphs
- Read words with consonant blends and digraphs
- Review consonant blends and digraphs

Materials and Supplies:

- Teacher's Guide and Student Workbook
- White board or chart paper
- Phonics flashcards
- Reader: "The Princess Who Slept On A Pea"

Teaching Tips:

Review for Mastery. Discuss and review any work from the previous lesson that was assigned as homework. Check for completion of the activities and orally quiz the student for comprehension. Review any reading that was assigned, discussing the characters, setting, plot, theme, language, sequence, etc.

Strengthen fluency and phonemic awareness by reviewing words and sentences from the previous lessons. Build vocabulary skills by using some of the words in sentences. You may want to use the flashcards you created to review.

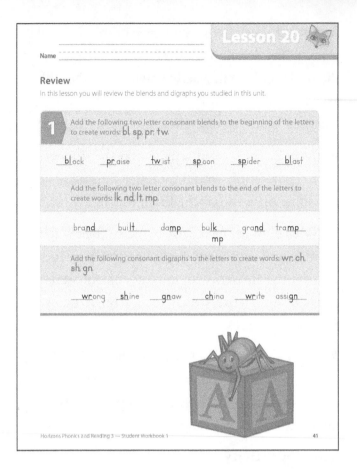

Activity 1. The student should turn to the Workbook and complete the first review activity. In this activity the student will add two letter consonant blends or digraphs to complete words. Answers: **block, praise, twist, spoon, spider, blast, brand, built, damp, bulk/bump, grand, tramp, wrong, shine, gnaw, china, write, assign.**

Activity 2. Turn to the second activity. Ask the student to identify the word in each line which does not contain a consonant blend or digraph. Answers: **seen, cookie, bacon, gallon, salad.**

Activity 3. In the final activity, the student must choose the correct word with a consonant blend to complete each sentence. Read the correct sentences with the class.

Answers:

1. Hope likes to **draw** pictures of dogs.
2. Matt and John like to **sled** during the winter.
3. The **crow** sat in the tree branch.
4. Jenny picked a **flower** for her mother.
5. Ben likes to **splash** in the pool.

Reading Activity.

1. Ask the student to turn to the selection "The Princess Who Slept On A Pea."

2. The student should read the selection for his/her personal enjoyment.

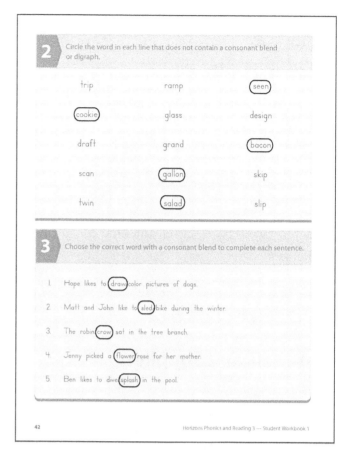

Test 2

Lessons 11-20

Overview:

- Define a consonant blend
- Read words with double and triple consonant blends
- Identify words with initial and final consonant blends
- Recognize words with beginning, middle and end consonant digraphs

Materials and Supplies:

- Student Test

Teaching Tips:

Review for Mastery. Discuss and review any work from the previous lesson that was assigned as homework. Check for completion of the activities and orally quiz the student for comprehension. Review any reading that was assigned.

Lesson Introduction. This lesson tests the material the student learned in the unit. Before the test you may want to ask the student if he/she has any final questions. There may be questions from the review the student will want to go over again. Remind the student that the final test follows a similar format as the review.

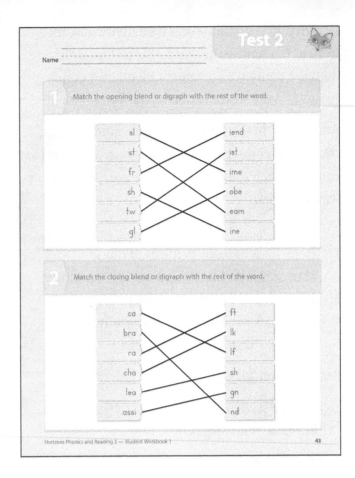

Activity 1. Match the opening blend or digraph with the rest of the word. Answers: **slime, steam, friend, shine, twist, globe**.

Activity 2. Match the closing blend or digraph with the rest of the word. Answers: **calf, brand, raft, chalk, leash, assign**.

Activity 3. Underline ten consonant blends and digraphs in the paragraph. Answer:

Each spring Joseph **helps** his **grandpa plant** a garden. **They** enjoy working **together planting** seeds in **the ground. They plant** beans, tomatoes, **and sweet** peas. All summer **Joseph** enjoys eating food **that** is **grown** in **the** garden.

Underline at least ten consonant blends and digraphs in the following paragraph.

Each spring Joseph helps his grandpa plant a garden. They enjoy working together planting seeds in the ground. They plant beans, tomatoes, and sweet peas. All summer Joseph enjoys eating food that is grown in the garden.

44   Horizons Phonics and Reading 3 — Student Workbook 1

Lesson 21

Vowel Digraphs: ai, ay

Overview:

- Define a vowel digraph
- Read words with long ā digraphs
- Recognize that the letter combinations **ai** and **ay** are long ā digraphs
- Form words with digraphs

Materials and Supplies:

- Teacher's Guide and Student Workbook
- White board or chart paper
- Phonics flashcards
- Reader: "The Frog Prince: Part I"

Teaching Tips:

Lesson Introduction. Ask the student to think of a word with a long ā vowel sound. Examples may include **ate, cave,** and **acorn.** Tell the student that sometimes two vowels work together to make the long ā sound. These are called digraphs. In this lesson the student will study the digraphs **ai** and **ay.** The letter **y** will be considered a vowel in the lesson. Write on the board the words **braid** and **lay.** Have the student pronounce the words emphasizing the long ā vowel sound. Ask for other examples of words with the long ā sound expressed as the digraphs **ay** and **ai.** Examples may include: **wait, plain, day,** and **may.**

You may want to create flashcards of words with the **ai** and **ay** digraphs. The student can study these throughout the unit.

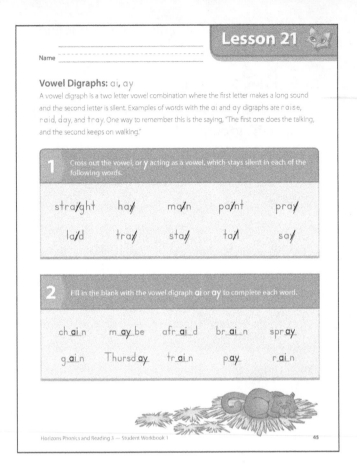

Activity 1. Take out the activity sheet accompanying this lesson. Read through the definition at the top of the page. Consider writing the phrase, "The first one does the talking, and the second keeps on walking," on the board. In this activity, the student should cross out the second letter of each vowel digraph. Answers: **straight, hay, main, point, pray, laid, tray, stay, tail, say.**

Activity 2. The student should fill in the blank with the correct vowel digraph either **ai** or **ay** to complete each word. Remind the student that all of the words will have the long ā sound where the blank occurs. Answers are: **chain, maybe, afraid, brain, spray, gain, Thursday, train, pay, rain.**

Activity 3. Using words with the vowel digraph **ai** or **ay**, the student should fill in each sentence. Answers are: **play, slay, praise, raised, way, plain, Friday, waited.**

Reading Activity.

1. The student should read "The Frog Prince: Part I."

2. Once the student has read the selection, have the student answer the following questions. Describe the princess. **(She is beautiful, people recognize her beauty, and her favorite toy is a golden ball.)** Describe the frog. **(He is old, ugly, and helpful.)** How did the princess respond to the frog's kindness? **(She promised to be the frog's friend, but she ran off once she had her ball.)**

3. Ask the student to predict what he/she thinks will happen next. **(Answers will vary.)**

4. Find three words in the selection which have **ai** or **ay** digraphs. (Answers include: **wailed, wait, maiden, play.**)

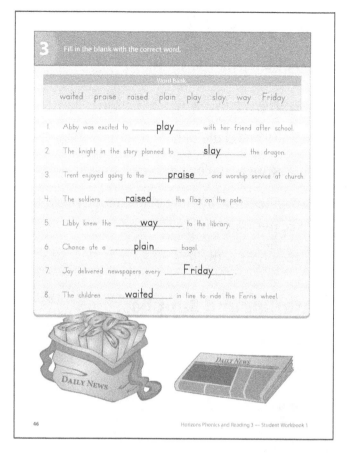

3 Fill in the blank with the correct word.

Word Bank

waited   praise   raised   plain   play   slay   way   Friday

1. Abby was excited to _____play_____ with her friend after school.

2. The knight in the story planned to _____slay_____ the dragon.

3. Trent enjoyed going to the _____praise_____ and worship service at church.

4. The soldiers _____raised_____ the flag on the pole.

5. Libby knew the _____way_____ to the library.

6. Chance ate a _____plain_____ bagel.

7. Joy delivered newspapers every _____Friday_____.

8. The children _____waited_____ in line to ride the Ferris wheel.

46

Horizons Phonics and Reading 3 — Student Workbook 1

Lesson 22

Vowel Digraphs: ei, ie

Overview:

- Define a vowel digraph
- Read words with long ē digraphs
- Recognize that the letter combinations **ei** and **ie** make the long ē or long ī sound
- Form words with digraphs

Materials and Supplies:

- Teacher's Guide and Student Workbook
- White board or chart paper
- Phonics flashcards
- Reader: "The Frog Prince: Part II"

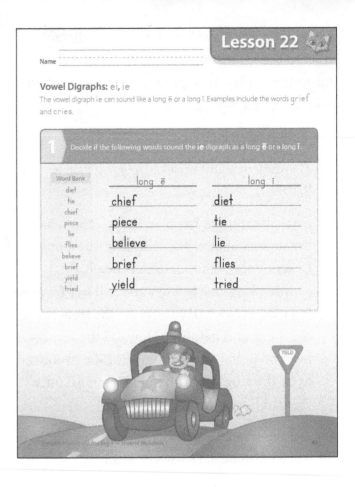

Teaching Tips:

Review for Mastery. Discuss and review any work from the previous lesson that was assigned as homework. Check for completion of the activities and orally quiz the student for comprehension. Review any reading that was assigned, discussing the characters, setting, plot, theme, language, sequence, etc.

Strengthen fluency and phonemic awareness by reviewing words and sentences from the previous lessons. Build vocabulary skills by using some of the words in sentences.

You may want to create flashcards of words with the **ei** and **ie** digraphs. The student can study these throughout the unit.

Lesson Introduction. Remind the student that in the previous lesson words with the vowel digraph **ai** and **ay** sounding ā were studied. In this lesson, the student will look at digraphs that make the long ē or long ī sound. These are spelled **ei** and **ie**. Write the words **seize, tie** and **brief** on the board. Discuss how each **ie** or **ei** letter digraph forms the long ē or long ī sound.

Activity 1. Turn to the activity sheet accompanying this lesson. Read through the list of words with the student. Ask the student to put the words in the correct column depending on if the digraph has a long ē or long ī sound.

long ē	long ī
chief	diet
piece	tie
believe	lie
brief	flies
yield	tried

Activity 2. Read together with the student the words in the Word Bank he/she will use to fill in the blanks. Have the student emphasize the digraphs' long ē or long ī sounds. This will reinforce what the student worked on in the previous activity. Go over the correct answers together: **tie, receipt, tried, weird, ceiling, seize, dried, chief, fried, cried**.

Activity 3. Ask the student to fill in the blank with either the **ie** or **ei** digraph. The student may wish to have a piece of scratch paper nearby. This way the student can practice spelling the word before filling in the blank on the activity sheet. Answers are: **ceiling, either, fried, tries, skies, receipt, grief, tried, priest, piece**.

Reading Activity.

1. Ask the student to read "The Frog Prince: Part II."

2. Discuss the selection with your student. How did the princess respond to seeing the frog again? (**She shut the door on him and struck him with her knife at the dinner table.**) Why do you think she acted this way? (**She may have thought the frog ugly or not wanted to admit the frog helped her.**) What does the king tell the princess to do when she shuts the door in the frog's face? (**He tells her to let the frog in.**) Why? (**A princess is not to tell a lie.**) Why was the young prince turned into a frog? (**A wicked woman was jealous of his mother.**) Why does the frog love the princess? (**She saved him and let him eat at the table. Because of her, he was turned from a frog into a prince.**) Tell the student you will finish discussing the selection in the next lesson.

3. Find three examples of **ie** or **ei** digraphs in the reading. (Examples include: **lie, friends, received, cried.**)

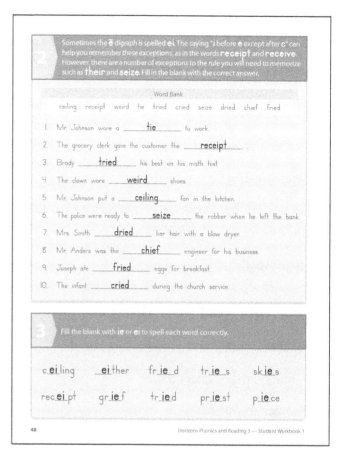

Lesson 23

Vowel Digraphs: ee, ea, ey

Overview:

- Define a vowel digraph
- Read words with long **ē** digraphs
- Recognize that the letter combinations **ee**, **ea**, and **ey** make the long **ē** sound
- Form words with digraphs

Materials and Supplies:

- Teacher's Guide and Student Workbook
- White board or chart paper
- Phonics flashcards
- Reader: "The Frog Prince"

Teaching Tips:

Review for Mastery. Discuss and review any work from the previous lesson that was assigned as homework. Check for completion of the activities and orally quiz the student for comprehension. Review any reading that was assigned, discussing the characters, setting, plot, theme, language, sequence, etc.

Strengthen fluency and phonemic awareness by reviewing words and sentences from the previous lessons. Build vocabulary skills by using some of the words in sentences.

You may want to create flashcards of words with the **ee, ea,** and **ey** digraphs. The student can study these throughout the unit.

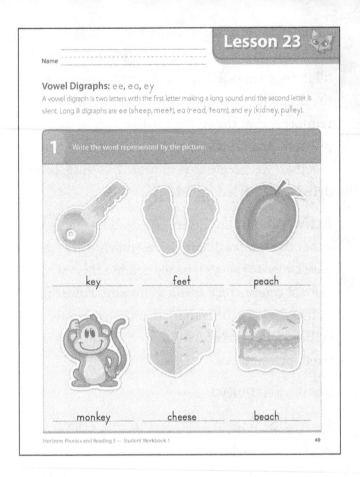

Name

Vowel Digraphs: ee, ea, ey
A vowel digraph is two letters with the first letter making a long sound and the second letter is silent. Long ē digraphs are ee (sheep, meet), ea (read, team), and ey (kidney, pulley).

1 Write the word represented by the picture.

key   feet   peach

monkey   cheese   beach

Horizons Phonics and Reading 3 — Student Workbook 1   49

Lesson Introduction. On the board write the words **flee**, **read**, and **key**. Ask the student which vowel is doing the talking and which vowel is doing the walking in each word. The student should remember that in a vowel digraph the first letter speaks while the second letter is silent. Remind the student that in the previous lessons words with the vowel digraphs made the long **ā**, **ē**, or **ī** sound. These were spelled **ai**, **ay**, **ei**, and **ie**. Have the student look at the words on the board. Which sounds are these digraphs making? They are making the long **ē**. How is the long **ē** being spelled? It is being spelled **ee**, **ea**, and **ey**.

Activity 1. Turn to the accompanying activity sheet. Read through the information and examples listed on the top. Together identify each of the pictures. The student should write the word with a vowel digraph that identifies each picture. The answers are: **key, feet, peach, monkey, cheese, beach.**

Activity 2. The lesson continues with the student identifying the silent letter in each vowel digraph. Answers: **free, honey, steam, meet, heat, alley, dream, clean, sleep, volley.**

Activity 3. The lesson concludes with a word search. Before the student searches for the words, have him/her read each word emphasizing the long ē vowel sound found in each. Answers: **creep, weak, chimney, screen, teacher, squeak, steep, trolley, week, donkey.**

Reading Activity.

1. Finish your discussion of "The Frog Prince." Fairy tales often end "happily ever after." How does this fairy tale end happily ever after? (Examples include: **The frog was turned back into a prince, the prince and princess married, and the kingdom loved the couple.**) Fairy tales often have lessons that the reader or listener is to learn. What lessons are taught in this fairy tale? (The student should identify some of the following themes: **Jealousy turned the prince into a frog, telling a lie caused the frog's good deed to go unrewarded, kindness turned the frog back into a prince.**) A well-known saying is that, "You shouldn't judge a book by its cover." How is this saying shown in the selection? (**The frog appeared ugly but was really a handsome prince.**) How can you keep from "judging a book by its cover?" (**Answers will vary.**)

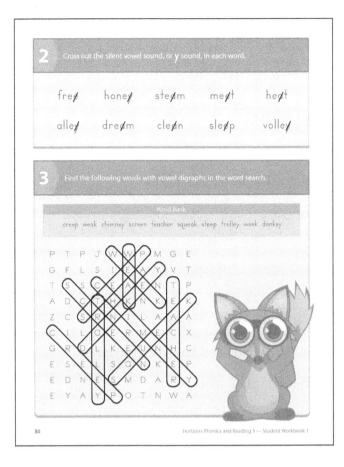

2. (At the end of the discussion relate the following Bible verse to students: 1 Samuel 16:7 (NIV) "But the LORD said to Samuel, 'Do not consider his appearance or his height, for I have rejected him. The LORD does not look at the things man looks at. Man looks at the outward appearance, but the LORD looks at the heart.'"

3. The student should locate five words having the digraphs **ee, ea,** and **ey.** (Examples include: **heard, creeping, sweet, eat, break, heart, beauty, ceased, beautiful.**)

Lesson 24

Vowel Diphthongs: ew, ow

Overview:

- Define a vowel diphthong

- Read words with diphthongs

- Recognize that the letter combinations **ow** and **ew** make diphthongs

- Form words with diphthongs

Materials and Supplies:

- Teacher's Guide and Student Workbook

- White board or chart paper

- Phonics flashcards

- Reader: "Jackie Robinson"

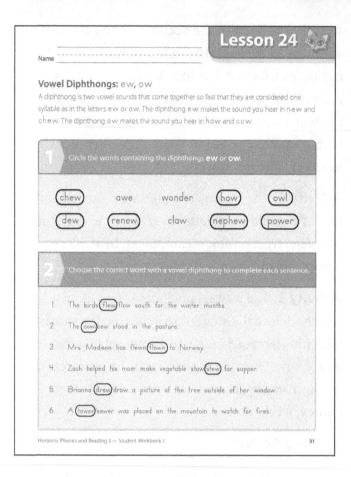

Teaching Tips:

Review for Mastery. Discuss and review any work from the previous lesson that was assigned as homework. Check for completion of the activities and orally quiz the student for comprehension. Review any reading that was assigned discussing the characters, setting, plot, theme, language, sequence, etc.

Strengthen fluency and phonemic awareness by reviewing words and sentences from the previous lessons. Build vocabulary skills by using some of the words in sentences.

You may want to create flashcards of words with the **ew** and **ow** diphthongs. The student can study these throughout the unit.

Lesson Introduction. Begin by having the student say the **ew** and **ow** diphthong sounds. Explain that a diphthong is two vowel sounds that come together so fast that they are considered one vowel. Once the student understands the unique sound, have the student think of words having the **ew** or **ow** sound. Examples include: **blew, threw, brow,** and **chow.**

Activity 1. Have the student turn to the activity sheet accompanying this lesson. The student should circle **ew** or **ow** diphthongs. While there may be other diphthongs in the activity, the student should only circle those sounding **ew** or **ow**. Answers are: **chew, how, owl, dew, renew, nephew, power.**

Activity 2. The next section asks the student to identify the correctly used and spelled diphthongs which will complete each sentence. You may want to have the student read each sentence with both word options before choosing the correct one. Answers: **flew, cow, flown, stew, drew, tower.**

Activity 3. Read the psalm together with the student. You may want to read responsively with you reading one line and the student the next. Discuss the psalm with your student. Talk about the creation God has made and the ways in which He cares for it. Look at the images in the psalm, as in the phrase, "the hills are clothed with gladness." After discussing the psalm, the student should locate words using either the **ew** or **ow** diphthong. Answers include: **vows, showers, crown.** Words with long **o** digraph: **furrows, overflow, meadows.** For added practice have the student find some of the other double vowel words in the psalm.

Reading Activity.

1. Have the student read the selection "Jackie Robinson."

2. Discuss the selection with the student. Why was there a Negro baseball league? (**Major League Baseball (MLB) did not allow African-Americans to play with them.**) How was the Negro League different than MLB? (**The players in the Negro league earned less, traveled more, and stayed in less comfortable motels.**) Why did the Brooklyn Dodgers want Jackie Robinson on their team? (**They wanted an African-American player as well as a great baseball player.**) What warnings did the Brooklyn Dodgers give Jackie Robinson? (**They told him he would probably receive boos and have things thrown at him. They also warned him that people would probably yell mean things at him.**) What do you think it might have been like for Jackie Robinson to play his first MLB game? (Answers may include: **He was nervous, afraid, proud.**)

3. Ask the student to find two words in the selection that have **ew** or **ow** diphthongs. (Answers include: **throw, knew, following.**)

Lesson 25

Vowel Diphthongs: oi, oy, ou

Overview:

- Define a vowel diphthong
- Read words with diphthongs
- Recognize that the letter combinations **oi**, **oy**, and **ou** make diphthongs
- Form words with diphthongs

Materials and Supplies:

- Teacher's Guide and Student Workbook
- White board or chart paper
- Phonics flashcards
- Reader: "Jackie Robinson"

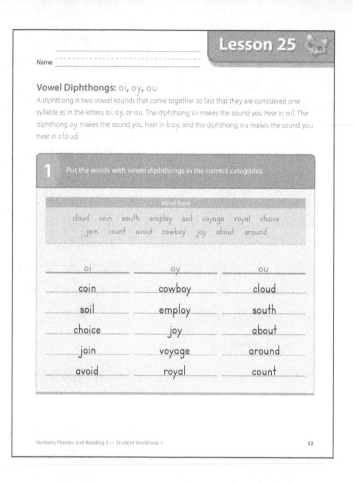

Teaching Tips:

Review for Mastery. Discuss and review any work from the previous lesson that was assigned as homework. Check for completion of the activities and orally quiz the student for comprehension. Review any reading that was assigned, discussing the characters, setting, plot, theme, language, sequence, etc.

Strengthen fluency and phonemic awareness by reviewing words and sentences from the previous lessons. Build vocabulary skills by using some of the words in sentences.

You may want to create flashcards of words with the **oi**, **oy**, and **ou** diphthongs. The student can study these throughout the unit.

Lesson Introduction. Remind the student of his/her study of diphthongs in the previous lesson. Ask the student to define diphthong. (**A diphthong**

is two vowel sounds that come together so fast that they are considered one syllable.) Have the student sound the diphthongs **oi**, **oy**, and **ou** for this lesson. Brainstorm words featuring these diphthongs: **boil, boy,** and **bound.**

Activity 1. Turn to the activity sheet which accompanies this lesson. Read through the words which will be used in the activity. Have the student emphasize the diphthong as he/she reads. The student should continue by putting the words in the correct categories.

oi	oy	ou
coin	cowboy	cloud
soil	employ	south
choice	joy	about
join	voyage	around
avoid	royal	count

Activity 2. The student continues the study of diphthongs by circling words in each sentence which contain diphthongs. You may choose to have the student read the sentences aloud so he/she can hear the diphthong. For added practice find the other double vowel words.

1. The **cowboy** rode his horse **around** the field.
2. Andres **enjoys** playing with his birthday **toys**.
3. The **loud sound** frightened the child.
4. The **loyal** dog **found** his favorite bone in the **soil**.
5. The **playground** was located on the **south** side of **town**.

Activity 3. The student should continue by filling in the blanks with the correct vowel digraph. You may want to have scratch paper so the student can experiment with writing the word correctly with appropriate diphthongs before filling in the activity sheet. The answers for the activity are: **ground, loyal, bound, joy, coil, soil, outside, voyage, choice, about.**

Reading Activity.

1. The student should review the selection "Jackie Robinson." In this lesson, the student will focus on Jackie Robinson rather than MLB.

2. Ask the student the following questions. When was Jackie Robinson born? **(He was born in 1919.)** What did you learn about his life before baseball? **(He lived in Georgia, went to college at UCLA, he played many sports and he was in the Army in WWII.)** What accomplishments did Jackie Robinson have as a professional baseball player? **(He was named Rookie of the Year, MVP (Most Valuable Player), and elected to MLB's Hall of Fame.)** Why do you think Jackie Robinson

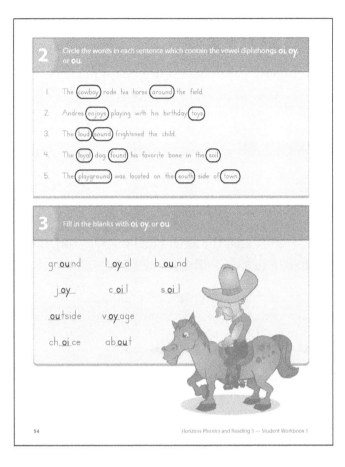

chose to be the first African-American to play MLB in almost 60 years? (Answers may include: **He wanted to show people that African-American athletes were as good as white athletes. He may have wanted to pave the way for other African-American baseball players. He may have wanted to compete against other excellent players.**)

3. Have the student find three words with the diphthongs **oi, oy,** and **ou.** (Answers include: **joined, youngest, could, you.**)

Lesson 26

Wild Colt Endings: old, ild, olt, ost, ind, oll

Overview:

- Define a Wild Colt ending
- Read words with Wild Colt endings
- Recognize that the letter combinations **old**, **ild**, **olt**, **ost**, **ind**, and **oll** form Wild Colt endings
- Form words with Wild Colt endings

Materials and Supplies:

- Teacher's Guide and Student Workbook
- White board or chart paper
- Phonics flashcards
- Reader: "The Star-Nosed Mole"

Teaching Tips:

Review for Mastery. Discuss and review any work from the previous lesson that was assigned as homework. Check for completion of the activities and orally quiz the student for comprehension. Review any reading that was assigned, discussing the characters, setting, plot, theme, language, sequence, etc.

Strengthen fluency and phonemic awareness by reviewing words and sentences from the previous lessons. Build vocabulary skills by using some of the words in sentences.

You may want to create flashcards of words with the Wild Colt endings. The student can study these throughout the unit.

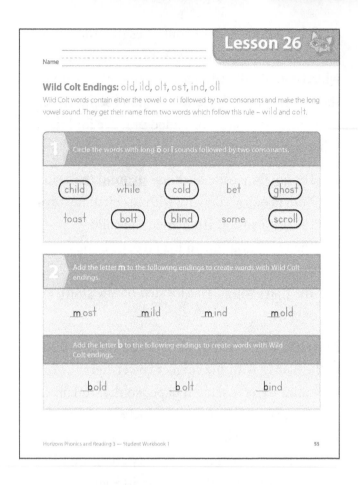

Lesson Introduction. Write the words **find, bolt,** and **mild** on the board. Ask the student if the vowel sound is long or short in the word. (The vowel sound is long). Ask the student to note the types of letters following the long vowel sound. (The letters are consonants). Explain that when the vowel **o** or **i** is followed by two consonants like **nd, st, lt, ld, ll,** and **ld** it is generally long. These are called Wild Colt endings because the words **wild** and **colt** are examples of the rule. As a challenge, ask the student if he/she could think of a sentence with these types of words to help remember the rule. (Example: **The cold child ate rolls.**)

Activity 1. The student should turn to the accompanying activity sheet. Read through the information at the top of the page about Wild Colt endings. Have the student identify the words in the activity which follow the rules of Wild Colt endings. Answers are: **child, cold, ghost, bolt, blind, scroll**.

Activity 2. The student will continue the activity by forming words with Wild Colt endings. The answers are: **most, mild, mind, mold, bold, bolt, bind**. When the student has completed this section, he/she may want to add other beginnings to form Wild Colt words.

Activity 3. The final activity asks the student to use words with Wild Colt endings to complete sentences. Have the student read the sentences with the correct words included. The answers are: **told, find, remind, rolls, fold, rind, kind**.

Reading Activity.

1. Ask the student to read the selection "The Star-Nosed Mole."

2. Discuss the selection with the student by asking the following questions. Where does the star-nosed mole live? **(It lives in eastern North America, near lakes and also near rivers.)** How did the mole get its name? **(The mole's nose is covered with tentacles in a star-like shape which is how the mole received its name.)** Describe the physical appearance of the star-nosed mole. **(It is small with large feet and claws. It has tentacles on his nose and brown-black fur.)**

3. The only word with a Wild Colt ending in the selection is in the second sentence. Ask the student to find it. **(Most)**

4. Have the student draw a picture of the star-nosed mole.

Fill in the blank with the correct word.

Word Bank

remind   fold   rolls   rind   kind   told   find

1. Jeremy ____told____ his mother he needed to go to the library.

2. Brianna couldn't ____find____ her rain boots.

3. The teacher needed to ____remind____ her students about tomorrow's test.

4. Mrs. Dickens served ____rolls____ with supper.

5. Carson helped his mom ____fold____ the laundry.

6. Lindsey threw away her watermelon ____rind____

7. The ____kind____ child helped her dad clean the garage.

56   Horizons Phonics and Reading 3 — Student Workbook 1

Lesson 27
Schwa Sound

Overview:

- Define the schwa sound
- Read words with the schwa sound
- Recognize the schwa sound when heard in words
- Form words with the schwa sound

Materials and Supplies:

- Teacher's Guide and Student Workbook
- White board or chart paper
- Phonics flashcards
- Reader: "The Star-Nosed Mole"

Teaching Tips:

Review for Mastery. Discuss and review any work from the previous lesson that was assigned as homework. Check for completion of the activities and orally quiz the student for comprehension. Review any reading that was assigned, discussing the characters, setting, plot, theme, language, sequence, etc.

Strengthen fluency and phonemic awareness by reviewing words and sentences from the previous lessons. Build vocabulary skills by using some of the words in sentences.

You may want to create flashcards of words with the schwa sound. The student can study these throughout the unit.

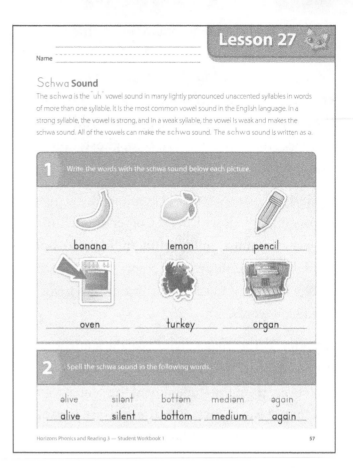

Lesson Introduction. Ask the student what he/she thinks is the most common vowel sound in the English language. After the student has made his/her guesses, tell him/her that the most common vowel sound is **uh**. Have the student make the sound with you. Every vowel can make the schwa sound. Write words with the schwa sound on the board: **afraid** (schwa a), **bushel** (schwa e), **ribbon** (schwa o), and **circus** (schwa u). After the student has pronounced the words, ask the student to compile a list of his/her own words featuring the schwa sound.

Activity 1. The student should have a copy of the activity sheet for this lesson. Read through the definition for the schwa sound at the top of the worksheet. Have the student identify the pictures in the first activity. Below each picture the student should write the word with the schwa sound. The answers are: **banana, lemon, pencil, oven, turkey, organ.**

Activity 2. Explain to the student that the schwa sound is spelled **ə**. The student should replace the **ə** with the correct vowel. Answers: <u>a</u>live, sil<u>e</u>nt, bott<u>o</u>m, medi<u>u</u>m, <u>a</u>gain, eas<u>i</u>ly, doct<u>o</u>r, tok<u>e</u>n, foc<u>u</u>s, crat<u>e</u>r.

Activity 3. The final activity on the sheet is a crossword puzzle. Before beginning the activity, have the student pronounce each word in the Word Bank emphasizing the schwa sound. The student should complete the crossword puzzle.

Across:	Down:
4. **dozen**	1. **cousin**
6. **circus**	2. **medium**
7. **enemy**	3. **doctor**
9. **tailor**	5. **present**
10. **sofa**	8. **drama**

Reading Activity.

1. Have the student turn to the selection "The Star-Nosed Mole."

2. At the end of the article about the star-nosed mole, the author wrote, "God has given it unique abilities to survive in its habitat." Ask the student to re-read the selection looking for examples of how the star-nosed mole was created to live in its habitat. **(It is an excellent swimmer, its tentacles help it feel for food at the bottom of the stream, it can swim underwater, its fur repels water, its tail stores food for the winter months, and its large feet and claws enable it to dig in the mud.)**

3. The student should write a paragraph in which he/she describes how another animal has been created by God to survive in its habitat.

4. The student should find three words in the first paragraph which have the schwa sound. (Examples include: **Eastern, America, Canada, other, tunnels, rivers.**)

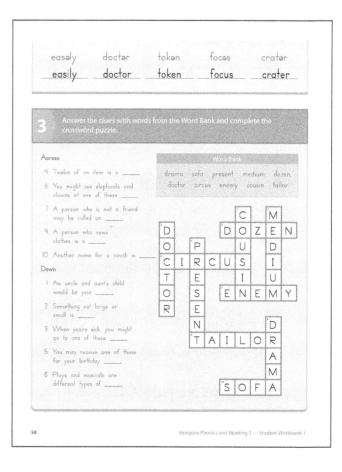

Lesson 28

Final Schwa Sound followed by l, r

Overview:

- Define the schwa sound

- Practice the schwa sound followed by **l** or **r**

- Read words with the schwa sound followed by **l** or **r**

- Recognize the schwa sound followed by **l** or **r** when heard in words

- Form words with the schwa sound followed by **l** or **r**

Materials and Supplies:

- Teacher's Guide and Student Workbook

- White board or chart paper

- Phonics flashcards

- Reader: "My Shadow"

Teaching Tips:

Review for Mastery. Discuss and review any work from the previous lesson that was assigned as homework. Check for completion of the activities and orally quiz the student for comprehension. Review any reading that was assigned, discussing the characters, setting, plot, theme, language, sequence, etc.

Strengthen fluency and phonemic awareness by reviewing words and sentences from the previous lessons. Build vocabulary skills by using some of the words in sentences.

You may want to create flashcards of words with the schwa sound followed by **l** or **r**. The student can study these throughout the unit.

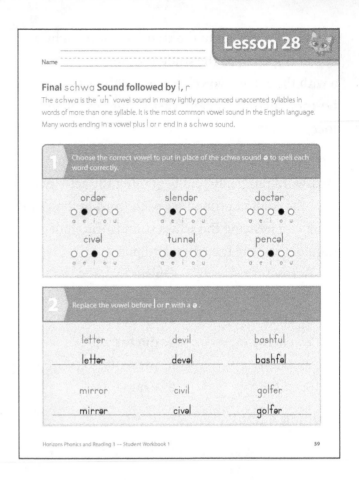

Lesson Introduction. Recall with the student the /uh/ sound of the schwa. Explain that many words ending in a vowel plus **l** or **r** have the vowel make the schwa sound. Write the words **fossil**, **channel**, **grader**, and **calendar**. Have the student say the words emphasizing the /uh/ sound before the final consonant.

Activity 1. The student should find the activity sheet which accompanies this lesson. Read the definition for the schwa sound at the top of the page. The student will choose the correct vowel to put in place of the ə symbol. The correct answers are: **order, slender, doctor, civil, tunnel, pencil**.

Activity 2. The next activity asks the student to do the opposite of what he/she did in the previous activity. The student must replace the vowel with the ə symbol. Answers for the activity are: **lettər, devəl, bashfəl, mirrər, civəl, golfər**.

Activity 3. The final activity asks the student to demonstrate his/her use of words with the schwa sound. The student must write sentences using words with a schwa sound. Sample sentences:

1. **The explorer hoped to discover a new mountain.**
2. **The evil villain tried to harm the hero.**
3. **Emma and Alice are sisters.**
4. **I sang a Christmas carol at church.**
5. **A red and blue banner was hung outside of the library.**

Reading Activity.

1. Before reading the selection, have the student go outside or in a well-lit room and play with his/her shadow. You could also make shadow puppets using a flashlight in a darkened room.

2. The student should turn to the selection "My Shadow." Explain that the selection was written over 100 years ago by a famous writer named Robert Louis Stevenson. Because of this, some of the wording may be challenging. Write the following words on the board: **India-rubber ball**, **nursie**, and **errant**. Define these words for the student. An India-rubber ball is a small bouncing ball made from rubber from India. A nursie would be a nickname for a childhood nurse or nanny. The word errant means straying from the proper course. For example, the baseball player threw an errant pitch. This means the ball did not go where it was intended.

3. Read through the selection with the student. It's best to hear poetry rather than only see it on the page.

4. Ask the student the following general questions about the poem. What does the author notice about his shadow? (**It goes everywhere he does. The shadow gets larger and smaller depending on where he is.**) What complaints does the boy have about his shadow? (**The shadow stays too close to him or sometimes stays behind in bed. The shadow also doesn't seem to know how to play with others.**)

5. In the second stanza of the poem, ask the student to locate two words with schwa sound followed by **r**. (**proper, taller**)

Lesson 29

Long Vowels a and i spelled eigh and igh

Overview:

- Identify words with the long **a** and **i** vowel sounds spelled **eigh** or **igh**

- Read words with the long **a** and **i** vowel sound spelled **eigh** or **igh**

- Form words with the long **a** and **i** vowel sound spelled **eigh** or **igh**

Materials and Supplies:

- Teacher's Guide and Student Workbook

- White board or chart paper

- Phonics flashcards

- Reader: "My Shadow"

Teaching Tips:

Review for Mastery. Discuss and review any work from the previous lesson that was assigned as homework. Check for completion of the activities and orally quiz the student for comprehension. Review any reading that was assigned, discussing the characters, setting, plot, theme, language, sequence, etc.

Strengthen fluency and phonemic awareness by reviewing words and sentences from the previous lessons. Build vocabulary skills by using some of the words in sentences.

You may want to create flashcards of words with the long **a** and **i** vowel sounds spelled **eigh** or **igh**.

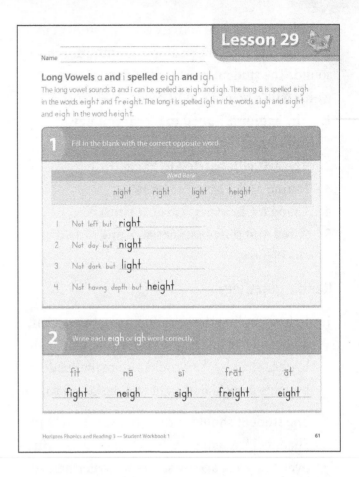

Lesson Introduction. Have the student say the words **fight** and **fine**. Ask the student what long vowel sound is being said in each word (**ī**). Have the student spell the words **fight** and **fine** on the board. Note how the long **i** is being spelled in each of the words. Explain to the student that the long **a** and **i** can be spelled **eigh** or **igh**. See if the student can come up with examples of words spelled these ways. Examples may include: **eight** and **right**.

Activity 1. The student should take out the activity sheet for this lesson. The student will be asked to fill in the blank with a word that means the opposite of the given word. A Word Bank is provided to assist the student. Answers are: **right**, **night**, **light**, **height**.

Activity 2. In this activity, the word is spelled with either a long **a** or **i** vowel sound and the student must spell it correctly with **eigh** or **igh**. The answers are: **fight, neigh, sigh, freight, eight**.

Activity 3. The final activity asks the student to fill in the blank with the correct word. A Word Bank is provided to assist the student. The answers are: **knight, bright, eight, freight**.

Reading Activity.

1. Reread the poem "My Shadow" with the student.

2. Ask the student to notice how the lines of the poem rhyme. Write out the end rhymes on the board. (**me/see, head/bed, grow/slow, ball/all, play/way, see/me, up/buttercup, head/bed**)

3. The author uses images and comparisons to show what the shadow looks and acts like. What comparisons did the student notice? (Examples include: **Like an India-rubber ball, coward, and stayed asleep in bed.**)

4. Have the student draw a picture featuring himself or herself with a shadow.

Lesson 30

Review

Overview:

- Identify and sound out vowel digraphs spelled **ai**, **ay**, **ei**, **ie**, **ee**, **ea**, and **ey**

- Identify and sound out vowel diphthongs **ew**, **ow**, **oi**, **oy**, and **ou**

- Recognize and correctly use Wild Colt endings **old**, **ild**, **olt**, **ost**, **ind**, and **oll**

- Recall vowels which sound the schwa

- Write the long **a** and **i** vowel sounds spelled **eigh** or **igh**

Materials and Supplies:

- Teacher's Guide and Student Workbook

- White board or chart paper

- Phonics flashcards

- Reader: "The Search for a Good Child"

Teaching Tips:

Review for Mastery. Discuss and review any work from the previous lesson that was assigned as homework. Check for completion of the activities and orally quiz the student for comprehension. Review any reading that was assigned, discussing the characters, setting, plot, theme, language, sequence, etc.

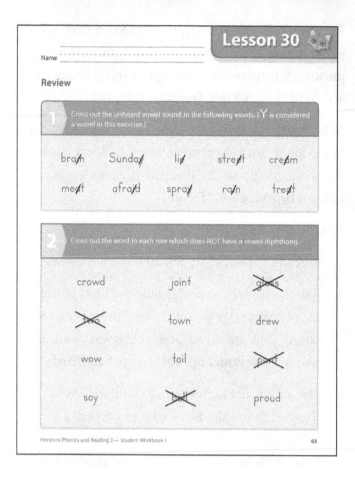

Strengthen fluency and phonemic awareness by reviewing words and sentences from the previous lessons. Build vocabulary skills by using some of the words in sentences.

You may want to review flashcards made for words in this unit.

Activity 1. Have the student turn to the review activity sheet. The review begins with the student recognizing the heard and unheard vowel sound in the words. The student will be asked to cross out the vowel which is not sounded. The answers are: **brain, Sunday, lie, street, cream, meat, afraid, spray, rain, treat.**

Activity 2. The review continues by looking at words which are diphthongs. The student must identify the word which is not a diphthong in each line. The words **glass**, **two**, **punt**, **ball** do not contain diphthongs.

Activity 3. This review activity asks the student to spell words correctly based on their vowel pronunciations. The words are: **weigh**, **night**, **freight**, **light**, **another**, **apron**.

Activity 4. The final review activity asks the student to identify words with Wild Colt endings. Have the student identify the words which follow the rules of Wild Colt endings. Answers are: **most**, **child**, **mind**, **grind**, **hold**, **troll**, **post**.

Reading Activity. The student should take out the selection, "The Search for a Good Child" and read it for pleasure.

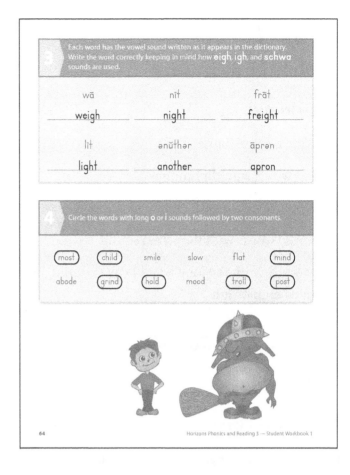

Test 3

Lessons 21-30

Overview:

- Define a vowel digraph
- Read words with diphthongs
- Recognize words with Wild Colt endings
- Identify words with the schwa sound
- Use words with the long **a** and **i** vowel sound spelled **eigh** or **igh**

Materials and Supplies:

- Student Test

Teaching Tips:

Review for Mastery. Discuss and review any work from the previous lesson that was assigned as homework. Check for completion of the activities and orally quiz the student for comprehension. Review any reading that was assigned.

Lesson Introduction. This lesson tests the material the student learned in the unit. Before the test you may want to ask the student if he/she has any final questions. There may be questions from the review the student will want to look over again. Remind the student that the final test follows the same format as the review.

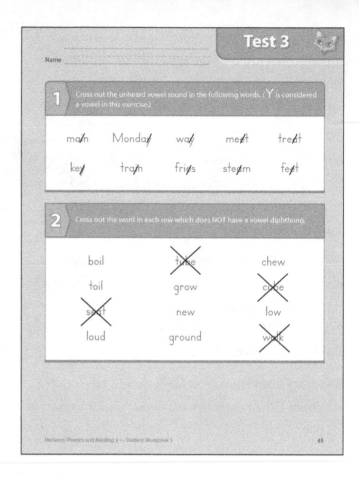

Activity 1. The student will be asked to cross out the unheard vowel. Answers: **main, Monday, way, meet, treat, key, train, fries, steam, feet**.

Activity 2. The student should cross out the word in each row which does not have a vowel diphthong. The answers are: **tube, cube, seat, walk**.

Activity 3. Each word has the vowel sound written as it appears in the dictionary. Answers: **height, flight, other, alike, ribbon, sigh.**

Activity 4. The student is to circle the words which follow the rules of Wild Colt endings. Answers are: **gold, scroll, wild, mind.**

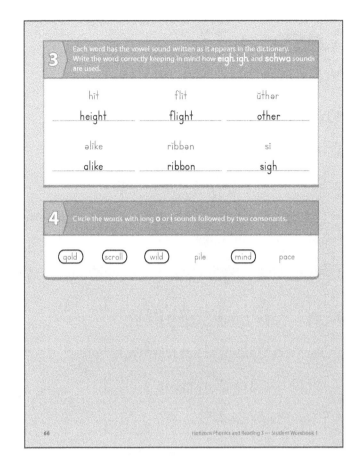

Lesson 31
Vowel Diphthongs: au, oo

Overview:

- Define a vowel diphthong

- Read words with vowel diphthongs

- Recognize that the letter combinations **au** and **oo** are vowel diphthongs

- Write sentences with words with diphthongs

Materials and Supplies:

- Teacher's Guide and Student Workbook

- White board or chart paper

- Phonics flashcards

- Reader: "The Happy Prince: Part I"

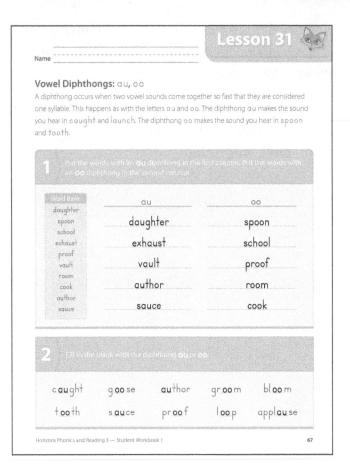

Teaching Tips:

Lesson Introduction. Ask the student to recall the lessons on vowel diphthongs he/she learned in the previous unit. The student may remember studying the vowel diphthongs **oi**, **oy**, and **ou**. Have the student think of words that were made with these diphthongs. Answers may include: **soil, boy, cloud.** Tell the student that in this lesson he/she will study two more vowel diphthongs: **au** and **oo**. Write the words **vault** and **pool** on the board. Explain that these two words have vowel diphthongs where the two vowel sounds come together so quickly that they are considered one syllable. See if the student can brainstorm other words with either the **au** or **oo** diphthong sound.

You may want to create flashcards of words with the **au** and **oo** diphthongs. Students can study these throughout the unit.

Activity 1. The student should turn to the activity sheet which accompanies this lesson. Read through the definition at the top of the page with the student. The student should take the listed words with vowel diphthongs and put them in the correct column. It might be helpful to have the student read each of the words aloud before completing the activity. This would help the student to hear the sound as well as see it.

au	oo
daughter	spoon
exhaust	school
vault	proof
author	room
sauce	cook

Activity 2. Have the student continue by filling in the blank with the diphthong **au** or **oo** in order to form words. Again, you may want to have the student read the word aloud so that the word can be both seen and heard. Answers: **caught, goose, author, groom, bloom, tooth, sauce, proof, loop, applause.**

Activity 3. Finally, the student will be asked to write sentences using each of the listed vowel diphthong words. If time permits, you may want to ask the student to write additional sentences using other diphthongs found on the activity sheet. (Answers will vary.)

Reading Activity.

1. The student should read "The Happy Prince: Part I."

2. After the student has read the first part, have the student describe the two main characters: the Happy Prince and the swallow. (**The Happy Prince was a beautiful statue that looked over the city. In life he was always happy because he faced no difficulties. As a statue he saw the pain of the people who lived in the city. The swallow was a small bird who did not head south soon enough for the winter. He was an ordinary bird who rested on the statue.**) Have the student describe the city in which the story took place. (**It was a city that had many people who were sad and hurting.**)

3. Discuss with the student the first person the Happy Prince and swallow assisted. (**They helped a seamstress and her sick child.**) What help did they give? (**The Prince gave the ruby from his statue, so they had money to buy what they needed. The swallow used his wings to cool off the feverish boy.**) What did the swallow feel like after helping the family? (**He was happy, and he felt warm even though it was cold.**) How was the attitude of the Prince different from the princess living in the palace? (**The princess thought the seamstress was lazy. She did not understand the difficulties of the seamstress' life. The Prince now understood the difficulties of the lives of people like the seamstress.**)

4. Continue by discussing the second person the swallow and Happy Prince assisted. Ask the student to describe the second person helped. (**The Prince and swallow helped a young man who was writing a play. He lived in a poor apartment that did not have enough heat.**) How did the swallow and Prince help this person? (**They gave him one of the Prince's sapphire eyes. This allowed the writer to have money to live and finish his play.**)

5. Ask the student to predict what he/she thinks will happen next in the selection. (**Encourage the student to make his/her predictions based on what has happened in the selection.**)

6. The student should find three **oo** diphthong words in the selection. (Examples include: **stood, balloon, looks, bedroom, moonlight, choose, cool, noon, room.**)

Lesson 32

Vowel Digraphs: oe, oa

Overview:

- Define a vowel digraph
- Read words with long ō digraphs
- Recognize that the letter combinations **oe** and **oa** make the long ō sound
- Identify words with vowel digraphs

Materials and Supplies:

- Teacher's Guide and Student Workbook
- White board or chart paper
- Phonics flashcards
- Reader: "The Happy Prince: Part II"

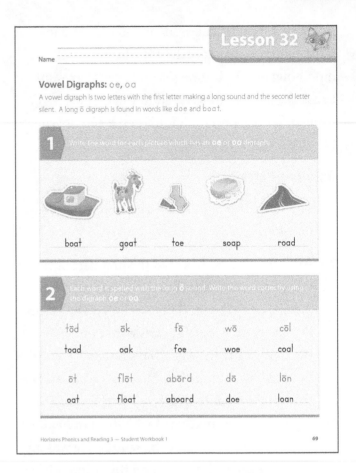

Teaching Tips:

Review for Mastery. Discuss and review any work from the previous lesson that was assigned as homework. Check for completion of the activities and orally quiz the student for comprehension. Review any reading that was assigned, discussing the characters, setting, plot, theme, language, sequence, etc.

Strengthen fluency and phonemic awareness by reviewing words and sentences from the previous lessons. Build vocabulary skills by using some of the words in sentences.

You may want to create flashcards of words with the **oa** and **oe** digraphs. The student can study these throughout the unit.

Lesson Introduction. Remind the student that in the previous unit he/she studied vowel digraphs like **ai**, **ay**, **ei**, and **ie**. Write the words **seize**, **tie**, **slay**, and **said** on the board. Discuss how the two letters form the vowel digraph. The first vowel makes the sound and the second is silent.

Explain that in this lesson two more vowel digraphs will be studied. These make the long ō sound. Write the words **boat**, **soap**, **toe**, and **foe** on the board. Ask the student to identify the two vowel digraphs that are used in these words: **oa** and **oe**.

Activity 1. Ask the student to turn to the activity sheet for this lesson. Read through the definition and examples of the **oe** and the **oa** vowel digraphs at the top of the page. Ask the student to identify each of the pictures at the top of the page. After the student has correctly identified the picture, he/she should write the correct word with the vowel digraph underneath. Answers: **boat, goat, toe, soap, road.**

Activity 2. The student will find in the next activity that the vowel sound has been written phonetically. The student should write the word correctly with the digraph **oe** or **oa**. Answers: **toad, oak, foe, woe, cool, oat, float, aboard, doe, loan.**

Activity 3. In the final activity, the student will be asked to complete sentences using words with vowel digraphs. While both word choices may correctly complete the sentence, only the one containing the vowel digraph will be correct. Answers: **hoe, toast, mosquitoes, Aboard, toe.**

Reading Activity.

1. Before reading "The Happy Prince: Part II" the student should review what he/she learned in Part I of the selection.

2. After reading Part II, discuss the selection with the student. Who received the final sapphire from the Prince? (**A girl who was selling matches.**) Why did the Prince want her to receive this gift? (**She had dropped the matches she was selling and her father would be angry with her. Her family needed money.**) What happened to the gold that covered the Prince? (**The bird took pieces of it and gave it to people in need.**) How did the Mayor and Town Council react when they saw the Happy Prince after all his jewels and gold were gone? (**They wanted the statue torn down and a new one put in its place. Each person thought the new statue should be about him or her.**) Why did the swallow keep telling the Prince he needed to go to Egypt? (**He needed to join his friends, and he needed to be where the weather was warm.**) Why didn't the swallow leave? (**At the beginning he stayed because he wanted to help the Prince. Later he stayed because he loved the Prince.**) What happened because the swallow refused to leave? (**He comforted**

the Prince by telling him stories. He also died in the cold weather.**) Why do you think the author added the part about God and the angels at the end of the selection? (**The author may have wanted to make sure that the reader understood that the Prince and the swallow behaved in a manner which pleased God.**)

3. Very few words in this part of the selection have **oe** or **oa** vowel digraphs, so students will not be asked to search for them.

Lesson 33

Review: Vowel Diphthongs and Digraphs

Overview:

- Define a vowel diphthong
- Define a vowel digraph
- Read diphthongs and digraphs
- Recognize that the letter combinations **au, oo, oi, oy**, and **ou** are diphthongs
- Recognize that the letter combinations **oe, oa, ai, ay, ee, ea**, and **ey** are digraphs

Materials and Supplies:

- Teacher's Guide and Student Workbook
- White board or chart paper
- Phonics flashcards
- Reader: "The Happy Prince: Parts I and II"

Teaching Tips:

Review for Mastery. Discuss and review any work from the previous lesson that was assigned as homework. Check for completion of the activities and orally quiz the student for comprehension. Review any reading that was assigned, discussing the characters, setting, plot, theme, language, sequence, etc.

Strengthen fluency and phonemic awareness by reviewing words and sentences from the previous lessons. Build vocabulary skills by using some of the words in sentences.

You may want to create flashcards of words with vowel digraphs and diphthongs. The student can study these throughout the unit.

Lesson Introduction. Ask the student to define the terms vowel digraph and vowel diphthong. A digraph is two letters with the first letter making a long sound and the second letter remaining silent. A vowel

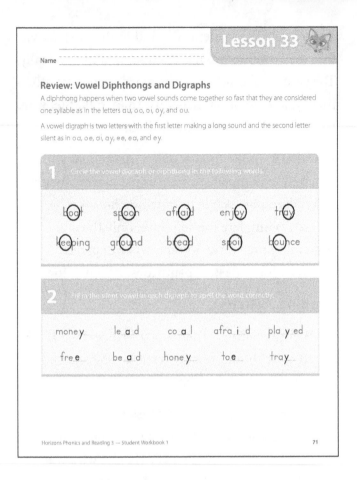

diphthong is when two vowel sounds come together so quickly that they are considered one syllable.

Have the student give examples of words with vowel digraphs. Examples include: **key, read**, and **load**. Have the student give examples of words with vowel diphthongs. These include the words: **toy, boil**, and **book**.

Activity 1. The student should refer to the activity sheet for this lesson. Have the student read the definitions at the top of the page. The student should go on to identify words with vowel digraphs or diphthongs. **See image for answers.**

Activity 2. The next activity focuses only on vowel digraphs. The student should fill in the silent letter for each word. This is the letter that is not pronounced in the vowel digraph. **See image for answers.**

Activity 3. Completing a crossword puzzle is the final activity. Ask the student to first answer the clues and then use them to complete the puzzle. A Word Bank is provided to help the student complete the activity. **See image for answers.**

Reading Activity.

1. Briefly review the story "The Happy Prince" with your student.

2. Lead a discussion about the main themes of the selection. Use some of the following questions to begin the discussion. How did the Happy Prince's view of the city change from when he was alive to when he was a statue? (**When he was alive he was isolated in the castle and did not realize the difficulties that people in the city faced.**) How did the Prince care for the needs of the people of the city? (**He gave them all that he had. He gave away his jewels and the gold which covered him.**) How did the officials of the city care for the needs of the people? (**They didn't.**) What lessons do you think the author wanted the reader to learn? (Answers may include: **Treating others kindly and caring for the needs of the poor. Students may also recognize the value of friendship that is shown in the relationship of the sparrow and Prince.**)

3. Read to students Jesus' parable of "The Sheep and the Goats" from Matthew 25:31-45:

    "When the Son of Man comes in his glory, and all the angels with him, he will sit on his throne in heavenly glory. All the nations will be gathered before him, and he will separate the people one from another as a shepherd separates the sheep from the goats. He will put the sheep on his right and the goats on his left.

    Then the King will say to those on his right, 'Come, you who are blessed by my Father; take your inheritance, the kingdom prepared for you since the creation of the world. For I was hungry and you gave me something to eat, I was thirsty and you gave me something to drink, I was a stranger and you invited me in, I needed clothes and you clothed me, I was sick and you looked after me, I was in prison and you came to visit me.'

    Then the righteous will answer him, 'Lord, when did we see you hungry and feed you, or thirsty and give you something to drink? When did we see you a stranger and invite you in, or needing clothes and clothe you? When did we see you sick or in prison and go to visit you?'

    The King will reply, 'I tell you the truth, whatever you did for one of the least of these brothers of mine, you did for me.'

    Then he will say to those on his left, 'Depart from me, you who are cursed, into the eternal fire prepared for the devil and his angels. For I was hungry and you gave me nothing to eat, I was thirsty and you gave me nothing to drink, I was a stranger and you did not invite me in, I needed clothes and

you did not clothe me, I was sick and in prison and you did not look after me.'

    They also will answer, 'Lord, when did we see you hungry or thirsty or a stranger or needing clothes or sick or in prison, and did not help you?'

    He will reply, 'I tell you the truth, whatever you did not do for one of the least of these, you did not do for me.'"

4. After reading the parable, discuss how Jesus wants people to treat others. (**Point out that Jesus wants His people to help those who are poor and in need. Sometimes we ignore those people who don't look or act like us. It becomes clear in this parable that Jesus wants Christians to treat all people with compassion.**) You may also want to discuss how the story "The Happy Prince" reflects Christ's teaching.

5. Ask the student to find three vowel digraphs and three vowel diphthongs in the selection. Vowel digraphs include the words: **waiting, faint, eye, money, day.** Vowel diphthongs include the words: **round, cause, paused, cloud, thought.**

Lesson 34
Soft and Hard c sounds

Overview:

- Recall the soft and hard sounds the letter **c** can make

- Read words which use the soft and hard /c/ sounds

- Recognize the patterns of words with the soft and hard /c/ sounds

- Form words using both the soft and hard /c/ sounds

Materials and Supplies:

- Teacher's Guide and Student Workbook

- White board or chart paper

- Phonics flashcards

- Reader: "The Alpaca"

Teaching Tips:

Review for Mastery. Discuss and review any work from the previous lesson that was assigned as homework. Check for completion of the activities and orally quiz the student for comprehension. Review any reading that was assigned, discussing the characters, setting, plot, theme, language, sequence, etc.

Strengthen fluency and phonemic awareness by reviewing words and sentences from the previous lessons. Build vocabulary skills by using some of the words in sentences.

You may want to create flashcards of words with soft and hard /c/ sounds. The student can study these throughout the unit.

Lesson Introduction. Write the word **circus** on the board. Ask the student what sounds the letter **c** makes in the word. The student should identify both the soft and hard /c/ sounds. Brainstorm a list

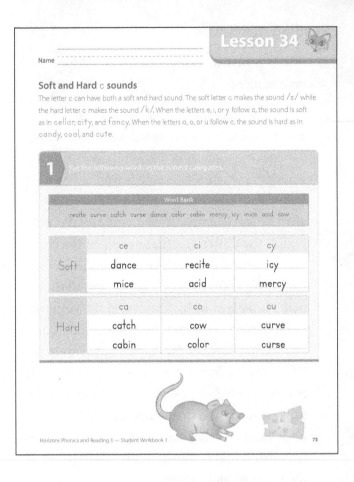

of words with both the soft and hard /c/ sounds. Examples include: **cancel**, **council**, and **cancer**.

Activity 1. Turn to the activity sheet for this lesson. Read with the student the definition and examples at the top of the page. After the student has read the rules, he/she should put the given words in the correct categories.

Soft:	ce	ci	cy
	dance	recite	icy
	mice	acid	mercy

Hard:	ca	co	cu
	catch	cow	curve
	cabin	color	curse

Activity 2. In the next activity the student will be asked to identify which words have soft /c/ sounds, hard /c/ sounds, or both. You may find it helpful to do the first word, circus, together identifying it as having both hard and soft /c/ sounds. Words with soft /c/ sounds in this activity are: **circus, cancel, notice, pencil, cycle, icicle, spicy, civil**. Words with hard /c/ sounds are: **circus, cancel, cycle, coin, cut, icicle**.

Activity 3. Read through the directions of the final activity with the class. Emphasize that only words with the soft /c/ sound should be used to fill in the blank. There will be words with hard /c/ sounds in the Word Bank, so the student will need to pay careful attention when filling in the blank. The correct words for the activity are: **balance, cement, icy, piece, Cindy, spicy.**

Reading Activity.

1. Direct the student to read the selection "The Alpaca." After students have read the selection, give a short true and false quiz to assess what the student learned in the selection. Discuss those questions the student did not answer correctly.

   - Llamas and alpacas share many similarities. **(True)**

   - Alpaca fur is used to make yarn. **(True)**

   - An alpaca is a much larger animal than a llama. **(False)**

   - Alpacas live in the mountains of Europe. **(False)**

   - A happy alpaca makes a clicking or chirping sound. **(True)**

2. Continue your discussion of the alpaca with the student. Use the following questions in your discussion. Where are alpacas generally found? **(They make their home in the Andes Mountains in South America. However, some farmers in North America also raise alpacas.)** What makes the wool of an alpaca special? **(The wool is warm, not prickly, comes in 22 different colors, and is soft.)** What is the diet of an alpaca? **(The alpaca eats hay, grass, and about everything else. This creates a problem because the alpaca will eat plastic bottles and fencing.)** How does the alpaca express itself if it's happy or angry? **(If it's angry it will spit partially digested food. If it's happy it will cluck and click.)** Why would a person want to

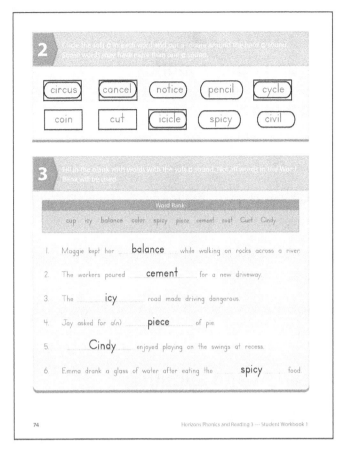

raise alpacas? **(They are small animals, take little room to live, and have valuable wool.)**

3. If you know of a place which raises alpacas or llamas, you may want to plan a visit with your student. Another idea would be to visit a person who knits garments using alpaca fur. You may be able to purchase yarn made from alpaca fur at a hobby store. The student could feel the difference in texture between yarn made from the fur of an alpaca and yarn made from cotton, synthetics, or wool.

4. Ask the student to look at the selection for words with soft and hard /c/ sounds. Ask the student to find three words with the hard /c/ sound. **(Examples include: alpaca, camel, colors, carry, can.)** Find one word with the soft /c/ sound. **(Fencing and once both have soft /c/ sounds.)**

Lesson 35
Soft and Hard g sounds

Overview:

- Recall the soft and hard sounds the letter **g** can make

- Read words which use the soft and hard /g/ sounds

- Recognize the patterns of words with the soft and hard /g/ sounds

- Form words using both the soft and hard /g/ sounds

Materials and Supplies:

- Teacher's Guide and Student Workbook

- White board or chart paper

- Phonics flashcards

- Reader: "The Wind and the Sun"

Teaching Tips:

Review for Mastery. Discuss and review any work from the previous lesson that was assigned as homework. Check for completion of the activities and orally quiz the student for comprehension. Review any reading that was assigned, discussing the characters, setting, plot, theme, language, sequence, etc.

Strengthen fluency and phonemic awareness by reviewing words and sentences from the previous lessons. Build vocabulary skills by using some of the words in sentences.

You may want to create flashcards of words with soft and hard /g/ sounds. The student can study these throughout the unit.

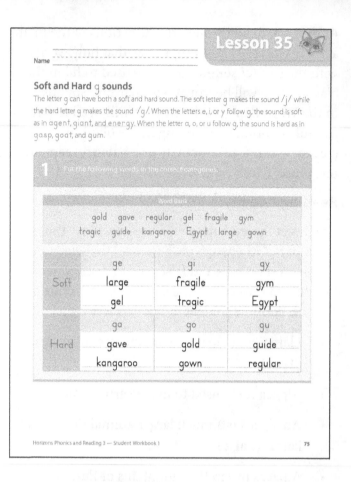

Lesson Introduction. Write the word **circus** on the board. Remind the student that in the previous lesson he/she studied words with the soft and hard /c/ sounds. Remind the student that the letter /c/ was hard when followed by the vowels **a**, **o**, or **u**. The letter /c/ was soft when followed by the vowels **e**, **i**, or **y**. In this lesson the student will study words with the soft and hard /g/ sounds. The rules for the soft and hard /g/ sound are the same as those for the soft and hard /c/ sound.

Ask the student to think of words that have either the soft and hard /g/ sounds. Answers may include: **gum**, **gym**, and **guest.**

Activity 1. Turn to the activity sheet for this lesson. Read with the student the definition and examples at the top of the page. After the student has read the rules, he/she should put the given words in the correct categories.

<u>Soft:</u>   <u>**ge**</u>   <u>**gi**</u>   <u>**gy**</u>
        gel   fragile   gym
        large   tragic   Egypt

<u>Hard:</u>   <u>**ga**</u>   <u>**go**</u>   <u>**gu**</u>
        gave   gold   regular
        kangaroo   gown   guide

Activity 2. The student should continue to the next activity where he/she is asked to identify words with either the soft or hard /g/ sound. Some of the words will have both. Words with the soft /g/ sound are: **large, allergy, garage, gem, cage, religion, gauge.** Words with the hard /g/ sound are: **guitar, goose, figure, garage, gauge.**

Activity 3. The lesson concludes with a word search. The student will be asked to find words with soft and hard /g/ sounds in the word search. A Word Bank is provided to assist the student. **See image for the answers.**

Reading Activity.

1. The student should read the selection "The Wind and the Sun."

2. After reading the selection, ask the student to describe the argument between the wind and the sun. (**The sun and wind want to determine which is the stronger of the two.**) How did each try to win? (**The wind used its strength to try to force the man's coat off of him. The sun used its strength to gently warm the man so he removed his coat.**)

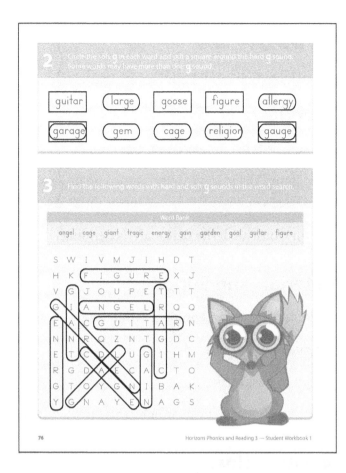

3. Ask the student what lessons can be learned from the fable. (**A lesson can be learned that kindness and gentleness go much farther than force. The student should also recognize that in life a kind word and action can have better results than forceful responses.**) Share with students the Bible verse, "A gentle answer turns away wrath, but a harsh word stirs up anger." (Proverbs 15:1). Help the student to connect the words of Scripture with the fable the student read in today's lesson.

4. Conclude by asking the student to find three words with the hard **g** sound. (Examples include: **stronger, along, long, began, give.**)

Lesson 36

Endings: age and dge

Overview:

- Read words having **-age** and **-dge** endings

- Recognize the soft /g/ sound at the end of **-age** and **-dge** words

- Form words with the **-age** and **-dge** endings

Materials and Supplies:

- Teacher's Guide and Student Workbook

- White board or chart paper

- Phonics flashcards

- Reader: "How the Leaves Came Down"

Teaching Tips:

Review for Mastery. Discuss and review any work from the previous lesson that was assigned as homework. Check for completion of the activities and orally quiz the student for comprehension. Review any reading that was assigned, discussing the characters, setting, plot, theme, language, sequence, etc.

Strengthen fluency and phonemic awareness by reviewing words and sentences from the previous lessons. Build vocabulary skills by using some of the words in sentences.

You may want to create flashcards of words with the **-age** and **-dge** endings. The student can study these throughout the unit.

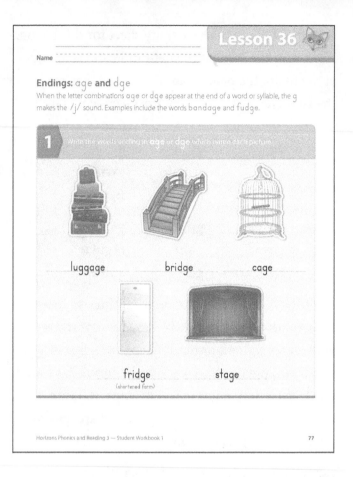

Name

Endings: age **and** dge
When the letter combinations age or dge appear at the end of a word or syllable, the g makes the /j/ sound. Examples include the words bandage and fudge.

1 Write the words ending in age or dge which name each picture.

luggage   bridge   cage

fridge   stage
(shortened form)

Horizons Phonics and Reading 3 — Student Workbook 1   77

Lesson Introduction. As an extension of the lesson on soft and hard /g/ sounds, the student will focus on the **-age** and **-dge** endings of words. Write the two endings on the board. Ask the student to identify if the sounds of /g/ are soft or hard. (**The sounds are soft.**) Challenge the student to come up with words that have the **-age** or **-dge** ending. Examples may include: **page**, **cage**, **fridge**, and **ridge**.

Activity 1. Ask the student to turn to the activity sheet for this lesson. The student will need to identify the items pictured that end in **-age** or **-dge.** The student should write the name of each object below the picture. You may want to ask the student to correctly identify each object first before writing its name below. The objects are: **luggage, bridge, cage, fridge, stage**.

Activity 2. In this activity the student needs to add the correct ending, either -**age** or -**dge**, to each word beginning. The student may want to write each word on scratch paper before filling in the blank on the activity sheet. The correct spellings are: **ridge**, **average**, **cabbage**, **dodge**, **postage**, **page**.

Activity 3. The final activity asks the student to complete sentences using words ending in -**age** or -**dge**. A Word Bank is provided to assist the student. The correct answers are: **garbage**, **bridge**, **rage**, **luggage**, **hedge**, **bandage**, **cabbage**, **fridge**.

Reading Activity.

1. Together read the poem "How the Leaves Came Down." You may want to read it more than once.

2. Ask the student to describe the setting of the poem. (**The poem is set in autumn at the time leaves fall to the ground.**) Have the student identify the main characters. (**The main characters are the tree and the leaves.**) How is the tree described? (**The tree is described as great and as a father.**) How are the leaves described? (**The leaves are described as sleepy children.**)

3. Write the word "anthropomorphism" on the board. Explain to the student that anthropomorphism means giving human characteristics to something which is not human. For example the stories of "The Berenstain Bears," "Arthur," and "Winnie the Pooh" all have animal characters who act and talk like people. Ask the student to think of other examples of anthropomorphism in books, television, or movies. (Examples may include: **"Toy Story," "Ratatouille," and "Thomas the Tank Engine."**)

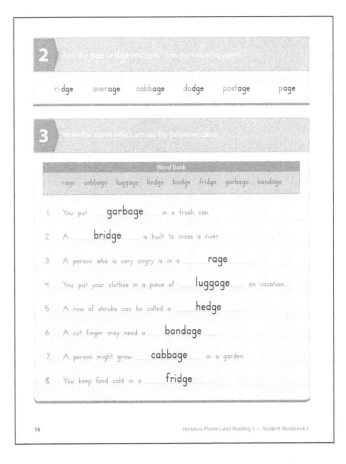

4. Tell the student that in this poem the author used anthropomorphism to describe the tree and the leaves. Have the student find examples of anthropomorphism used in the poem. (Examples include: **The tree speaks to the leaves, the tree calls the leaves his children, the leaves dance and whisper, and the tree puts the leaves to bed.**)

Lesson 37

Sounds of s: /s/, /z/, /zh/

Overview:

- Recall the letter **s** make the sound /s/, /z/, or /zh/

- Read words with the letter **s** sounded /s/, /z/, or /zh/

- Form words with the letter **s**

Materials and Supplies:

- Teacher's Guide and Student Workbook

- White board or chart paper

- Phonics flashcards

- Reader: "How the Leaves Came Down"

Teaching Tips:

Review for Mastery. Discuss and review any work from the previous lesson that was assigned as homework. Check for completion of the activities and orally quiz the student for comprehension. Review any reading that was assigned, discussing the characters, setting, plot, theme, language, sequence, etc.

Strengthen fluency and phonemic awareness by reviewing words and sentences from the previous lessons. Build vocabulary skills by using some of the words in sentences.

You may want to create flashcards of words with the letter /s/ sound. The student can study these throughout the unit.

Lesson Introduction. Write the words **slippery, raise,** and **casual** on the board. Ask the student how the /s/ sounds in each of the words. The student should recognize that in **slippery,** the letter

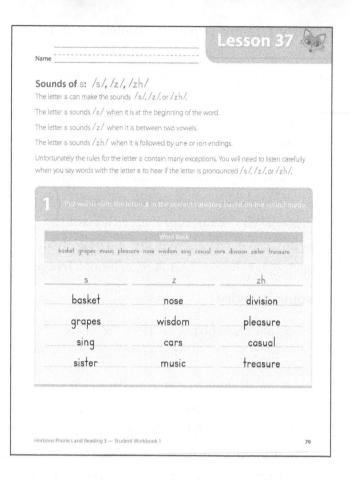

s makes the /s/ sound. In the word **raise**, the letter **s** makes the /z/ sound. In the word **casual**, the letter **s** makes the /zh/ sound. Tell the student that in this lesson he/she will study words with the letter **s**. The letter **s** will make the sounds /s/, /z/, and /zh/.

Activity 1. Direct the student to turn to the activity sheet. In the first activity, the student will be asked to categorize the words based on the sound of **s**. The student may find it helpful to say the words aloud rather than silently in order to hear the sound. The words should be put in the following categories:

s	z	zh
basket	nose	division
grapes	wisdom	pleasure
sing	cars	casual
sister	music	treasure

Activity 2. The student will continue to work on identifying the /s/ sounds in words. Each line in the activity has a sound the student needs to identify in one of the words. There is only one correct answer in each row. Again, it may be helpful to have the student say the words in order to better hear the sounds. The answers are: **television, vision, seal, socks, was, praise**.

Activity 3. In the final activity, the student will read a number of verses from Psalm 11. Only two of the **s** sounds, /s/ and /z/, will be identified in the psalm. Read the psalm together with your student. You may want to take turns reading lines or read it together. Words with the /s/ sound include: **assembly, works, majestic, glorious, deeds, endures, wonders, precepts, understanding, righteousness, gracious**. Optional words with the /s/ sound include: **Selected, Verses, Psalm**. Words with the /z/ sound are: **praise, his, has caused, belongs, wisdom**. The word **compassionate** has the /zh/ sound.

Reading Activity.

1. Turn again to the poem "How the Leaves Came Down." Once again read the poem with your student.

2. Briefly review anthropomorphism and the action of the poem.

3. Tell the student that as he/she looks at the poem this time, you would like the student to focus on how the poem was written. Explain to the student that the poem is divided into stanzas of five lines. Point out a line and a stanza. The student should note that each stanza focuses on an action. Ask the student to look at the first stanza. What is the theme of this stanza? **(It sets the mood of the poem. It also identifies the main characters.)** What lines of the stanza rhyme?

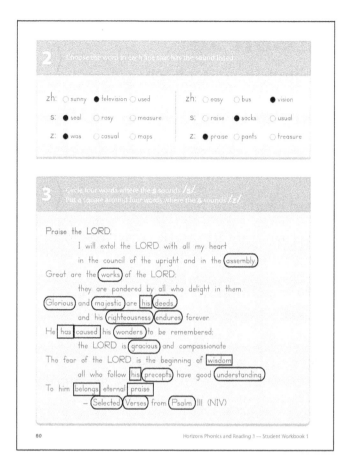

(Explain the rhyme scheme of the poem is ababb.) Have the student count the number of syllables in each line. **(Most of the lines have 8 syllables.)** Explain that this is another method that poets use in their work.

4. Read the poem a final time enjoying the rhythm, rhyme, and descriptions of the selection.

5. Ask the student to find three **s** words with /s/ sound. (Answers include: **said, sleepy, yes, silly, us.**) Find two **s** words with the /z/ sound. (Answers include: **leaves, is, 'tis, clothes.**)

Lesson 38

Spelling /k/: c, k, ck, ch

Overview:

- Recall the /k/ sound can be spelled **c, k, ck**, or **ch**

- Read words with the /k/ sound

- Recognize the letters **c, k, ck**, and **ch** can make the /k/ sound

- Form words which spell the /k/ sound **c, k, ck,** or **ch**

Materials and Supplies:

- Teacher's Guide and Student Workbook

- White board or chart paper

- Phonics flashcards

- Reader: "Mother Teresa"

Teaching Tips:

Review for Mastery. Discuss and review any work from the previous lesson that was assigned as homework. Check for completion of the activities and orally quiz the student for comprehension. Review any reading that was assigned, discussing the characters, setting, plot, theme, language, sequence, etc.

Strengthen fluency and phonemic awareness by reviewing words and sentences from the previous lessons. Build vocabulary skills by using some of the words in sentences.

You may want to create flashcards of words with the **c, k, ck,** and **ch** sounds. The student can study these throughout the unit.

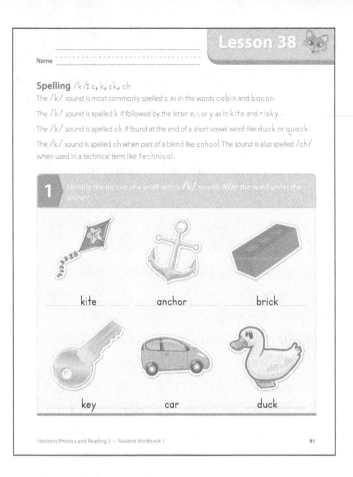

Lesson Introduction. Write on the board the words **can, like, lack,** and **technology.** Ask the student what common sound is found in each of these words. (**The /k/ sound.**) Continue by asking the student how the /k/ sound is spelled in each of the words. (It is spelled **c, k, ck,** and **ch.**) Have the student think of other words that have the /k/ sound. After the student has brainstormed a list of words, divide them into the different ways the /k/ sound is spelled.

Activity 1. Turn to the sheet which accompanies this lesson. The student will begin by identifying pictures. After the student has correctly identified the picture, he/she should correctly write the word underneath the picture. Make sure the student focuses on how the /k/ sound is spelled. The answers are: **kite, anchor, brick, key, car, duck.**

Activity 2. The student will be asked to put each word into the category in which the /k/ sound is spelled. While the student can do this by looking at each word, it would also be helpful for the student to say each word so he/she can hear the /k/ sound.

c	k	ck	ch
cake	cake	chick	echo
could	kind	attack	Christ
cook	cook	flock	character
character	kick	kick	ache

Activity 3. In the last activity, the student will see that each word has the letter **k** listed for each time the /k/ sound appears in the word. The student will need to spell each word correctly with the **k** spelled **c**, **k**, **ck**, or **ch**. Some of the words will be spelled correctly. The answers are: **cut, crack, school, park, cash, truck, stomach, kept, come, desk**.

Reading Activity.

1. The student should read the selection "Mother Teresa." Before reading, you may want to show the student pictures of Mother Teresa and her work among the poor in India.

2. Discuss the selection with the student using the following questions. What was Mother Teresa's life like before she moved to India? **(She was born in Eastern Europe and her father died when she was 8. She felt God's call to become a missionary when she was 12 and left home to become a nun at 18. She lived in Ireland where she learned English.)** Why did Mother Teresa start the Missionaries of Charity? **(She saw the need for someone to work among the poorest of the poor in India. She saw that no one was caring for the basic needs of the sick and suffering.)** Are Missionaries of Charity only located within India? **(No, there are chapters around the world. They too work with the poorest of the poor.)** What international award did Mother Teresa receive? **(She was awarded the Nobel Peace Prize.)**

3. Have students locate three words in the selection that have the /k/ sound spelled **c**, **k**, **ck**, or **ch**. (Answers include: **sick, Catholic, compassion, Christian, calling, could, Calcutta, take, working.**)

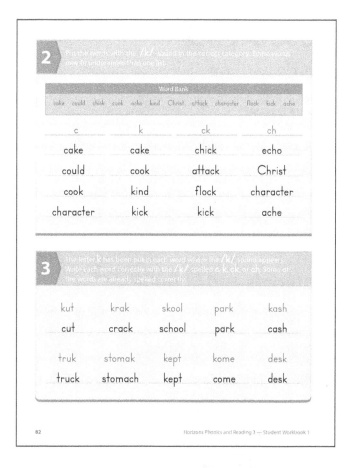

Lesson 39

Words with qu

Overview:

- Identify words with the **qu** letter combination

- Read words with the **qu** letter combination

- Form words which contain the **qu** letter combination

Materials and Supplies:

- Teacher's Guide and Student Workbook

- White board or chart paper

- Phonics flashcards

- Reader: "Mother Teresa"

Teaching Tips:

Review for Mastery. Discuss and review any work from the previous lesson that was assigned as homework. Check for completion of the activities and orally quiz the student for comprehension. Review any reading that was assigned, discussing the characters, setting, plot, theme, language, sequence, etc.

Strengthen fluency and phonemic awareness by reviewing words and sentences from the previous lessons. Build vocabulary skills by using some of the words in sentences.

You may want to create flashcards of words with the letters **qu**. The student can study these throughout the unit.

Activity 1. The student should turn to the activity sheet on **qu** words. The student will be asked to identify which **qu** word is pictured. After the student has completed the activity, go over the answers together. The correct answers are: **quack**, **quilt**, **quarter**, **liquid**, **queen**.

Activity 2. The student will continue the study of **qu** words by creating **qu** words. The student will need to fill in the blank with the letters **qu** to form the words. After the student has completed filling in the blank, ask him/her to read each word. Point out that not all **qu** words begin with the letters. Sometimes the letters appear in the middle of words. The answers are: **quiz**, **queen**, **squeak**, **question**, **request**, **require**, **quit**, **quack**, **quote**, **liquid**.

Activity 3. Finally, the student should complete each sentence with a **qu** word. A Word Bank is provided to assist the student in completing the sentences. The answers are: **equal, quickly, squeaked, quiet, quest, question, required, frequently**.

Reading Activity.

1. Ask the student to return to the selection "Mother Teresa." Briefly review the main facts of the selection the student previously studied.

2. Discuss the themes and the lessons that can be learned from the selection. How did God prepare Mother Teresa to work among the poor in India? (**Mother Teresa had faced her own struggles as a child. This made her compassionate to others. She also sensed God's call at an early age to become a missionary and dedicated her life to His service.**) What needs did Mother Teresa see among the Indian people? (**She saw there was no one to care for the needs of the poorest in Calcutta. There was no system to help those who were poor and dying.**)

3. Continue by discussing the global impact of Mother Teresa's work. Why do you think other people started Missionaries of Charity in their countries? (**They also saw there were poor and needy people among them who needed to be shown the love of Christ. They saw the good work that Mother Teresa was doing and wanted to do it as well.**) How did God bless Mother Teresa's work? (**He blessed the people to whom she ministered. He also let others see her good work and glorify Him. The work she did to assist the poor was copied by others. She received the Nobel Peace Prize which also brought her work to the world's attention.**)

Ask the student if he/she can think of stories where Jesus helped the poor. (Answers may include: **Jesus healing lepers or giving sight to blind Bartimaeus.**) Ask the student what Christians can learn from the life of Mother Teresa. (Answers may include: **Christians need to care for all of God's people, especially the poor. We need to let others know we are Christians by how we treat the poor among us.**)

Lesson 40

Review

Overview:

- Identify the hard and soft /g/ and /c/ sounds in words

- Determine the correct spelling of the /k/ sound

- Recall the correct **s** spelling of the sounds /s/, /z/, and /zh/

- Choose the correct spelling of digraphs and diphthongs

Materials and Supplies:

- Teacher's Guide and Student Workbook

- White board or chart paper

- Phonics flashcards

- Reader: "Casey at the Bat"

Teaching Tips:

Review for Mastery. Discuss and review any work from the previous lesson that was assigned as homework. Check for completion of the activities and orally quiz the student for comprehension. Review any reading that was assigned, discussing the characters, setting, plot, theme, language, sequence, etc.

Strengthen fluency and phonemic awareness by reviewing words and sentences from the previous lessons. Build vocabulary skills by using some of the words in sentences.

You may want to review flashcards made for words in this unit.

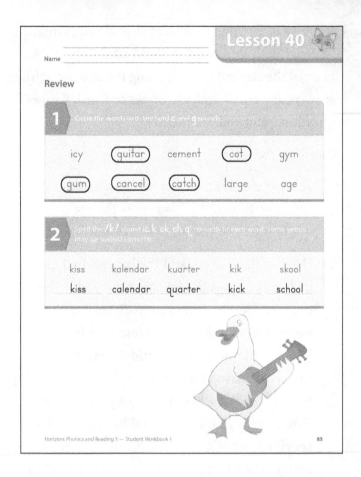

Activity 1. The student should turn to the review activity sheet. Begin by reviewing with the student the hard and soft /g/ and /c/ sounds. Ask the student to make each sound before completing the review activity. The words which have the hard /g/ and /c/ sounds are: **guitar, cot, gum, cancel, catch.**

Activity 2. Next, the student will review the /k/ sound. Review with the student the various ways the /k/ sound can be spelled including **c, k, ck, ch,** and **qu.** The student should rewrite each word with the /k/ sound spelled correctly. The correct spellings are: **kiss, calendar, quarter, kick, school.**

Activity 3. The letter **s** makes the sound /s/, /z/, and /zh/. The sounds the letter **s** makes are spelled out in this activity. Students will need to identify the sound and correctly rewrite the word using the letter **s**. The correct spelling of the words are: **vision, raise, sister, nose, usual**.

Activity 4. Finally the student will review digraphs and diphthongs. The student will be given two choices of how each word with a digraph or diphthong is spelled. The student will need to make the correct choice. The answers are: **taught, look, float, toe, author, spoon, board, foe**.

Reading Activity.

1. The student should turn to the selection "Casey at the Bat."

2. The student will be given the opportunity to read for pleasure in this lesson. The text will not be discussed.

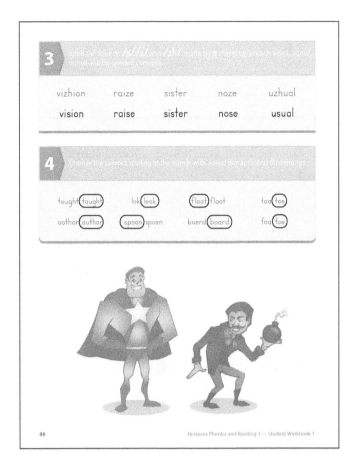

Test 4

Lessons 31-40

Overview:

- Identify the hard and soft /g/ and /c/ sounds in words

- Determine the correct spelling of the /k/ sound

- Recall the correct **s** spelling of the sounds /s/, /z/, and /zh/

- Choose the correct spelling of digraphs and diphthongs

Materials and Supplies:

- Student Test

Teaching Tips:

Review for Mastery. Discuss and review any work from the previous lesson that was assigned as homework. Check for completion of the activities and orally quiz the student for comprehension. Review any reading that was assigned, discussing the characters, setting, plot, theme, language, sequence, etc.

Check if the student has any final questions about the review before taking the test. The test is formatted like the review. Different words will be used in the test than what appeared in the review.

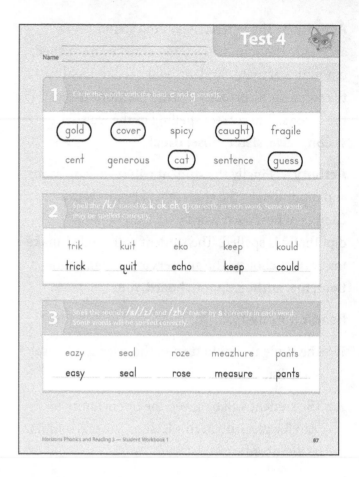

Activity 1. The first activity asks the student to correctly identify words with hard and soft /c/ and /g/ sounds. The student will do this by circling only the words with hard /c/ and /g/ sounds. The answers are: **gold, cover, caught, cat, guess**.

Activity 2. The student will continue with the test by correctly spelling words with the /k/ sound spelled **c, k, ck, ch,** or **qu**. The correct answers are: **trick, quit, echo, keep, could**.

Activity 3. The letter **s** makes the sound /s/, /z/, and /zh/. The sounds the letter **s** makes are spelled out in this activity. Students will need to identify the sound and correctly rewrite the word using the letter **s.** The answers are: **easy, seal, rose, measure, pants.**

Activity 4. Finally the student will be tested on digraphs and diphthongs. The student will be given two choices of how each word with a digraph or diphthong is spelled. The student will need to make the correct choice. The answers are: **caught, tooth, goat, hoe, doe, sauce, oak, booth.**

Lesson 41

R-controlled vowels: ar, ir

Overview:

- Define R-controlled vowels
- Read words with R-controlled vowels
- Recognize words with and without R-controlled vowels
- Use words with R-controlled vowels in sentences

Materials and Supplies:

- Teacher's Guide and Student Workbook
- White board or chart paper
- Phonics flashcards
- Reader: "The Emperor's New Clothes"

Teaching Tips:

Lesson Introduction. Write the words **far, fare,** and **fat** on the board. Ask the student what sound the vowel **a** makes in each of the words. In the word **fare,** the vowel **a** is long. In the word **fat,** the vowel sound is short. In the word **far,** the vowel sound is neither long nor short. Explain that when a vowel is followed by an **r** in the same syllable, that vowel is R-controlled. It is neither long nor short. In an R-controlled vowel, an **r** after the vowel makes the vowel sound differently.

Write the letters **ar** on the board. Ask the student to think of letters that can be placed in front of **ar** to form other words that have R-controlled vowels. Answers may include **bar, car, jar,** and **tar.**

Write the letters **ir** on the board. Ask the student to think of letters that can be placed in front of **ir** to form other words that have R-controlled vowels. Answers may include **fir, stir, whir,** and **sir.**

In this lesson the student will explore words where the vowels **a** and **i** are controlled by the letter **r.**

You may want to create flashcards of words with R-controlled vowels **a** and **i.** The student can study these throughout the unit.

Activity 1. The student should turn to the activity sheet accompanying this lesson. The student will be asked to identify pictures of words with R-controlled vowels. Ask the student to identify each picture and write the word underneath. The words pictured are: **skirt, yarn, star, shirt, harp.**

Activity 2. The next activity asks the student to fill in the blank with the letter **a** or **i** to form words with R-controlled vowels. You may want to do the first one together so the student understands the activity. After the student has completed the activity, read the words together taking note of the R-controlled vowels. The answers are: **first, arm, cart, chirp, park, smart, tart, market, part, thirteen.**

Name _____

R-controlled vowels: ar, ir

When a vowel is followed by an r in the same syllable, that vowel is R-controlled. It is neither long nor short. In an R-controlled vowel, an r after the vowel makes the vowel sound different from a short or long sound as in first or park.

1 Identify the picture with an R-controlled vowel.

skirt   yarn   star   shirt   harp

2 Fill in the blank with a or i for the R-controlled vowel.

f i rst   arm   c a rt   ch i rp   p a rk

sm a rt   t a rt   m a rket   p a rt   th i rteen

Horizons Phonics and Reading 3 — Student Workbook 1   89

Activity 3. The student will continue the study of R-controlled vowels by using words with R-controlled vowels in sentences. Together read the list of words that will be used in the sentences. Take note of the R-controlled vowel in each. Ask the student to complete the activity by putting the correct word in each sentence. Finish by reading the sentences with the correctly placed words. The answers are: **garden, dirt, artist, thirsty, carpet, apartment, squirt, harvest.**

Reading Activity.

1. Direct the student to read the selection "The Emperor's New Clothes." You could also read it together and take turns reading the dialogue.

2. Discuss the main characters and actions of the selection. Use the following questions to assist your discussion. Describe the Emperor. **(He ruled a kingdom but did not appear to be wise. He thought a great deal of himself. He liked clothes and wanted to impress people by what he wore.)** Describe the weavers. **(They were dishonest men who took advantage of the Emperor. They recognized the Emperor's pride and knew how to use it against him.)** Describe the type of people the Emperor chose to help him lead his kingdom. **(He chose people who would agree with what he said. They did not think for themselves but did what the Emperor asked.)** How did the weavers describe the fabric? **(They said it was made of beautiful colors, gold thread, and incredible patterns. They also told the Emperor that only people worthy of their offices or wise would be able to see the fabric. Later, they said the fabric was light as air.)** Who finally stated that the Emperor's clothes did not exist? **(A child.)** What happened as a result? **(The rest of the people admitted the truth.**

The Emperor wanted to maintain his pride, so he acted as if he was wearing a beautiful robe.)

3. In this lesson, the student studied words with the R-controlled vowels **a** and **i**. Find three words in this selection that have **a** or **i** R-controlled vowels. (Answers include: **large, charm, arms, first, sir, shirt.**)

Lesson 42

R-controlled vowels: er, or, ur

Overview:

- Define R-controlled vowels

- Read words with R-controlled vowels

- Recognize words with and without R-controlled vowels

- Use words with R-controlled vowels in sentences

Materials and Supplies:

- Teacher's Guide and Student Workbook

- White board or chart paper

- Phonics flashcards

- Reader: "The Emperor's New Clothes"

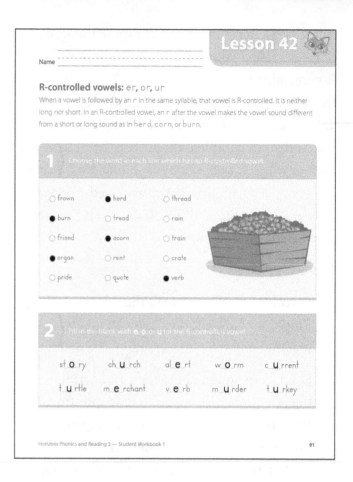

Teaching Tips:

Review for Mastery. Discuss and review any work from the previous lesson that was assigned as homework. Check for completion of the activities and orally quiz the student for comprehension. Review any reading that was assigned, discussing the characters, setting, plot, theme, language, sequence, etc.

Strengthen fluency and phonemic awareness by reviewing words and sentences from the previous lessons. Build vocabulary skills by using some of the words in sentences.

You may want to create flashcards of words with the R-controlled vowels **e**, **o**, and **u**. The student can study these throughout the unit.

Lesson Introduction. Write the words **far** and **fir** on the board. Remind the student of what he/she learned in the previous lesson about R-controlled vowels. An **r** after the vowel makes the vowel sound differently.

Write the letters **er**, **or**, and **ur** on the board. Ask the student to think of letters that can be placed in front of **er**, **or**, and **ur** to form other words that have an R-controlled vowel. Answers may include: **her**, **for**, and **fur**.

Explain that in this lesson the student will explore words where the vowels **e**, **o**, and **u** are controlled by the letter **r**.

Activity 1. Ask the student to turn to the activity sheet which accompanies this lesson. Read the words in each line and have the student determine which word has an R-controlled vowel. While the student can read the words silently, it may be helpful to read the words aloud. The answers are: **herd, burn, acorn, organ, verb**.

Activity 2. In the next activity, the student will be asked to fill in the blanks with the vowel **e**, **o**, or **u** in order to create words. The student may want to have a piece of scratch paper available in order to practice the words before writing them in the activity sheet. The answers are: **story, church, alert, worm, current, turtle, merchant, verb, murder, turkey.**

Activity 3. The final activity is a word search where the student is asked to locate R-controlled words. **See image for answers.**

Reading Activity.

1. Direct the student to return to the selection "The Emperor's New Clothes." You may want to briefly review the selection and main characters before continuing your discussion of the story.

2. Continue your discussion of "The Emperor's New Clothes." Ask the student to define the word "vanity." Vanity means unworthy pride in oneself. How did the Emperor show vanity? **(He loved wearing the newest and most beautiful clothes. He thought he was wise and yet the cheating weavers took advantage of him.)** Discuss how the student, or people in general, can struggle with vanity. **(Allow for a variety of answers.)** Because the weavers knew of the Emperor's pride and vanity, how were they able to take advantage of him? **(They played on the Emperor's pride by telling him only people who were wise or worthy of office would be able to see the fabric.)** The Emperor only surrounded himself with people who would agree with him. Why was this dangerous? **(These people did not tell him the truth. They told him what he wanted to hear. They wanted to protect their high offices and didn't really care about what was best for the Emperor.)** What can you learn about the types of friends and people with whom you should surround yourself? **(Talk about the need for people who encourage you but also tell you the truth.)**

3. In this lesson, the student studied words with the R-controlled vowels **e, o,** and **u.** Find three words in this selection that have **e, o,** or **u** R-controlled vowels. (Answers include: **emperor, government, visitor, tailor, return, turning.**)

Lesson 43

R-controlled vowels: are, air

Overview:

- Define R-controlled vowels
- Read words with R-controlled vowels
- Recognize that R-controlled vowels can be spelled **are** or **air**
- Use words with R-controlled vowels in sentences

Materials and Supplies:

- Teacher's Guide and Student Workbook
- White board or chart paper
- Phonics flashcards
- Reader: "Bed in Summer"

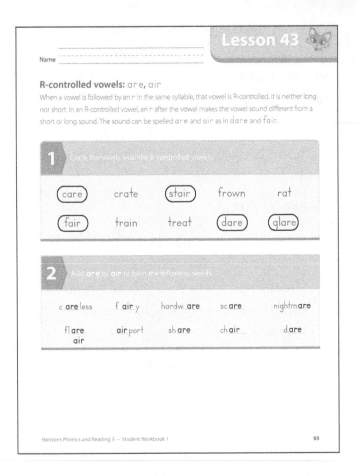

Teaching Tips:

Review for Mastery. Discuss and review any work from the previous lesson that was assigned as homework. Check for completion of the activities and orally quiz the student for comprehension. Review any reading that was assigned, discussing the characters, setting, plot, theme, language, sequence, etc.

Strengthen fluency and phonemic awareness by reviewing words and sentences from the previous lessons. Build vocabulary skills by using some of the words in sentences.

You may want to create flashcards of words with **are** and **air** R-controlled vowels. The student can study these throughout the unit.

Lesson Introduction. Tell the student that the /ar/ sound can also be spelled **are** or **air**. Write the words **care**, **chair**, and **rare** and the board. Ask the student to say these words. The student should note the /ar/ sound in each word.

Activity 1. The student should turn to the activity sheet for this lesson. Read through the definitions about R-controlled vowels at the top of the sheet. Together read the words in the first activity. Emphasize the R-controlled vowel sounds where found. The student should circle only the words with R-controlled vowel sounds. These words are: **care, stair, fair, dare, glare**.

Activity 2. Next the student will be asked to add the /ar/ sound to words. The /ar/ sound will be spelled either **are** or **air**. The student may want to have a piece of scratch paper to write out the word first before filling in the blanks on the activity sheet. The answers are: **careless, fairy, hardware, scare, nightmare, flare/flair, airport, share, chair, dare.**

Activity 3. The student will continue by choosing the correct R-controlled vowel word to fill in the blank in each sentence. You may want to read each sentence aloud with the correct word. The answers are: **square, hair, stairs, pair, shared, airport, prepare, chair, nightmare, fair.**

Reading Activity.

1. Read the poem "Bed in Summer" with your student. You may want to read it to the student first and then have the student read it to you.

2. Discuss the themes in the poem using the following discussion starters. How does the poet describe going to bed in winter? (**The author says that it is dark and he must dress by candlelight.**) What is it like to go to bed in the summer? (**In the summer it is still light and the author can see and hear the birds and people moving.**) What would the author rather be doing at bedtime during the summer months? (**The author would rather be playing outside.**) Ask the student to describe the difference for him/her in going to bed in the summer vs. the winter. (**Answers will vary.**)

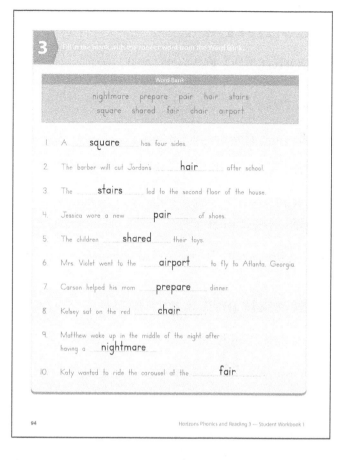

3. Study the rhythm and rhyme schemes of the poem with your student. How many syllables are in each line of the poem? (**There are 8 syllables per line.**) What words at the end of each line rhyme? (**The first two lines rhyme and the third and fourth lines rhyme.**) Read through the rhyming words with the student so he/she hears the rhyme.

Lesson 44

R-controlled vowels: ear, eer

Overview:

- Define R-controlled vowels

- Read words with R-controlled vowels

- Recognize that R-controlled vowels can be spelled **ear** or **eer**

- Use words with R-controlled vowels in sentences

Materials and Supplies:

- Teacher's Guide and Student Workbook

- White board or chart paper

- Phonics flashcards

- Reader: "Dikembe Mutombo"

95

Teaching Tips:

Review for Mastery. Discuss and review any work from the previous lesson that was assigned as homework. Check for completion of the activities and orally quiz the student for comprehension. Review any reading that was assigned, discussing the characters, setting, plot, theme, language, sequence, etc.

Strengthen fluency and phonemic awareness by reviewing words and sentences from the previous lessons. Build vocabulary skills by using some of the words in sentences.

You may want to create flashcards of words with **eer** and **ear** R-controlled vowels. The student can study these throughout the unit.

Lesson Introduction. Tell the student that the /er/ sound can be spelled **eer** or **ear**. Write the words **cheer**, **fear**, and **dear** on the board. Ask the student to say these words. The student should note the /er/ sound in each word.

Activity 1. The student should turn to the activity sheet for this lesson. Read through the definitions at the top of the sheet. The student should identify each of the pictures at the top of the page. After the pictures are identified, have the student write the correct word underneath. As an added activity, you may ask the student to underline the **ear** or **eer** letter combinations in each word. The correct words for the pictures are: **ear**, **beard**, **deer**, **tear**, **gear**.

Activity 2. The student should form words with **ear** and **eer**. The student may want to have a piece of paper to write the words out first before filling in the blanks on the activity sheet. The correct answers are: **spear**, **reindeer**, **appear**, **weary**, **pioneer**, **swear**, **clear**, **career**.

Activity 3. The student will need to choose the correct word from each pair to complete the sentences in the final activity. The student may want to read the sentence with each possible word before deciding on the correct one. Remind the student that both words may fit, but only one word will have an R-controlled vowel sound. The correct answers are: **weary**, **pearl**, **gear**, **earache**, **volunteer**, **steer**, **year**, **pioneers**, **near**, **clear**.

Reading Activity.

1. The student should turn to the selection "Dikembe Mutombo." Pronounce the name of this athlete for the student.

2. After the student has read the selection, discuss the main points. Ask the student to describe Dikembe Mutombo. **(He is a former National Basketball Association (NBA) player. He is 7'2" tall and grew up in the Democratic Republic of Congo.)** Describe Mutombo's childhood. **(His dad was a high school principal. He grew up in Kinshasa. He was also one of nine children.)** How did Mutombo become interested in basketball? **(His father told him he should play. His height made him appear to be a natural basketball player.)** Describe Mutombo as an NBA player. **(He was an excellent shot blocker and rebounder. He had quick reflexes. He was a frequent all-star and defensive player of the year.)**

3. Tell the student that you will continue your study of Dikembe Mutombo in the next lesson.

4. Ask the student to find three words in the selection with the R-controlled vowel spelled **ear**. (Answers include: **year**, **near**, **learn**, **earn**.)

Lesson 45

Final e: a_e

Overview:

- Define a "sneaky" or "bossy" **e**

- Read words with long /a/ sounds because of final **e**'s

- Form words with long /a/ sounds because of final **e**'s

- Use words with "sneaky" or "bossy" **e**'s in phrases

Materials and Supplies:

- Teacher's Guide and Student Workbook

- White board or chart paper

- Phonics flashcards

- Reader: "Dikembe Mutombo"

Teaching Tips:

Review for Mastery. Discuss and review any work from the previous lesson that was assigned as homework. Check for completion of the activities and orally quiz the student for comprehension. Review any reading that was assigned, discussing the characters, setting, plot, theme, language, sequence, etc.

Strengthen fluency and phonemic awareness by reviewing words and sentences from the previous lessons. Build vocabulary skills by using some of the words in sentences.

You may want to create flashcards of words with long **a** sounds because of final silent **e**'s. The student can study these throughout the unit.

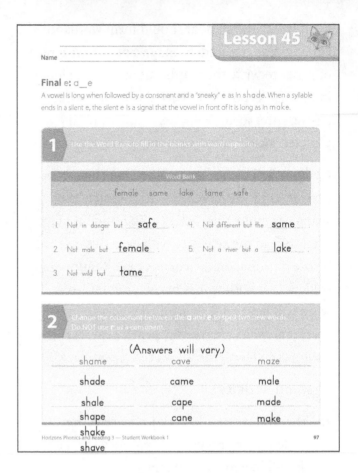

Lesson Introduction. Remind the student of how you studied long vowel sounds with different spellings in previous lessons. Another rule for a long vowel sound is a "sneaky" or "bossy" **e**. Write the words **save** and **came** on the board. Point out the long /a/ vowel sound and the silent **e** at the end of the words. In this lesson, the student will be asked to look for words with "sneaky" **e**'s at the end of words.

Continue by writing the words **cave** and **care** on the board. Notice how the R-controlled vowel is even stronger than the "sneaky" **e**. Words with R-controlled vowels do not follow the "sneaky" or "bossy" **e** rule.

Activity 1. The student should turn to the accompanying activity sheet. Read through the definition at the top of the page. Read through the words used in the first activity. The student should read each clue and insert the correct **a_e** word. The answers are: **safe, female, tame, same, lake**.

Activity 2. The student will continue by creating new words with the **a_e** pattern. You may want to complete one as an example before the student completes the activity. An example would be the word **lame**, which could become the word **lake** by changing the final consonant. Ask the student to complete the activity and find two new words which can be made from each example. Possible answers for the activity are: **shade, shake, shale, shape, shave, came, cape, cane, male, made, make.** Keep in mind the student's answers may vary.

Activity 3. Next the student will be asked to complete a crossword puzzle. The student should first use the Word Bank to answer the clues before placing them on the crossword puzzle. Answers to the clues are:

Across:	Down:
1. **cage**	2. **gate**
4. **hate**	3. **save**
5. **fame**	5. **frame**
6. **shape**	7. **sale**
7. **shade**	
8. **blade**	

Reading Activity.

1. The student should return to the selection "Dikembe Mutombo."

2. Continue your discussion of the selection with the following questions. How did God prepare Mutombo to become a basketball player? (**He blessed Mutombo with great height and coordination.**) What did Mutombo want to do when he came to the U.S. for college? (**He wanted to become a doctor. He wanted to help the people in his country.**) Why did Mutombo think it would be better to be a professional basketball player than a doctor? (**He realized he would be able to help more people in his home country with the money and fame he earned**

in the NBA.**)** How did Mutombo express his thankfulness to God for the success he had in the NBA? (**Mutombo used his money to build the first modern hospital in the Democratic Republic of Congo in 40 years.**) What can Christians learn from Dikembe Mutombo? (Answers include: **Christians can learn to be generous with the many gifts that God has given them. Christians can also learn the importance of serving others and caring for God's people.**)

3. Ask the student to find one word in the selection with the long **a** vowel sound because of the "sneaky" **e**. (Answers include: **game, named.**)

Lesson 46

Final e: e_e, i_e

Overview:

- Define a "sneaky" or "bossy" **e**
- Read words with long **e** or **i** sounds because of final **e**'s
- Form words with long **e** or **i** sounds because of final **e**'s
- Use words with "sneaky" or "bossy" **e**'s in phrases

Materials and Supplies:

- Teacher's Guide and Student Workbook
- White board or chart paper
- Phonics flashcards
- Reader: "The Sun Bear"

Teaching Tips:

Review for Mastery. Discuss and review any work from the previous lesson that was assigned as homework. Check for completion of the activities and orally quiz the student for comprehension. Review any reading that was assigned, discussing the characters, setting, plot, theme, language, sequence, etc.

Strengthen fluency and phonemic awareness by reviewing words and sentences from the previous lessons. Build vocabulary skills by using some of the words in sentences.

You may want to create flashcards of words with long **e** or **i** sounds because of final silent **e**'s. The student can study these throughout the unit.

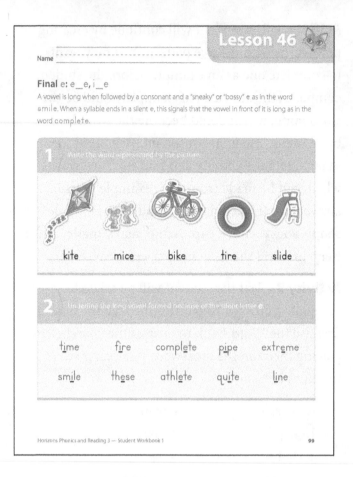

Lesson Introduction. Remind the student of how you studied long vowel sounds in previous lessons. One rule for a long vowel sound was if the word had a "sneaky" or "bossy" **e**. Write the words **tide** and **extreme** on the board. Point out the long **i** and **e** vowel sounds and the silent **e**'s at the end of the words. In this lesson, the student will be asked to look for words with "sneaky" **e**'s.

Activity 1. Turn to the activity sheet which accompanies the lesson. Read through the definition at the top of the page. The student should identify each of the pictures on the activity sheet. They are all words with long **i** vowel sounds because of "bossy" **e**'s at the end. The student should identify the pictures as: **kite, mice, bike, tire, slide**.

Activity 2. The student will identify the long **e** or **i** vowel sounds in the words because of final **e**'s. You may find it helpful to have the student read aloud each word before underlining the long **e** or **i**. The answers are: t**i**me, f**i**re, compl**e**te, p**i**pe, extr**e**me, sm**i**le, th**e**se, athl**e**te, qu**i**te, l**i**ne.

Activity 3. The student will be asked to fill in the blank in each sentence with a word from the Word Bank. Each word has either a long **e** or **i** sound because of a final **e**. The correct answers for the activity are: **supreme, dive, athlete, Eve, line, these, time, hike.**

Reading Activity.

1. The student should turn to the selection "The Sun Bear." Direct the student in reading the selection either with you or alone.

2. After reading the selection, discuss "The Sun Bear" with your student. Ask the student to describe the sun bear's physical appearance. (**The bear is the smallest member of the bear family weighing about 150 pounds and standing 4 feet tall. It has black or brown fur with an area of orange on its chest and around its nose and eyes. The bear has a long tongue, and a good sense of smell, but poor eyes. The bear is also shy.**) How is the sun bear different from other bears? (**It is smaller, does not hibernate, and is nocturnal.**) What is the habitat of the sun bear? (**It is native to the tropical rain forests of India and China. It sleeps above the forest floor.**) What food does the bear eat? (**It eats lizards, birds, fruit, and honey.**) What story character is modeled after the sun bear? (**Winnie the Pooh**) What main danger does the sun bear face? (**They have few predators. People are cutting down the rain forests in which they live. They are also hunted by people. Others kill mother bears so the cubs can be raised as pets.**)

3. Ask the student to find three words in the selection with long **e** or **i** sounds because of the "sneaky" **e**. (Answers include: **size, like, unlike, hives, eyes.**)

4. As an added activity, have the student draw or find pictures of the sun bear.

Lesson 47

Final e: o_e

Overview:

- Recall that the "bossy" **e** can make a vowel sound long
- Read words with long **o** vowel sounds because of "sneaky" **e**'s
- Use words with long **o** vowel sounds because of "sneaky" **e**'s in sentences

Materials and Supplies:

- Teacher's Guide and Student Workbook
- White board or chart paper
- Phonics flashcards
- Reader: "Trees"

Teaching Tips:

Review for Mastery. Discuss and review any work from the previous lesson that was assigned as homework. Check for completion of the activities and orally quiz the student for comprehension. Review any reading that was assigned, discussing the characters, setting, plot, theme, language, sequence, etc.

Strengthen fluency and phonemic awareness by reviewing words and sentences from the previous lessons. Build vocabulary skills by using some of the words in sentences.

You may want to create flashcards of words with the long **o** vowel sounds because of the "sneaky" **e**. The student can study these throughout the unit.

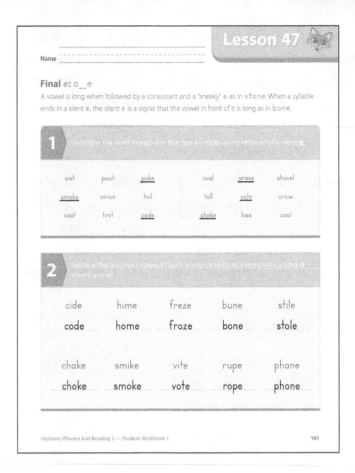

Lesson Introduction. Ask the student what vowels they have studied that became long when followed by a "sneaky" or "bossy" **e**. (The student has studied the vowels **a**, **e**, and **i**.) Explain that in this lesson the student will study the long **o** sound formed because of a "sneaky" **e** at the end of a word. See if the student can think of words with long **o** sounds because of the "sneaky" **e**. Answers include: **rode**, **froze**, and **choke**.

Activity 1. Turn to the activity sheet which accompanies the lesson. Read through the definition at the top of the activity sheet. Tell the student to underline the word in each line which has a long **o** vowel sound because of a final **e**. The answers are: **poke, smoke, code, arose, vote, choke**.

Activity 2. In the next activity, each word has an incorrect vowel in place of the long **o** sound. The student should rewrite each word using the correct long **o** vowel sound. The correct answers are: **code, home, froze, bone, stole, choke, smoke, vote, rope, phone**.

Activity 3. Five words with long **o** vowel sounds are listed. The student should write a sentence for each of the words. Sample answers are:

1. James used the <u>phone</u> to call his mom.
2. Brianna liked to jump <u>rope</u> at recess.
3. Ellie walked <u>home</u> from the library.
4. Kenton had a <u>stone</u> in his shoe.
5. Tori gave her mom a <u>rose.</u>

Reading Activity.

1. Ask the student, "If you were to write a poem about a tree, what descriptions would you use?" Give the student time to brainstorm a list of things about a tree that he/she would want to describe.

2. Read the poem "Trees" to your student. After you have read it once, have the student join you to read it a second time.

3. Discuss the poem with the student. What parts of a tree did the author appreciate? (**The author spoke of how the tree received nourishment from the soil, had leaves, and held a robin's nest. The author described how the tree looked during different seasons of the year.**) What conclusion did the author make about a tree and a poem? (**While an author can write about a tree, only God can make a tree.**) Look at the poetic form of the selection. (**The student should note the rhyming couplets of eight syllables.**)

Lesson 48

Final e: u_e

Overview:

- Recall that a "sneaky" or "bossy" **e** makes a preceding vowel long

- Read words with long **u** sounds because of final **e**'s

- Recognize how the final **e** affects the **u** vowel sound

- Form words with long **u** vowel sounds because of "sneaky" **e**'s

Materials and Supplies:

- Teacher's Guide and Student Workbook

- White board or chart paper

- Phonics flashcards

- Reader: "The Swiss Family Robinson"

Teaching Tips:

Review for Mastery. Discuss and review any work from the previous lesson that was assigned as homework. Check for completion of the activities and orally quiz the student for comprehension. Review any reading that was assigned, discussing the characters, setting, plot, theme, language, sequence, etc.

Strengthen fluency and phonemic awareness by reviewing words and sentences from the previous lessons. Build vocabulary skills by using some of the words in sentences.

You may want to create flashcards of words with long **u** vowel sounds because of "sneaky" **e**'s. The student can study these throughout the unit.

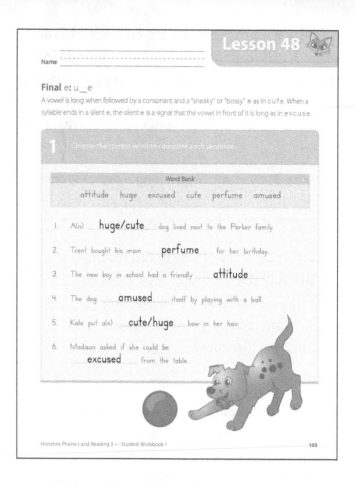

Lesson Introduction. Tell the student in this lesson he/she will study the long **u** vowel sounds that result from "sneaky" **e**'s. See if the student can think of words with long **a**, **e**, **i**, and **o** because of "sneaky" **e**'s. These may be words studied in previous lessons. Examples may include **bake**, **extreme**, **like**, and **rose**. Ask the student to brainstorm a list of words that have long **u** vowel sound because of silent **e**'s. Answers include: **amuse**, **cube**, and **volume**.

Activity 1. Turn to the activity sheet which accompanies the lesson. Read through the definition at the top of the activity sheet. Next read the words with long **u** vowel sounds found in the Word Bank. The student will use these words to complete the sentences. You may want to note that there may be more than one correct answer for some of the questions. The answers are: **huge/cute**, **perfume**, **attitude**, **amused**, **cute/huge**, **excused**.

Activity 2. Next the student should identify the word in each line which has a long **u** vowel sound because of a "sneaky" **e**. Only one word in each line will be correct. The answers are: **cube, amuse, produce, excuse, volume, distribute**.

Activity 3. Finally, the student will need to find the word or words in each of the sentences provided which have a long **u** vowel sounds because of "sneaky" or "bossy" **e**'s. The correct answers are:

1. The doctor said the medicine would **<u>cure</u>** Elmer's cold.
2. Mr. Bridge turned up the **<u>volume</u>** on the radio.
3. Mrs. Dobson had a **<u>huge</u>** addition problem to **compute**.
4. The difficult math problem **<u>confused</u>** Rachel.
5. The water in the river was **<u>pure</u>** and clear.
6. Mr. Carter **<u>reused</u>** the paper bag.

Reading Activity.

1. Ask the student to read the entire selection of "The Swiss Family Robinson." You may want to read the selection together and take turns reading the dialogue. Because of the length of the selection, the majority of the discussion will take place during the next lesson.

2. Discuss the main characters and setting of the selection with your student. (**The main characters are the mother, father, Fritz, Ernest, Jack, and Franz. The setting is an island after a shipwreck.**)

3. Ask the student to identify two words in the selection which have a long **u** sounds because of a silent **e** at the end of the word or syllable. (Answers are: **use, huge, plumes**.)

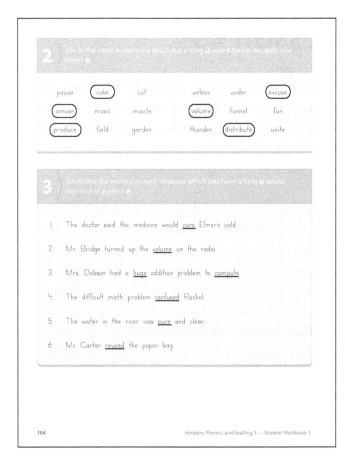

Lesson 49
Final e

Overview:

- Identify words with long **a**, **e**, **i**, **o**, or **u** sounds because of a "sneaky" or "bossy" **e**

- Read words with long vowel sounds because of silent **e** endings

- Form words correctly with long **a**, **e**, **i**, **o**, or **u** sounds because of a "sneaky **e**

Materials and Supplies:

- Teacher's Guide and Student Workbook

- White board or chart paper

- Phonics flashcards

- Reader: "The Swiss Family Robinson"

Teaching Tips:

Review for Mastery. Discuss and review any work from the previous lesson that was assigned as homework. Check for completion of the activities and orally quiz the student for comprehension. Review any reading that was assigned, discussing the characters, setting, plot, theme, language, sequence, etc.

Strengthen fluency and phonemic awareness by reviewing words and sentences from the previous lessons. Build vocabulary skills by using some of the words in sentences.

You may want to review just the flashcards the student made for words with long vowel sounds because of a "sneaky" **e**.

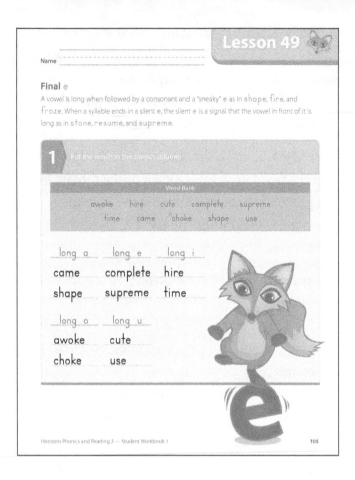

Lesson Introduction. Write the following series of words on the board: **dim**, **dime**, and **dome**. Ask the student which one of the words does not belong in the series (**dim**). Why shouldn't this word be included? (**It does not have a long vowel sound formed because of a "sneaky" or "bossy" e.**) Explain that in this lesson the student will review words with long vowel sounds because of a "sneaky" or "bossy" **e**.

Activity 1. Turn to the activity sheet which accompanies the lesson. Read through the definition and examples at the top of the page. The student will be asked to put words with long vowel sounds in the correct categories. You may find it helpful to read through the words with the student before he/she places them in the correct column. That way the student can hear the long vowel sound as well as see it.

long a	long e	long i	long o	long u
came	complete	hire	awoke	cute
shape	supreme	time	choke	use

Activity 2. The student will be asked to fill in the missing vowel in each of the words. It may be helpful to have a piece of paper for the student to practice each word with a chosen vowel before choosing the correct one. The answers for the activity are: **phone, frame, trade, cube, blade, shape, supreme, smoke, excuse, slide**.

Activity 3. Read through the Bible passage found on the activity sheet. The student should listen for words with long vowel sounds because of a "sneaky" or "bossy" **e**. Have the student underline words in the Bible passage which fit the pattern of words studied in this lesson. The answers are: **life** and **name**. The words love and live have short vowel sounds.

Reading Activity.

1. Return to the selection "The Swiss Family Robinson."

2. Ask the student what problems a family would face after being shipwrecked on an island. (Answers include: **What to eat, where to sleep, and how to stay safe.**) How did the family face some of the problems the student raised? (**The family gathered supplies from the ship that had not yet sunk. They were able to get weapons, tools, food, livestock, and clothes. They decided to make their home in a very large tree where they would be safe from wild animals. The weapons along with the location of their home kept them safe from danger.**) What interesting things did the family discover on the island? (**They learned that it would be easy to get coconuts if the monkeys dropped them from the tree. The boys also discovered a flamingo.**) What dangers did the family face? (**First of all they faced the danger of the shipwreck and getting safely to the island. Later they faced danger from a shark.**) At the end of the story, you read that the parents wanted to be rescued but not the boys. Why do you think the boys did not want to be

rescued? (**The boys enjoyed the adventure and excitement of the island. The boys may not have realized what things they were missing at home.**)

3. The author wrote "The Swiss Family Robinson" to teach his four sons the importance of being resourceful as well as being good Christian men. How do you see these themes in the selection you read? (Answers may include: **The family stayed together and cared for each other. The boys in the story learned to solve problems in interesting ways such as the monkeys and the coconuts as well as where to build a house.**)

4. The selection contains many words that have long vowel sounds because of a "sneaky" or "bossy" **e**. Ask the student to find five words that have a "sneaky" or "bossy" **e**. (Answers include: **side, lives, alone, take, use, safe, made, rode, hoped, safely, axe, size, surprise.**)

Lesson 50

Review

Overview:

- Identify words with R-controlled vowels
- Determine the correct spelling of /ar/ and /er/ sounds
- Recall words with long vowel sounds because of a "sneaky" or "bossy" **e**

Materials and Supplies:

- Teacher's Guide and Student Workbook
- White board or chart paper
- Phonics flashcards
- Reader: "All Things Bright and Beautiful"

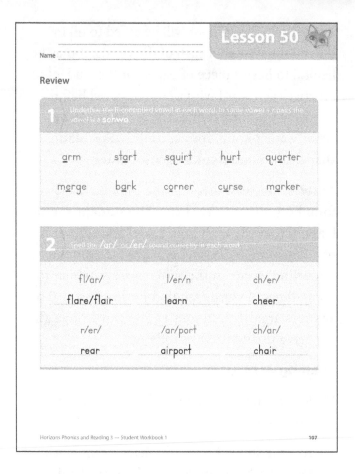

Teaching Tips:

Review for Mastery. Discuss and review any work from the previous lesson that was assigned as homework. Check for completion of the activities and orally quiz the student for comprehension. Review any reading that was assigned, discussing the characters, setting, plot, theme, language, sequence, etc.

Strengthen fluency and phonemic awareness by reviewing words and sentences from the previous lessons. Build vocabulary skills by using some of the words in sentences.

You my want to review flashcards made for words in this unit.

Lesson Introduction. Have the student think of the phonics rules he/she learned in this unit. The student should remember studying R-controlled vowels, alternate ways of spelling the /ar/ and /er/ sounds, and words with long vowel sounds because of a "sneaky" or "bossy" **e**.

Write each of the topics on the board. Ask the student to brainstorm words that would fit under each category. For examples, words with R-controlled vowels include: **farmer, storm**, and **hurt**. Words with alternate spellings of /ar/ and /er/ include the words: **stair, pear**, and **mare**. Words with long vowel sounds because of silent **e**'s at the end of the syllable include: **stake, line**, and **tone**.

Activity 1. The student should turn to the review sheet accompanying this lesson. The first activity reviews R-controlled vowels. Read the instructions with the student and have him/her underline the R-controlled vowel in each word. Remind the students that not all vowel+r combinations are R-controlled. Some are a schwa. The correct answers are: **a̱rm**, **sta̱rt**, **squi̱rt**, **hu̱rt**, **qua̱rter**, **me̱rge**, **ba̱rk**, **co̱rner**, **cu̱rse**, **ma̱rker**. Go over the correct answers with the student. Explain that the activity on the test will be exactly like this only different words will be used.

Activity 2. The student will continue by reviewing words with alternate spellings of /ar/ or /er/ sounds. Remind the student that these alternate spellings are: **air**, **are**, **ear**, and **eer**. You may want to write these on the board so the student can refer to them during the activity. The correct answers are: **flare/ flair**, **learn**, **cheer**, **rear**, **airport**, **chair**.

Activity 3. The student will continue the review by underlining words in sentences which have long vowel sounds because of "sneaky" **e**'s. You may want to read through each sentence together before the student completes the activity. In this way the student may be able to hear the long vowel sounds. The answers are:

1. Mrs. Thomas could not find the **remote** control for her television.
2. **Kade** dug a **hole** in the sandbox.
3. Mr. Titus **used** a **rope** to **tie** the **luggage** to the top of his car.
4. Max threw a **stone** in the **lake**.
5. Mrs. Allen told her children it was **time** for bed.
6. A **sale** on **bike tires** was held on Wednesday.

3   Underline the word(s) in each sentence with the long vowel sound(s) because of the silent e.

1. Mrs. Thomas could not find the <u>remote</u> control for her television.
2. <u>Kade</u> dug a <u>hole</u> in the sandbox.
3. Mr. Titus <u>used</u> a <u>rope</u> to <u>tie</u> the <u>luggage</u> to the top of his car.
4. Max threw a <u>stone</u> in the <u>lake</u>.
5. Mrs. Allen told her children it was <u>time</u> for bed.
6. A <u>sale</u> on <u>bike</u> <u>tires</u> was held on Wednesday.

Horizons Phonics and Reading 3 — Student Workbook 1

Reading Activity.

1. Ask the student to turn to the poem "All Things Bright and Beautiful." Some may be familiar with the poem through the hymn setting of the words.

2. Let the student read through the poem while enjoying its images.

Test 5

Lessons 41-50

Overview:

- Identify words with R-controlled vowels

- Determine the correct spelling of /ar/ and /er/ sounds

- Recall words with long vowel sounds because of a "sneaky" or "bossy" **e**

Materials and Supplies:

- Student Test

Teaching Tips:

Review for Mastery. Discuss and review any work from the previous lesson that was assigned as homework. Check for completion of the activities and orally quiz the student for comprehension. Review any reading that was assigned, discussing the characters, setting, plot, theme, language, sequence, etc.

Lesson Introduction. Check if the student has any final questions from the review before taking the test. The test is formatted like the review. Different words will be used in the test than what appeared in the review.

Activity 1. The first section of the test asks the student to recall words with R-controlled vowels. Each word in the activity has an R-controlled vowel, but it is possible that a word will have more than one R-controlled vowel. It may be helpful for you to read the instructions for the activity with the student before he/she completes the activity. The answers are: **b**o**rn, occu**r**, rad**a**r, f**o**rl**o**rn, p**u**rple, ch**i**rp, ad**o**rable, s**e**rvant, h**a**rd, m**e**rchant.**

Activity 2. The student will be asked to spell words correctly with /ar/ and /er/ sounds. The ways in which these sounds can be spelled are not on the test. As a teacher, you may decide whether or not you want to give these spellings to the student. They are **air**, **are**, **ear**, and **eer**. The correct answers are: **care, clear, pioneer, gear, airplane, hair**.

Activity 3. The final section of the test asks the student to identify words with long vowel sounds because of "sneaky" **e**'s. The student may find it helpful to be able to read the sentences aloud before identifying the correct words. However, not all classroom situations will permit this. The correct answers are:

1. **Hope** needed new **tires** on her **bike**.
2. Dawson called his grandma on the **phone**.
3. The **smoke** from the **fire** went straight into the air.
4. Mr. Jansen ordered a **supreme** pizza for his family.
5. Mrs. Daniels **made** plans to **vote** in the next election.
6. Ava walked through the garden **gate**.

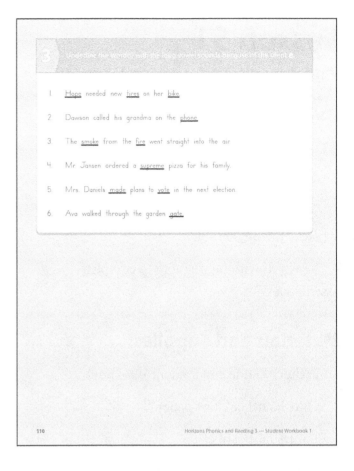

Lesson 51

Patterns with ng: ang, eng, ing

Overview:

- Define the **ng** digraph

- Read words with the **ng** digraph

- Recognize words with the vowels **a, e,** and **i** before the **ng** digraph

- Use words with **ng** digraphs to complete sentences

Materials and Supplies:

- Teacher's Guide and Student Workbook

- White board or chart paper

- Phonics flashcards

- Reader: "How Brother Rabbit Fooled the Whale and the Elephant"

Teaching Tips:

Lesson Introduction. This is the first of a series of lessons on the **ng** and **nk** consonant digraphs. In this lesson the student will learn about the **ng** digraph. In particular, the student will look at the **ng** digraph as it follows the vowels **a, e,** and **i.** Write the endings **-ang, -eng,** and **-ing** on the board. See if the student can think of words which have these letter combinations forming the **ng** digraph. Answers may include: **English, sang,** and **thing.**

You may want to create flashcards of words with **ng** digraphs. The student can study these throughout the unit.

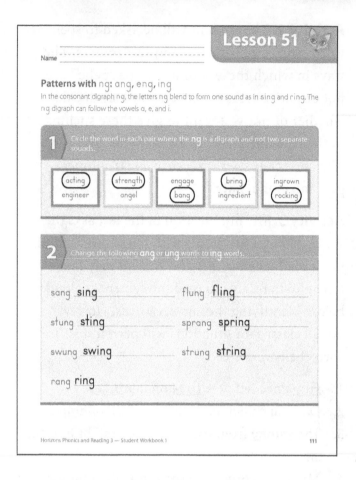

Activity 1. The student should turn to the accompanying activity sheet. Read through the definitions at the top of the page with the student. In the first activity the student will be asked to differentiate between words with the **ng** sound as a digraph and as two separate sounds. If possible have the student read the words aloud so he/she can hear the difference in the digraph and separate sounds. Words with the **ng** digraph are: **acting, strength, bang, bring, rocking.**

Activity 2. As the lesson continues, the student will be asked to change words with the **ng** digraph preceded by **a** or **u** to words with the **ng** digraph preceded by **i.** Do an example with the student. The word **sung** would be changed to **sing.** Have the student complete the activity making the necessary changes. Go over the correct answers with the student. Answers are: **sing, fling, sting, spring, swing, string, ring.**

Activity 3. The student should continue by using words with **ng** digraphs in sentences. The student should read each sentence and fill in the blank with a word with an **ng** digraph. A Word Bank is provided to assist the student. The answers are: **length, rang, sang, cooking, wing, rocking, parking, amazing, strength, banged.**

Reading Activity.

1. The Student should read the selection "How Brother Rabbit Fooled the Whale and the Elephant."

2. Discuss the main points of the story with the student. This will be a preliminary discussion. The student will finish discussing the selection in the next lesson. The student should begin by describing the main characters. (**Brother Rabbit was clever. He didn't want to have the Whale and Elephant boss him or other animals around. The Elephant and Whale were strong, proud animals.**) What was the setting? (**The story is set somewhere near an ocean and an elephant's habitat. It may have been set in Africa or Asia.**) What is the problem or conflict in the selection? (**The Whale and the Elephant want to rule the animals and Brother Rabbit didn't want this.**)

3. The student should find examples of five words in the selection containing the **ng** digraph preceded by the vowel **i**. (Answers include: **running, talking, saying, thing, sliding, making, pulling, slipping.**)

3 Fill in the blank with the correct **ng** word.

Word Bank

sang   parking   amazing   cooking   banged
length   strength   wing   rocking   rang

1. The table was two feet in **length**
2. The church bell **rang** 30 minutes before the service.
3. Parker **sang** in the church choir.
4. Mrs. Hummel was **cooking** a roast for supper.
5. The bird had an injured **wing**
6. The two-year-old loved to ride her **rocking** horse.
7. There were no **parking** spots near the library.
8. April was a(n) **amazing** dancer.
9. The climber needed a lot of **strength** to climb the mountain.
10. The drummer **banged** the drum during the song.

Lesson 52

Patterns with ng: ong, ung

Overview:

- Define the **ng** digraph
- Read words with the **ng** digraph
- Recognize words with the vowels **o** and **u** before the **ng** digraph
- Use words with **ng** digraphs to complete sentences

Materials and Supplies:

- Teacher's Guide and Student Workbook
- White board or chart paper
- Phonics flashcards
- Reader: "How Brother Rabbit Fooled the Whale and the Elephant"

Teaching Tips:

Review for Mastery. Discuss and review any work from the previous lesson that was assigned as homework. Check for completion of the activities and orally quiz the student for comprehension. Review any reading that was assigned, discussing the characters, setting, plot, theme, language, sequence, etc.

Strengthen fluency and phonemic awareness by reviewing words and sentences from the previous lessons. Build vocabulary skills by using some of the words in sentences.

You may want to create flashcards of words with the **ng** digraphs preceded by **o** and **u**. The student can study these throughout the unit.

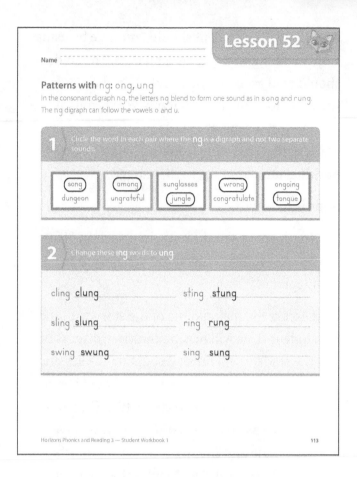

Lesson Introduction. Write the words **string** and **rang** on the board. Ask the student if he/she could make a new word by placing **o** or **u** in place of the **i** or **a** in each word. New words created would be: **strong**, **strung**, and **rung**.

Tell the student that in this lesson he/she will be looking at **ng** digraphs with the vowels **o** or **u** in front of them.

Activity 1. The student should turn to the accompanying activity sheet. Ask the student to read the definition for an **ng** digraph at the top of the sheet. The student will then be asked to identify the word in each pair where the consonant combination **ng** is being used as a digraph and not two separate sounds. The answers are: **song**, **among**, **jungle**, **wrong**, **tongue**.

Activity 2. In the next activity, the student will be asked to change **ing** words to **ung.** The answers are: **clung, stung, slung, rung, swung, sung.** As an added activity, ask the student to say or write sentences using the new word.

Activity 3. The final activity asks the student to conduct a word search of words with **ong** and **ung** digraphs. In the word search the student should find the words from the Word Bank. **See image for answers.**

Reading Activity.

1. The student should return to the selection "How Brother Rabbit Fooled the Whale and the Elephant." Review the main characters and the setting of the selection.

2. Spend time discussing the selection. Review the plan of the Whale and the Elephant to rule over the animal kingdom. (**They planned to use their strength and power to rule the other animals.**) What was Brother Rabbit's plan to stop them from ruling? (**He was going to get them to unknowingly compete against each other. He asked each of them to help get his cow out of the mud.**) How did Brother Rabbit get the two animals to agree to help him? (**He flattered them and told them how kind and strong they were.**) How did he carry out his plan? (**He tied the two animals together in a tug of war. They did not realize they were competing against each other.**) What was the result of the tug of war? (**Both animals became frustrated because they couldn't accomplish the task. They became angry with each other because they thought the other was in on the trick. They no longer wanted to work together to rule the animals.**) What lessons can you learn from this story? (Answers may include: **Strength doesn't always win the battle. Pride brings people low.**)

3. Find two words in the selection with the **ng** preceded by the vowel **o.** (Answers include: **along, long, strong.**)

Lesson 53

Patterns with nk: ank, enk, ink, onk, and unk

Overview:

- Define the **nk** digraph
- Read words with the **nk** digraph
- Recognize words with vowels before the **nk** digraph
- Use words with **nk** digraphs to complete sentences

Materials and Supplies:

- Teacher's Guide and Student Workbook
- White board or chart paper
- Phonics flashcards
- Reader: "Count that Day Lost"

Teaching Tips:

Review for Mastery. Discuss and review any work from the previous lesson that was assigned as homework. Check for completion of the activities and orally quiz the student for comprehension. Review any reading that was assigned, discussing the characters, setting, plot, theme, language, sequence, etc.

Strengthen fluency and phonemic awareness by reviewing words and sentences from the previous lessons. Build vocabulary skills by using some of the words in sentences.

You may want to create flashcards of words with **nk** digraphs. The student can study these throughout the unit.

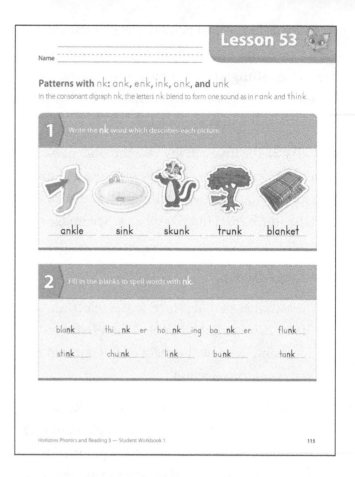

Lesson Introduction. Write the word **ink** on the board. Ask the student what letters can be added to the word **ink** to make new words. Answers include: **link, stink, sink,** and **wink.** Ask the student to make the sound of the digraph **nk.** Have the student think of other words with the **nk** digraph that are preceded by a vowel. To help the student get started you may want to write on the board the words: **blank, honk,** and **trunk.**

Activity 1. The student should turn to the activity sheet which accompanies the lesson. Read with the student the definition of the **nk** digraph at the top of the page. The student should go on to identify each picture and write the name of the **nk** word which describes each picture. The answers are: **ankle, sink, skunk, trunk, blanket.**

Activity 2. The student should fill in the blank with the digraph **nk** to spell words. You may want to have the student rewrite each word on a separate piece of paper for additional practice. The answers to the activity are: **blank, thinker, honking, banker, flunk, stink, chunk, link, bunk, tank.**

Activity 3. The final activity asks the student to fill in a crossword puzzle. The student should first answer the clues to the puzzle before filling in the puzzle. You may want to go over the correct answers to the clues before the student completes the puzzle. The answers to the clues are:

Across:
3. **honk**
5. **thank**
6. **trunk**
7. **wrinkled**
9. **sink**
10. **flunk**
11. **pink**

Down:
1. **bank**
2. **shrink**
4. **chipmunk**
8. **ink**
9. **skunk**

Reading Activity.

1. Together read the poem "Count that Day Lost." You may want to read it to the student first and then read it together.

2. Discuss the poem with the student. What is being compared in the poem? (**A meaningful and a meaningless day.**) What does the author say makes a day meaningful? (Examples include: **putting others first, saying kind words, looking kindly at others.**) What makes a day meaningless or lost? (Answers include: **cheering no one, causing no one to smile, not doing any good deeds.**) The author speaks of doing small acts of kindness to cheer others. What are some small acts you can do to cheer others or brighten their day? (Answers may include: **smiling, sharing, saying please and thank you, setting a table.**)

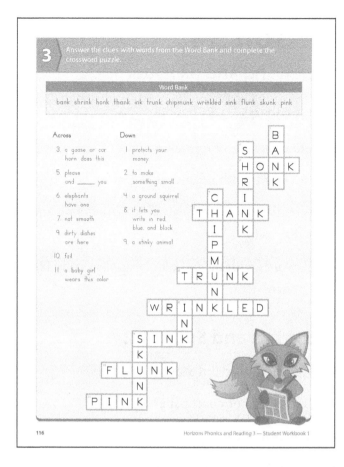

3. Study the way the poem was written. Which words in the poem rhyme? (**The rhyme scheme is aabccbdd.**) How many syllables are in the various lines? (**The scheme for the number of syllables is 88488488.**)

Lesson 54

Review: ng and nk Patterns

Overview:

- Define **ng** and **nk** digraphs

- Read words with **ng** and **nk** digraphs

- Recognize words with vowels before the **ng** and **nk** digraphs

- Use words with **ng** and **nk** digraphs to complete sentences

Materials and Supplies:

- Teacher's Guide and Student Workbook

- White board or chart paper

- Phonics flashcards

- Reader: "Two Little Kittens"

Teaching Tips:

Review for Mastery. Discuss and review any work from the previous lesson that was assigned as homework. Check for completion of the activities and orally quiz the student for comprehension. Review any reading that was assigned, discussing the characters, setting, plot, theme, language, sequence, etc.

Strengthen fluency and phonemic awareness by reviewing words and sentences from the previous lessons. Build vocabulary skills by using some of the words in sentences.

You may want to review the flashcards of words with **ng** and **nk** digraphs.

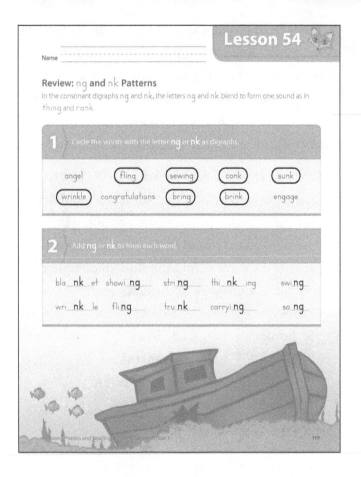

Lesson Introduction. Ask the student to give you an example of a word with an **ng** digraph. Answers may include: **string** or **bang**. Ask the student to give you an example of a word with an **nk** digraph. Examples may include: **bank** or **link**. Tell the student that in this lesson he/she will be reviewing words with **ng** and **nk** digraphs.

Activity 1. The student should turn to the activity sheet which accompanies this lesson. In the first activity the student should circle the words containing the **ng** or **nk** digraph. You may want to remind the student that a digraph makes a single sound. Answers are: **fling, sewing, conk, sunk, wrinkle, bring, brink**.

Activity 2. The digraph **ng** or **nk** needs to be added to form the words in this activity. The student may want to write the words out on a piece of paper before filling in the blanks on the activity sheet. The answers are: **blanket, showing, string, thinking, swing, wrinkle, fling, trunk, carrying, song.**

Activity 3. The student will need to identify the words in each sentence which have either an **ng** or **nk** digraph. It may help the student to identify the words by reading the sentences aloud. The answers are as follows:

1. **thanked, finding**
2. **falling, trunk**
3. **Bing, honked**
4. **carrying, sink**
5. **drank**
6. **string**
7. **rang**
8. **chipmunk**
9. **ironing, wrinkles**
10. **dunk**

Reading Activity.

1. Read the poem "Two Little Kittens" to your student. Next have the student read the poem with you.

2. Discuss the poem with your student. What is the setting of the poem? (**The poem is set in a house on a very stormy night.**) Who are the main characters? (**They are an old woman and two kittens.**) What caused the kittens to fight? (**The two were fighting over a mouse.**) Why did the old woman sweep them out of her house? (**The two kittens were arguing.**) What was the weather like outside? (**The weather was cold, snowy, and miserable.**) What did the kittens learn from the experience?

(**They learned that it's better to be indoors and not fight.**) What lesson do you think the author was trying to teach? (Answers include: **The need to get along and when people fight there are consequences.**)

3. What is the rhyme scheme of the poem? (**aabb**) What is the syllable scheme of the poem?

   1st stanza 9, 9, 9, 9
   2nd stanza 9, 9, 10, 10
   3rd stanza 10, 11, 9, 11
   4th stanza 9, 12, 11, 11
   5th stanza 9, 9, 11, 11

Lesson 55
Regular Plurals: adding s

Overview:

- Define a regular plural
- Form words with regular plurals which add **s**
- Identify words with regular plurals formed by adding **s**

Materials and Supplies:

- Teacher's Guide and Student Workbook
- White board or chart paper
- Phonics flashcards
- Reader: "The Atlantic Puffin"

Teaching Tips:

Review for Mastery. Discuss and review any work from the previous lesson that was assigned as homework. Check for completion of the activities and orally quiz the student for comprehension. Review any reading that was assigned, discussing the characters, setting, plot, theme, language, sequence, etc.

Strengthen fluency and phonemic awareness by reviewing words and sentences from the previous lessons. Build vocabulary skills by using some of the words in sentences.

You may want to create flashcards of words with regular **s** plurals. The student can study these throughout the unit.

Lesson Introduction. Write the following list of words on the board: **word, phone, window, book,** and **table**. Ask the student to name the plural of each word. After naming the plural, ask the student to write the plural of each word. The student should notice that each word becomes plural by adding **s**. The plural words would be: **words, phones, windows, books,** and **tables**. Explain that in this lesson the student will study words which become plural by adding the letter **s**.

Activity 1. Read with the student the definition at the top of the activity sheet. Remind the student that most words are regular plurals ending in **s**. Ask the student to identify the pictures in the first activity. The student should then write the plural words. The answers are: **birds, dogs, ants, chairs, keys**.

Activity 2. In the next activity, the student should rewrite the words so they are plural. The correct answers: **pencils, books, violins, lakes, tickets, fingers, computers, shoes, flowers, windows.**

Activity 3. The student should read each sentence and then circle the regular plural words. Each sentence has two regular plural words. The answers to the activity are:

1. **birds, trees**
2. **cars, roads**
3. **noses, girls**
4. **books, desks**
5. **pillows, beds**
6. **pumpkins, fields**
7. **horses, stalls**
8. **builders, houses**

Reading Activity.

1. The student should turn to the selection "The Atlantic Puffin." After reading the selection, discuss the selection with the student.

2. Use the following questions to begin your discussion. What is the physical appearance of the puffin? (**An Atlantic Puffin is about 10 inches long and weighs one pound. It has orange webbed feet, black and white feathers, and a colorful red, blue, and yellow bill.**) Where do most other types of puffins live? (**The three other types of puffins live in the Pacific Ocean.**) Where do Atlantic Puffins live? (**They live in the northern Atlantic Ocean. They are often found on the coasts of Russia, England, Iceland, and Canada.**) How do Atlantic Puffins protect their nests and young? (**They burrow into rocky cliffs and soil to make their nests. They line nests with grass, seaweed, and**

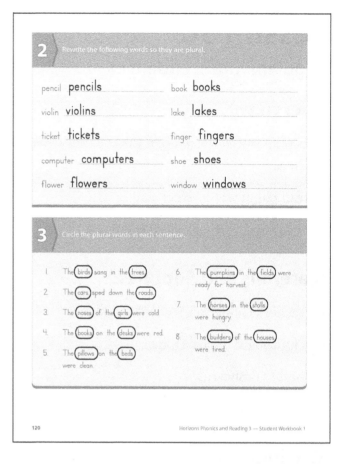

feathers. Both parents care for the eggs.**) Where and how do puffins fly? (**They fly in the air and on the water. They use their wings as paddles and their webbed feet to steer. In the air they can travel about 55 mph.**) What do puffins eat? (**They eat fish. They are good divers and scoop up many fish.**)

3. Extend the lesson by asking the student to find pictures of Atlantic Puffin. Have the student draw a picture of these unique animals.

Lesson 56

Regular Plurals: adding es

Overview:

- Identify words which are regular plurals which add **es**

- Read plural words which add **es**

- Form words with **es** plural endings

Materials and Supplies:

- Teacher's Guide and Student Workbook

- White board or chart paper

- Phonics flashcards

- Reader: "Sojourner Truth"

Teaching Tips:

Review for Mastery. Discuss and review any work from the previous lesson that was assigned as homework. Check for completion of the activities and orally quiz the student for comprehension. Review any reading that was assigned, discussing the characters, setting, plot, theme, language, sequence, etc.

Strengthen fluency and phonemic awareness by reviewing words and sentences from the previous lessons. Build vocabulary skills by using some of the words in sentences.

You may want to create flashcards of words with regular **es** plurals. The student can study these throughout the unit.

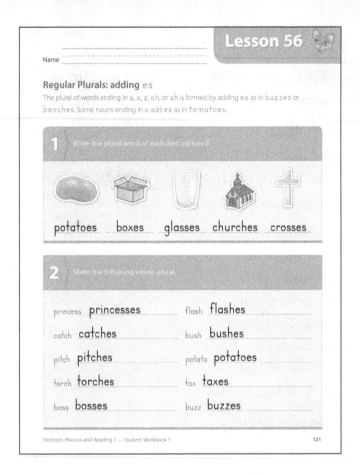

Lesson Introduction. Remind the student of how he/she formed regular plurals in the previous lesson. Write the words **letter**, **plate**, and **frog** on the board. Have the student direct you in how these plurals should be formed. The answers are: **letters**, **plates**, and **frogs**. Tell the student that other words form regular plurals by adding **es** to the endings. Words ending in **s, x, z, ch,** or **sh** form plurals by adding **es** to the end. Some words ending in **o** add **es** to become plural. Write the words **box, dress, potato,** and **beach** on the board. Ask the student to form the plurals of these words. The answers are: **boxes, dresses, potatoes,** and **beaches**.

Activity 1. Read through the definition at the top of the page. The student should recognize that words ending in **s**, **x**, **z**, **ch**, or **sh** form plurals by adding **es**. Some words ending with **o** add **es**. Identify the pictures in the first activity. After the student identifies the pictures, have him/her write the plurals. The answers are: **potatoes, boxes, glasses, churches, crosses**.

Activity 2. The student should make the words in the next activity plural. The plurals are: **princesses, flashes, catches, bushes, pitches, potatoes, torches, taxes, bosses, buzzes**.

Activity 3. The student should read the sentences in the next activity. One word in the sentence is underlined. The student should rewrite the word to be plural. After the word is rewritten, the sentence will be correct. The answers to the activity are: **bushes, flashes, patches, taxes, bosses, arches, potatoes, foxes, compasses, porches**.

Reading Activity.

1. The student should turn to the selection "Sojourner Truth." Before the student reads the selection, explain that Sojourner Truth was the name of a real woman who lived in the U.S. at a time when slavery was permitted.

2. After the student has read the selection, begin a short discussion. The student will discuss the selection in more depth in the next lesson. Ask the student the details of Sojourner Truth's early life. **(She was born into slavery in 1797. She was one of 13 children. Her birth name was Isabella Baumfree. As a young girl she was sold for $100 and a flock of sheep.)**

3. You may want to extend the lesson by having the student find pictures of Sojourner Truth.

3	Rewrite the underlined word so that the sentence makes sense.	
1.	bushes	Mr. Burns planned to trim all the <u>bush</u> in front of his house.
2.	flashes	There were many <u>flash</u> of lightning during the thunderstorm.
3.	patches	Mrs. Carson put a number of <u>patch</u> on her childrens pants.
4.	taxes	The citizens paid their <u>tax</u> each year.
5.	bosses	Miss Tucker has three <u>boss</u> at work.
6.	arches	The building had seven <u>arch</u> in the front.
7.	potatoes	Mr. Davidson peeled five <u>potato</u> for dinner.
8.	foxes	The woods were filled with <u>fox</u>.
9.	compasses	The store carried many different types of <u>compass</u>.
10.	porches	The Mason family had front and back <u>porch</u> on their home.

Lesson 57
Regular Plurals: adding s, es

Overview:

- Recall the two types of regular plurals **s** and **es**
- Read words with regular plurals
- Form words with regular plurals

Materials and Supplies:

- Teacher's Guide and Student Workbook
- White board or chart paper
- Phonics flashcards
- Reader: "Sojourner Truth"

Teaching Tips:

Review for Mastery. Discuss and review any work from the previous lesson that was assigned as homework. Check for completion of the activities and orally quiz the student for comprehension. Review any reading that was assigned, discussing the characters, setting, plot, theme, language, sequence, etc.

Strengthen fluency and phonemic awareness by reviewing words and sentences from the previous lessons. Build vocabulary skills by using some of the words in sentences.

You may want to review the two types of regular plurals with **s** and **es.**

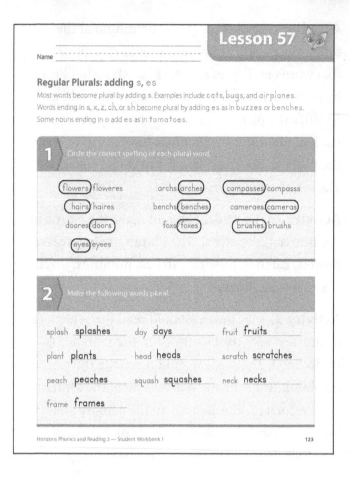

Lesson Introduction. Before the student goes on to learn about irregular plurals, the student will review regular plural words. Write the following list of words on the board: **color**, **match**, **can**, and **tax**. Ask the student to make each word plural. The answers are: **colors**, **matches**, **cans**, and **taxes**. Continue by asking the student what makes one word add an **es** to become plural, while another adds only **s**. The student should remember that words ending in **s**, **x**, **z**, **ch**, **sh**, and sometimes **o** add the letters **es**.

Activity 1. The student will be asked to form plurals of words. All of the words are regular plurals but some will add **s** and others **es**. The correct answers are: **flowers, arches, compasses, hairs, benches, cameras, doors, foxes, brushes, eyes.**

Activity 2. In this activity the student will need to form words which are plural by adding either **s** or **es**. The correct answers are: **splashes, days, fruits, plants, heads, scratches, peaches, squashes, necks, frames**.

Activity 3. In the final activity, the student is to identify plural words which have been formed incorrectly. The answers are: **shirts, hamburgers, peaches, birds, foxes, lawns, boxes, rabbits, teachers, flags**.

Reading Activity.

1. The student should return to the selection "Sojourner Truth." You may want to ask the student to read the first sentence of each paragraph in order to review.

2. Discuss the rest of the selection with your student. Use the following questions to lead your discussion. What was Sojourner Truth's life like as a slave? **(She was beaten, sold, and had no say as to whom she would marry. Her child was also taken from her.)** Describe her appearance. **(She was an extremely tall woman for that time period. She was six feet tall.)** What happened to her son Robert? **(When he was little, he was illegally sold as a slave to a person in Alabama. Sojourner Truth needed to go to court in order to get him back.)** Why was the Van Wagener family important to Sojourner Truth? **(They helped her get her son Robert back. They also told her more about Christ.)** What message did Sojourner Truth preach? **(She preached equality for slaves and women. She believed that God wanted all people to be treated equally.)**

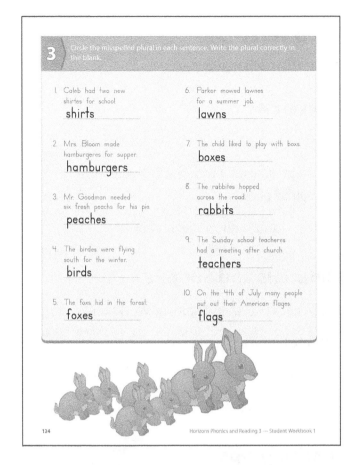

3. Have the student think about why Isabella Baumfree changed her name to "Sojourner Truth." **(If needed, explain that a person who travels is sometimes called a "sojourner." Sojourner Truth did a great deal of traveling to tell others about the evils of slavery and the need for all people to be treated equally. She also spoke the "truth" about slavery and equal rights for all of the people God created.)**

4. Have the student find three words in the selection which are regular plurals. Answers include: **slaves, others, crowds, leaders, rights.**

5. You may want to extend the lesson by having the student find and read a copy of Sojourner's speech "Ain't I a Woman?"

Lesson 58

Irregular Plurals: f-v, y-i

Overview:

- Identify words which are irregular plurals
- Recognize word endings which will form irregular plurals
- Form words with irregular plurals

Materials and Supplies:

- Teacher's Guide and Student Workbook
- White board or chart paper
- Phonics flashcards
- Reader: "The Blue Rose"

Teaching Tips:

Review for Mastery. Discuss and review any work from the previous lesson that was assigned as homework. Check for completion of the activities and orally quiz the student for comprehension. Review any reading that was assigned, discussing the characters, setting, plot, theme, language, sequence, etc.

Strengthen fluency and phonemic awareness by reviewing words and sentences from the previous lessons. Build vocabulary skills by using some of the words in sentences.

You may want to create flashcards of words with the irregular plurals **f-v** and **y-i**. The student can study these throughout the unit.

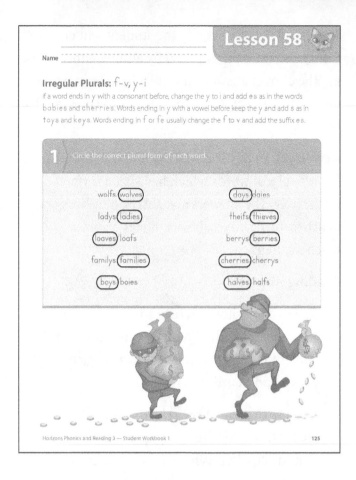

Lesson Introduction. Ask the student to recall how regular plural words are formed. The student may remember that most plurals are formed by adding **s** or **es** to the end. Tell the student that not all words follow this regular pattern. Write the word **shelf** on the board. The student may remember that **shelf** becomes plural by changing the **f** to a **v** and adding **es** as in **shelves**. Next write the word **family** on the board. Ask the student how the word **family** becomes plural. The student may remember that the **y** changes to an **i** and **es** is added as in **families**. Write the word **boy** on the board. Ask the student how this word is made plural. Explain that **boy** only adds an **s** to become **boys**. Words ending in **y** which are preceded by a vowel become plural by adding **s**.

Activity 1. The student should turn to the activity sheet which accompanies this lesson. Read through the definitions at the top of the activity sheet. Make sure the student is clear as to how words become plural by changing **f-v** and adding **es** and **y-i** and adding **es**. If the student is struggling with the concept, do the first few words of this activity together. Not all of the words in the activity will be irregular plurals. The correct plural forms of the words are: **wolves, days, ladies, thieves, loaves, berries, families, cherries, boys, halves.**

Activity 2. The lesson continues with the student creating plural words. Again, not all of the words will be irregular plurals. The correct answers are: **wives, stories, trays, scarves, lives, candies, keys, activities, knives.**

Activity 3. The final activity asks student to use plural words in phrases. The student should identify which plural word completes the phrase. The answers are: **babies, victories, ladies, knives, thieves, halves, cries, enemies.**

Reading Activity.

1. The student should turn to the selection "The Blue Rose." Direct the student in reading the selection.

2. Begin a short discussion on the selection. The student will discuss more of the story in the next lesson. What is the setting of the story? **(The story is set in China in the Emperor's palace.)** Describe the Emperor's daughter. **(She was beautiful, with small feet. She had lovely eyes and a delightful laugh.)** Who did the princess say she would marry? **(She would marry the man who brought her the blue rose.)**

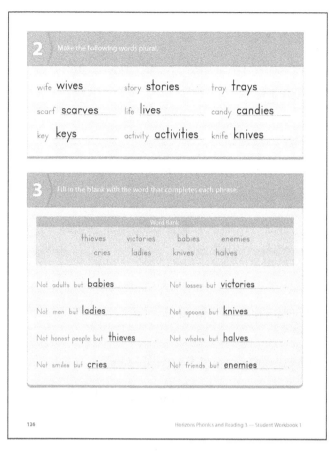

Lesson 59

Irregular Plurals: no change and great change

Overview:

- Identify words which do not change when they become plural
- Identify words which become new words when they become plural
- Read words which are irregular plurals
- Form irregular plural words

Materials and Supplies:

- Teacher's Guide and Student Workbook
- White board or chart paper
- Phonics flashcards
- Reader: "The Blue Rose"

Teaching Tips:

Review for Mastery. Discuss and review any work from the previous lesson that was assigned as homework. Check for completion of the activities and orally quiz the student for comprehension. Review any reading that was assigned, discussing the characters, setting, plot, theme, language, sequence, etc.

Strengthen fluency and phonemic awareness by reviewing words and sentences from the previous lessons. Build vocabulary skills by using some of the words in sentences.

You may want to review just the flashcards the student made for words with irregular plurals.

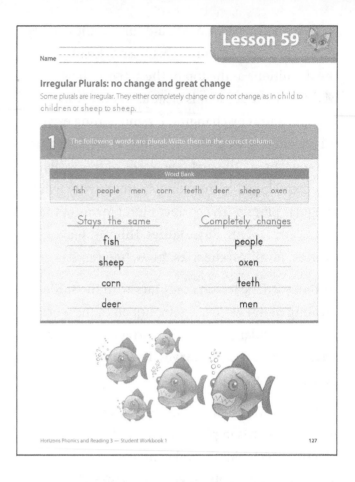

Lesson Introduction. Review with the student again how regular words become plural. Most words become plural by adding **s** or **es**. Have the student write a list of a few words which form regular plurals such as **chairs**, **pens**, and **papers**. Next review with the student the previous lesson in which irregular plurals were studied. Write the words **leaf** and **country** on the board. Ask the student to make these words plural. The answers are: **leaves** and **countries**. Tell the student that other irregular plurals change their spelling completely or do not change at all. For example, the word **fish** is plural, and so are other fish names such as **trout** and **salmon.** Other words change from **child** to **children** and **person** to **people.** In this lesson the student will study these types of irregular plurals.

Activity 1. The student should turn to the accompanying activity sheet. Read through the definition at the top of the activity sheet. The student will need to identify the plural words which remain the same and those which change completely. The words which stay the same are: **fish, sheep, corn, deer.** Those which change are: **people, oxen, teeth, men.**

Activity 2. The next activity asks the student to make words plural. Some of these words will change completely and others will remain the same. The answers to the activity are: **children, deer, oxen, mice, wheat, trout, women, feet.**

Activity 3. An incorrectly spelled plural occurs in each of the sentences. The student needs to identify the incorrectly spelled plural as well as write it correctly. The answers to the activity are: **equipment, teeth, women, geese, corn, children, people, mice.**

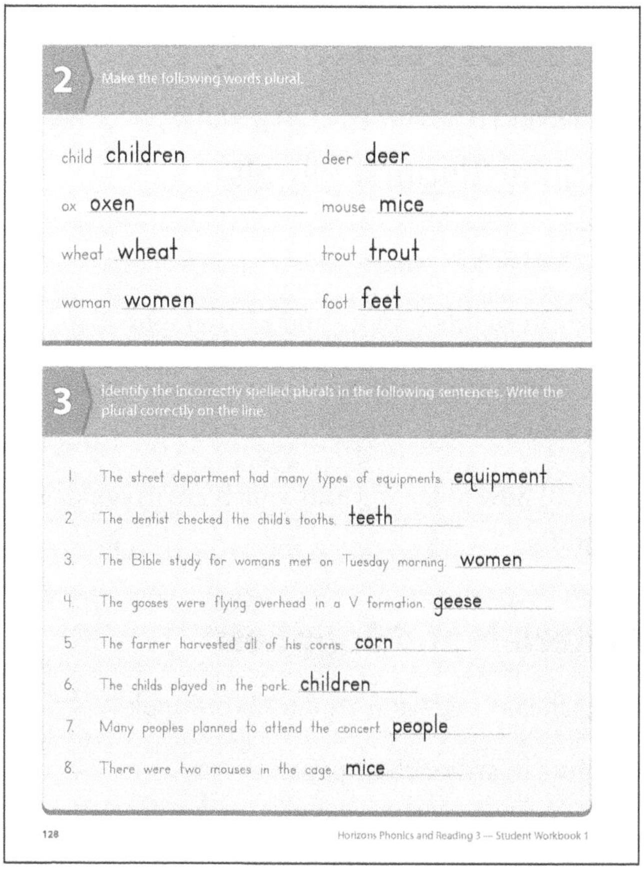

Reading Activity.

1. The student should turn to the selection "The Blue Rose."

2. Continue your discussion of the selection. How did Ti-Fun-Ti try to find a blue rose? (**He went to a shopkeeper for help.**) How did the shopkeeper try to help him? (**The shopkeeper searched for a blue rose but was unable to find one. Eventually the shopkeeper dyed a white rose blue.**) Why did the Princess reject this blue rose? (**She knew it was a dyed rose. She said that if a butterfly had landed on the rose it would have been poisoned.**) How did the warrior try to find a blue rose? (**He went to the King of the Five Rivers. The King gave him a rose made from a large sapphire, which is a blue jewel.**) How did the Princess like this blue rose? (**She said that it was a stone and not a real rose. She rejected it.**) What was the Lord Chief Justice's plan for bringing a blue rose? (**He hired an artist to paint a blue rose on China.**) How did the Princess react to this blue rose? (**She said it was beautiful, but she rejected it as a blue rose.**) What did her friend the musician bring as a blue rose? (**He brought a "regular" rose.**) Why did she accept this rose? (**She loved the musician and wanted to marry him.**) Why did the Emperor permit this? (**He loved his daughter and trusted her choice and decision.**)

3. Ask the student to find five plural words in the selection. He/she should explain if each word is a regular or irregular plural. Examples of regular plurals include: **chimes, suitors, roses, sunshades, petals.** Irregular plural examples are: **feet, horsemen, apologies.**

The following reproduces the student workbook page shown at upper right.

2 Make the following words plural.

child	children	deer	deer
ox	oxen	mouse	mice
wheat	wheat	trout	trout
woman	women	foot	feet

3 Identify the incorrectly spelled plurals in the following sentences. Write the plural correctly on the line.

1. The street department had many types of equipments. **equipment**
2. The dentist checked the child's tooths. **teeth**
3. The Bible study for womans met on Tuesday morning. **women**
4. The gooses were flying overhead in a V formation. **geese**
5. The farmer harvested all of his corns. **corn**
6. The childs played in the park. **children**
7. Many peoples planned to attend the concert. **people**
8. There were two mouses in the cage. **mice**

128   Horizons Phonics and Reading 3 — Student Workbook 1

Lesson 60

Review: ng and nk Digraphs, Irregular/Regular Plurals

Overview:

- Identify words with **ng** and **nk** digraphs

- Determine the spelling of words with regular plurals

- Recall how to form words which are irregular plurals

Materials and Supplies:

- Teacher's Guide and Student Workbook

- White board or chart paper

- Phonics flashcards

- Reader: "The Loaf of Bread"

Teaching Tips:

Review for Mastery. Discuss and review any work from the previous lesson that was assigned as homework. Check for completion of the activities and orally quiz the student for comprehension. Review any reading that was assigned, discussing the characters, setting, plot, theme, language, sequence, etc.

Strengthen fluency and phonemic awareness by reviewing words and sentences from the previous lessons. Build vocabulary skills by using some of the words in sentences.

You may want to review flashcards made for words in this unit.

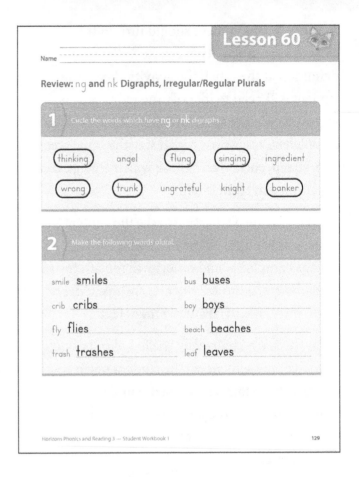

Lesson Introduction. In this lesson the student will review all of the material from this unit on **ng** and **nk** digraphs as well as regular and irregular plurals. The review will be formatted in the same way as the test. This should help the student feel better prepared for the test which follows.

Activity 1. The student should turn to the review sheet which accompanies this lesson. The first activity asks the student to identify words which have **ng** or **nk** digraphs. If possible, have the student say the words aloud so he/she can hear the digraph. The answers are: **thinking, flung, singing, wrong, trunk, banker**.

Activity 2. The next activity asks the student to make words plural. These words are examples of regular and irregular plurals. The answers are: **smiles, buses, cribs, boys, flies, beaches, trashes, leaves**.

Activity 3. The last activity asks the student to choose the correct plural in each sentence. Examples are of both regular and irregular plurals. The answers are: **doors, dresses, boxes, cherries, sheep**.

Reading Activity.

1. Direct the student to read "The Loaf of Bread."

2. This reading will be done for pleasure. If you want, you may discuss the selection with your student.

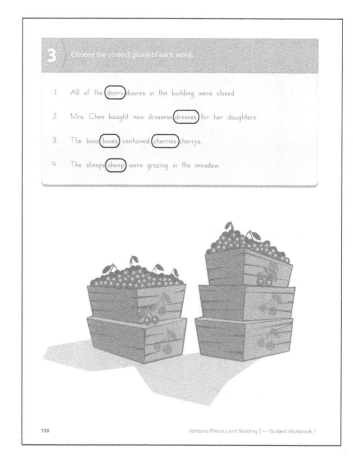

3 Choose the correct plural of each word.

1. All of the (doors) doores in the building were closed

2. Mrs. Chen bought new dressess (dresses) for her daughters

3. The boxs (boxes) contained (cherries) cherrys.

4. The sheeps (sheep) were grazing in the meadow.

130   Horizons Phonics and Reading 3 — Student Workbook 1

Test 6

Lessons 51-60

Overview:

- Identify words with **ng** and **nk** digraphs
- Determine the spelling of words with regular plurals
- Recall how to spell words which are irregular plurals

Materials and Supplies:

- Student Test

Teaching Tips:

Review for Mastery. Discuss and review any work from the previous lesson that was assigned as homework. Check for completion of the activities and orally quiz the student for comprehension. Review any reading that was assigned, discussing the characters, setting, plot, theme, language, sequence, etc.

Lesson Introduction. Check if the student has any final questions from the review before taking the test. The test is formatted like the review. Different words will be used in the test than what appeared in the review.

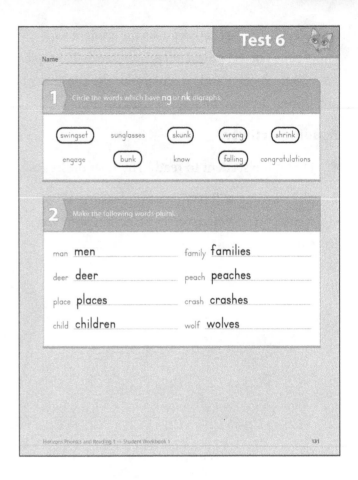

Activity 1. The student should turn to the test which accompanies this lesson. The first activity asks the student to identify words which have **ng** or **nk** digraphs. If possible, have the student say the words aloud so he/she can hear the digraph. The answers are: **swingset, skunk, wrong, shrink, bunk, falling**.

Activity 2. The next activity asks the student to make words plural. These words are examples of regular and irregular plurals. The answers are: **men, families, deer, peaches, places, crashes, children, wolves**.

Activity 3. The last activity asks the student to choose the correct plural in each sentence. Examples are of both regular and irregular plurals. The answers are: **churches, drums, leaves, mice, branches**.

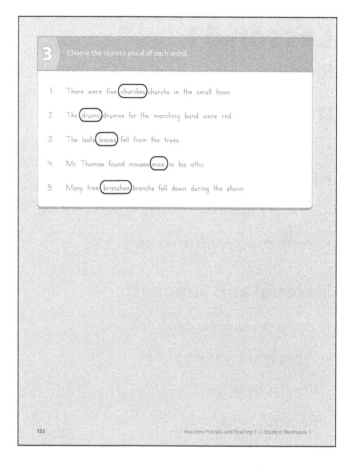

Lesson 61
Rhyming Words: Regular Spelling

Overview:

- Define rhyming words
- Hear words that rhyme
- Identify rhyming words with regular spellings
- Use rhyming words in sentences

Material and Supplies:

- Teacher's Guide and Student Workbook
- White board or chart paper
- Phonics flashcards
- Reader: "Daisies"

Teaching Tips:

Lesson Introduction. This is the first of a series of lessons on rhyming words. In this lesson the student will learn about rhyming words which share a spelling pattern. Write the words **black**, **cat**, **track**, and **rat** on the board. Ask the student which words rhyme with each other. The student should identify **black** and **track** along with **cat** and **rat**. Ask the student what he/she notices about the end of each word. The student should note that the ends of the words are spelled similarly. Tell the student that words which rhyme often share the same spelling in the final syllable. Write the word **blister** on the board. Ask the student to think of other words which share the same ending rhyme. Examples include **sister** and **mister**. Highlight the similar spelling.

You may want to create flashcards of words which have regular spelling rhymes. The student can study these throughout the unit.

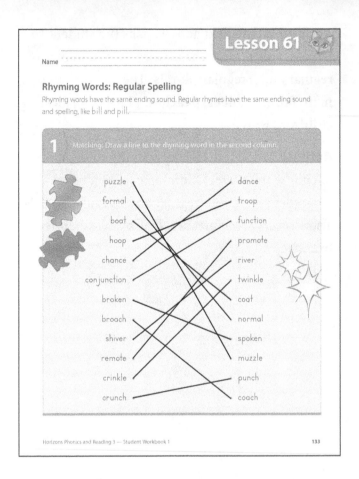

Activity 1. The student should turn to the activity sheet and read the definition of regular rhyming words at the top of the page. In the first activity, the student is asked to draw a line from the rhyming words in the first column to those in the second. If possible, have the student read the rhyming words aloud before drawing the line between the words. This way the student will be able to both see and hear the words which rhyme.

The words which match are as follows:

puzzle	muzzle
formal	normal
boat	coat
hoop	troop
chance	dance
conjunction	function
broken	spoken
broach	coach
shiver	river
remote	promote
crinkle	twinkle
crunch	punch

Activity 2. The student will continue working with rhyming words in the next activity. The first word in each line is in boldface. The student will need to identify other words in the line which rhyme with the first word. The word must also share the same spelling at the end. If needed, complete the first example together with the student. Again, it is helpful if the student can both hear and see the words which rhyme. The answers for each line are as follows:

tender:	**render**, **fender**
cake:	**bake**, **take**
funny:	**bunny**
cabbage:	**garbage**, **manage**
yellow:	**fellow**

Activity 3. The final activity asks the student to complete proverbs which have internal rhymes. The student will use the words in the Word Bank to complete each proverb rhyme. When the student has finished the activity, read the proverbs together. As an added activity, have the student think of other proverbs or sayings which rhyme. The answers are:

1. An apple a **day** keeps the doctor away.
2. A friend in **need** is a friend indeed.
3. Birds of a **feather** flock together.
4. When the cat's **away** the mice will play.
5. Early to bed and early to **rise**, makes a man healthy, wealthy, and wise.
6. No **gain** without pain.
7. A man of words and not of **deeds** is like a garden full of weeds.

Reading Activity.

1. Before reading the poem, write the word **metaphor** on the board. Explain to the student that a metaphor is a comparison of two objects. For example, a person might say, "A tree is a soldier, standing straight and tall." In the poem the student is to read for today, the author

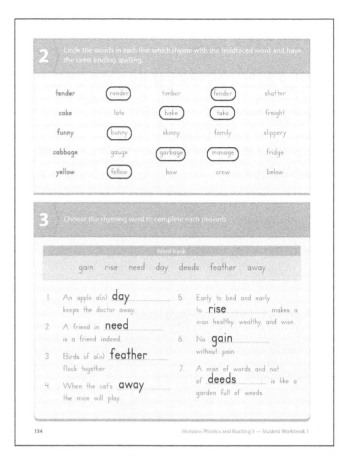

will compare stars to something else. Ask the student to think of things with which he/she would compare a star. Examples may include: **a night-light** or **a firefly**.

2. Direct the student to the poem "Daisies." Read the poem to the student while he/she reads along in the book. Next have the student join you in reading the poem.

3. Discuss the poem with your student. What does the poet compare the stars to? (**daisies**) What metaphor does the author use for the moon? (**A lady picking daisies.**) Why are there no stars left in the morning? (**The woman has picked all the daisies.**)

4. Discuss the techniques the author uses in the poem. What is the pattern of end rhymes in the poem? (**aabb**) What examples of regular ending rhymes are in the poem? (**so** and **go**; **down** and **town**)

Lesson 62

Rhyming Words: Irregular Spelling

Overview:

- Define rhyming words that are spelled similarly and dissimilarly
- Read differently spelled rhyming words
- Be able to hear words which rhyme
- Use irregularly spelled rhyming words in sentences

Material and Supplies:

- Teacher's Guide and Student Workbook
- White board or chart paper
- Phonics flashcards
- Reader: "The Duel"

Teaching Tips:

Review for Mastery. Discuss and review any work from the previous lesson that was assigned as homework. Check for completion of the activities and orally quiz the student for comprehension. Review any reading that was assigned, discussing the characters, setting, plot, theme, language, sequence, etc.

Strengthen fluency and phonemic awareness by reviewing words and sentences from the previous lessons. Build vocabulary skills by using some of the words in sentences.

You may want to create flashcards of words which rhyme but are spelled differently. The student can study these throughout the unit.

Lesson Introduction. Write the words **flower** and **power** on the board. Discuss how these two words rhyme and share a similar spelling. Now write the words **power** and **flour** on the board. Ask the student if these two words rhyme. The student should note that the two words rhyme even though their ending spelling is different.

Explain to the student that rhyming words can be spelled similarly or differently. The important thing is that their sounds are the same. This is why it is

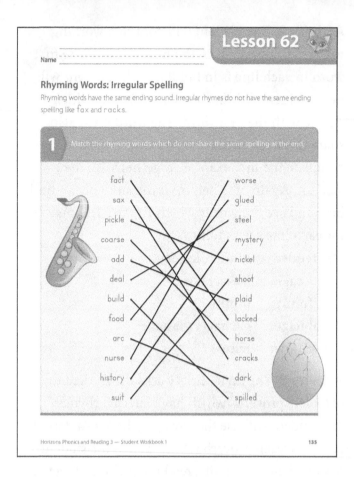

important to see words that rhyme and not just hear them.

Write the word **cord** on the board. Ask the student to say words that rhyme with cord like **board**, **sword**, **poured**, and **roared**. After the student has said a series of words, write them on the board. The student should notice how even though these words rhyme, their end spelling differs. In this lesson the student will study rhyming words which are spelled differently.

Activity 1. The student should turn to the accompanying activity sheet. Read through the definition at the top of the sheet. The first activity asks the student to match words which rhyme. For this activity it will be important that the student can hear the words as well as read them. The sound of the rhyme will be the indicator of a match. The words which match are as follows:

fact	lacked
sax	cracks
pickle	nickel
coarse	horse
add	plaid
deal	steel
build	spilled

food	glued
arc	dark
nurse	worse
history	mystery
suit	shoot

Activity 2. The student will continue working with rhyming words in the next activity. The first word in each line is in boldface. The student will need to identify other words in the line which rhyme with the first word. If needed, complete the first example together with the student. Again, it is helpful if the student can both hear and see the words which rhyme. The answers for each line are as follows:

sunny:	**funny, honey**
include:	**seafood, pursued, conclude**
flower:	**sour, flour, shower**
flock:	**chalk, squawk**
billed:	**rebuild, skilled**
said:	**head, red, shed**

Activity 3. The final activity asks the student to fill in the blank with the word that best completes the sentence and rhymes with the underlined word. If possible have the student read the sentences aloud.

1. The horse said "**neigh**" when he saw his **hay**.
2. Every night at **six** the dog likes to do some **tricks**.
3. Tom needed a **nickel** to pay for a **pickle**.
4. Kari needed to **tune** her violin very **soon**.
5. Beth left her favorite **comb** at **home**.
6. At the end of the **hour** the battery would be out of **power**.
7. It is well **known** that every dog likes a **bone**.
8. The church **choir** wore matching **attire**.
9. The new hotel **guest** wore a purple **vest**.
10. Let me **guess**; you don't play **chess**.

Reading Activity.

1. Direct the student to read the poem "The Duel." After the student has read the poem to him or herself, read the poem aloud.

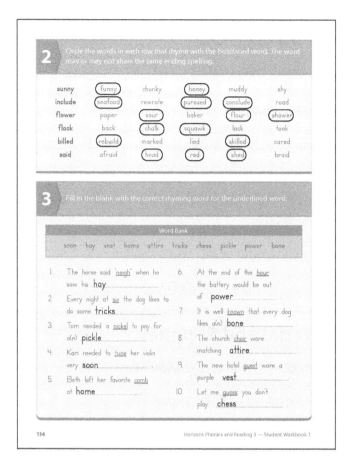

2. Discuss the content of the poem with the student. Who was fighting in the poem? (**The gingham dog and the calico cat.**) You may want to explain that gingham and calico are types of fabrics. Why did the two animals fight? (**The poet doesn't tell us. However, we know that they hadn't slept or recently talked to each other.**) What was the result of the fight? (**The two tore each other into shreds and ate each other up.**) How did the speaker learn of the story? (**The Old Dutch clock and the Chinese plate.**) How does the poet use humor? (**He makes little comments about how he heard the story.**)

3. Discuss the poetic format with the student. How many lines are in each stanza? (**9**) What is the rhyme scheme? (**The first stanza is aabbccacc and the rest are aabbccadd.**) What are some examples of regular rhymes? (**cat and sat; claw and saw; day and away**) What are some examples of irregular rhymes? (**so and know; you and true; blue, do, and flew**)

Lesson 63

Review: Rhyming Words

Overview:

- Define rhyming words that are spelled similarly and dissimilarly
- Review rhyming words spelled similarly and dissimilarly
- Hear rhyming words when spoken
- Use rhyming words in sentences

Material and Supplies:

- Teacher's Guide and Student Workbook
- White board or chart paper
- Phonics flashcards
- Reader: "To God Be the Glory"

Teaching Tips:

Review for Mastery. Discuss and review any work from the previous lesson that was assigned as homework. Check for completion of the activities and orally quiz the student for comprehension. Review any reading that was assigned, discussing the characters, setting, plot, theme, language, sequence, etc.

Strengthen fluency and phonemic awareness by reviewing words and sentences from the previous lessons. Build vocabulary skills by using some of the words in sentences.

You may want to create flashcards of words with rhyming words. The student can study these throughout the unit.

Lesson Introduction. Write the word **file** on the board. Ask the student what words rhyme with **file**. Words include: **pile, dial**, and **aisle**. Ask the student which words share spellings and which ones are regular or are irregular. The student should

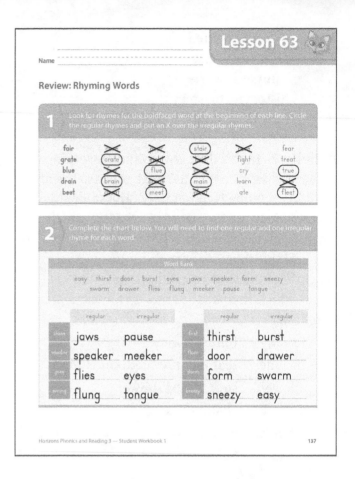

identify **file** and **pile** as regular and **dial** and **aisle** as irregular.

Activity 1. The student should take out the activity sheet which accompanies the lesson. The first activity asks the student to identify rhyming words in each line. The student should read the first word and then identify those words in the line which rhyme with it. Those which are regular rhymes should be circled and those which are irregular rhymes should have an X placed over them.

fair:	~~care~~	~~pear~~	(stair)	~~rare~~	fear
grate:	(crate)	~~eight~~	~~bait~~	fight	treat
blue:	~~few~~	(flue)	~~crew~~	cry	(true)
drain:	(brain)	~~crane~~	(main)	learn	~~vein~~
beet:	~~cheat~~	(meet)	~~pleat~~	ate	(fleet)

Activity 2. The review continues with the student finding the rhyming words for the boldfaced word in each line. The student will need to find one regular and one irregular rhyme for each word.

	Regular	Irregular
claws	**jaws**	**pause**
sneaker	**speaker**	**meeker**
pies	**flies**	**eyes**
swung	**flung**	**tongue**
first	**thirst**	**burst**
floor	**door**	**drawer**
dorm	**form**	**swarm**
breezy	**sneezy**	**easy**

Activity 3. Next, ask the student to read the poem on the activity sheet. The student should focus on just the ending rhymes of the lines. Together decide on the rhyme scheme of the poem to help the student notice which end rhymes will be paired. The rhyme scheme to the poem/hymn is **aabb**. The student should circle the regular rhymes at the end of each line and draw a square around the irregular rhymes at the end of lines.

Count Your Blessings by Johnson Oatman, Jr.

> When upon life's billows you are tempest tossed,
> When you are discouraged, thinking all is lost,
> Count your many blessings, name them one by one,
> And it will surprise you what the Lord hath done
>
> Are you ever burdened with a load of care?
> Does the cross seem heavy you are called to bear?
> Count your many blessings, every doubt will fly,
> And you will keep singing as the days go by.
>
> When you look at others with their lands and gold,
> Think that Christ has promised you His wealth untold;
> Count your many blessings. Wealth can never buy
> Your reward in heaven, nor your home on high.
>
> So, amid the conflict whether great or small,
> Do not be disheartened, God is over all;
> Count your many blessings, angels will attend,
> Help and comfort give you to your journey's end.

Reading Activity.

1. Explain that the poem the student is about to read is a famous hymn written by Fanny Crosby. The student will learn more about the author in the next lesson. If possible listen to a recording of the

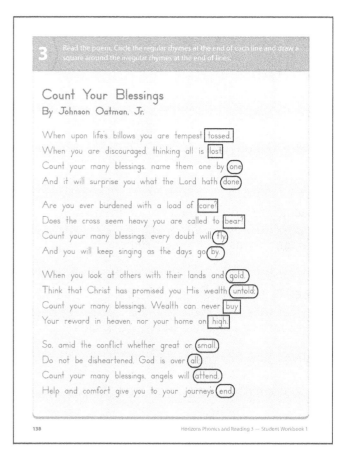

song "To God Be the Glory" as the student follows along in the book.

2. Discuss the themes of the song with your student. What are some of the great things the writer says that God has done? (**He sent Jesus who died for the sins of His people. He loved the world so much He sent Christ.**) What should the Christian's response be for what God has done? (**The poem speaks of rejoicing and praising the Lord. The Christian should give God glory.**) Who has Christ come to save? (**God came to save all who believe in Him. Even the worst offender, if he/she believes in God, is saved.**) How will the rejoicing of God's people increase? (**Their joy will increase when they go to heaven and see Jesus.**)

3. Discuss the poetic rhyme scheme and pattern with your student. What is the rhyme scheme of the verses? (**aabb**) What is the rhyme scheme of the chorus? (**ababcc**) What are two examples of regular rhymes? (**voice and rejoice; sin and in**) What are two examples of irregular rhymes? (**be and see; done and Son**)

Lesson 64

Antonyms

Overview:

- Define antonym
- Identify words which are antonyms
- Recognize words which are antonyms
- Use antonyms to complete sentences

Material and Supplies:

- Teacher's Guide and Student Workbook
- White board or chart paper
- Phonics flashcards
- Reader: "Fanny Crosby"

Teaching Tips:

Review for Mastery. Discuss and review any work from the previous lesson that was assigned as homework. Check for completion of the activities and orally quiz the student for comprehension. Review any reading that was assigned, discussing the characters, setting, plot, theme, language, sequence, etc.

Strengthen fluency and phonemic awareness by reviewing words and sentences from the previous lessons. Build vocabulary skills by using some of the words in sentences.

You may want to create flashcards of words which are antonyms. The student can study these throughout the unit.

Lesson Introduction. Write the word **antonym** on the board. Ask the student if he/she knows the meaning of the word. An antonym is a word which means the opposite of another word. Write the word **night** on the board. Ask the student what would be an antonym of the word **night**. The

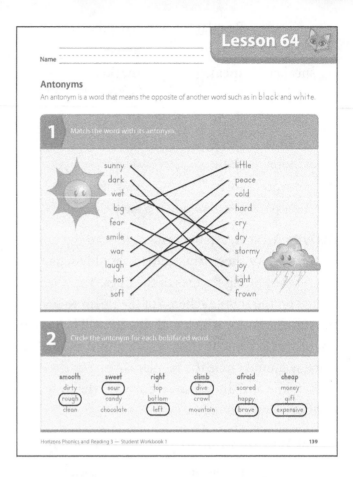

word **day** would be an antonym. See if the student can come up with other pairs of words which are antonyms. Answers may include: **rich and poor, sick and well,** and **happy and sad.**

Activity 1. The student should turn to the activity sheet which accompanies this lesson. Read through the definition of antonym at the top of the page. In the first activity the student will be asked to pair a word with its antonym. You may want to do one together as a sample. The correct pairs are as follows:

sunny	**stormy**
dark	**light**
wet	**dry**
big	**little**
fear	**joy**
smile	**frown**
war	**peace**
laugh	**cry**
hot	**cold**
soft	**hard**

Activity 2. The student should continue by circling the antonym for each boldfaced word. There is only one correct answer in each line.

smooth:	**rough**
sweet:	**sour**
right:	**left**
climb:	**dive**
afraid:	**brave**
cheap:	**expensive**

Activity 3. The final activity asks the student to use clues to fill in the answers to a crossword puzzle. A Word Bank is provided to help the student with this activity.

Across:	Down:
1. **sick**	1. **strong**
2. **loser**	3. **open**
5. **loud**	4. **robber**
6. **awake**	6. **away**
8. **enemy**	7. **remember**
9. **comedy**	
10. **clean**	

Reading Activity.

1. The student should turn to the selection "Fanny Crosby." Remind the student of the poem/hymn he/she read in the previous lesson. Have the student recall some of the themes of "To God Be the Glory." Tell the student that in this lesson he/she will learn more about the woman who wrote these lyrics.

2. After the student has read the selection, lead a discussion using some of the following questions. How did Fanny Crosby become blind? (**A man pretending to be a doctor treated her for a cold. The treatment he gave her ended up causing her to lose her sight.**) How did her grandmother and mother prepare her to write hymns? (**They had her memorize Scripture, which prepared her for using these themes in her hymns.**) What role did the New York Institute for the Blind play

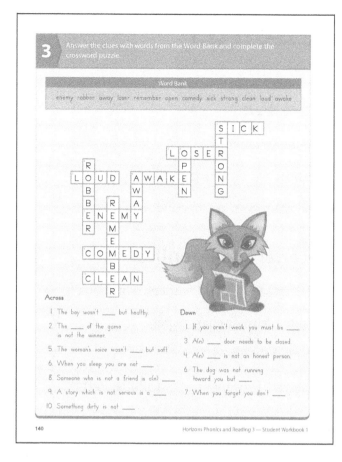

in her life? (**Fanny Crosby started school there at the age of 15. She would meet her husband at the school. She would also teach at the school. Fanny Crosby would spend 35 years of her life associated with the school.**) Why was Fanny Crosby an unusual hymn writer? (**Fanny wrote more hymns than most writers. Some days she wrote about 6-7. She also had an agreement in which three of her hymns each week would be published.**)

3. Conclude by asking the student what he/she could learn from the example of Fanny Crosby? (Answers may include: **Being thankful for the gift of sight. The importance of memorizing Scripture. Finally the student may comment on using the talents God has given him/her for God's glory.**)

Lesson 65

Synonyms

Overview:

- Define synonyms

- Identify words which are synonyms

- Use synonyms to complete sentences

Material and Supplies:

- Teacher's Guide and Student Workbook

- White board or chart paper

- Phonics flashcards

- Reader: "The Story of Dr. Dolittle: Part I"

Teaching Tips:

Review for Mastery. Discuss and review any work from the previous lesson that was assigned as homework. Check for completion of the activities and orally quiz the student for comprehension. Review any reading that was assigned, discussing the characters, setting, plot, theme, language, sequence, etc.

Strengthen fluency and phonemic awareness by reviewing words and sentences from the previous lessons. Build vocabulary skills by using some of the words in sentences.

You may want to create flashcards of words with synonyms. The student can study these throughout the unit.

Lesson Introduction. Review with the student the definition of the word antonym. Explain that antonym means the opposite of a given word. For example, **big** is the opposite of **little**. Tell the student that the opposite of an antonym is a synonym. A word which is a synonym of another word has about the same meaning as the given word. For example the words **big** and **large** are synonyms. **Little** and **small** are also synonyms.

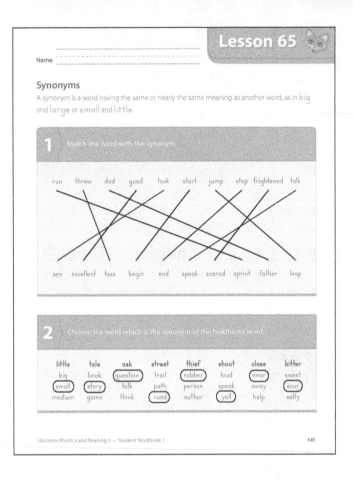

Write the words **dirty** and **talk** on the board. Ask the student to think of words which are synonyms of these two words. Synonyms of **dirty** include **filthy** or **unclean.** Synonyms of **talk** include **speak** and **say.**

Activity 1. Ask the student to turn to the accompanying activity sheet. Read through the definition of synonym together. In the first activity the student will be asked to match the word in the first column with its synonym in the second. The answers for this activity follow.

run	sprint
throw	toss
dad	father
good	excellent
look	see
start	begin
jump	leap
stop	end
frightened	scared
talk	speak

Activity 2. In the next activity, the student will need to choose the word that is the synonym of the boldfaced word. There is one correct answer per line.

little: **small**

tale: **story**

ask: **question**

street: **road**

thief: **robber**

shout: **yell**

close: **near**

bitter: **sour**

Activity 3. The final activity is a series of sentences. Each sentence has an underlined word. The student will need to replace the underlined word with a synonym from the Word Bank.

1. A **portion** of the road was closed to traffic.
2. The **loyal** dog came when his master called.
3. The family had a **great** time at the party.
4. Devin **desired** a cookie.
5. The **scene** from the mountain was beautiful.
6. The **small** dog barked loudly.
7. Brooke **created** a painting in art class.
8. Jacob was **exhausted** after running the race.
9. Emma **ran** to the ice cream store.
10. The **powerful** man lifted the heavy weight.
11. The **right** answer to the question was true.
12. Isaiah was **sick** on Friday.

Reading Activity.

1. The student should turn to the selection "The Story of Dr. Dolittle: Part I." The student should read this part of the selection.

2. After reading the selection, discuss it with the student. Ask the student to describe the setting of the story. (**The story is set in Puddleby-on-the-Marsh, a long time ago.**) Describe the main character of the story. (**The main character is Dr. Dolittle. He wore a tall hat and children especially liked him. He also had lots of animals in and around his home.**) What kinds of pets did Doctor Dolittle have? (**He had rabbits, a**

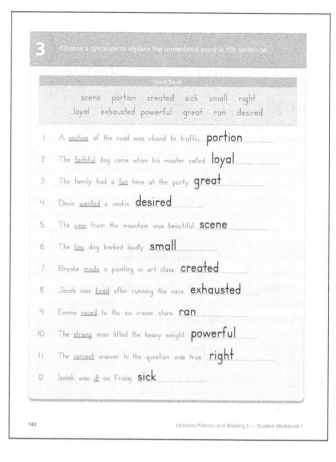

hedgehog, chickens, a duck, and an owl. He loved his many animals even though they drove away his patients.) Why didn't people want to see the doctor? (**They didn't care to have all the pets around when he was examining them.**)

3. Ask the student to predict what they think will happen next in the selection. You may want to use some of the following questions to prod their thinking. (**How will Dr. Dolittle earn money if people don't come to him as a doctor? Will he be able to keep all of his animals? Will the children continue to like him as he walks through the town? If the animals could come up with a solution, what do you think it would be?**)

4. Write on the board a number of words that come from the selection, "Dr. Dolittle." Challenge the student to come up with synonyms for the words. Word examples may include: **tall, little, untidy.** Following is a list of words that could be synonyms of the given words—tall: **high, big**; little: **small, tiny**; untidy: **messy, dirty.**

Lesson 66

Review: Antonyms and Synonyms

Overview:

- Define antonyms and synonyms

- Recognize antonyms and synonyms in sentences

- Use antonyms and synonyms in sentences

Material and Supplies:

- Teacher's Guide and Student Workbook

- White board or chart paper

- Phonics flashcards

- Reader: "The Story of Dr. Dolittle: Part II"

Teaching Tips:

Review for Mastery. Discuss and review any work from the previous lesson that was assigned as homework. Check for completion of the activities and orally quiz the student for comprehension. Review any reading that was assigned, discussing the characters, setting, plot, theme, language, sequence, etc.

Strengthen fluency and phonemic awareness by reviewing words and sentences from the previous lessons. Build vocabulary skills by using some of the words in sentences.

Lesson Introduction. Review with the student the definitions for the words antonym and synonym. The student should remember that words which are antonyms are the opposite and synonyms are the same. Write the words **bitter, short,** and **single** on the board. Ask the student to think of both an antonym and a synonym for each word. Antonyms for the words include **sweet, tall,** and **plural.** Synonyms are **sour, small,** and **one.**

Activity 1. The student should turn to the review lesson on antonyms and synonyms. The first activity asks the student to write an antonym and synonym for each of the given words. A Word Bank is provided.

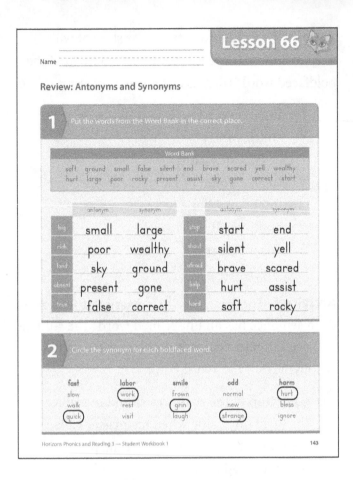

	Antonym	Synonym
big	**small**	large
rich	**poor**	wealthy
land	**sky**	ground
absent	**present**	gone
true	**false**	correct
stop	**start**	end
shout	**silent**	yell
afraid	**brave**	scared
help	**hurt**	assist
hard	**soft**	rocky

Activity 2. The next activity asks the student to only look at synonyms. The student needs to identify the synonym for each of the boldfaced words. The answers are: fast: **quick,** labor: **work,** smile: **grin,** odd: **strange,** harm: **hurt.**

Activity 3. In an activity similar to the previous one, the student will be asked to identify antonyms. The student will be asked to identify the antonym for each of the boldfaced words. The answers are: few: **many,** dark: **light,** enter: **exit,** straight: **crooked,** cruel: **kind.**

Activity 4. The final review activity asks the student to choose the antonym or synonym that best completes each sentence. A Word Bank is provided to assist the student.

1. The glass was not **empty** but full.
2. The children were happy and not **sad**.
3. The guests at the wedding put their **presents** and gifts on the table.
4. The weather was sunny and warm and not cloudy and **cold**.
5. Lilly could not sleep and was wide **awake**.
6. The car was **old** and not new.
7. Carson was so excited he could not stop **smiling** and grinning.
8. The museum visitors **gazed** and looked at the display.
9. The winding road was **crooked** and not straight.
10. The dessert was **sweet** and not sour.

Reading Activity.

1. The student should return to the selection "The Story of Dr. Dolittle: Part II." First review with the student what he/she learned about Dr. Dolittle in Part I of the selection. After reviewing, the student should read Part II of the selection.

2. Discuss the selection with the student. What advice did the butcher give Dr. Dolittle for his financial problems? (**The butcher told him that he should become an animal doctor. The doctor knew more about animals than most vets. The doctor also had written a book about cats which showed he clearly understood them.**) How did the butcher say he would help the doctor get more animal patients? (**He said he would make the animals sick.**) What was Dr. Dolittle's response? (**He said he didn't think it was a good idea.**) What can we learn about the doctor from his response? (**We can learn that he cared about the animals and didn't want them ill. He also cared about the animals more than money. He was willing to make less money if that would benefit the animals.**) What did the doctor learn from the parrot? (**He learned that animals also talk.**) How did the parrot help the doctor? (**The parrot taught the doctor animal-language. The parrot also taught the doctor that animals also speak in gestures and**

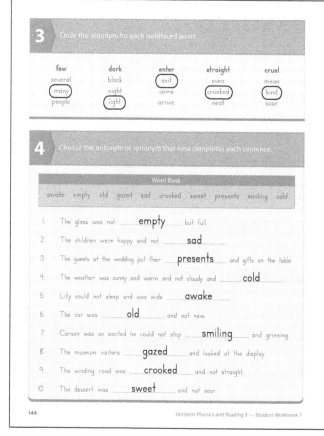

looks. For example, dogs use their noses to ask questions.) What happened when Dr. Dolittle started taking animal patients? (**He was overrun with animals. He needed to put extra doors in his house to accommodate the different sizes and types of patients.**) How did the doctor combine his knowledge of being a people doctor with how he treated his animal patients? (**He solved their problems in ways you would for a person. For example, he fitted a horse with glasses. Soon other animals also received glasses.**) How did word of the doctor's skills spread? (**Animals let each other know that Dr. Dolittle understood them. As birds flew to different parts of the world, they also spoke about Dr. Dolittle.**) Do you think the doctor was happier as a doctor for people or animals? Why? (**Allow for personal reflection.**)

3. Ask the student to turn to the second to the last paragraph. The words **sick**, **glad**, and **say** appear in this paragraph. Ask the student to think of an antonym and a synonym for each of these words. Possible responses are: sick: **well**, **ill**; glad: **sad**, **happy**; say: **silent**, **speak**.

Lesson 67

Homonyms

Overview:

- Define homonyms
- Identify words which are homonyms
- Read sentences with homonyms
- Form word combinations with homonyms

Material and Supplies:

- Teacher's Guide and Student Workbook
- White board or chart paper
- Phonics flashcards
- Reader: "The Kangaroo"

Teaching Tips:

Review for Mastery. Discuss and review any work from the previous lesson that was assigned as homework. Check for completion of the activities and orally quiz the student for comprehension. Review any reading that was assigned, discussing the characters, setting, plot, theme, language, sequence, etc.

Strengthen fluency and phonemic awareness by reviewing words and sentences from the previous lessons. Build vocabulary skills by using some of the words in sentences.

You may want to make flashcards of words which are homonyms. The student can study these throughout the unit.

Lesson Introduction. Write the words **hole** and **whole** on the board. Ask the student to say the words. Afterwards, ask the student what he/she noticed about how the two words sounded. The student should note that the two words sounded the same. Ask the student if the two words are spelled the same and if they mean the same thing. **(No)** Tell the student that the words **hole** and **whole** are homonyms. This means

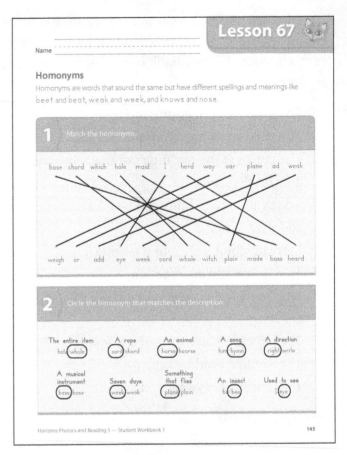

that even though the words sound alike they have different spellings and meanings. Tell the student that in this lesson and the next the student will learn more examples of words which are homonyms.

Activity 1. The student should turn to the activity sheet on homonyms. Ask the student to read the definition of homonym at the top of the page. The student should match the words in the first column with their homonyms in the second column. If possible provide a place where the student can say the words to hear their similar sound.

base	bass
chord	cord
which	witch
hole	whole
maid	made
I	eye
herd	heard
way	weigh
oar	or
plane	plain
ad	add
weak	week

Activity 2. The next activity focuses not on the different spellings of homonyms but on their different meanings. The student will be given two homonyms and the definition of one. The object of the activity is to match the definition with one of the homonyms. The correct answers are: **whole, cord, horse, hymn, right, bass, week, plane, bee, eye.**

Activity 3. In the next activity pairs of homonyms are listed in the Word Bank. The student will need to choose the correct homonym to complete the sentences listed below.

1. Joshua couldn't **be** at the game.
2. The congregation sang a beautiful **hymn**.
3. Alyssa couldn't **hear** the announcement.
4. Matt's voice was **hoarse** from cheering at the game.
5. Betsy needed to **write** her name at the top of the paper.
6. The **horse** enjoyed running in the pasture.
7. The **bee** landed on the flower.
8. Cassie shouted, "**Here** is my missing book!"
9. Mr. Peterson turned **right** at the intersection.
10. Simon was sad the present wasn't for **him**.

Reading Activity.

1. The student should turn to the reading "The Kangaroo" which accompanies this lesson. Either read the poem together or have the student read the poem aloud.

2. Have the student discuss kangaroos after reading the poem. What are the physical characteristics of a kangaroo? (**A kangaroo is about five feet tall. It has large back legs as well as a tail. Because of its build, a kangaroo can hop 20 mph and jump a 30 foot wall.**) Where does a kangaroo live? (**The kangaroo is native to Australia.**) What types of food does a kangaroo eat? (**A kangaroo eats grasses, shrubs, but not meat. In other words, a kangaroo is an herbivore.**) Kangaroos are known to be nocturnal animals. What do you think the word nocturnal means? (**A nocturnal animal is awake**

during the night and sleeps during the day.) What did you learn about a kangaroo's baby? (**A baby kangaroo is called a joey. The joey lives in the pouch of its mother for about a year. A kangaroo gives birth to a single baby unlike puppies or cats who have litters.**)

3. Ask the student to look at the rhyme scheme of the poem. Which lines in the poem rhyme? (**The rhyming pattern is aabbcc…**) Tell the student that in this lesson he/she learned about homonyms. Tell the student you want them to find two words in the selection which have homonyms. You may want to give the example that if the word **there** was in the selection you would list the homonyms **their** and **they're**. Possible answers for the poem are: **night: knight, tail: tale, hour: our, no: know.**

---

3   Fill in the blank with the correct word.

Word Bank

be   bee   hymn   him   here   hear   horse   hoarse   write   right

1. Joshua couldn't ____**be**____ at the game.
2. The congregation sang a beautiful ____**hymn**____
3. Alyssa couldn't ____**hear**____ the announcement.
4. Matt's voice was ____**hoarse**____ from cheering at the game.
5. Betsy needed to ____**write**____ her name at the top of the paper.
6. The ____**horse**____ enjoyed running in the pasture.
7. The ____**bee**____ landed on the flower.
8. Cassie shouted, "____**Here**____ is my missing book!"
9. Mr. Peterson turned ____**right**____ at the intersection.
10. Simon was sad the present wasn't for ____**him**____

146   Horizons Phonics and Reading 3 — Student Workbook 1

Lesson 68

Homonyms

Overview:

- Define homonyms
- Identify words which are homonyms
- Read sentences with homonyms
- Form word combinations with homonyms

Material and Supplies:

- Teacher's Guide and Student Workbook
- White board or chart paper
- Phonics flashcards
- Reader: "Androcles and the Lion"

Teaching Tips:

Review for Mastery. Discuss and review any work from the previous lesson that was assigned as homework. Check for completion of the activities and orally quiz the student for comprehension. Review any reading that was assigned, discussing the characters, setting, plot, theme, language, sequence, etc.

Strengthen fluency and phonemic awareness by reviewing words and sentences from the previous lessons. Build vocabulary skills by using some of the words in sentences.

You may want to create additional flashcards of words which are homonyms. The student can study these throughout the unit.

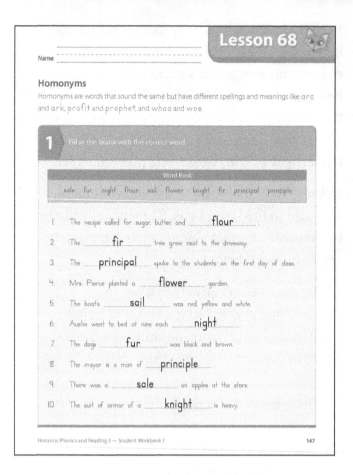

Lesson Introduction. Ask the student to recall the meaning of the word homonym. If needed, remind the student that words which are homonyms sound the same but have different spellings and meanings. See if the student can give you an example of a homonym. Examples could include: **I: eye, horse: hoarse,** or **be: bee.** Tell the student in this lesson they will look at other examples of homonyms.

Activity 1. The student should turn to the activity sheet which accompanies the lesson. The student should read through the definition of homonym at the top of the page. In the first activity, the student will be asked to fill in sentences with homonyms. A Word Bank of pairs of homonyms is provided. The student should choose the correct word to fill in the blank.

1. The recipe called for sugar, butter, and **flour**.
2. The **fir** tree grew next to the driveway.
3. The **principal** spoke to the students on the first day of class.
4. Mrs. Pierce planted a **flower** garden.
5. The boat's **sail** was red, yellow and white.
6. Austin went to bed at nine each **night**.
7. The dog's **fur** was black and brown.
8. The mayor is a man of **principle**.
9. There was a **sale** on apples at the store.
10. The suit of armor of a **knight** is heavy.

Activity 2. In this activity the student will need to choose the word or words which are a homonym of the boldfaced word in each line. The answers are: waist: **waste**, sew: **so, sow**, peace: **piece**, for: **four**, their: **there, they're**, two: **to, too**, know: **no**, male: **mail**, son: **sun**, pair: **pear**.

Activity 3. The final activity asks the student to complete a word search. In the word search are pairs of homonyms. The student will need to find both homonyms in the word search. A Word Bank is provided. **See image for answers.**

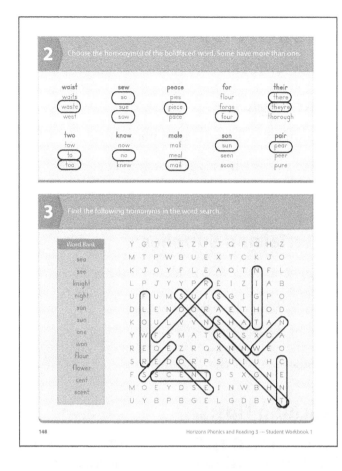

Reading Activity.

1. The student should turn to the story "Androcles and the Lion" which accompanies this lesson. The student will read the selection in this lesson and then discuss it in the next.

2. Have the student turn to the first paragraph of the selection. Ask the student to find three words in the paragraph that have homonyms. The student should write down both the word in the paragraph and the accompanying homonym. Answers include: **no: know, die: dye, in: inn, by: buy, I: eye, be: bee.**

Lesson 69

Homographs

Overview:

- Identify words which are homographs
- Read words which are homographs
- Form word combinations with homographs

Material and Supplies:

- Teacher's Guide and Student Workbook
- White board or chart paper
- Phonics flashcards
- Reader: "Androcles and the Lion"

Teaching Tips:

Review for Mastery: Discuss and review any work from the previous lesson that was assigned as home-work. Check for completion of the activities and orally quiz the student for comprehension. Review any reading that was assigned, discussing the characters, setting, plot, theme, language, sequence, etc.

Strengthen fluency and phonemic awareness by reviewing words and sentences from the previous lessons. Build vocabulary skills by using some of the words in sentences.

You may want to create flashcards for words which are homographs. The student can study these throughout the unit.

Lesson Introduction. Review with the student the definition for a homonym. The student should recall that a homonym is a word which has the same sound as another word but is spelled differently and has a different meanings. Write the word **homograph** on the board. Explain to the student that a homograph is when words are spelled the same although they may be pronounced differently. The words also have different meanings.

Write the word **live** on the board. Pronounce the word **live** as in to be **alive** and **live** as in **living**. Tell

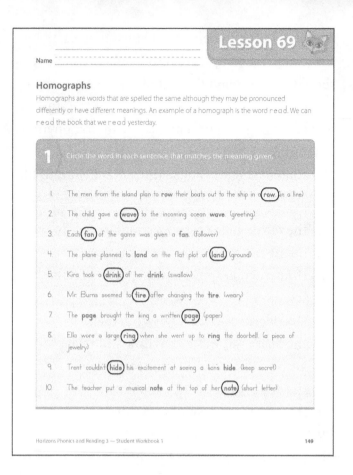

the student in this lesson he/she will be exploring words which are homographs.

Activity 1. The student should take out the activity sheet which accompanies this lesson. The student should read the definition at the top of the page. In the first activity, two words which are homographs are used in each sentence. The student will need to circle the underlined word which matches the definition given.

1. The men from the island plan to **row** their boats out to the ship in a **row**.
2. The child gave a **wave** to the incoming ocean **wave**.
3. Each **fan** of the game was given a **fan**.
4. The plane planned to **land** on the flat plot of **land**.
5. Kira took a **drink** of her **drink**.
6. Mr. Burns seemed to **tire** after changing the **tire**.
7. The **page** brought the king a written **page**.
8. Ella wore a large **ring** when she went up to **ring** the doorbell.
9. Trent couldn't **hide** his excitement at seeing a lion's **hide**.
10. The teacher put a musical **note** at the top of her **note**.

Horizons Phonics and Reading 3 — Teacher's Guide

Activity 2. The activity sheet continues with the student identifying whether or not an underlined pair of words in a sentence is an example of a homonym or a homograph. It may be helpful to have the student read the sentences aloud so that he/she can better hear the sounds of the words.

1. homonym 2. homonym 3. homograph 4. homonym
5. homonym 6. homograph 7. homograph 8. homonym
9. homonym 10. homonym

Activity 3. The student will be asked to choose three pairs of homonyms or homographs from the Word Bank and write sentences for each. Examples for six pairs:

> I couldn't wait to see the sea.
> > The knight rode his horse into the night.
> Sam could not untie the knot.
> > The bow hunter took a bow.
> The gold mine was mine.
> > Andrew felt well after drinking from the well.

Reading Activity.

1. The student should turn to the selection "Androcles and the Lion." In the previous lesson, the student read the selection. In this lesson, the student will discuss the selection.

2. Use some of the following questions to assist your discussion. Why did Androcles leave his master? **(His life was miserable as a slave. He did not see any way out of his suffering other than to run away.)** Where did Androcles go when he escaped? **(He fled to a forest and found shelter in a cave.)** What was life like for Androcles after his escape? **(His life continued to be challenging and difficult. He went from being miserable as a slave, to being miserable free.)** What did Androcles find in the cave? **(He found a huge lion.)** What was Androcles' first reaction to seeing the lion? **(He was afraid and assumed the lion would kill him.)** Why didn't the lion kill him? **(The lion was wounded and needed help. He had a thorn in his paw that was causing him great pain. He was unable to take the thorn out of his paw.)** How did the lion react after the thorn was removed? **(He treated Androcles as a much-loved guest. He even brought food for Androcles to eat.)**

3. Continue by discussing how Androcles was caught by the soldiers. Tell the student that at this

time slavery was permitted. Slaves who had run away were punished by death. As unbelievable as it is, people went to large arenas where they would watch people being killed by lions. The people of the time saw this as a form of entertainment, like we might call watching a basketball game or a movie. What did the crowd expect to happen to Androcles when the lion was turned loose? **(They expected the lion would tear Androcles apart and kill him.)** How did the lion react? **(The lion saw it was Androcles and sat at his feet. The lion looked up at Androcles with devotion.)** How did Androcles explain the lion's reaction to the crowd? **(He told that the story of how he cared for the lion and they became friends.)** What did Androcles receive instead of death? **(He received his freedom along with the lion.)**

4. Tell the student that this selection is a fable. This means that the story teaches people lessons about life. What lessons do you think people can learn from the story of "Androcles and the Lion?" (Answers include: **The need to be kind to all people and animals. Sometimes being kind to a person or animal may have unexpected benefits.)**

---

2 Mark whether the underlined words are homographs or homonyms.

		homograph	homonym
1.	A _pair_ of _pears_ was on the counter.	○	●
2.	James wanted to _buy_ the candy _by_ the cereal boxes.	○	●
3.	My _great_-grandmother is _great_.	●	○
4.	Julia _rode_ her bike on the _road_.	○	●
5.	Our _mail_ was delivered by a _male_.	○	●
6.	The man received a _fine_ for not driving _fine_.	●	○
7.	Mallory couldn't _bear_ to see the scary _bear_.	●	○
8.	Aunt Carmen told a _tale_ about a dog with no _tail_.	○	●
9.	The boys were _too_ tired _to_ go sledding.	○	●
10.	A _dear_ looking _deer_ crossed the road.	○	●

3 Choose among the pairs of homographs and homonyms from the Word Bank to write three of your own sentences.

Word Bank
sea/sea
night/knight
not/knot
bow/bow
well/well
mine/mine

1. _____ (Answers will vary.)
2.
3.

Lesson 70

Review

Overview:

- Identify rhyming words which have regular and irregular spellings

- Practice using words which are antonyms and synonyms

- Recall words which are homographs and homonyms

Material and Supplies:

- Teacher's Guide and Student Workbook

- White board or chart paper

- Phonics flashcards

- Reader: "The Endless Tale"

Teaching Tips:

Review for Mastery. Discuss and review any work from the previous lesson that was assigned as homework. Check for completion of the activities and orally quiz the student for comprehension. Review any reading that was assigned, discussing the characters, setting, plot, theme, language, sequence, etc.

Strengthen fluency and phonemic awareness by reviewing words and sentences from the previous lessons. Build vocabulary skills by using some of the words in sentences.

You may want to review flashcards made for words in this unit.

Lesson Introduction. In this lesson the student will review all of the material from this unit. These lessons will review rhyming words, antonyms, synonyms, homonyms, and homographs. The activities will follow the pattern of the text.

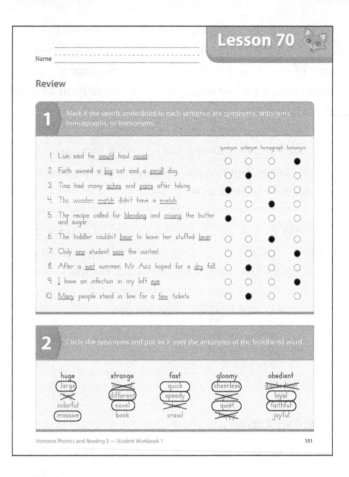

Activity 1. The student should turn to the activity sheet which accompanies this lesson. The first activity reviews many of the materials the student studied in the unit. The student will be asked to identify if the pair of underlined words in a sentence are antonyms, synonyms, homonyms, or homographs. The answers to the activity are as follows:

1. Luis said he <u>would</u> haul <u>wood.</u> (**homonym**)
2. Faith owned a <u>big</u> cat and a <u>small</u> dog. (**antonym**)
3. Tina had many <u>aches</u> and <u>pains</u> after hiking. (**synonym**)
4. The wooden <u>match</u> didn't have a <u>match</u>. (**homograph**)
5. The recipe called for <u>blending</u> and <u>mixing</u> the butter and sugar. (**synonym**)
6. The toddler couldn't <u>bear</u> to leave her stuffed <u>bear</u>. (**homograph**)
7. Only <u>one</u> student <u>won</u> the contest. (**homonym**)

8. After a <u>wet</u> summer, Mr. Aziz hoped for a <u>dry</u> fall. (**antonym**)

9. <u>I</u> have an infection in my left <u>eye</u>. (**homonym**)

10. <u>Many</u> people stood in line for a <u>few</u> tickets. (**antonym**)

Activity 2. The lesson continues with the student identifying antonyms and synonyms. Each line will have a word in boldfaced type. The student will need to circle the words which are synonyms and place an X over the words which are antonyms. Not all words will be synonyms or antonyms.

huge: (large) ~~tiny~~ colorful (massive)

strange: ~~normal~~ (different) (novel) book

fast: (quick) (speedy) ~~slow~~ crawl

gloomy: (cheerless) grin (quiet) happy

obedient: ~~disobedient~~ (loyal) (faithful) ~~joyful~~

Activity 3. The lesson continues with a closer review of homonyms. The student will be asked to match the word in the first column with its homonym in the second.

pair	pear
rode	road
dear	deer
buy	by
bear	bare
fur	fir
write	right
sew	so

Activity 4. The final review activity focuses on rhyming words. The student will be asked to identify both regular and irregular rhyming words which rhyme with the initial boldfaced words.

thicker: (quicker) (wicker) curse (slicker)

judicial: (initial) while (official) canal

air: (blare) care (stair) bar

activity: beauty (captivity) (festivity) duty

tune: (moon) (dune) (bloom) (noon)

compute: polite (lawsuit) (recruit) (pollute)

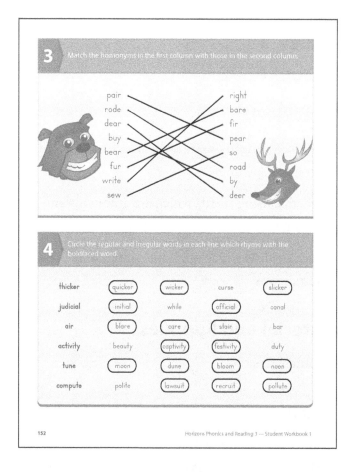

Reading Activity.

1. Ask the student to turn to the selection "The Endless Tale."

2. Tell the student that this selection will be read for pleasure and not discussed.

Test 7

Lessons 61-70

Overview:

- Identify rhyming words which have regular and irregular spellings

- Practice using words which are antonyms and synonyms

- Recall words which are homographs and homonyms

Material and Supplies:

- Student Test

Teaching Tips:

Review for Mastery. Discuss and review any work from the previous lesson that was assigned as homework. Check for completion of the activities and orally quiz the student for comprehension. Review any reading that was assigned, discussing the characters, setting, plot, theme, language, sequence, etc.

Lesson Introduction. Check if the student has any final questions from the review before taking the test. The test is formatted like the review. Different words will be used in the test than what appeared in the review.

Activity 1. The student should turn to the test which accompanies this lesson. In the first activity the student will read sentences which contain synonyms, antonyms, homonyms, or homographs. The student will need to identify the underlined pair of words and identify if they are synonyms, antonyms, homonyms, or homographs.

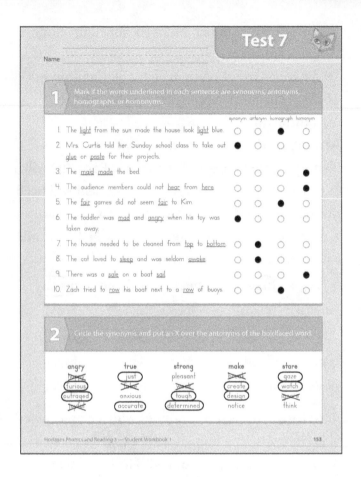

1. The <u>light</u> from the sun made the house look <u>light</u> blue. (**homograph**)
2. Mrs. Curtis told her Sunday school class to take out <u>glue</u> or <u>paste</u> for their projects. (**synonym**)
3. The <u>maid</u> <u>made</u> the bed. (**homonym**)
4. The audience members could not <u>hear</u> from <u>here</u>. (**homonym**)
5. The <u>fair</u> games did not seem <u>fair</u> to Kim. (**homograph**)
6. The toddler was <u>mad</u> and <u>angry</u> when his toy was taken away. (**synonym**)
7. The house needed to be cleaned from <u>top</u> to <u>bottom</u>. (**antonym**)
8. The cat loved to <u>sleep</u> and was seldom <u>awake</u>. (**antonym**)
9. There was a <u>sale</u> on a boat <u>sail</u>. (**homonym**)
10. Zach tried to <u>row</u> his boat next to a <u>row</u> of buoys. (**homograph**)

Activity 2. The student will continue the test by identifying synonyms and antonyms. The student will read the boldfaced word in each line and then place an X over the words which are antonyms and circle the words which are synonyms.

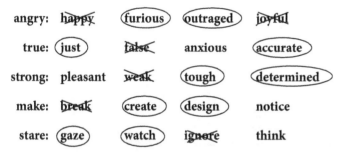

angry: ~~happy~~   (furious)   (outraged)   ~~joyful~~

true: (just)   ~~false~~   anxious   (accurate)

strong: pleasant   ~~weak~~   (tough)   (determined)

make: ~~break~~   (create)   (design)   notice

stare: (gaze)   (watch)   ~~ignore~~   think

Activity 3. The next activity asks the student to match words in the first column with their homonyms in the second column. There is one correct match for each word.

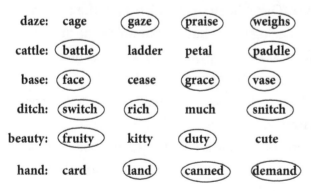

heal	heel
cent	scent
merry	Mary
vain	vein
son	sun
great	grate
days	daze
plane	plain

Activity 4. The last activity asks the student to identify rhyming words. At the beginning of each line is a boldfaced word. The student will identify other words which match with the first one.

daze: cage   (gaze)   (praise)   (weighs)

cattle: (battle)   ladder   petal   (paddle)

base: (face)   cease   (grace)   (vase)

ditch: (switch)   (rich)   much   (snitch)

beauty: (fruity)   kitty   (duty)   cute

hand: card   (land)   (canned)   (demand)

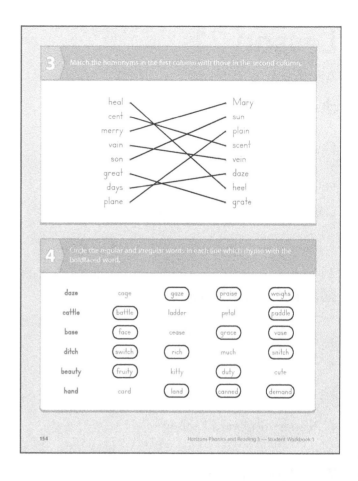

Lesson 71

Analogies: parts of a whole, size/degree, category/type

Overview:

- Define analogies
- Recognize types of analogies
- Identify words which complete analogies

Material and Supplies:

- Teacher's Guide and Student Workbook
- White board or chart paper
- Phonics flashcards
- Reader: "Rudyard Kipling"

Teaching Tips:

Lesson Introduction. This is the first of a series of lessons on analogies. Write the words **finger**, **hand**, **foot**, and **toe** on the board. Ask the student how the words relate to each other. Through the discussion, help the student notice that **finger** and **toe** are parts of a larger thing such as **hand** and **foot**. Explain that analogies are comparisons when two word pairs illustrate how the pairs relate to one another. Analogies are often used on tests as a way to recognize how well a student understands how words relate to one another.

You may want to create flashcards of analogies. The student can study these throughout the unit.

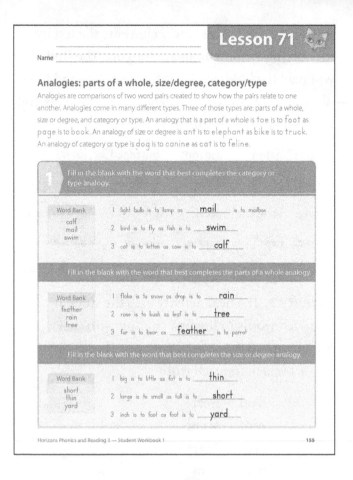

Activity 1. The student should turn to the activity sheet which accompanies this lesson. Read with the student the definition and examples at the top of the page. You may find it helpful to write out the analogy examples on the board and see if the student can make additional ones. For example: **toe is to foot as page is to book.** Other similar analogies might include: **keyboard to computer or roof to house.** Once the student understands the concept of an analogy, have him/her complete the first set of activities. These activities have a limited number of answers which will help to reinforce the concept of analogies. The answers to analogies of category or type are: **mail, swim, calf.** The answers to analogies of parts of a whole are: **rain, tree, feather.** The answers to analogies of size or degree are: **thin, short, yard.**

Activity 2. The student should go on to the second main activity on the sheet. In this activity, the student will have a variety of types of analogies to complete. Three possible answers are provided for each. The student will need to choose the word that best completes the analogy. The correct answers are: **b, c, b, c, c, c, b, c, a, c.**

Reading Activity.

1. All of the reading activities in this unit will relate to the author Rudyard Kipling. Four of the lessons will focus on his well-known story "Rikki-Tikki-Tavi." In this lesson, the student will be introduced to the author Rudyard Kipling. The student will learn about his childhood and life as a writer.

2. Direct the student to read the selection "Rudyard Kipling." Once the student has completed the reading, discuss it. Ask the student to describe Kipling's parents. (**They lived and worked in India but they were from England.**) What was Kipling's childhood experience in England like? (**He lived with a couple from England whom he didn't know. He did not enjoy living with them. He also studied at a boarding school.**) When Kipling returned to India at age 16, what did he do? (**He worked as a newspaper reporter, he began writing short stories, and he also wrote poetry.**) What was the significance of Kipling winning the Nobel Prize? (**He was the first person from England to win a Nobel Prize in literature. He was also the youngest winner.**) Ask the student if he/she is familiar with any of the books Kipling wrote. (**The student may be familiar with the movie *The Jungle Book*.**)

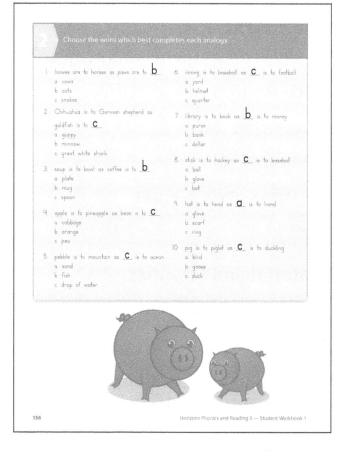

3. Create some analogies based on the selection. Have the student complete them. Some examples are provided:

   - composer is to music as _____ is to book (**author**)

   - _____ is to Asia as the U.S. is to North America (**India**)

   - World Series is to baseball as the _____ is to writing (**Nobel Prize**)

Lesson 72

Analogies: synonyms/antonyms, function/use, and grammar

Overview:

- Define analogies
- Recognize types of analogies
- Identify words which complete analogies

Material and Supplies:

- Teacher's Guide and Student Workbook
- White board or chart paper
- Phonics flashcards
- Reader: "The Camel's Hump"

Teaching Tips:

Review for Mastery. Discuss and review any work from the previous lesson that was assigned as homework. Check for completion of the activities and orally quiz the student for comprehension. Review any reading that was assigned, discussing the characters, setting, plot, theme, language, sequence, etc.

Strengthen fluency and phonemic awareness by reviewing words and sentences from the previous lessons. Build vocabulary skills by using some of the words in sentences.

You may want to create flashcards of words which are analogies. The student can study these throughout the unit.

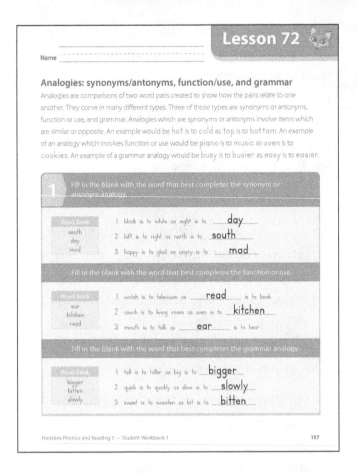

Lesson Introduction. This lesson continues with the study of analogies. In this lesson the student will study synonym, antonym, function, use, and grammar analogies. Ask the student to define or give an example of an analogy. For example: **garage is to car as house is to people**. Tell the student in this lesson he/she will learn about other types of analogies. Write on the board: **whipped cream is to pie as butter is to _____**. Ask the student to complete the analogy. The student could complete the analogy with the words: **bread, roll,** or **bun**.

Activity 1. The student should turn to the activity sheet which accompanies this lesson. The student should read the definition of an analogy at the top of the sheet.

Direct the student to complete the first three fill in the blank activities on the sheet. These activities take the student through synonym, antonym, function or use, and grammar analogies. A Word Bank is provided to help the student to have success in recognizing these different types of analogies.

Answers: **day, south, mad**
Answers: **read, kitchen, ear**
Answers: **bigger, slowly, bitten**

Activity 2. The student should look at the final activity on the sheet. The student will need to choose the best word to complete each analogy. The different types of analogies studied in this lesson are all used in this section. The student will need to choose the best word to complete each analogy.

The answers are: **b, a, b, a, c, b, c, c, a, c.**

Reading Activity.

1. Ask the student to read the poem "The Camel's Hump." After the student has read the poem, read the poem together, listening to the rhythm and sound of the words.

2. Discuss the selection with the student. Is the poet saying that people have real humps on their backs? (**No**) What kinds of humps do people have? (**They have humps from not doing enough work. They have humps of laziness.**) How does the author describe the protests people make when they do not want to work? (**They don't want to get out of bed. They growl and scowl at everything they are asked to do.**) What does the author say is the cure for the hump that is black and blue? (**Work! The author says it is not relaxing with a book but**

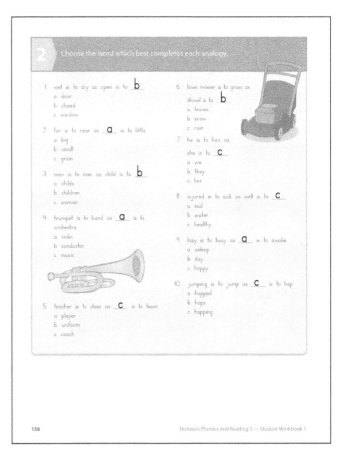

shoveling, digging, and sweating.) Do you think this poem gives good advice? Why or why not? (**Allow for a personal response.**)

3. Continue by discussing the structure of the poem? How many lines are in each stanza? (**Four or five lines.**) Explain how the five line stanzas act as a chorus. Analyze the rhyme scheme of the poem. In the four line stanzas the second and third lines rhyme making for an **abcb** rhyme scheme. In the five line stanzas the rhyme scheme is either **aabba** or **abccb**. Ask the student to read the words which rhyme at the end of some of the lines.

4. Challenge the student to create analogies from some of the words or ideas from the poem. For example: **hump is to camel as trunk is to elephant** or **busy is to lazy as awake is to tired.**

Lesson 73
Contractions with not and would

Overview:

- Define contractions
- Learn how to form contractions
- Identify words which are contractions
- Use contractions in sentences

Material and Supplies:

- Teacher's Guide and Student Workbook
- White board or chart paper
- Phonics flashcards
- Reader: "I Keep Six Honest Serving Men"

Teaching Tips:

Review for Mastery. Discuss and review any work from the previous lesson that was assigned as homework. Check for completion of the activities and orally quiz the student for comprehension. Review any reading that was assigned, discussing the characters, setting, plot, theme, language, sequence, etc.

Strengthen fluency and phonemic awareness by reviewing words and sentences from the previous lessons. Build vocabulary skills by using some of the words in sentences.

You may want to create flashcards of words which are contractions. The student can study these throughout the unit.

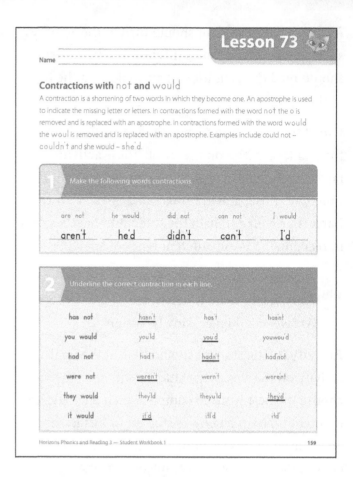

Lesson Introduction. This lesson begins a study of contractions. In this lesson the student will study contractions formed with **not** and **would**. Ask the student to define or give an example of a contraction. For example: **can't**, **she's**, or **they'd**. Tell the student in this lesson he/she will learn about words formed with the contractions **not** and **would**. Write on the board the words **can not** and **she would**. See if the student can determine how contractions can be made of the two words. Show the student how the apostrophe is used to indicate the missing letters in **can't** and **she'd**.

Activity 1. The student should turn to the activity sheet accompanying this lesson. Read with the student the definition of contraction at the top of the sheet. The first activity asks the student to make a series of word contractions. You may want to do the first one with the student to make sure he/she understands what is expected in the activity. The answers are: **aren't, he'd, didn't, can't, I'd.**

Activity 2. The next activity asks the student to determine the correct formation of a contraction. Three possible answers are given but only one will be correct. Again, you may find it helpful to do the first example with the student so he/she understands the activity. The answers are: **hasn't, you'd, hadn't, weren't, they'd, it'd.**

Activity 3. The final activity asks the student to replace the underlined words in each sentence with a contraction. This allows the student to see how contractions are used in everyday writing. The answers for the activity are: **How'd, isn't, Why'd, didn't, wasn't, Who'd, doesn't, don't, hasn't, he'd.**

Reading Activity.

1. Lead a short discussion on questions before reading the poem. Ask the student to list for you some question words. (These include **who, what, when, where, why,** and **how.**) Continue by asking the student what question words he/she has used today. (Answers may include: **Asking what page an assignment was on or how many more minutes until recess.**) Ask the student what he/she has learned from asking questions either today or in the past. (**Allow for individual answers.**)

2. Read the poem "I Keep Six Honest Serving Men" to the student while he/she follows along. When you have finished, have the student read the poem to you.

3. Discuss the poem with the student. What are the names of the serving men? (**What, Why, When, How, Where, Who**) When don't the servers work? (**They don't work when he eats or during the work day.**) What do the serving men do? (**They answer questions and teach him about people, places, and things.**) How does the woman in the poem make use of her servers? (**She asks even more questions and does so all day.**)

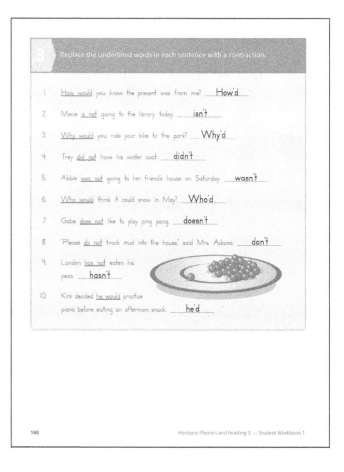

4. Talk about the way in which the poem is written. How many syllables are in each line? (**In the first two stanzas the pattern is 8686 etc. The final stanza has an irregular form.**) What is the rhyme scheme of the poem? (**The rhyme scheme in the stanzas varies. Point out the words which do rhyme. The pattern of the first stanza is ababcdcd.**)

5. Write the question words from the poem on the board: **what, why, when, how, where,** and **who.** Ask the student to form contractions with the question words by adding would. Answers are: **what'd, why'd, when'd, how'd, where'd, who'd.**

Lesson 74

Contractions with will, am, had, have, has

Overview:

- Define contractions

- Learn how to form contractions

- Identify words which are contractions

- Use contractions in sentences

Material and Supplies:

- Teacher's Guide and Student Workbook

- White board or chart paper

- Phonics flashcards

- Reader: "The King Cobra"

Teaching Tips:

Review for Mastery. Discuss and review any work from the previous lesson that was assigned as homework. Check for completion of the activities and orally quiz the student for comprehension. Review any reading that was assigned, discussing the characters, setting, plot, theme, language, sequence, etc.

Strengthen fluency and phonemic awareness by reviewing words and sentences from the previous lessons. Build vocabulary skills by using some of the words in sentences.

You may want to create flashcards of words which are contractions. The student can study these throughout the unit.

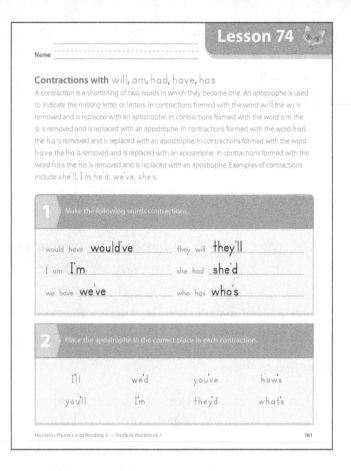

Lesson Introduction. This lesson continues a study of contractions. In this lesson the student will study contractions formed with **will**, **am**, **had**, **have**, and **has**. Ask the student to define or give an example of a contraction. For example: **can't**, **she's**, or **they'd**. Tell the student in this lesson he/she will learn about words formed with the contractions **will**, **am**, **had**, **have**, and **has**. Write on the board the words **I am** and **he has**. See if the student can determine how contractions can be made from the two words. Show the student how the apostrophe is used to indicate the missing letters in **I'm** and **he's**.

Activity 1. The student should turn to the activity sheet which accompanies this lesson. In the first activity, the student will need to take two words and make them into a contraction. The answers are: **would've, they'll, I'm, she'd, we've, who's.**

Activity 2. The lesson continues with the student choosing where an apostrophe should go in each contraction. Before the student begins, remind him/her that the apostrophe is placed to indicate where the missing letters would be. The answers are: **I'll**, **we'd**, **you've**, **how's**, **you'll**, **I'm**, **they'd**, **what's**.

Activity 3. The final activity asks the student to recognize the incorrectly formed contraction in each sentence. The student will be asked to write the contraction correctly at the end of each line. The answers are: **Who'll**, **should've**, **may've**, **might've**, **he's**, **We've**, **I'm**, **that'd**, **I'll**, **she's**.

Reading Activity.

1. Ask the student to read the selection "The King Cobra." This selection will give them some background knowledge about cobras before reading "Rikki-Tikki-Tavi."

2. Discuss the selection with your student. Where is the natural habitat of the king cobra? **(India, southern Asia, and China.)** What characteristics does the king cobra have that make it unique? (Answers include: **It's the largest of the cobra family, builds nests for its young, guards nest, longest of the venomous snakes, and makes more of a growl than a hiss.)** What does the king cobra eat? **(It eats snakes, lizards, small animals, and eggs.)** Who are the king cobra's predators? **(Their predators are people and mongooses.)**

3. Have the student write two sentences telling what they learned about the cobra. Each sentence should include a contraction.

Horizons Phonics and Reading 3 — Teacher's Guide   **197**

Lesson 75

Contractions with is, are, did, could

Overview:

- Define contractions

- Learn how to form contractions

- Identify words which are contractions

- Use contractions in sentences

Material and Supplies:

- Teacher's Guide and Student Workbook

- White board or chart paper

- Phonics flashcards

- Reader: "The Mongoose"

Teaching Tips:

Review for Mastery. Discuss and review any work from the previous lesson that was assigned as homework. Check for completion of the activities and orally quiz the student for comprehension. Review any reading that was assigned, discussing the characters, setting, plot, theme, language, sequence, etc.

Strengthen fluency and phonemic awareness by reviewing words and sentences from the previous lessons. Build vocabulary skills by using some of the words in sentences.

You may want to create flashcards of words which are contractions. The student can study these throughout the unit.

Lesson Introduction. This lesson continues a study of contractions. In this lesson the student will study contractions formed with **is**, **are**, **did**, and **could**. Ask the student to define or give an example of a contraction. For example: **can't**, **she's**, or **they'd**. Tell the student in this lesson he/she will learn about words formed with the contractions **is**, **are**, **did**, and **could**. Write the words **she is** and **they did** on the board. See if the student can determine how contractions can be made from the two words. Show the student how the apostrophe is used to indicate the missing letters in **she's** and **they'd.**

Activity 1. Ask the student to take out the activity sheet which accompanies this lesson. Once again ask the student to read the definition at the top of the sheet. As on the other contraction activity sheets, the student will be asked to take two words and form a contraction. The answers are: **he's, we're, they'd, I'd, you're, I'd.**

Activity 2. The student should continue with the activity sheet by completing a matching activity. The student will be asked to match two words with the correct contraction. The answers are as follows:

why did	**why'd**
who could	**who'd**
she is	**she's**
they are	**they're**
he could	**he'd**
how is	**how's**
how are	**how're**
what did	**what'd**

Activity 3. The activity asks the student to apply what he/she has learned about contractions. The student must choose the correct contraction to complete each sentence. It will be important that the student can determine what the words are if they weren't contractions. The answers to the activity are: **Who's, We're, How'd, Why'd, she'd, she's, How's, he'd.**

Reading Activity.

1. The student should read the selection "The Mongoose." This selection will provide the student with some background information before reading "Rikki-Tikki-Tavi."

2. After reading the selection, discuss it with the student. To what parts of the world are mongooses native? **(Africa, Asia, and southern Europe.)** How did God uniquely make the mongoose? **(The animal is quick, it doesn't easily tire, and it is unaffected by venom.)** How do mongooses live? **(They live in the burrows of other animals. They live in groups or separately.)** What is the diet of a mongoose? **(It eats insects, crabs, snakes, and chickens.)** Why did some countries import mongooses? **(The mongooses were imported to control the population of snakes and other pests.)** Why was this a bad idea? **(The mongooses controlled the pests but in the process became pests themselves.)**

3. Ask the student to write two sentences comparing or contrasting the mongoose and cobra. The student should include a contraction in each sentence.

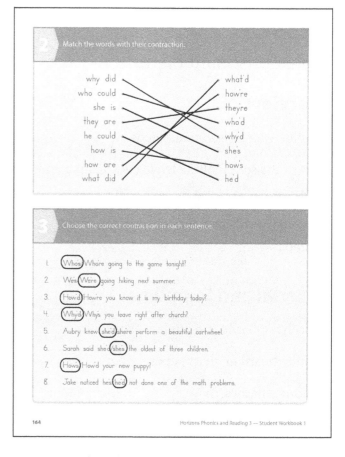

Lesson 76

Triple Consonant Blend: tch

Overview:

- Define triple consonant blends

- Learn the sound of the triple consonant blend **tch**

- Identify words containing triple consonant blends

Material and Supplies:

- Teacher's Guide and Student Workbook

- White board or chart paper

- Phonics flashcards

- Reader: "Rikki-Tikki-Tavi: Part I"

Teaching Tips:

Review for Mastery. Discuss and review any work from the previous lesson that was assigned as homework. Check for completion of the activities and orally quiz the student for comprehension. Review any reading that was assigned, discussing the characters, setting, plot, theme, language, sequence, etc.

Strengthen fluency and phonemic awareness by reviewing words and sentences from the previous lessons. Build vocabulary skills by using some of the words in sentences.

You may want to create flashcards of words with triple consonant blends. The student can study these throughout the unit.

Lesson Introduction. This lesson begins a study of triple consonant blends, also called a trigraph or cluster. In this lesson the student will study the triple consonant blend **tch**. Write the words **match, hitch,** and **pitch** on the board. See if the student can determine the connection among the

words. Explain that the student has learned about double consonant blends such as **bl, sn,** or **ng**. In this lesson and the one that follows the student will learn about three letter consonant blends.

Activity 1. The student should turn to the activity sheet accompanying this lesson. Ask the student to read the explanation of **tch** consonant blends at the top of the page. In this activity the student will be asked to complete each sentence with the correct word containing the three letter consonant blend **tch**. A Word Bank is provided. The answers are: **catch, match, itch, batch, fetch, hatched, pitch, Dutch, patch, latch.**

Activity 2. In this activity, the student will be asked to form words by adding a consonant and then vowel to the three letter consonant blend **tch**. You may want to do one of the activities together before having the student complete the activity individually. Answers are: **hatch, hitch, watch, witch, patch, pitch, match.**

Activity 3. The final section of the activity sheet asks the student to complete a word search. Words with the **tch** consonant blend will be found in the word search. A Word Bank is provided. **See image for answers.**

Reading Activity.

1. Explain to the student that in the previous two lessons, he/she learned about the mongoose and king cobra. In this lesson, the student will begin reading a story about the conflict between two king cobras and a mongoose. The selection is entitled "Rikki-Tikki-Tavi," which is the name of the mongoose. The selection is long so the student will read and study the lesson in four parts. If you feel the selection is too challenging for your student to read on his/her own, read the selection to the student. He/she can follow along as you read. This will also encourage the student to concentrate on the themes and characters of the story.

2. Direct the student to the selection "Rikki-Tikki-Tavi: Part I." The student should read or listen to the first part of the selection.

3. After reading the selection, discuss it with your student. How is Rikki-Tikki-Tavi like the mongooses you studied earlier? **(His appearance is that of a typical mongoose. His behavior seems like that of a mongoose.)** How does Rikki-Tikki-Tavi end up in the home of the family? **(He was carried away in a summer flood. The boy found him and thought he was dead. The father cared for the mongoose and he stayed to live with the family.)** What do you learn about the family? **(They had recently moved from England, they lived in a bungalow, and they seemed to be caring people.)** What is the setting of the selection? **(The selection takes place in India, which isn't noted in the text. The action is in the bungalow (small house) and the surrounding garden.)**

4. Discuss the literary technique of foreshadowing. Why does the father say it's a good thing for the mongoose to sleep in Teddy's room? **(The mongoose will protect him. No snake will get**

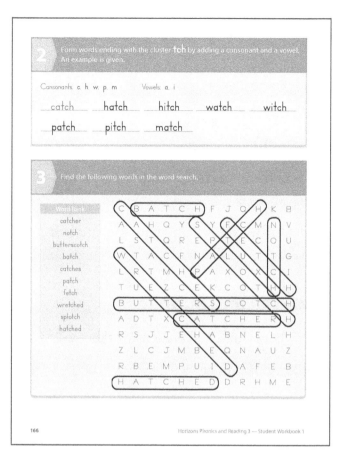

near Teddy as long as Rikki-Tikki is around.) Explain that the father's comments are an example of foreshadowing. Foreshadowing occurs when the author hints at an action or event that is going to be important later.

5. Continue with your discussion. When Rikki-Tikki explores the garden what does he learn? **(He talks to the tailor bird Darzee. He learns that one of Darzee's babies was eaten by Nag the snake.)** Describe Rikki-Tikki's first encounter with Nag. **(The student should note that Nag had a wicked expression. Nag also tried to get Rikki-Tikki relaxed so that his wife could attack the mongoose.)** At the end of the section, the author makes it clear who are the good "guys" and who are the bad "guys." Who are the good characters? **(The family, Rikki-Tikki, and Darzee.)** Who are the bad characters? **(The villains are Nag and his wife Nagaina.)**

6. Have the student find two examples of words with the triple consonant blend **tch**. Examples include: **scratch, tikkitchk, ditch, watch.**

Lesson 77

Triple Consonant Blends: nch, rch

Overview:

- Define triple consonant blends

- Learn the sound of the triple consonant blends **nch** and **rch**

- Identify words containing triple consonant blends

Material and Supplies:

- Teacher's Guide and Student Workbook

- White board or chart paper

- Phonics flashcards

- Reader: "Rikki-Tikki-Tavi: Part II"

Teaching Tips:

Review for Mastery. Discuss and review any work from the previous lesson that was assigned as homework. Check for completion of the activities and orally quiz the student for comprehension. Review any reading that was assigned, discussing the characters, setting, plot, theme, language, sequence, etc.

Strengthen fluency and phonemic awareness by reviewing words and sentences from the previous lessons. Build vocabulary skills by using some of the words in sentences.

You may want to create flashcards of words with triple consonant blends. The student can study these throughout the unit.

Lesson Introduction. This lesson continues a study of triple consonant blends, also called a trigraph or cluster. In this lesson the student will study the triple consonant blends **nch** and **rch**. On the board write the triple consonant blends

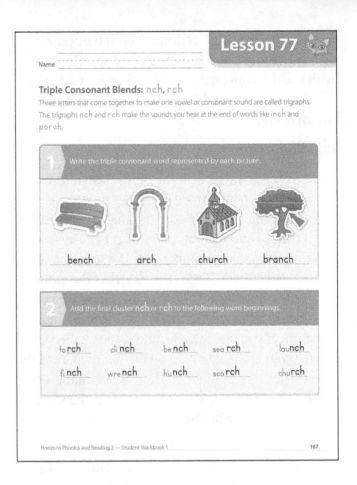

nch and rch. Also write the letters **be** and **bi**. Have the student match the front of the word with the correct three letter consonant blend. The student should write the words **bench** and **birch**.

Activity 1. Ask the student to turn to the activity sheet accompanying this lesson. The student should read the definition at the top of the page before beginning any activities. In the first activity, the student will need to identify the pictures. Each picture represents a word ending in **rch** or **nch**. The answers are: **bench**, **arch**, **church**, **branch**.

Activity 2. The lesson continues with the student adding either **nch** or **rch** to the end of letter combinations. This activity is similar to what the student did in the lesson introduction. It may be helpful to complete one of the examples together before the student completes the rest. The answers are: **torch, clinch, bench, search, launch, finch, wrench, hunch, scorch, church.**

Activity 3. The final activity on the sheet asks the student to complete sentences using words with three letter consonant blends. The student may find it helpful to read the sentences aloud to determine the correct word for completion. The answers are: **punch, birch, perched, church, munch, searched, inch, lunch, wrench, bench.**

Reading Activity.

1. The student should return to the selection "Rikki-Tikki-Tavi." The student should read "Rikki-Tikki-Tavi: Part II."

2. What does Rikki-Tikki learn from Chuchundra? **(He learns that Nag and Nagaina are planning something. He also learns that the two snakes are entering the house.)** What conversation between Nag and Nagaina does Rikki-Tikki hear? **(He overhears the snakes discussing how they plan to kill the people in the home so they can rule the garden. He also learns that the two of them are about to have children. They assume that if the family is gone the mongoose will be as well.)** How does Nag plan to kill the big man? **(He hides in the water jar used to fill the bathtub. When the man picks up the water jar, he will strike.)** How did Rikki-Tikki prepare to fight Nag? **(He waited until Nag was asleep and planned to attack the snake by its head.)** Describe the battle between Rikki-Tikki and Nag. **(Rikki-Tikki attacked Nag just as he planned. The snake was fierce and whipped Rikki-Tikki around. At the last minute the big man shot the snake with a gun.)** Was Rikki-Tikki's reaction to the fight what you expected? **(Allow for individual answers.)**

Choose the correct word with the **nch** or **rch** blend to complete each sentence.

1. Maggie wanted pink (punch) lunch for her birthday party.
2. Mr. Potter planted a lurch (birch) tree in his backyard.
3. The bird was (perched) launched on the branch.
4. The arch (church) steeple was the highest point in the town.
5. Adam liked to pinch (munch) on popcorn during a movie.
6. Mrs. Maya hunched (searched) for her car keys.
7. The math problem asked the student to measure the line to the nearest bench (inch).
8. Ham sandwiches were served at (lunch) lurch.
9. The mechanic used a (wrench) crunch to fix the car.
10. A black (bench) porch was placed under the oak tree at the park.

168   Horizons Phonics and Reading 3 — Student Workbook 1

3. Have the student predict what he/she thinks will happen when Nagaina hears of her husband's death. **(Allow for individual responses.)**

Lesson 78

Triple Consonant Blends: nth, rth, mpt

Overview:

- Define triple consonant blends
- Learn the sound of the triple consonant blends **nth, rth,** and **mpt**
- Identify words containing triple consonant blends

Material and Supplies:

- Teacher's Guide and Student Workbook
- White board or chart paper
- Phonics flashcards
- Reader: "Rikki-Tikki-Tavi: Part III"

Teaching Tips:

Review for Mastery. Discuss and review any work from the previous lesson that was assigned as homework. Check for completion of the activities and orally quiz the student for comprehension. Review any reading that was assigned, discussing the characters, setting, plot, theme, language, sequence, etc.

Strengthen fluency and phonemic awareness by reviewing words and sentences from the previous lessons. Build vocabulary skills by using some of the words in sentences.

You may want to create flashcards of words with triple consonant blends. The student can study these throughout the unit.

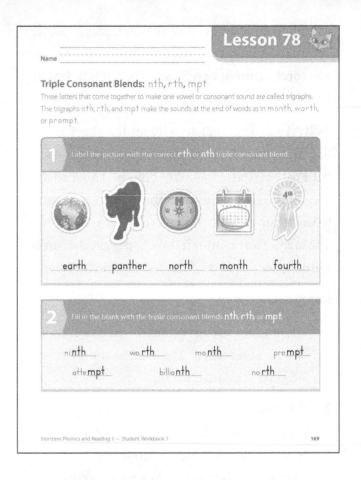

Lesson Introduction. This lesson continues a study of triple consonant blends. In this lesson the student will study the triple consonant blends **nth, rth,** and **mpt**. On the board write the triple consonant blends **nth, rth,** and **mpt**. Write the vowel **o** in front of each of the blends. See if the student can think of a consonant or consonants that can be put in front of each vowel and blended to form words. Words which can be formed include: **month, forth,** and **prompt**.

Activity 1. The student should turn to the accompanying activity sheet for this lesson. Read with the student the definition at the top of the sheet. The student should go on to the first activity on the sheet. Ask the student to label the picture with the correct word with an **rth** or **nth** triple consonant blend. No words with an **mpt** consonant blend will be used. The answers for this activity are: **earth, panther, north, month, fourth.**

Activity 2. The second activity asks the student to fill in the blanks with the triple consonant blends **nth, rth,** or **mpt.** The student may wish to have a piece of blank paper nearby so that he/she can practice writing the words with the ending before placing them on the activity sheet. The correct answers are: **ninth, worth, month, prompt, attempt, billionth, north.**

Activity 3. The activity sheet concludes with the student completing a crossword puzzle. A Word Bank is provided to help the student complete the clues. The student should answer the clues before filling in the crossword puzzle. The answers to the crossword puzzle are:

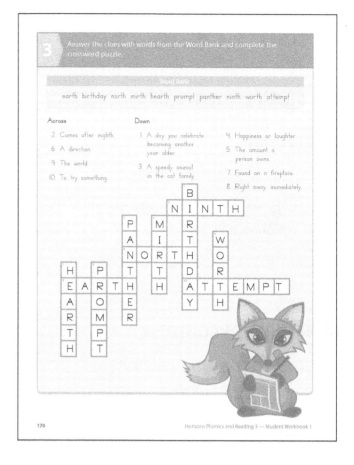

Across:	Down:
2. **ninth**	1. **birthday**
6. **north**	3. **panther**
9. **earth**	4. **mirth**
10. **attempt**	5. **worth**
	7. **hearth**
	8. **prompt**

Reading Activity.

1. The student should turn to Part III of "Rikki-Tikki-Tavi." Before reading, review with the student the action up to this point in the selection. Discuss the main characters, the death of Nag, and the upcoming arrival of Nagaina's babies.

2. After reading, discuss the selection with the student. The author describes Darzee as a "featherbrained little fellow who could never hold more than one idea at a time in his head." Why does the author describe him this way? **(Darzee didn't realize that baby snakes come out of snake eggs. He kept singing about Rikki-Tikki's triumph even when Rikki-**

Tikki wanted him to stop. He had a hard time realizing the importance of the information Rikki-Tikki needed.)** What does Rikki-Tikki learn from Darzee? **(He learns the location of the eggs.)** What role does Darzee's wife play in Rikki-Tikki's plan to destroy the eggs? **(She pretends she has a broken wing so she can lead Nagaina away from her eggs.)** What stops Rikki-Tikki from destroying all the eggs. **(He hears Darzee's wife screaming that Nagaina is on the veranda by the family.)**

3. Ask the student to predict how they think the story will end. **(Allow for individual answers.)**

Lesson 79

Review: Triple Consonant Blends nth, rth, mpt, nch, rch, tch

Overview:

- Define triple consonant blends
- Recall the sound of the triple consonant blends **nth**, **rth**, **mpt**, **nch**, **rch**, and **tch**
- Identify words containing triple consonant blends

Material and Supplies:

- Teacher's Guide and Student Workbook
- White board or chart paper
- Phonics flashcards
- Reader: "Rikki-Tikki-Tavi: Part IV"

Teaching Tips:

Review for Mastery. Discuss and review any work from the previous lesson that was assigned as homework. Check for completion of the activities and orally quiz the student for comprehension. Review any reading that was assigned, discussing the characters, setting, plot, theme, language, sequence, etc.

Strengthen fluency and phonemic awareness by reviewing words and sentences from the previous lessons. Build vocabulary skills by using some of the words in sentences.

You may want to review flashcards of words with triple consonant blends. The student can study these throughout the unit.

Lesson Introduction. This lesson reviews triple consonant blends. In this lesson the student will

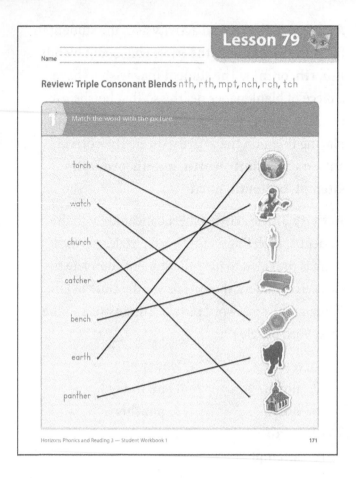

Name

Review: Triple Consonant Blends nth, rth, mpt, nch, rch, tch

1 Match the word with the picture.

torch

watch

church

catcher

bench

earth

panther

review the triple consonant blends **nth**, **rth**, **mpt**, **nch**, **rch**, and **tch**. On the board write the triple consonant blends **nth**, **rth**, **mpt**, **nch**, **rch**, and **tch**. Ask the student if he/she can think of words formed with each of the triple consonant blends. Examples include: **month**, **starch**, **prompt**, **bench**, **birch**, and **latch**.

Activity 1. The student should turn to the review activity sheet for this lesson. In the first activity the student will be asked to match the word with a triple consonant blend to the correct picture. Read through the words first before the student matches them with the picture. The words for this section are: **torch**, **watch**, **church**, **catcher**, **bench**, **earth**, **panther**.

Activity 2. The second activity asks the student to unscramble letters to form words with triple consonant blends. The student should recognize the letter combinations of the triple consonant blends and begin forming each word with one of them. The answers are: **pitch**, **branch**, **hatch**, **search**, **eleventh**, **birth**, **prompt**, **crunch**, **wrench**, **scratch**.

Activity 3. The final activity asks the student to underline words in each sentence which have triple consonant blends. Some sentences will have more than one. If this activity is challenging to your student, have him/her find only one triple consonant blend word in each sentence.

1. The dog **scratched** the **itch** behind his right ear.
2. After **lunch** Evan planned to practice his baseball **pitch**.
3. Our **church** added two new **benches**.
4. The **earth** has **north** and south poles.
5. Amy turned eight on the **ninth**.
6. A **finch** was **perched** on the tree **branch**.
7. Carson **stretched** before exercising.
8. Mrs. Russell put her **watch** on before she left for work.
9. Carla was looking forward to her **eighteenth birthday**.
10. The **panther** is a beautiful, swift animal.

Reading Activity.

1. You may want to review the selection "Rikki-Tikki-Tavi." Have the student briefly describe the main characters and action of the selection. The student should read the exciting conclusion of "Rikki-Tikki-Tavi: Part IV."

2. Discuss the selection with the student. How does Rikki-Tikki keep Nagaina from biting Teddy? (**He distracts her with the one egg he did not destroy.**) How does Darzee's wife continue to help Rikki-Tikki? (**She tries to slow down the snake by flapping her wings near Nagaina.**) What do we learn about the character of Rikki-Tikki from his encounter with Nagaina? (Answers include: **The mongoose was brave by going after Nagaina**

in the tunnel. Rikki-Tikki was also clever which was illustrated by how he used the egg to lure Nagaina away from the family. He didn't rest after killing Nagaina and her egg but he continued to keep the garden safe. He was also loyal to the family.**) How did the family show its appreciation for what Rikki-Tikki did? (**The family gave him an abundance of food. Notice that Rikki-Tikki ate the food because he wasn't worried about defeating the snakes anymore. The family also let him stay with them and sleep with Teddy.**) This story has been popular for over 100 years. Why do you think people still enjoy it? (**Allow for individual answers.**)

3. Have the student look for two examples of words with triple consonant blends in the final section of "Rikki-Tikki-Tavi." Examples include: **empty, earth, clenched, catch, watch.**

Lesson 80

Review

Overview:

- Define analogies
- Identify words which complete analogies
- Correctly form contractions
- Recall the sound of the triple consonant blends **nth**, **rth**, **mpt**, **nch**, **rch**, and **tch**
- Create words containing triple consonant blends

Material and Supplies:

- Teacher's Guide and Student Workbook
- White board or chart paper
- Phonics flashcards
- Reader: "The Elephant's Child"

Teaching Tips:

Review for Mastery. Discuss and review any work from the previous lesson that was assigned as homework. Check for completion of the activities and orally quiz the student for comprehension. Review any reading that was assigned, discussing the characters, setting, plot, theme, language, sequence, etc.

Strengthen fluency and phonemic awareness by reviewing words and sentences from the previous lessons. Build vocabulary skills by using some of the words in sentences.

You may want to review flashcards made for words in this unit.

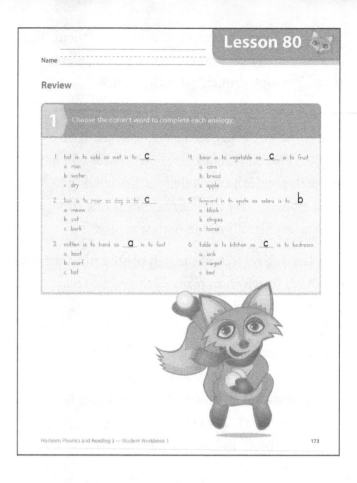

Lesson Introduction. This lesson reviews the material the student learned in the unit. Brainstorm with the student the themes of the unit. The student should recall learning about analogies, contractions, and three letter consonant blends. Ask the student to fill in the following analogy: **Stop is to go, as left is to _____ (right).** Ask the student to explain to you how analogies are formed. Make sure the student understands that analogies follow a logical pattern and can be formed using a variety of methods. Continue by writing on the board words which the student will need to make into contractions. Examples may include: **we would (we'd), I am (I'm), who is (who's),** and **could not (couldn't).** Finally review words with three letter consonant blends. Write the words **match, much, prompt,** and **faith** on the board. Ask the student which words have three letter consonant blends. The student should identify **match** and **prompt.**

Activity 1. The student should turn to the activity sheet which accompanies this lesson. The first activity asks the student to complete each analogy by choosing the correct word. The correct answers are: **c, c, a, c, b, c**.

Activity 2. The review continues with the next activity. In this activity, the student will take words and make them into contractions. The correct contractions are: **I'm, he'd, you're, who's, they'd, didn't**.

Activity 3. The next section is the first of two activities on three letter consonant blends. This first activity asks the student to fill in the blank with either an **rth** or **rch** ending. You may want to allow the student to have a piece of scratch paper in order to practice the word with each ending before filling the blank on the activity sheet. The correct answers are: **porch, perch, fourth, march, torch, earth**.

Activity 4. The final activity continues the review of triple consonant blends. In this activity the student will be asked to fill in the blank with the correct **tch** or **nch** ending. The correct answers are: **branch, hatch, punch, hitch, scratch, wrench/wretch**.

Reading Activity.

1. The student will read the selection "The Elephant's Child" for pleasure.

2. However, before the student reads the selection, tell the student that the poem "I Keep Six Honest Serving Men" was written as an introduction to the selection. As the student reads the story, he/she should think about why this poem is fitting for the selection.

Test 8

Lessons 71-80

Overview:

- Define analogies

- Identify words which complete analogies

- Correctly form contractions

- Recall the sound of the triple consonant blends **nth**, **rth**, **mpt**, **nch**, **rch**, and **tch**

- Create words containing triple consonant blends

Material and Supplies:

- Student Test

Teaching Tips:

Review for Mastery. Discuss and review any work from the previous lesson that was assigned as homework. Check for completion of the activities and orally quiz the student for comprehension. Review any reading that was assigned, discussing the characters, setting, plot, theme, language, sequence, etc.

Lesson Introduction. This lesson tests the material the student learned in the unit. Before the test you may want to ask the student if he/she has any final questions. There may be questions from the review the student will want to review. Remind the student that the final test follows the same format as the review.

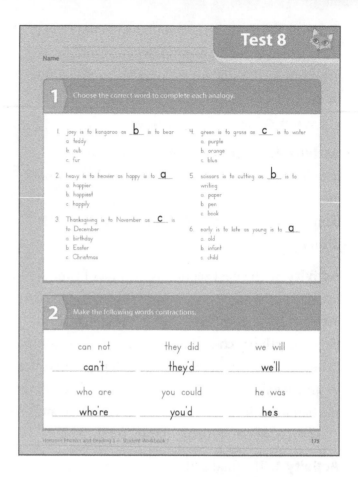

Activity 1. The student should turn to the test. The first activity asks the student to complete each analogy by choosing the correct word. The correct answers are: **b, a, c, c, b, a.**

Activity 2. The test continues with the next activity. In this activity, the student will take words and make them into contractions. The correct contractions are: **can't, they'd, we'll, who're, you'd, he's.**

Activity 3. The next section is the first of two activities on three letter consonant blends. This first activity asks the student to fill in the blank with either an **rth** or **rch** ending. You may want to allow the student to have a piece of scratch paper in order to practice the word with each ending before filling the blank on the test. The correct answers are: **arch, worth, birthday, search, church, forth**.

Activity 4. The final activity continues the testing of triple consonant blends. In this activity the student will be asked to fill in the blank with the correct **tch** or **nch** ending. The correct answers are: **patch, branch, match, hatch, punch, launch**.

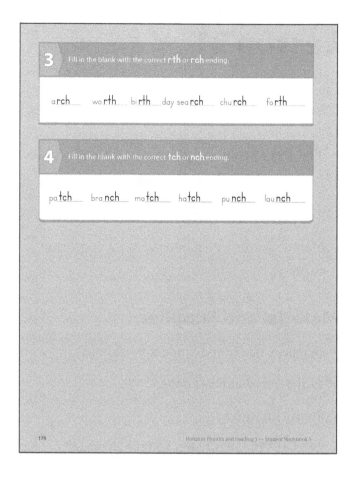

Lesson 81
Spelling Adjacent Clusters: rk, rm, rn, rt

Overview:

- Locate adjacent clusters **rk**, **rm**, **rn**, and **rt**
- Recognize adjacent clusters in words
- Identify words which have adjacent consonant clusters

Material and Supplies:

- Teacher's Guide and Student Workbook
- White board or chart paper
- Phonics flashcards
- Reader: "The Blind Men and the Elephant"

Teaching Tips:

Lesson Introduction. Write the words **shark**, **farm**, **corn**, and **part** on the board. Underline the letters **rk**, **rm**, **rn**, and **rt** in the words. Ask the student what sounds are made by the **r** letter clusters. Through the discussion help the student notice the sounds these letter combinations make. Ask the student to think of other words that have these letter combinations.

You may want to create flashcards of **rk**, **rm**, **rn**, and **rt** letter combinations. The student can study these throughout the unit.

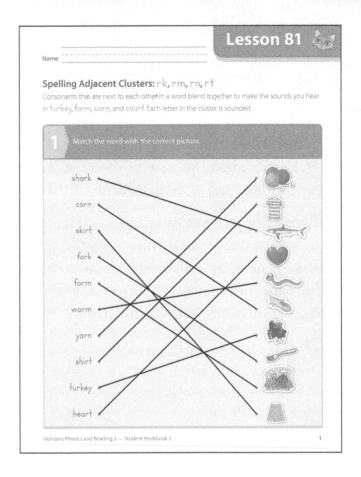

Activity 1. Ask the student to turn to the activity sheet which accompanies this lesson. Read through the definition of adjacent consonant clusters with the student. The student should then match the words with the pictures. Each of the words pictured contains a consonant blend with the letter **r**. The pictures are: **yarn**, **shirt**, **shark**, **heart**, **worm**, **corn**, **turkey**, **fork**, **farm**, **skirt**.

Activity 2. The student should continue to the next activity on the sheet. The student will be asked to fill in the blanks with the letter cluster **rk**, **rm**, **rn**, or **rt**. You may want to have the student use a piece of scratch paper to write out the words with possible letter clusters before filling in the blanks on the sheet. The answers to the activity are: **shark**, **dessert**, **sparkle**, **germ**, **heart**, **learn**, **clerk**, **thorn**, **platform**, **turkey**, **court**, **dirk/dirt**.

Activity 3. The student will need to choose the correct word to complete each sentence. Two choices are given for each sentence. The correct answers are: **turn, bark, dirt, fork, storm, art, barked, uniforms, acorn, concert.** After the student has completed the activity, have him/her read the sentences aloud.

Reading Activity.

1. Ask the student to turn to the reading for this lesson which is, "The Blind Men and the Elephant." Have the student read the selection.

2. After reading the selection, ask the student the following questions. How did the blind men decide they would discover what an elephant looked like? **(They decided to go to an elephant and use their hands to see.)** How was each person's description of the elephant accurate and inaccurate? **(They each described the part of the elephant they felt accurately. However, they did not get the entire picture.)** If you put all the men's descriptions together would you get an accurate picture? **(Allow for an individual response.)** What do you think is the meaning of the story? **(The story tells that people need to look at the whole picture and not just the parts. For example, the student may focus on how he/she spelled a word incorrectly rather than on the wonderful story he/she wrote.)**

3. As an added activity, ask the student to draw an elephant like the one the men described. The student can compare this with what an elephant really looks like.

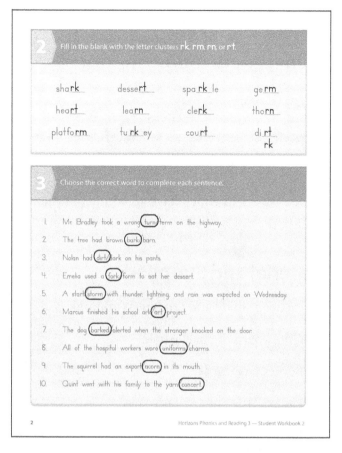

Lesson 82

Silent Letters: mb, bt, rh, kn, mn

Overview:

- Locate adjacent clusters **mb**, **bt**, **rh**, **kn**, and **mn**

- Recognize adjacent clusters in words

- Identify words which have adjacent consonant clusters

Material and Supplies:

- Teacher's Guide and Student Workbook

- White board or chart paper

- Phonics flashcards

- Reader: "The Sugar-Plum Tree"

Teaching Tips:

Review for Mastery. Discuss and review any work from the previous lesson that was assigned as homework. Check for completion of the activities and orally quiz the student for comprehension. Review any reading that was assigned, discussing the characters, setting, plot, theme, language, sequence, etc.

Strengthen fluency and phonemic awareness by reviewing words and sentences from the previous lessons. Build vocabulary skills by using some of the words in sentences.

You may want to create flashcards of words which contain **mb**, **bt**, **rh**, **kn**, and **mn**. The student can study these throughout the unit.

Lesson Introduction. Ask the student how he/she has changed in the previous year. For example the student may have grown taller, learned to play an instrument, or received glasses. Tell the student that just like people change over time so

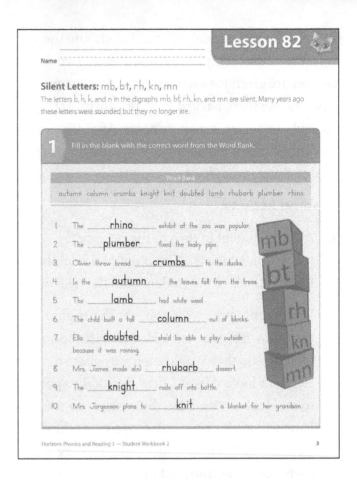

does the way words are spelled or pronounced. Write the words **eft** and **betwenan** on the board. Ask the student to pronounce the words. Then ask the student if he/she knows what the words mean. The first word **eft** means back and the word **betwenan** means between. This is how these words were written and pronounced over 1000 years ago. Explain that language and spelling changes over time. The words in today's lesson have silent letters. At one time, these silent letters were pronounced, but they are no longer sounded today.

Write the words **numb**, **doubt**, **rhyme**, **know**, and **autumn** on the board. Ask the student what letters are silent in the letters on the board. The student should recognize that the letters **b**, **h**, **k**, and **n** are not pronounced. This lesson will focus on other words which have these silent letters.

Activity 1. The student should turn to the activity sheet which accompanies this lesson. Read through the definition regarding silent letters. The student should look at the first section of the activity sheet. The student will fill in the blanks with words that complete each sentence. A Word Bank is provided. The correct answers are: **rhino, plumber, crumbs, autumn, lamb, column, doubted, rhubarb, knight, knit.**

Activity 2. The student will be asked to fill in the blank with the letter combinations **mb, bt, rh, kn,** and **mn.** The student may want to have a piece of scratch paper available to practice writing the word before filling in the blanks on the activity sheet. The answers are: **debt, knuckle, climb, column, bomb, knit, thumb, limb, rhyme, doubt, hymn, rhythm.**

Activity 3. The final activity is a word search. All the words for the word search have silent letters. You may want to have the student read each of the words before completing the word search. As an added activity, have the student choose three words to use in sentences. **See image for answers.**

Reading Activity.

1. Ask the student to turn to the selection, "The Sugar-Plum Tree." Read the selection to the student as he/she follows along in the book. Explain any words the student may not know or understand. Next, ask the student to read the selection with you. Finally, have the student read the poem to you.

2. After reading the poem to you, ask the student the following questions. Who is telling the story? **(The story is probably being told by a mom or dad.)** At what time would the parent tell the story? How do you know? **(The parent would probably tell the story at night before the child goes to bed. At the end the words "nightcap and gown" are used, hinting that the poem would be read before bedtime.)** What is "Shut-

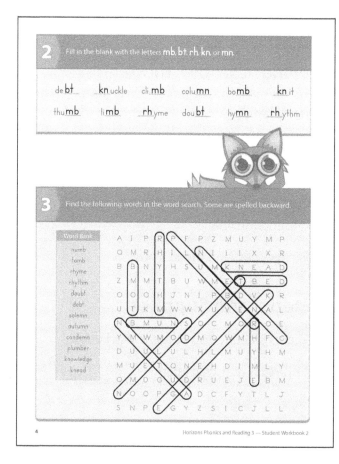

Eye Town?" **(This represents sleep or dreams.)** What does Shut-Eye town look like? **(There are trees and a lake lined with fruit and candy. The children are happy. There is a chocolate cat and a gingerbread dog.)** Give an example of a description in the poem you liked. **(Allow for a personal reflection.)**

3. Continue by asking the student to look at how the poem is arranged. Direct the student in recognizing the poem has stanzas of four lines. How many syllables are in each line? **(The first and third lines have eight syllables and the second and fourth lines have eleven syllables.)** What is the rhyme scheme of the poem? **(The rhyme scheme of each stanza is abab.)** What is an example of this rhyme scheme? **(The student can give an example like around/ground and that/cat.)** Finally ask the student to find a word that uses the silent letter **b.** (Examples are: **climb, limb.)**

Lesson 83

Spelling: nge, pse, mpse

Overview:

- Learn how to form words with **nge**, **pse**, and **mpse** letter combinations

- Identify words with **nge**, **pse**, and **mpse** combinations

- Use **nge**, **pse**, and **mpse** words

Material and Supplies:

- Teacher's Guide and Student Workbook

- White board or chart paper

- Phonics flashcards

- Reader: "The Months"

Teaching Tips:

Review for Mastery. Discuss and review any work from the previous lesson that was assigned as homework. Check for completion of the activities and orally quiz the student for comprehension. Review any reading that was assigned, discussing the characters, setting, plot, theme, language, sequence, etc.

Strengthen fluency and phonemic awareness by reviewing words and sentences from the previous lessons. Build vocabulary skills by using some of the words in sentences.

You may want to create flashcards of words which have the letter combinations **nge**, **pse**, and **mpse**. The student can study these throughout the unit.

Lesson Introduction. Write the word endings **nge**, **pse**, and **mpse** on the board. Tell the student that sometimes these letter combinations work together to form the ends of words. Write the vowel **a** in front of **nge** and **pse** and see if the

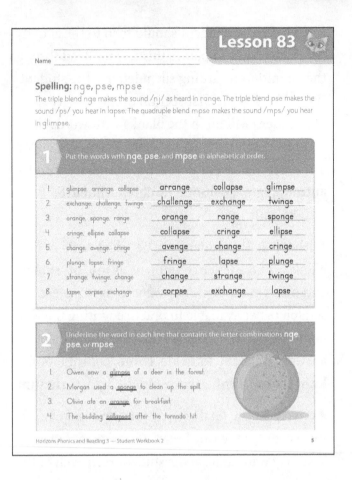

student can think of words that have these endings. For example: **strange**, **range**, and **lapse** are words that can be formed. Tell the student in this lesson he/she will study other words formed with these letter combinations.

Activity 1. The student should turn to the activity sheet which accompanies the lesson. Read through the definition at the top of the sheet. The student will then go on to complete the first section of the activity sheet. Read through the words in each line and then ask the student to put them in alphabetical order. Reading the words first will help the student hear the three and four letter combinations. The answers are:

1. **arrange, collapse, glimpse**
2. **challenge, exchange, twinge**
3. **orange, range, sponge**
4. **collapse, cringe, ellipse**
5. **avenge, change, cringe**

6. **fringe, lapse, plunge**

7. **change, strange, twinge**

8. **corpse, exchange, lapse**

Activity 2. The lesson continues with the student identifying words with the **nge**, **pse**, and **mpse** in sentences. You may want to read each sentence to the student and then ask him/her to underline the appropriate word or words. The correct answers are: **glimpse, sponge, orange, collapsed, arranged, eclipse, change, twinge.**

Activity 3. The final lesson activity is a crossword puzzle. The student is provided with a Word Bank for the activity. Have the student identify the words that go with the clues and fill in the crossword puzzle. The answers are:

Across:	Down:
3. **glimpse**	1. **collapse**
5. **arrange**	2. **fringe**
8. **challenge**	4. **orange**
9. **change**	6. **exchange**
10. **eclipse**	7. **range**

Reading Activity.

1. Ask the student his/her birth month. How would the student describe the month of his/her birth? Write the descriptions on the board. Tell the student you will come back to the descriptions later.

2. Ask the student to turn to the selection, "The Months." Read the selection with the student.

3. After the student has read the selection, discuss it with your student. Ask the student to describe the different months as presented by the author. Ask the student if he/she disagrees with any of the descriptions. Help the student to recognize that the descriptions are more fitting to people living in northern climates where the seasons clearly change. Go back to the description the student wrote about his/her birth month. Have

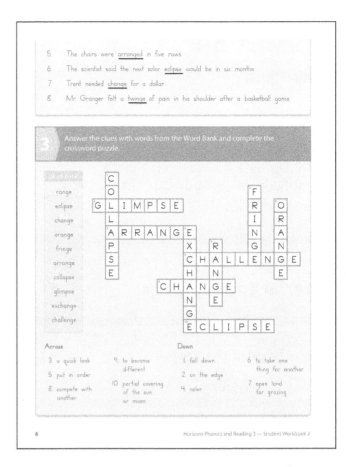

the student compare the author's description with his/her own.

4. Look at the style in which the poem was written. The student should notice that the poem is written in rhyming couplets. Each line has seven syllables.

5. As an added activity, have the student write his/her own couplets like those in the poem.

Lesson 84

Spelling: nce

Overview:

- Learn how to sound the letter combination **nce**

- Identify the /ns/ sound made by the letter combination **nce**

- Use words with **nce** in sentences

Material and Supplies:

- Teacher's Guide and Student Workbook

- White board or chart paper

- Phonics flashcards

- Reader: "The Magic Thread: Part I"

Teaching Tips:

Review for Mastery. Discuss and review any work from the previous lesson that was assigned as homework. Check for completion of the activities and orally quiz the student for comprehension. Review any reading that was assigned, discussing the characters, setting, plot, theme, language, sequence, etc.

Strengthen fluency and phonemic awareness by reviewing words and sentences from the previous lessons. Build vocabulary skills by using some of the words in sentences.

You may want to create flashcards of words which contain the letter combination **nce**. The student can study these throughout the unit.

Lesson Introduction. Write the word **chance** on the board. Ask the student if he/she can think of any words that rhyme with **chance**. Answers include: **dance, prance,** and **France**. Tell the student in this lesson he/she will study words ending with **nce**. Not all will be preceded by the letter **a**.

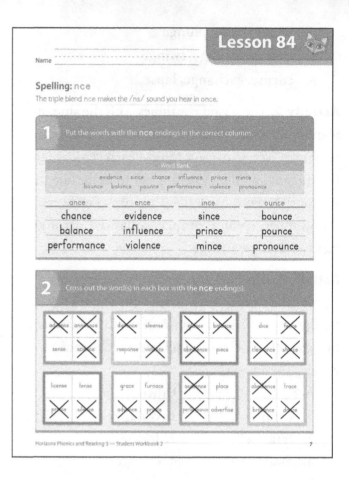

Activity 1. The student should turn to the activity sheet which accompanies this lesson. Ask the student to read the words listed which have **nce** endings. The student will need to put the words in columns based on the vowel that precedes the **nce** ending. The answers for the activity are as follows:

ance	ence	ince	ounce
chance	evidence	since	bounce
balance	influence	prince	pounce
performance	violence	mince	pronounce

Activity 2. The next activity asks the student to identify the words in each box which have **nce** endings. Read through the words within the box with the student. The student should cross out the words with the **nce** endings. The answers to the activity are as follows:

- **advance, announce, science**
- **distance, violence**
- **glance, balance, obedience**
- **fence, clearance, stance**
- **prince, silence**
- **advance, prince**
- **audience, performance**
- **obedience, brilliance, dance**

Activity 3. The final activity asks the student to choose the best word to complete each sentence. You may want to have the student read the sentences with each possible answer before the student circles the correct answer. The answers for the activity are: **audience, distance, lance, bounced, pounced, ambulance, attendance, entrance.**

Reading Activity.

1. Have the student turn to the selection, "The Magic Thread." Ask the student to read Part I of the selection.

2. After reading the selection, discuss it with the student. Who was the main character? (**Peter**) Describe him. (**He was a young boy who went to school.**) What did he like? (**He enjoyed daydreaming and thinking about the future. He liked Liese.**) What didn't he like? (**He didn't seem to like anything he was doing at the time.**) What happened when he went to the

woods? (**He met an old woman with a silver ball and thread.**) If he pulled the thread, what would happen? (**If he pulled the thread, time would move more quickly. If he did nothing, time would move at the same speed.**) What would be the advantage or disadvantage of having time move slower or faster? (**Allow the student to provide individual responses.**)

3. Have the student predict what he/she thinks Peter will do. Ask the student why he/she has that opinion. (**Allow for individual responses.**)

Lesson 85

Spelling: ture

Overview:

- Learn how to pronounce words with **-ture** endings
- Identify words which contain **-ture**
- Use words with **-ture** in sentences

Material and Supplies:

- Teacher's Guide and Student Workbook
- White board or chart paper
- Phonics flashcards
- Reader: "The Magic Thread: Part II"

Teaching Tips:

Review for Mastery. Discuss and review any work from the previous lesson that was assigned as homework. Check for completion of the activities and orally quiz the student for comprehension. Review any reading that was assigned, discussing the characters, setting, plot, theme, language, sequence, etc.

Strengthen fluency and phonemic awareness by reviewing words and sentences from the previous lessons. Build vocabulary skills by using some of the words in sentences.

You may want to create flashcards of words which contain **-ture** words. The student can study these throughout the unit.

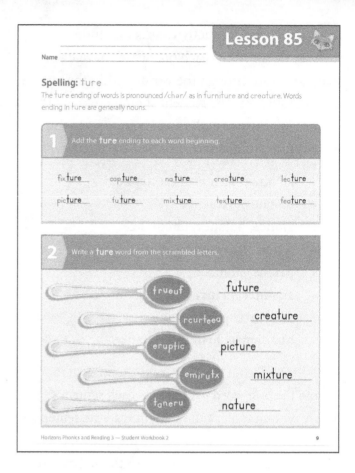

Lesson Introduction. On the board write the word **creature**. Ask the student how the **-ture** part of the word sounds. The sound is **(chər)**. In this lesson the student will study words that make the **(chər)** sound and end in **ture**. See if the student can think of other words that would fit the pattern. Examples include: **feature**, **future**, and **nature**.

Activity 1. The student should turn to the activity sheet which accompanies this lesson. The first activity asks the student to add the **-ture** ending to word beginnings. After the student has written the words, have him/her pronounce them. The answers to the activity are: **fixture, capture, nature, creature, lecture, picture, future, mixture, texture, feature**.

Activity 2. The next activity asks the student to take scrambled letters and create words. The student should recognize the **-ture** endings for the words. The answers to the activity are: **future, creature, picture, mixture, nature**.

Activity 3. The final activity asks the student to complete sentences using -**ture** words. A Word Bank is provided to assist the student in this activity. Have the student read the sentences after he/she has chosen the correct word. The answers to the sentences are: **Scripture, posture, creature, future, picture, temperature, culture, capture, mixture, structure**.

Reading Activity.

1. The student should return to the selection, "The Magic Thread." You may want to review the main characters and plot before having the student read Part II.

2. Since the second section of the reading is long, there will not be time for an extended discussion about it with the student. Instead, take some time and read along with the student. You may want to ask clarifying questions as you read through the story.

3. At the conclusion, ask the student what choice he/she thinks Peter will make. Have the student explain his/her answer.

Use the Word Bank to find words to fill in the blanks.

Word Bank

creature   culture   capture   Scripture   future
picture   structure   mixture   temperature   posture

1. The minister read a passage of ___Scripture___ from Luke.

2. Jacob stood straight and tall with excellent ___posture___.

3. Mrs. Roth couldn't find the ___creature___ that was hiding under her porch.

4. The teacher said there would be a math test sometime in the ___future___.

5. Devin took a ___picture___ of his sister next to an elephant.

6. The newspaper said that the ___temperature___ would only be 20 degrees F. on Monday.

7. Beth was studying Japanese ___culture___ in school.

8. The police planned to ___capture___ the escaped prisoner.

9. Mr. Tapper made a dessert which was a ___mixture___ of cake and ice cream.

10. The city planned to put up a large new ___structure___ in an empty lot.

10   Horizons Phonics and Reading 3 — Student Workbook 2

Lesson 86

Consonant –le Syllables: ble, dle, fle

Overview:

- Learn to sound the -**le** endings

- Identify words with -**le** endings

- Use words with -**le** endings

Material and Supplies:

- Teacher's Guide and Student Workbook

- White board or chart paper

- Phonics flashcards

- Reader: "The Magic Thread: Part III"

Teaching Tips:

Review for Mastery. Discuss and review any work from the previous lesson that was assigned as homework. Check for completion of the activities and orally quiz the student for comprehension. Review any reading that was assigned, discussing the characters, setting, plot, theme, language, sequence, etc.

Strengthen fluency and phonemic awareness by reviewing words and sentences from the previous lessons. Build vocabulary skills by using some of the words in sentences.

You may want to create flashcards of words with -**le** endings. The student can study these throughout the unit.

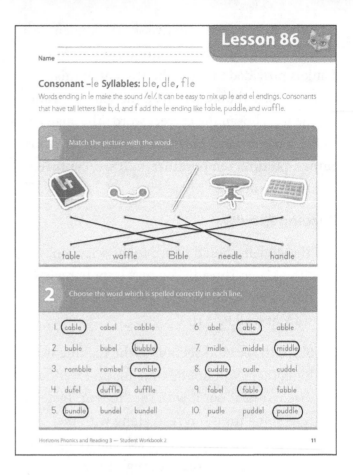

Lesson Introduction. Ask the student to come to the board and write the words **cradle** and **towel**. Have the student note that one word ends in -**le** and the other -**el**, although the endings sound the same. Explain that spelling -**le** and -**el** words can be confusing. The majority of words end in **le**. Words with a tall letter before the ending like **b**, **d**, and **f** add -**le**. Those are the words the student will study in this lesson.

Activity 1. The student should turn to the activity sheet which accompanies this lesson. Ask the student to read the explanation about words ending in -**le**. In the first activity the student will be asked to match the picture with the word. Have the student read the words first and then match the words with the picture. The pictured words are: **Bible, handle, needle, table, waffle.**

Activity 2. The next activity asks the student to identify the word which is spelled correctly in each line. Remind the student that first of all he/she should look for words ending in **-le**. It may be helpful to read each word first so that the student can both see and hear how the word is spelled. The answers are: **cable, bubble, ramble, duffle, bundle, able, middle, cuddle, fable, puddle**.

Activity 3. The final activity is a series of rhymes. A Word Bank is provided to help the student fill in the blanks. You may want to have the student complete this activity aloud rather than silently. Hearing the rhymes may help the student choose the correct response. The answers to the rhymes are: **fable, fiddle, riddle, handle, table, waffle, duffle, poodle, needle, fumble**.

Reading Activity.

1. The student will finish reading the selection "The Magic Thread: Part III."

2. After reading the selection, discuss it with your student. Why did Peter start pulling the thread? **(He wanted his school day to go faster.)** During what parts of his life did he pull the thread? **(He often pulled the thread when he was bored or life was difficult.)** What joyful events do you think he missed because he pulled the thread? **(He may have missed the daily events which bring a person joy such as a sunrise, sunset, or a funny story.)** In the end, he chose to have life go back as it had been before. Why do you think he did this? **(He realized what he had missed. He also noted how quickly life had passed.)** What lesson is the reader to learn from the selection? (Answers may include: **contentment in life, the brevity of life, the need to experience both the good and bad in life.)**

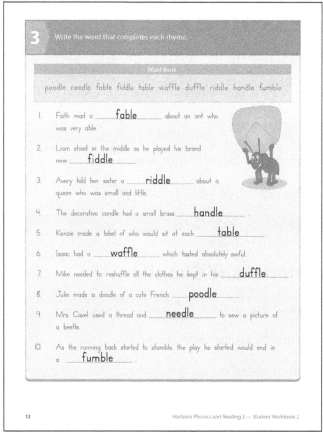

Lesson 87

Consonant -le Syllables: ple, sle, tle, zle

Overview:

- Learn to sound the **-le** endings
- Identify words with **-le** endings
- Use words with **-le** endings

Material and Supplies:

- Teacher's Guide and Student Workbook
- White board or chart paper
- Phonics flashcards
- Reader: "The Boy Who Cried Wolf"

Teaching Tips:

Review for Mastery. Discuss and review any work from the previous lesson that was assigned as homework. Check for completion of the activities and orally quiz the student for comprehension. Review any reading that was assigned, discussing the characters, setting, plot, theme, language, sequence, etc.

Strengthen fluency and phonemic awareness by reviewing words and sentences from the previous lessons. Build vocabulary skills by using some of the words in sentences.

You may want to create flashcards of words with **-le** endings. The student can study these throughout the unit.

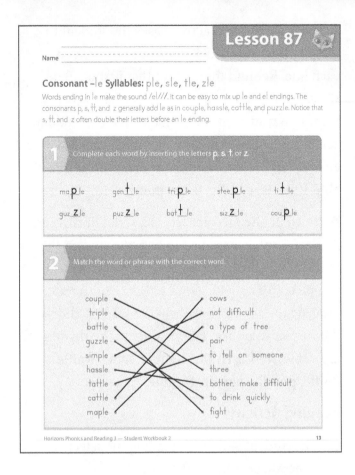

Lesson Introduction. Tell the student that the study of **-le** words will continue in this lesson. What words from the previous lesson did the student learn that end in **-le**? Answers include: **bubble** and **middle**. Other letters that often use **-le** endings include p, s, t, and z. See if the student can think of words ending in **-ple**, **-sle**, **-tle**, or **-zle**. Answers include: **apple, hassle, battle,** and **puzzle**. Note that many of these words double the consonant before the ending.

Activity 1. Ask the student to turn to the activity sheet which accompanies this lesson. The student should read the definition at the top of the page. The student should then complete the first activity. In it the student will be asked to insert the consonant **p, s, t,** or **z** before the **-le** ending to correctly spell the word. The answers are: **maple, gentle, triple, steeple, title, guzzle, puzzle, battle, sizzle, couple.**

Activity 2. The student should continue by matching words with **-le** endings with their correct descriptions. The answers are as follows:

couple	pair
triple	three
battle	fight
guzzle	to drink quickly
simple	not difficult
hassle	bother, make difficult
tattle	to tell on someone
cattle	cows
maple	a type of tree

Activity 3. The final activity on the sheet asks the student to circle the word in each sentence that contains a consonant and **-le** ending. Before the student completes the activity, have him/her read each of the sentences aloud. This will reinforce the sound the **-le** ending of words makes.

1. The baby had a **dimple** in his chin.
2. The **battle** took place outside the **castle** gates.
3. The child fixed a **simple puzzle**.
4. The church **steeple** was painted white.
5. A **gentle** rain fell during the night.
6. The **people** planted **maple** trees in the park.
7. Paul was an **apostle** of Jesus.
8. Mr. Banks hoped there was a **simple** solution to his car's **rattle**.

Reading Activity.

1. The student should turn to the poem, "The Boy Who Cried Wolf." Read the selection with the student. Have the student read one line and you the next. This will assist the student in noting the **abab** rhyme scheme.

2. After reading the poem, discuss its themes with the student. Use some of the following questions to assist your discussion. What was the young boy's job? **(He was to care for his family's flock of sheep.)** Why didn't he like his job? **(He thought it was boring. There was no one to talk to as he did his job.)** How did the boy decide to make his day more exciting? **(He said there was a wolf attacking his flock and he needed help.)** What reaction did he receive from the villagers? **(They dropped everything and came to help.)** What were the consequences of the boy's lies? **(When a wolf came, the villagers did not go to help. They assumed that it was another lie told by the boy. All of the sheep he was to care for were killed.)** What lesson should a reader take from this poem? **(The primary lesson is the importance of telling the truth.)**

3. Continue the discussion by analyzing how the poem is put together. **The poem is written in four line stanzas of 12 syllables of length. The rhyme scheme is abab.**

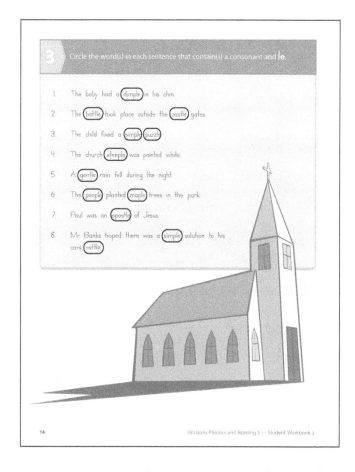

Lesson 88

Consonant -le Syllables: gle, cle, ckle, kle

Overview:

- Learn to sound the **-le** endings
- Identify words with **-le** endings
- Use words with **-le** endings

Material and Supplies:

- Teacher's Guide and Student Workbook
- White board or chart paper
- Phonics flashcards
- Reader: "The Green Sea Turtle"

Teaching Tips:

Review for Mastery. Discuss and review any work from the previous lesson that was assigned as homework. Check for completion of the activities and orally quiz the student for comprehension. Review any reading that was assigned, discussing the characters, setting, plot, theme, language, sequence, etc.

Strengthen fluency and phonemic awareness by reviewing words and sentences from the previous lessons. Build vocabulary skills by using some of the words in sentences.

You may want to create flashcards of words with **-le** endings. The student can study these throughout the unit.

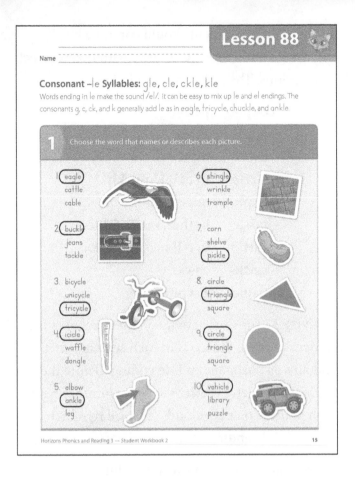

Lesson Introduction. Ask the student to recall words with **-le** endings. Ask the student what consonants went before these endings. The student should remember that consonants like **p** and **t** come before the **-le** ending. Tell the student that in this lesson the focus will be on the letters **g**, **c**, and **k** that come before **-le**. The student will also learn about the letter combination **ck** that comes before **-le** endings. Ask the student if he/she can think of any words that end in **-ckle** or **-gle**. Answers may include: **cackle** and **giggle**.

Activity 1. Have the student turn to the activity sheet which accompanies this lesson. Ask the student to read the definition at the top of the page. The student will then be asked to choose the word with a **-gle, -cle, -ckle,** or **-kle** ending that best describes each picture. It may be helpful to have the student identify the pictures before determining which word goes with each. The correct answers are: **eagle, buckle, tricycle, icicle, ankle, shingle, pickle, triangle, circle, vehicle.**

Activity 2. Ask the student to look at the next section of the activity sheet. Here the student will be asked to cross out the extra letter in each word. As the student works, he/she should remember that the endings of the words must always be **-gle, -cle, -ckle,** or **-kle.** After the student has completed the activity, have him/her read the words aloud. The correct spellings are: **ankle, circle, angle, beagle, buckle, jingle, wrinkle, pickle, twinkle, miracle.**

Activity 3. The final activity asks the student to answer questions with words ending in **-gle, -cle, -ckle,** or **-kle.** A Word Bank is provided to assist the student in answering each of the questions. The correct responses are: **giggle, twinkle, pickle, bicycle, wrinkle, icicle, eagle, jingle.**

Reading Activity.

1. The student should turn to the selection, "The Green Sea Turtle." Have the student read the selection and look for three interesting facts. You may want to have the student write down these facts.

2. After reading the selection, ask the student to share the facts he/she found.

3. Continue by highlighting some of the information contained in the selection. How are/aren't the turtles able to protect themselves from predators? (**Their shells provide protection. Their size also aids them in being able to protect themselves. On land the turtles are very slow which makes them vulnerable.**)

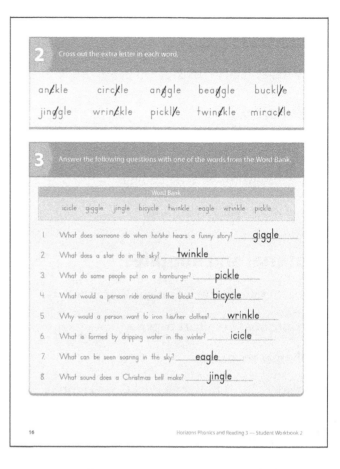

How did God make the turtles suitable for their lives in the ocean? (**The turtles have flippers which enable them to swim quickly in the ocean. Their eyes are also suited for seeing underwater. Finally, they were created so that they can stay underwater for long periods of time.**) What problems do these turtles face? (**The primary problem sea turtles face is that the beaches, where they lay eggs, are being developed.**)

4. As an added activity, have the student draw a picture of a green sea turtle.

Lesson 89

Review: Consonant –le Syllables

Overview:

- Learn to sound the **-le** endings
- Identify words with **-le** endings
- Use words with **-le** endings

Material and Supplies:

- Teacher's Guide and Student Workbook
- White board or chart paper
- Phonics flashcards
- Reader: "Puss in Boots: Puss Goes Hunting"

Teaching Tips:

Review for Mastery. Discuss and review any work from the previous lesson that was assigned as homework. Check for completion of the activities and orally quiz the student for comprehension. Review any reading that was assigned, discussing the characters, setting, plot, theme, language, sequence, etc.

Strengthen fluency and phonemic awareness by reviewing words and sentences from the previous lessons. Build vocabulary skills by using some of the words in sentences.

You may want to review flashcards of words with **-le** endings. The student can study these throughout the unit.

Lesson Introduction. Tell the student that in the previous lessons he/she has been studying words ending in a consonant plus **-le**. In this lesson, the student will review those various endings. Ask

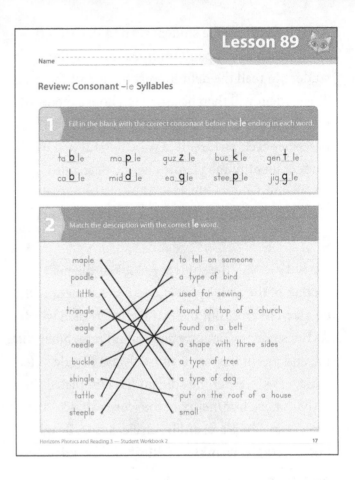

the student to brainstorm a list of all the endings he/she learned. If the student can't remember them all, remind him/her that they were **-ble, -dle, -fle, -ple, -sle, -tle, -zle, -gle, -cle, -ckle**, and **-kle**. Write the endings on the board and see if the student can list a word for each one. Answers would be: **Bible, puddle, waffle, apple, hassle, cattle, puzzle, wiggle, icicle, tackle**, and **ankle**.

Activity 1. Ask the student to turn to the activity sheet accompanying this lesson. In the first activity the student will need to fill in the blank with the correct consonant in order to form a word. You may want to have a piece of scratch paper available. The student can write out each word before filling in the blank on the sheet. After the student has correctly written each word, have the student read the words to you. The answers are: **table, maple, guzzle, buckle, gentle, cable, middle, eagle, steeple, jiggle**.

Activity 2. The next activity asks the student to match the description with the correct **-le** word. Have the student read through the words in the list first. The student can go on to complete the matching activity. The answers are as follows:

maple	a type of tree
poodle	a type of dog
little	small
triangle	a shape with three sides
eagle	a type of bird
needle	used for sewing
buckle	found on a belt
shingle	put on the roof of a house
tattle	to tell on someone
steeple	found on top of a church

Activity 3. The final section asks the student to identify the **-le** words in Bible passages. Read each Bible passage to your student as he/she follows along. The student should go on to identify the words ending in **-le** in each of the passages. The correct answers are: **needle, humble, gentle, stumble, eagles**.

Reading Activity.

1. The student should turn to the selection "Puss in Boots: Puss Goes Hunting." This selection has quite a few lines of dialogue. Your student may find it enjoyable to read the part of Puss and have you read the lines of the cat's master and the king. You can take turns reading the narrative section.

2. After reading the selection, discuss it with your student. Begin with the setting of the story. **(The story is set in the past in a rural kingdom.)** Who are the main characters? **(Puss, the youngest son, and the king.)** What problem is presented at the beginning of the

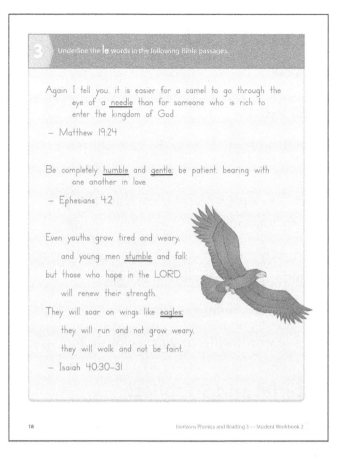

selection? **(The youngest son receives a cat as his inheritance.)** How does the cat show that he is clever? **(He captures food and brings it to the king. He arranges for the man not to have his dirty clothes on so the king can give him good ones. The cat acts as if his master is an important and wealthy man and the king treats him like one.)** What lesson does the youngest son learn? **(He learns that he shouldn't be quick to judge the people, or cats, by their looks. Often they have unknown or unseen abilities.)**

3. If time permits, have the student imagine another adventure for "Puss in Boots." You could have the student write the adventure, orally tell you the adventure, or draw the adventure.

Lesson 90

Review

Overview:

- Define words with adjacent letter clusters **rk**, **rm**, **rn**, and **rt**

- Identify words with the silent letter blends **mb**, **bt**, **rh**, **kn**, and **mn**

- Correctly form words with triple and quadruple blends **nge**, **pse**, **mpse**, and **nce**

- Recall words ending in **-ture**

- Create words with consonant plus **-le** endings

Material and Supplies:

- Teacher's Guide and Student Workbook

- White board or chart paper

- Phonics flashcards

- Reader: "Puss in Boots: Puss and the Lion"

Teaching Tips:

Review for Mastery. Discuss and review any work from the previous lesson that was assigned as homework. Check for completion of the activities and orally quiz the student for comprehension. Review any reading that was assigned, discussing the characters, setting, plot, theme, language, sequence, etc.

Strengthen fluency and phonemic awareness by reviewing words and sentences from the previous lessons. Build vocabulary skills by using some of the words in sentences.

You may want to review flashcards made for words in this unit.

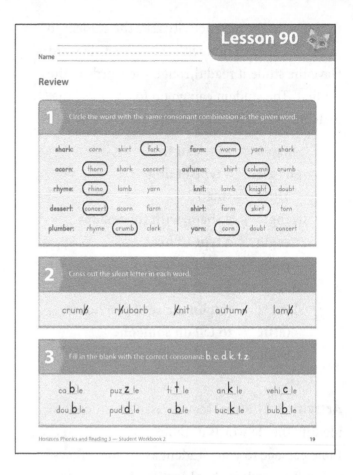

Lesson Introduction. This lesson reviews all of the material covered in the unit. Have the student recall the adjacent clusters he/she studied earlier. These include: **rk**, **rm**, **rn**, and **rt**. Ask the student to list words which match the letter clusters. Examples include: **park**, **farm**, **corn**, and **part**. Next remind the student of the silent letter clusters in the second lesson of the unit. These were **mb**, **bt**, **rh**, **kn**, and **mn**. Ask the student to think of words with these silent letter combinations. Examples include: **lamb**, **doubt**, **rhyme**, **know**, and **autumn**. The third and fourth lessons in the unit looked at triple and quadruple letter blends as in **nge**, **pse**, **nce**, and **mpse**. Again, ask the student for word examples. These include: **range**, **collapse**, **chance**, and **glimpse**. The student went on to learn about words ending with the **-ture** as in **creature**. The remainder of the lessons explored words ending with a consonant plus **-le**. These include the endings **-ble**, **-dle**, **-fle**, **-ple**, **-sle**, **-tle**, **-zle**, **-gle**, **-cle**, **-ckle**, and **-kle**. Again ask the student if he/she can think of words with these endings. Possible examples include: **cable, waddle, waffle, apple, hassle, title, puzzle, eagle, circle, chuckle,** and **ankle.** The review sheet will be arranged like the test.

Activity 1. Ask the student to turn to the activity sheet which accompanies this lesson. The first activity asks the student to circle the word with the same consonant combination as the given word. The answers are: **fork, thorn, rhino, concert, crumb, worm, column, knight, skirt, corn.**

Activity 2. The next activity reviews silent letter combinations. The student will need to cross out the silent letter in each word in the activity. The answers are: **b, h, k, n, b.**

Activity 3. The student should look at the next activity. Here the student should fill in the blank with the correct consonant before the **-le** endings. The answers are: **cable, puzzle, title, ankle, vehicle, double, puddle, able, buckle, bubble.**

Activity 4. The student should continue by matching the word with the picture. All of these are words with consonant plus **-le** endings. **See image for answers.**

Activity 5. The final activity asks the student to read sentences and fill in the blanks with words that best complete them. A Word Bank is provided to help the student. The answers are: **fixture, waffle, nature, plumber, fence, ankle, puddle, collapse, eagle, title.** After the student has completed the activity, have him/her read the questions aloud.

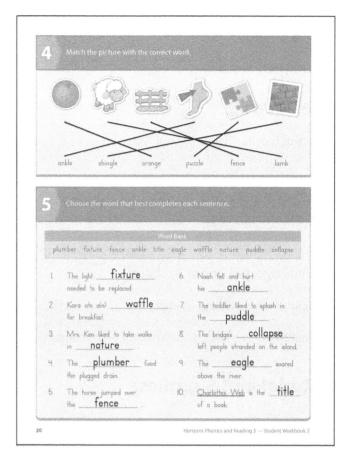

Reading Activity.

1. The selection for this lesson is a continuation of the story "Puss in Boots: Puss and the Lion." The student will read another short adventure of the colorful character introduced in the previous lesson.

2. The student will read this selection for pleasure.

Test 9

Lessons 81-90

Overview:

- Define words with adjacent letter clusters **rk**, **rm**, **rn**, and **rt**

- Identify words with the silent letter blends **mb**, **bt**, **rh**, **kn**, and **mn**

- Correctly form words with triple and quadruple blends **nge**, **pse**, **mpse**, and **nce**

- Recall words ending in **-ture**

- Create words with consonant plus **-le** endings

Material and Supplies:

- Student Test

Teaching Tips:

Review for Mastery. Discuss and review any work from the previous lesson that was assigned as homework. Check for completion of the activities and orally quiz the student for comprehension. Review any reading that was assigned, discussing the characters, setting, plot, theme, language, sequence, etc.

Lesson Introduction. This lesson tests using the material the student learned in the unit. Before the test you may want to ask the student if he/she has any final questions. There may be questions from the review the student will want to ask. Remind the student that the final test follows the same format as the review.

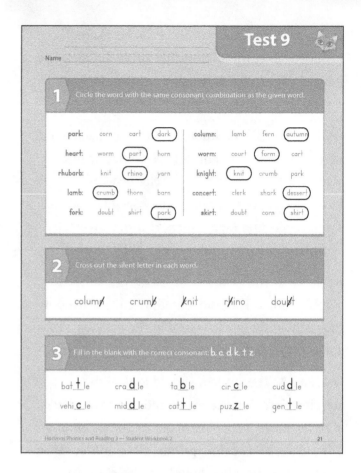

Activity 1. The first section asks the student to circle the word with the same consonant combination as the given word. The answers are: **dark, part, rhino, crumb, park, autumn, form, knit, dessert, shirt**.

Activity 2. The student should go on to the next activity in the test. Here the student is to cross through the silent letter in each word. The answers are: **n, b, k, h, b**.

Activity 3. The next section of the test asks the student to fill in the blank with the correct consonant before the -**le** ending. The answers are: **battle, cradle, table, circle, cuddle, vehicle, middle, cattle, puzzle, gentle**.

Activity 4. The test continues with the student matching words with pictures. The pictures are: **needle, circle, table, eagle, prince, waffle**.

Activity 5. The final activity has the student choose the word that best completes each sentence. A Word Bank is provided to assist the students. The answers are: **balance, license, Bible, bubble, lamb, circle, puzzle, battle, since, autumn**.

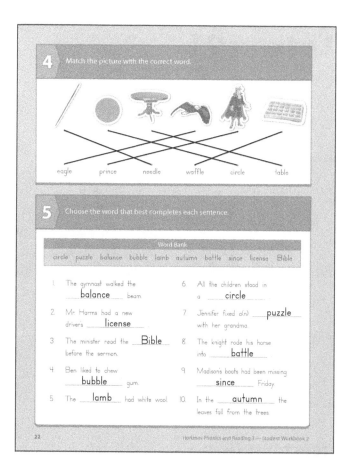

Lesson 91
CVC Pattern

Overview:

- Locate the CVC pattern in words
- Recognize words with the CVC pattern
- Identify the CVC pattern

Materials and Supplies:

- Teacher's Guide and Student Workbook
- White board or chart paper
- Phonics flashcards
- Reader: "The Caterpillar"

Teaching Tips:

Lesson Introduction. Explain to the student that in this unit the student will be studying consonant and vowel patterns in words. In this lesson the student will look at single syllable words which follow the consonant-vowel-consonant pattern. When a vowel is located between two consonants in a single syllable word, it has a short sound. Write the words **big** and **little** on the board. Ask the student which word follows the CVC pattern. The student should identify the word **big**. Have the student brainstorm other words with this pattern. Examples include: **bed, dig,** and **rid**.

You may want to create flashcards of words with CVC patterns. The student can study these throughout the unit.

Activity 1. Have the student turn to the activity sheet which accompanies this lesson. Read through the definition of the words with the CVC pattern at the top of the sheet. Ask the student to circle the short vowel sound in each of the words in the first activity. The answers are: **a, a, e, i, u, e**.

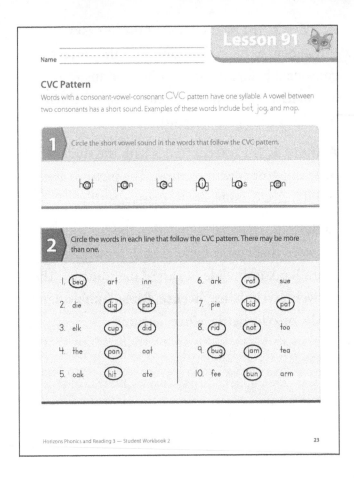

Activity 2. The next activity asks the student to circle the word in each line which follows the CVC pattern. Emphasize that the vowel needs to be between the two consonants in the word. You may want to have the student say each of the words in the line to hear the differences among those following the CVC pattern and those that do not. The answers to the activity are as follows:

1. **beg**
2. **dig, pat**
3. **cup, did**
4. **pan**
5. **hit**
6. **rot**
7. **bid, pat**
8. **rid, not**
9. **bug, jam**
10. **bun**

Activity 3. The final activity asks the student to identify CVC words in a Bible passage. Read through the Bible passage the first time with the student so he/she can hear the words. You may want to discuss the passage and its meaning with the student. Afterward, ask the student to locate those words within the passage that follow the CVC pattern. The answers are: **God, was, let**. Many are used more than once. The words day, now, and saw should not be underlined since they have vowel digraphs or dipthongs.

Reading Activity.

1. The student should read the poem "The Caterpillar." You may want to have the student read the poem aloud to you.

2. After reading the poem, ask the student the following questions. How does the poet describe the caterpillar? (**The caterpillar is brown, furry, and in a hurry.**) Where is the caterpillar going? (**It is going to a special leaf or stalk.**) What does the caterpillar try to avoid when it finds its place? (**It tries to avoid predators like toads and birds.**) What does the caterpillar do in its secret spot? (**It spins a web, dies, and becomes a butterfly.**) Are the images accurate to what you know about caterpillars? (**Allow for individual responses.**) What images would you add if you were to write about a caterpillar? (**Allow for individual responses.**)

3. How are the lines of the poem arranged? (**They are arranged in rhyming pairs. The first line is generally short and about three syllables while the second is longer and about seven syllables long.**)

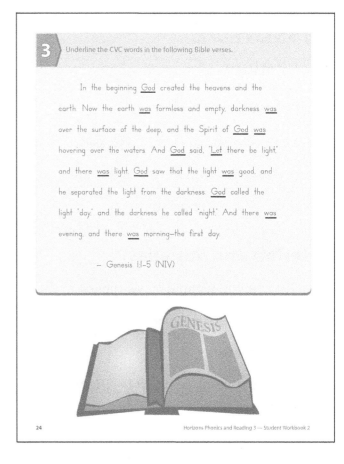

Lesson 92

CVCe Pattern

Overview:

- Locate words that follow the CVCe pattern
- Recognize words with the CVCe pattern
- Identify CVCe patterned words

Materials and Supplies:

- Teacher's Guide and Student Workbook
- White board or chart paper
- Phonics flashcards
- Reader: "Rumplestiltskin: Part I—The Miller's Boast"

Teaching Tips:

Review for Mastery. Discuss and review any work from the previous lesson that was assigned as homework. Check for completion of the activities and orally quiz the student for comprehension. Review any reading that was assigned, discussing the characters, setting, plot, theme, language, sequence, etc.

Strengthen fluency and phonemic awareness by reviewing words and sentences from the previous lessons. Build vocabulary skills by using some of the words in sentences.

You may want to create flashcards of words which contain the CVCe pattern. The student can study these throughout the unit.

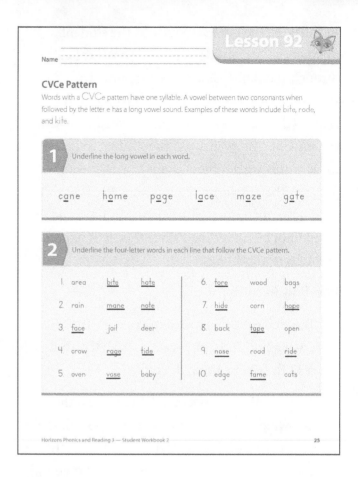

Lesson Introduction. Remind the student of the consonant-vowel-consonant pattern studied in the previous lesson. In this lesson, the student will study the same pattern but add the vowel **e** to the end of the pattern. This simple addition of the letter **e** changes the sound of the first vowel. Instead of the vowel having a short sound between two consonants, it has a long sound. Write the words **can**, **rid**, and **pan** on the board. Have the student pronounce these words with the short vowel sound. Now write the words on the board adding the letter **e** to the end. These words become **cane**, **ride**, and **pane**. Have the student pronounce the words and notice the long vowel sound.

Activity 1. The student should turn to the activity sheet which accompanies this lesson. Read through the definition of CVCe words at the top of the sheet. The student should underline the long vowel sound in each word. The answers are: **a, o, a, a, a, a.**

Activity 2. The student should continue the activity by underlining four-letter words in each line that follow the CVCe pattern. It may be helpful to read the words in each line so that the student can hear the long vowel sounds. The answers to the activity are as follows:

1. **bite, hate**
2. **mane, note**
3. **face**
4. **rage, tide**
5. **vase**
6. **tore**
7. **hide, hope**
8. **tape**
9. **nose, ride**
10. **fame**

Activity 3. The student should look at the last activity on the sheet. Read the verses from Psalm 31 with your student. Discuss them as well. Have the student underline the words in the passage which follow the CVCe pattern. The answers are: **face, save, love.** The student may also include: **times, shine, those.**

Reading Activity.

1. The student should turn to the selection, "Rumplestiltskin." The student should read Part I of the selection entitled, "The Miller's Boast." You may want to read the selection with your student. You can take turns reading the lines of dialogue.

2. After reading the selection, discuss the first part with the student. Who are the main characters in the selection? (**They are the miller, his daughter, the king, and a clever man.**) What problem did the miller's boasting cause? (**The miller's daughter went to live with the king. She must spin straw into gold in order to remain alive.**) What items does she give the

little man for his work? (**She gives him her necklace and her diamond ring.**) How does the king react when he sees the different piles of gold? (**He is very excited and asks the girl to spin even more straw into gold.**) Ask the student what he/she thinks will happen next in the story. (**Allow for individual responses.**)

Lesson 93

CV and VCC Patterns

Overview:

- Learn the CV and VCC word patterns
- Identify words with the CV and VCC patterns

Materials and Supplies:

- Teacher's Guide and Student Workbook
- White board or chart paper
- Phonics flashcards
- Reader: "Rumplestiltskin: Part II—A Strange Bargain"

Teaching Tips:

Review for Mastery. Discuss and review any work from the previous lesson that was assigned as homework. Check for completion of the activities and orally quiz the student for comprehension. Review any reading that was assigned, discussing the characters, setting, plot, theme, language, sequence, etc.

Strengthen fluency and phonemic awareness by reviewing words and sentences from the previous lessons. Build vocabulary skills by using some of the words in sentences.

You may want to create flashcards of words which have CV and VCC word patterns. The student can study these throughout the unit.

Lesson Introduction. Review the consonant vowel patterns the student learned in previous lessons. Recall the CVC pattern where the vowel had a short sound as in the words **let** and **fit**. Remind the student of the CVCe pattern where the vowel had a long sound as in the words **kite** and **like**. In this lesson the student will look at two

Name

CV and VCC Patterns

Words with a CV pattern have one syllable. The letter y will not be considered a vowel in this exercise. Examples of these words include go, do, and be. Words with a VCC pattern begin with a vowel and are often followed by blended consonants. Examples of these words include egg, old, and ash.

1 Put the CV and VCC words in alphabetical order.

1.	ark, do, art	ark	art	do
2.	be, ask, egg	ask	be	egg
3.	end, go, elf	elf	end	go
4.	ask, ink, art	art	ask	ink
5.	off, old, inn	inn	off	old
6.	he, end, to	end	he	to
7.	me, be, old	be	me	old
8.	ink, odd, he	he	ink	odd
9.	inn, ash, alp	alp	ash	inn
10.	do, go, egg	do	egg	go

more patterns that can be found in single syllable words. Write the words **me, do, art**, and **odd** on the board. Ask the student if he/she can determine the pattern. These patterns are CV and VCC.

Activity 1. The student should turn to the activity sheet which accompanies this lesson. Read through the definition of CV and VCC words at the top of the page. The first activity contains words which follow the CV and VCC patterns. By reading through this activity, the student will become familiar with words with the CV and VCC patterns. The student needs to put the words in each line in alphabetical order. The answers to the activity are as follows:

1. **ark, art, do**
2. **ask, be, egg**
3. **elf, end, go**
4. **art, ask, ink**
5. **inn, off, old**
6. **end, he, to**

7. **be, me, old**
8. **he, ink, odd**
9. **alp, ash, inn**
10. **do, egg, go**

Activity 2. The activity sheet continues with the student filling in the blanks with the correct vowels for the words. For the purpose of this activity, **y** is not considered a vowel. The answers are: **me, old, go, art, awl/owl, and/end, no, egg, ink, ask**.

Activity 3. The next activity asks the student to identify words in the sentences which follow the CV or VCC pattern. You may find it helpful to go through the sentences one at a time with the student rather than have him/her complete them all at once. By going through them one sentence at a time, you can better monitor whether or not the student understands the concept. The answers to the activity are as follows:

1. Clara liked the Bible story of Noah's **ark**.
2. Jay said **he** was going **to** the circus on Friday.
3. The **ink** in the pen was dry.
4. The chicken laid an **egg**.
5. Caleb turned **off** the lights.
6. Taylor was excited **to** hear the **end** of the story.
7. The **old** dog couldn't learn the new trick.
8. The barn **owl** hooted at night.
9. **Do** you want **to go** swimming?
10. The **elk** slowly walked across the road.

Reading Activity.

1. The student should read Part II of the selection "Rumplestiltskin." This section is entitled "A Strange Bargain." You may want to read the section with your student. You can take turns reading lines of dialogue.

2. After reading the selection, discuss this section with the student. In the next lesson, you will discuss the selection as a whole. Review how

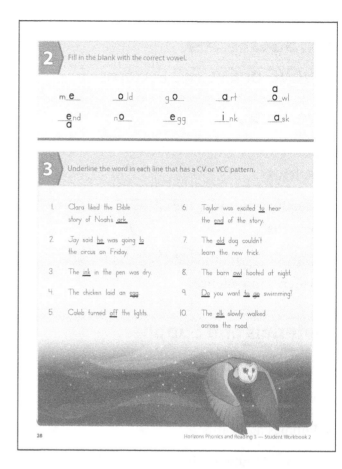

the miller's daughter came to live in the king's palace to spin straw into gold. What did the little man want if he spun the straw into gold a third time? **(He asked for the woman's firstborn child if she became queen.)** Why do you think she agreed to this arrangement? (Answers may include: **She didn't think she had a choice or she assumed she would never marry the king.**) Why do you think the woman was surprised when the little man showed up to collect her child? **(She probably thought he had forgotten or she may have forgotten the agreement.)** The little man says she may keep the baby if she can guess his name. How does she go about trying to guess the man's name? **(She sends messengers throughout the country.)** How does she learn his name? **(One messenger overhears a man singing in the forest.)** How did Rumplestiltskin react when the queen said his name? **(He was surprised and angry and went home without the child.)**

Lesson 94
CV/CVC or CVC/VC Patterns

Overview:

- Learn words with the CV/CVC and CVC/VC patterns
- Identify words with the CV/CVC and CVC/VC patterns
- Use words with the CV/CVC and CVC/VC patterns in sentences

Materials and Supplies:

- Teacher's Guide and Student Workbook
- White board or chart paper
- Phonics flashcards
- Reader: "Rumplestiltskin"

Teaching Tips:

Review for Mastery. Discuss and review any work from the previous lesson that was assigned as homework. Check for completion of the activities and orally quiz the student for comprehension. Review any reading that was assigned, discussing the characters, setting, plot, theme, language, sequence, etc.

Strengthen fluency and phonemic awareness by reviewing words and sentences from the previous lessons. Build vocabulary skills by using some of the words in sentences.

You may want to create flashcards of words which have the CV/CVC and CVC/VC patterns. The student can study these throughout the unit.

Lesson Introduction. In the previous lessons, the student has learned about consonant-vowel patterns in one-syllable words. In this lesson the student will look at the consonant-vowel patterns of two-

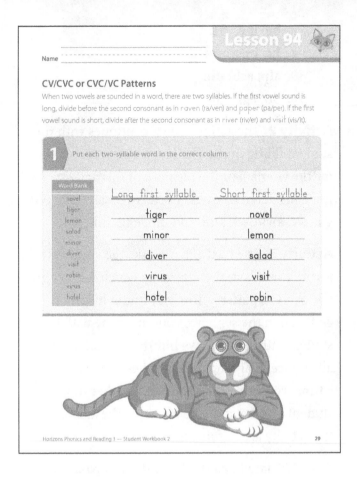

syllable words. One of the patterns is CVCVC. This consonant-vowel pattern can be divided into syllables in two different ways. Write the words **topaz** and **salad** on the board. Ask the student if the first vowel in the world has a long or short sound. In the word **topaz** the **o** is long and in the word **salad** the letter **a** is short. Explain that when a word has a long first vowel sound it is divided immediately after that letter as in **to/paz**. If the syllable sound is short, the word is divided after the second consonant of the word as in **sal/ad**. If the student is having trouble understanding this concept, give additional examples of words and have the student divide them into syllables. Additional word examples include: **ba/con, ru/ler, met/al, po/lar, su/per,** and **rab/id**.

Activity 1. The student should turn to the activity sheet which accompanies this lesson. Read through the definition at the top of the page. The opening activity asks the student to put the words in the correct column based on whether or not they have long or short first syllables. Read through the words with the student so he/she can hear their sounds. The correct answers are as follows:

Long first syllable	Short first syllable
tiger	novel
minor	lemon
diver	salad
virus	visit
hotel	robin

Activity 2. The second activity asks the student to take words and divide them into two syllables based on the CVC/VC or CV/CVC word pattern. Again, it may be helpful to have the student say the words before dividing them into syllables. The correct answers are: **lim/it, re/lax, ra/ven, pa/per, mod/el, mu/sic, doz/en, pi/lot, le/gal, to/ken.**

Activity 3. The final activity asks the student to choose the correct CVC/VC or CV/CVC word to complete each sentence. As an added activity, have the student divide the correct word into syllables. The answers for the activity are: **sal/ad, ho/tel, mod/el, lim/it, rob/in, doz/en, pa/per, riv/er, si/ren, re/lax.**

Reading Activity.

1. Explain to the student that you are going to discuss the entire selection of "Rumplestiltskin." Begin by discussing the characters. What kind of a person was the miller? **(He was boastful and didn't think of the consequences.)** How would you describe his daughter? **(She was put in a difficult position of saving her life by spinning straw into gold. She didn't tell the truth about the man who helped her. This was probably because she was trying to save her life.)** How would you describe the king? **(The king loved money and gold. He wanted to have as much as he could.)** How would you describe Rumplestiltskin? **(He was skilled in that he could spin straw into gold. He didn't work for free, and he expected something in return.)**

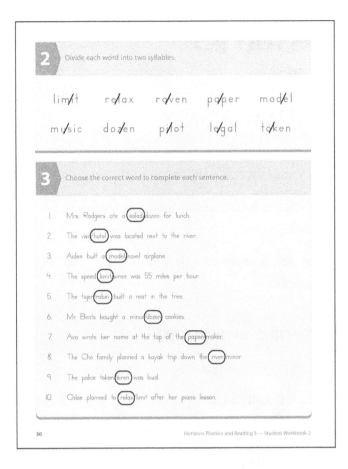

2. Continue by asking the student what the problems were in the story? **(The problems included the boasting of the miller, the king expecting the miller's daughter to turn straw to gold, and Rumplestiltskin wanting the queen's baby.)** How did the various problems get solved? **(Rumplestiltskin spun the straw into gold and the queen guessed his name so she could keep the child.)** How did the author build up the intensity for the queen guessing the little man's name? **(The reader knew that she had been told Rumplestiltskin's name, yet she guessed some other names before guessing the correct name.)** What lessons can be learned from this fairy tale? (They may include: **not boasting or loving money, telling the truth, and helping others without expecting anything in return.)**

Lesson 95

V/V Pattern

Overview:

- Learn how to divide words into syllables when they contain two adjacent sounding vowels

- Identify words with two adjacent sounding vowels

- Use words with two adjacent sounding vowels in sentences

Materials and Supplies:

- Teacher's Guide and Student Workbook

- White board or chart paper

- Phonics flashcards

- Reader: "My Loose Tooth"

Teaching Tips:

Review for Mastery. Discuss and review any work from the previous lesson that was assigned as homework. Check for completion of the activities and orally quiz the student for comprehension. Review any reading that was assigned, discussing the characters, setting, plot, theme, language, sequence, etc.

Strengthen fluency and phonemic awareness by reviewing words and sentences from the previous lessons. Build vocabulary skills by using some of the words in sentences. The student can study these throughout the unit.

You may want to create flashcards of words with two adjacent sounding vowels. The student can study these throughout the unit.

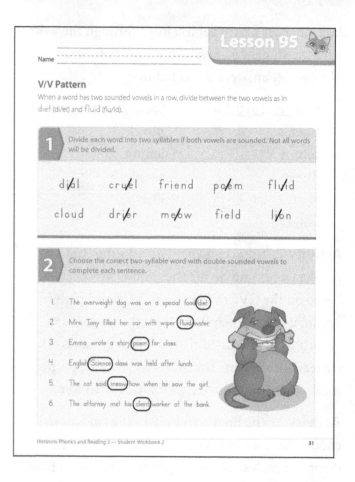

Lesson Introduction. This lesson will continue the study of two-syllable words. The words in this lesson will contain adjacent sounding vowels, for example **diet** and **cruel**. The student should notice that the words are divided into syllables between the vowels. The number of consonants before and after these vowel divisions will not be a focus of the lesson. Write the words **poem** and **drier** on the board. Ask the student to divide these two words into syllables. The student should note that the division occurs between the double vowels in the center of the words.

Activity 1. The student should turn to the activity sheet which accompanies the lesson. Read through the explanation of V/V words at the top of the sheet. Read with the student the words in the first activity. Have the student identify those words where the two vowels are sounded. The student may want to circle those words. Have the student divide the words with two vowel sounds into syllables. The answers are: **di/al, cru/el, po/em, flu/id, dri/er, me/ow, li/on.**

Activity 2. The student should continue with the activity where the student is asked to choose the words with a two syllable double vowel to complete each sentence. You may want to have the student read each sentence aloud. Have the student circle the correct response for each sentence. The answers are: **diet, fluid, poem, Science, meow, client, drier, duet, lion, flour.**

Activity 3. The final activity asks the student to complete a crossword puzzle. A Word Bank is provided to help the student fill in the clues. The answers are:

Across:	Down:
1. **duet**	1. **diet**
3. **poet**	2. **soil**
4. **dial**	4. **drier**
5. **boil**	7. **lion**
6. **cruel**	
8. **meow**	

Reading Activity.

1. The student should turn to the selection, "My Loose Tooth." The student should read the poem. After reading the poem, ask the student to read the poem aloud to you.

2. Discuss the poem with the student. What is the tone or mood of the poem? (**The poem is funny and clever.**) What is the story of the poem? (**The poem is about a child having a loose tooth, pulling it, and putting it under his/her pillow.**) How does the author make this basic story more interesting? (**The poet describes the tooth as wiggly and jiggly. The poet also repeats the phrase "loose tooth."**) Why does the person put the tooth under the pillow? (**The student may or may not be familiar with the idea of the tooth fairy. If a child loses a tooth and puts it under the pillow, the tooth fairy is supposed to come and take the tooth away and replace it with money or a gift. A mom or dad pretends to play this role.**)

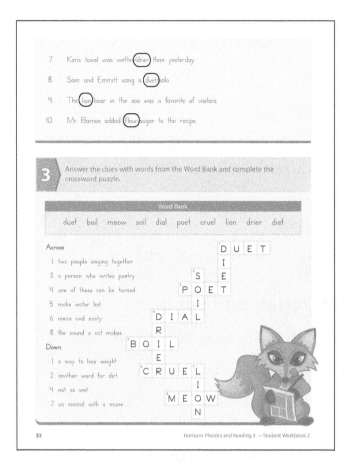

3. Discuss the way in which the poem was written. The poem was written in sets of two stanzas with many parallel lines. Have the student point out these matching rhymes. The poem makes use of repetition.

Lesson 96
CVC/CVC Patterns

Overview:

- Learn how words with two separated vowels form two syllables

- Identify words which follow the CVC/CVC pattern

- Use CVC/CVC words in sentences

Materials and Supplies:

- Teacher's Guide and Student Workbook

- White board or chart paper

- Phonics flashcards

- Reader: "The Traveling Musicians of Bremen: Part I—How They Set Out"

Teaching Tips:

Review for Mastery. Discuss and review any work from the previous lesson that was assigned as homework. Check for completion of the activities and orally quiz the student for comprehension. Review any reading that was assigned, discussing the characters, setting, plot, theme, language, sequence, etc.

Strengthen fluency and phonemic awareness by reviewing words and sentences from the previous lessons. Build vocabulary skills by using some of the words in sentences.

You may want to create flashcards with CVC/CVC patterns. The student can study these throughout the unit.

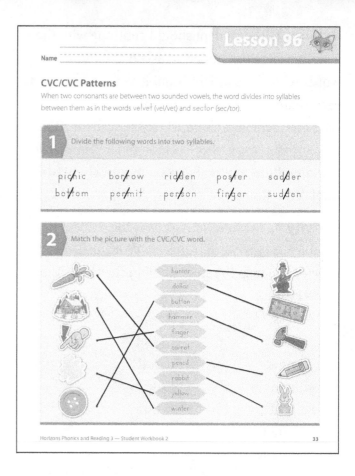

Lesson Introduction. Write the words **trick, sister,** and **lion** on the board. Ask the student how many syllables are in each word. **Trick** has one syllable, **sister** has two, and **lion** has two. Ask the student how many vowels are in each of the words. Help the student to see that the vowels in **sister** and **lion** are each sounded. This indicates that each vowel will be a part of one of the syllables. Remind the student that in the previous lesson, he/she learned that when two vowels are next to each other and each is sounded, the word is divided between the vowels. The word **sister** is the type of word that will be the focus of this lesson. In a word like **sister,** the word is divided between the double consonants **sis/ter**.

Activity 1. The student should turn to the activity sheet which accompanies this lesson. The student should read through the definition at the top of the page. The student should complete the first activity where words are divided into two syllables. The student should note the double consonants in the middle of the words. Have the student divide the words into two syllables. The answers are: **pic/nic, bor/row, rid/den, pos/ter, sad/der, bot/tom, per/mit, per/son, fin/ger, sud/den**.

Activity 2. The next activity asks the student to match CVC/CVC words with the appropriate pictures. As an added activity, you could ask the student to divide the words into two syllables. **See image for answers.**

Activity 3. The student will go on to fill in the blank with the word that best completes each sentence. All of the words are examples of the CVC/CVC pattern. You may want to have the student divide the words in the Word Bank into two syllables before completing the activity. The correct answers are: **bottom, carrot, sudden, person, butter, Turkey, corner, carpet, letter, helmet.**

Reading Activity.

1. Ask the student to turn to the selection, "The Traveling Musicians of Bremen." The student should read "Part I—How They Set Out."

2. After reading the first part of the selection, discuss it with the student. Why was each animal kicked out of its home? (**The donkey left because he was getting too old and couldn't work. The dog could no longer**

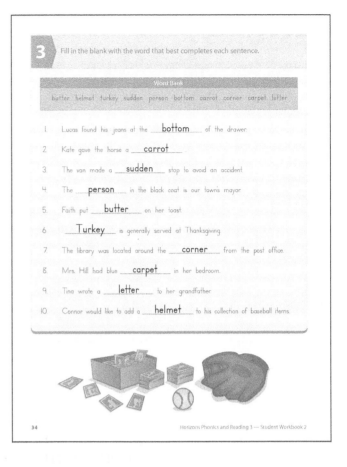

hunt. **The cat wanted to sleep and couldn't run after the mice. The rooster was going to be served as soup.**) What plan did the animals have? (**They were going to travel to the city and become musicians.**) Have the student predict what will happen next. What kind of music will the musicians play? Do you think people will want to listen? (**Allow for individual answers.**)

Lesson 97

Review One- and Two-Syllable Words

Overview:

- Review words with one and two syllables

- Identify the patterns of one- and two-syllable words

- Determine the correct division of two-syllable words

Materials and Supplies:

- Teacher's Guide and Student Workbook

- White board or chart paper

- Phonics flashcards

- Reader: "The Traveling Musicians of Bremen: Part II—How They Gave a Concert and Part III—How They Made Themselves at Home"

Teaching Tips:

Review for Mastery. Discuss and review any work from the previous lesson that was assigned as homework. Check for completion of the activities and orally quiz the student for comprehension. Review any reading that was assigned, discussing the characters, setting, plot, theme, language, sequence, etc.

Strengthen fluency and phonemic awareness by reviewing words and sentences from the previous lessons. Build vocabulary skills by using some of the words in sentences.

Lesson Introduction. Tell the student in this lesson he/she will review one- and two-syllable word patterns from the previous lesson. Write the following words on the board: **big, bigger, late, me, end, begin, salad,** and **poet.** Ask the student to list the patterns for these words. The patterns are CVC, CVCCVC, CVCe,

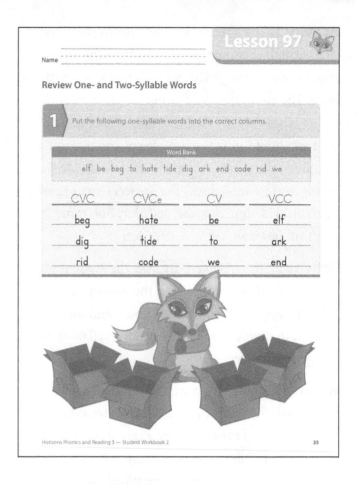

CV, VCC, CVCVC, CVCVC, and CVVC. Next ask the student to list another word for each form which follows the pattern. Examples could be **leg, borrow, gate, be, ark, relax, never,** and **duet.**

Activity 1. The student should turn to the activity sheet which accompanies this lesson. The first activity asks the student to put single syllable words in the columns with the correct pattern. The answers are as follows:

CVC	CVCe	CV	VCC
beg	**hate**	**be**	**elf**
dig	**tide**	**to**	**ark**
rid	**code**	**we**	**end**

Activity 2. The next activity asks the student to put two-syllable words in the columns with the correct pattern. The answers for this activity are as follows:

CVCVC	VV	CVCCVC
relax	cruel	borrow
novel	poem	bottom
tiger	quiet	magnet
dozen	dial	basket

Activity 3. The student will continue by dividing words into two syllables. It may be helpful to have the student say each word to hear the two syllables. The student can then divide the words into syllables after hearing the vowel sounds. The answers to the activity are: **sal/ad, but/ter, sud/den, lim/it, di/al, du/et, to/ken, pi/lot, di/et, se/cret.**

Activity 4. The final activity asks the student to fill in the blank with the correct vowel. The student should recognize the word patterns as he/she fills in the vowels. The answers to the activity are: **egg, diet, hate, go, inn, lion, tore, me, dial/dual, pilot.**

Reading Activity.

1. Have the student turn to the selection, "The Traveling Musicians of Bremen." The student should read "Part II—How They Gave a Concert and Part III—How They Made Themselves at Home."

2. After reading the selections, discuss them with the student. Where did the animals first go to sleep? **(They first went to sleep in the woods.)** Why did they move from the woods? **(They saw some lights in the distance, and they headed toward them.)** What did they find? **(They found a house where some robbers were living.)** How did they try to get into the house? **(They stood on one another's shoulders to look through the window. They began to sing to the robbers.)** What happened when they sang? **(The robbers took off running.)** Do you think the animals planned to get the robbers to leave through

their singing? **(Have the student explain his/ her answers.)** What happened when one of the robbers returned? **(He thought he was being attacked by monsters and others.)** Why didn't the musicians travel to the city? **(They decided to stay in the house the robbers abandoned.)**

3. As an added activity, have the student draw one of the scenes from the selection.

Lesson 98

Three-Syllable Words:
CVC/CVC/CVC and CVC/CVC/VC

Overview:

- Learn to divide words of three syllables
- Identify words with CVC/CVC/CVC and CVC/CVC/VC patterns
- Categorize words with CVC/CVC/CVC and CVC/CVC/VC patterns

Materials and Supplies:

- Teacher's Guide and Student Workbook
- White board or chart paper
- Phonics flashcards
- Reader: "The Magic Belt Buckle: Part I"

Teaching Tips:

Review for Mastery. Discuss and review any work from the previous lesson that was assigned as homework. Check for completion of the activities and orally quiz the student for comprehension. Review any reading that was assigned, discussing the characters, setting, plot, theme, language, sequence, etc.

Strengthen fluency and phonemic awareness by reviewing words and sentences from the previous lessons. Build vocabulary skills by using some of the words in sentences.

You may want to create flashcards of words with CVC/CVC/CVC and CVC/CVC/VC patterns. The student can study these throughout the unit.

Lesson Introduction. Remind the student that up to this point he/she has been studying the patterns of one- and two-syllable words. In this lesson and the next, the student will study words with three syllables. Tell the student that if a word has three

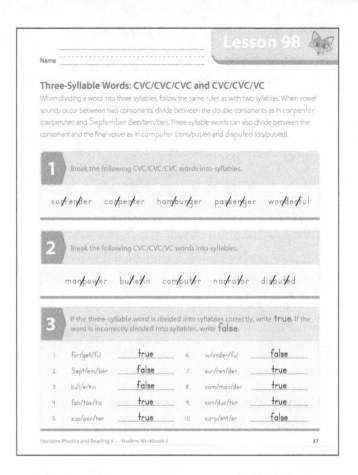

sounded vowels it will have three syllables. Help the student to see that the patterns he/she learned in earlier lessons also apply to three-syllable words. Write the word **wonderful** on the board. Now write the word **wonder** on the board. Ask the student how the word **wonder** would be divided into syllables. The student should note the word would be divided between the middle two consonants. It follows the CVCCVC pattern. The word divides as **won/der**. Now write the letters **derful** on the board. What is the pattern of these letters? The pattern is the same. The word divides between the middle two consonants. When put together, the word has three CVC patterns as **won/der/ful**.

Continue by writing the word **manpower** on the board. Write the word **power** on the board. The student should remember that a word like power divides before the final syllable when the first vowel is short as in **pow/er.** Now write the letters **manpow** on the board. The student should recognize that this follows the earlier pattern of CVCCVC. Put together it forms a new pattern, CVC/CVC/VC as in **man/pow/er**.

Activity 1. Ask the student to take out the activity sheet which accompanies this lesson. The student should read the information at the top of the sheet. The student should look at the first activity on the sheet. This activity focuses only on words with the CVC/CVC/CVC pattern. Ask the student to read the words and listen for the vowel sounds in the words. The student should go on to divide the words into syllables. The answers to the activity are: **sur/ren/der, car/pen/ter, ham/bur/ger, pas/sen/ger, won/der/ful**.

Activity 2. The student should continue by looking at words which follow the CVC/CVC/VC pattern. Have the student read the words aloud. The student should listen to the vowel sounds to determine where the words are divided. The answers are: **man/pow/er, bul/let/in, com/put/er, nar/rat/or, dis/put/ed**.

Activity 3. The next activity on the sheet asks the student to determine whether or not each given word is divided correctly into syllables. Once again, the student may find it helpful to read each word aloud before determining if the word is correctly divided. The student should write true for those words correctly divided and false for those which are incorrectly divided. The answers are: **true, false, false, true, true, false, true, true, true, false**.

Activity 4. The final activity asks the student to find three-syllable words in the word puzzle. As an added activity, you may want to have the student divide the words into three syllables. **See image for answers.**

Reading Activity.

1. The student should turn to Part I of the selection, "The Magic Belt Buckle." Have the student read the selection. You could read the selection with the student and when there is dialogue take turns.

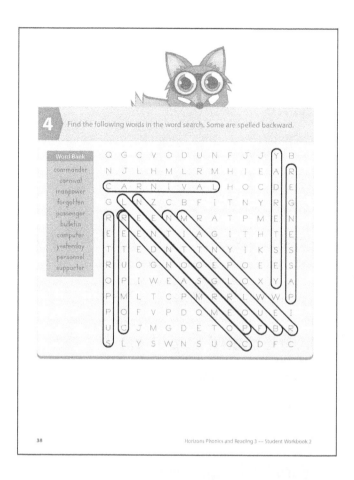

2. Discuss the selection with the student. Ask the student to describe the main character in the selection. (**The main character is a little blacksmith.**) Why did he make the belt buckle? (**He made it to remember or celebrate the time he killed ten flies that had landed on his lunch.**) Why do you think someone would celebrate that kind of event? (**Allow for individual responses.**) How did the bear and giant misinterpret the belt buckle's message? (**Each assumed that the message was directed at him. They could not imagine that such a message could relate to something as insignificant as a fly.**) How did he trick the giant? (**He sat in the tree branches and let the giant do the work.**) Ask the student to predict what they think would happen next. (**Allow for individual responses.**)

3. As an added activity, have the student draw a picture of the belt buckle.

Lesson 99

CVC/V/CVC and VC/CVC/CVCC Patterns

Overview:

- Learn words with the patterns CVC/V/CVC and VC/CVC/CVCC

- Identify three-syllable words with the CVC/V/CVC and VC/CVC/CVCC patterns

- Use three-syllable words in sentences

Materials and Supplies:

- Teacher's Guide and Student Workbook

- White board or chart paper

- Phonics flashcards

- Reader: "The Magic Belt Buckle: Part II"

Teaching Tips:

Review for Mastery. Discuss and review any work from the previous lesson that was assigned as homework. Check for completion of the activities and orally quiz the student for comprehension. Review any reading that was assigned, discussing the characters, setting, plot, theme, language, sequence, etc.

Strengthen fluency and phonemic awareness by reviewing words and sentences from the previous lessons. Build vocabulary skills by using some of the words in sentences.

You may want to create flashcards of words with CVC/V/CVC and VC/CVC/CVCC patterns. The student can study these throughout the unit.

Lesson Introduction. This lesson continues the study of three-syllable words following the pattern CVC/V/CVC and VC/CVC/CVCC. The words will have three sounded syllables. Write the word **attend** on the board. Ask the student how this word should be divided. The word would be divided between the two **t's**. Next write the word

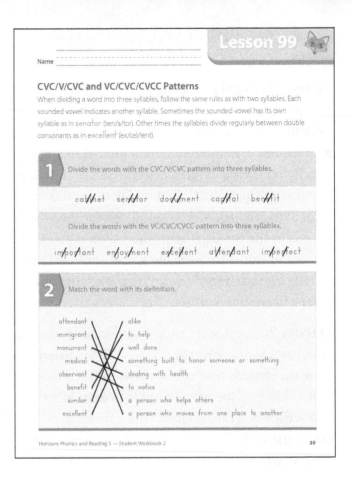

Name

CVC/V/CVC and VC/CVC/CVCC Patterns

When dividing a word into three syllables, follow the same rules as with two syllables. Each sounded vowel indicates another syllable. Sometimes the sounded vowel has its own syllable as in senator (sen/a/tor). Other times the syllables divide regularly between double consonants as in excellent (ex/cel/lent).

1 Divide the words with the CVC/V/CVC pattern into three syllables.

cab/i/net   sen/a/tor   doc/u/ment   cap/i/tal   ben/e/fit

Divide the words with the VC/CVC/CVCC pattern into three syllables.

im/por/tant   en/joy/ment   ex/cel/lent   at/ten/dant   im/per/fect

2 Match the word with its definition.

attendant — alike
immigrant — to help
monument — well done
medical — something built to honor someone or something
observant — dealing with health
benefit — to notice
similar — a person who helps others
excellent — a person who moves from one place to another

tendant on the board. How would this word be divided? The word would be divided between the consonants **n** and **d**. Write the word **attendant** on the board. Have the student divide the word into three syllables. The answer is **at/ten/dant**. This word follows the VC/CVC/CVCC pattern. Tell the student that some three-syllable words have **ant** and **ent** endings preceded by a vowel. These endings account for the double consonants at the end.

Continue by exploring the next pattern, which is CVC/V/CVC. Explain that these words have a vowel in the middle which forms its own syllable. Write the word **senator** on the board. The student should look at what vowel stands on its own. In this case the letter is **a**. The rest of the word follows the CVC pattern. The answer would be CVC/V/CVC as in **sen/a/tor**.

Activity 1. Ask the student to turn to the activity sheet which accompanies this lesson. The student should read the material at the top of the page. Ask the student to look at the first activity which focuses on words with the CVC/V/CVC pattern. The answers are: **cab/i/net, sen/a/tor, doc/u/ment, cap/i/tal, ben/e/fit.**

The student should continue with an activity similar to the first part, but this time he/she will focus on words which follow the VC/CVC/CVCC pattern. The student should read the words listed aloud. The student should listen for the sounded vowels. The answers are: **im/por/tant, en/joy/ment, ex/cel/lent, at/ten/dant, im/per/fect**.

Activity 2. The lesson continues with the student matching three-letter words with their definitions. The student should read the words first. As an added activity, the student could divide the words into three syllables. The answers to the matching activity are as follows:

attendant	a person who helps others
immigrant	a person who moves from one place to another
monument	something built to honor someone or something
medical	dealing with health
observant	to notice
benefit	to help
similar	alike
excellent	well done

Activity 3. The lesson continues with the student using three-syllable words in sentences. You may want to have the student read each of the words before looking at the sentences. The correct responses are as follows:

1. The church service started at its **regular** time of 10:30 a.m.
2. The **medical** team worked together to put a cast on Amy's broken leg.
3. Mrs. Garcia had a(n) **important** meeting at 10:00 a.m.
4. Joseph and Dave had **similar** winter coats.
5. Mr. Davis put the dishes in the **cabinet**.
6. Sarah was a(n) **citizen** of the United States.
7. Andrew worked hard and was a(n) **excellent** student.
8. Miss Kim signed a(n) **document** when she bought her house.
9. Swimming is a(n) **popular** summer activity.
10. The **immigrant** moved from Spain to the United States.

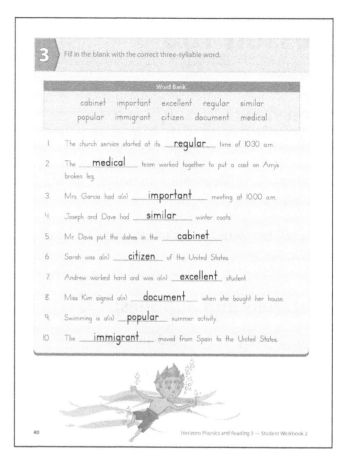

3 Fill in the blank with the correct three-syllable word.

Word Bank

cabinet   important   excellent   regular   similar
popular   immigrant   citizen   document   medical

1. The church service started at its _**regular**_ time of 10:30 a.m.
2. The _**medical**_ team worked together to put a cast on Amy's broken leg.
3. Mrs. Garcia had a(n) _**important**_ meeting at 10:00 a.m.
4. Joseph and Dave had _**similar**_ winter coats.
5. Mr. Davis put the dishes in the _**cabinet**_.
6. Sarah was a(n) _**citizen**_ of the United States.
7. Andrew worked hard and was a(n) _**excellent**_ student.
8. Miss Kim signed a(n) _**document**_ when she bought her house.
9. Swimming is a(n) _**popular**_ summer activity.
10. The _**immigrant**_ moved from Spain to the United States.

40   Horizons Phonics and Reading 3 — Student Workbook 2

Reading Activity.

1. Ask the student to recap the story and predictions made in the previous lesson. Have the student read the rest of the selection, "The Magic Belt Buckle: Part II."

2. After the student has read the selection, discuss it with him/her. What did the soldier assume about the little man? **(He assumed the blacksmith killed ten giants and ten bears.)** Why did the soldier assume this? **(He saw the giant's club and the bear's fur.)** What happened when the blacksmith went to battle? **(The commander assumed the belt was talking about him.)** How was the blacksmith rewarded? **(He was promised he would marry the princess and live happily ever after.)** How do you think the story would have been different if people had not assumed the belt was referencing them? **(Allow for a personal response.)** Why do you think the story had the blacksmith turning handsome? **(Talk about how many fairy tales have endings where there is a change in a person's appearance.)**

Lesson 100

Review

Overview:

- Identify words with one, two, and three syllables

- Correctly divide words with two and three syllables

- Recall how words with multiple syllables are divided

Materials and Supplies:

- Teacher's Guide and Student Workbook

- White board or chart paper

- Phonics flashcards

- Reader: "The Frogs' Travels"

Teaching Tips:

Review for Mastery. Discuss and review any work from the previous lesson that was assigned as homework. Check for completion of the activities and orally quiz the student for comprehension. Review any reading that was assigned, discussing the characters, setting, plot, theme, language, sequence, etc.

Strengthen fluency and phonemic awareness by reviewing words and sentences from the previous lessons. Build vocabulary skills by using some of the words in sentences.

You may want to review flashcards of words with one, two, and three syllables.

Lesson Introduction. This lesson reviews the material the student learned in the unit. The student will review single syllable and multi-syllable vowel consonant patterns. The test at the end of the unit follows the same format as the review.

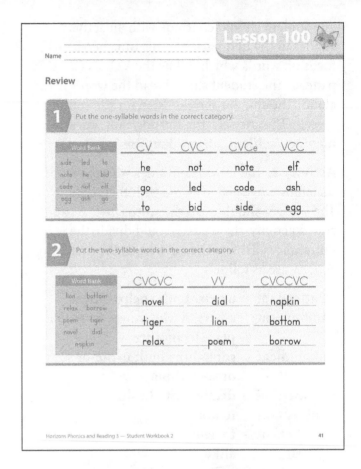

Before beginning, ask the student to list some of the consonant vowel patterns he/she learned in this unit. Start with the single syllable words. The student may remember the patterns CV, CVC, CVCe, and VCC. Have the student write a word which corresponds with each of the patterns. Examples include: **be, net, gate,** and **end**. Have the student think of patterns he/she learned for two-syllable words. Examples include: CVCVC, VV, and CVCCVC. Ask the student where the division between syllables would occur in each of these patterns. The CVCVC pattern can be divided either CV/CVC or CVC/VC. The other two patterns are divided V/V and CVC/CVC. The student should come up with examples of words for each of these patterns. These include: **cover, begin, duet,** and **beggar.** Finally, review the three-syllable patterns the student learned. These include CVCCVCCVC, CVCCVCVC, CVCVCVC, and VCCVCCVCC. Have the student indicate where the syllable breaks would occur in these patterns. They would appear as CVC/CVC/CVC, CVC/CVC/VC, CVC/V/CVC, and VC/CVC/CVCC. Have the student give an example of a word for each of the patterns. Examples include: **surrender**, **bulletin**, **senator**, and **important**.

Activity 1. The student should turn to the review activity sheet which accompanies this lesson. The student should look at the words in the Word Bank and place them under the correct heading. You may want to do one together to help the student understand the activity. The correct answers to the activity are as follows:

CV	CVC	CVCe	VCC
he	not	note	elf
go	led	code	ash
to	bid	side	egg

Activity 2. The student will continue the review by studying two-syllable words. The student should remember that each vowel sounded in a word creates a new syllable. Point out that in this activity the words which follow the pattern CV/CVC and CVC/VC will be placed in one column. Have the student read each word aloud before completing the activity. The answers to the activity are as follows:

CVCVC	VV	CVCCVC
novel	dial	napkin
tiger	lion	bottom
relax	poem	borrow

Activity 3. The student will continue the review of two-syllable words by dividing them into their separate syllables. The student should keep in mind the patterns studied in the previous activity. The answers to the activity are: **doz/en, le/gal, flu/id, per/mit, no/el, rid/den, fin/der, di/ner, dri/er, lem/on.**

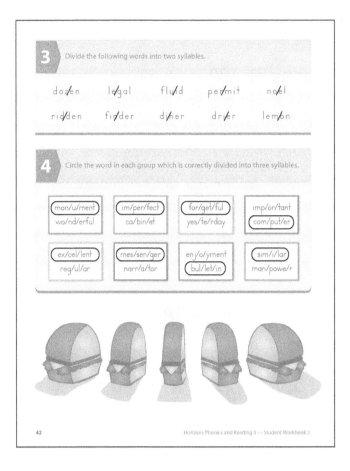

Activity 4. The final activity asks the student to divide words into three syllables. The student should recall at the beginning of the lesson when you reviewed the patterns for three-syllable words. Give the student the opportunity to say the words aloud so that the student can hear and then see where the division breaks should occur. The answers to the activity are: **mon/u/ment, im/per/fect, for/get/ful, com/put/er, ex/cel/lent, mes/sen/ger, bul/let/in, sim/i/lar.**

Reading Activity.

1. The selection for this lesson is, "The Frogs' Travels."

2. The student will read this selection for pleasure.

Test 10

Lessons 91-100

Overview:

- Identify words with one, two, and three syllables
- Correctly divide words with two and three syllables
- Recall how words with multiple syllables are divided

Materials and Supplies:

- Student Test

Teaching Tips:

Review for Mastery. Discuss and review any work from the previous lesson that was assigned as homework. Check for completion of the activities and orally quiz the student for comprehension. Review any reading that was assigned, discussing the characters, setting, plot, theme, language, sequence, etc.

Lesson Introduction. This lesson tests the material the student learned in the unit. Before the test you may want to ask the student if he/she has any final questions. There may be questions from the review the student will want to ask. Remind the student that the final test follows the same format as the review.

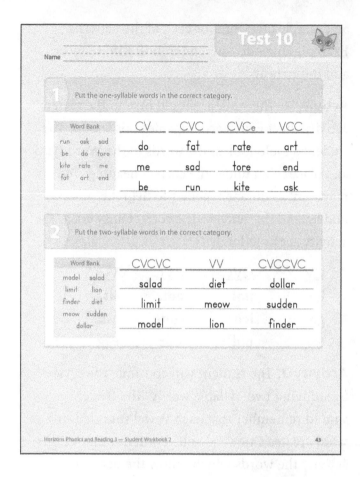

Activity 1. The student will begin the test by placing words with one syllable in the correct columns. The student will look at words with the patterns CV, CVC, CVCe, and VCC. The correct answers are as follows:

CV	CVC	CVCe	VCC
do	fat	rate	art
me	sad	tore	end
be	run	kite	ask

Activity 2. The student will continue by placing words with two syllables in the correct columns. Words which follow the pattern CV/CVC and CVC/VC will be listed in one column. The correct answers are as follows:

<u>CVCVC</u>	<u>VV</u>	<u>CVCCVC</u>
salad	diet	dollar
limit	meow	sudden
model	lion	finder

Activity 3. The next part of the test asks the student to divide words into two syllables. If your testing area permits, you may want to consider having the student say the words as he/she divides them into two syllables. This way the student can hear the long and short vowel sounds. The correct answers are as follows:

**re/gal   sum/mit fin/der   can/dle   po/em
mi/nor   di/et   du/et   bot/tom lim/it**

Activity 4. The final activity asks the student to circle the words that are correctly divided into three syllables. Again, if your testing area permits, you may want to consider having the student say the words as he/she divides them into three syllables. This way the student can hear the long and short vowel sounds. The correct answers are as follows:
won/der/ful, en/joy/ment, pas/sen/ger, nar/rat/or, fan/tas/tic, pop/u/lar, for/get/ful, im/por/tant.

Divide the following words into two syllables.

re/gal   sum/mit   fin/der   can/dle   po/em
mi/nor   di/et   du/et   bot/tom   lim/it

Circle the word in each group which is correctly divided into three syllables.

excel/le/nt   en/joy/ment   doc/ume/nt   nar/rat/or
won/der/ful   me/dic/al   pas/sen/ger   imp/er/fect

ca/bin/et   pop/u/lar   for/get/ful   im/por/tant
fan/tas/tic   di/sput/ed   supp/or/ter   ca/pit/al

44   Horizons Phonics and Reading 3 — Student Workbook 2

Lesson 101

Spelling Words Ending in eer and ation

Overview:

- Understand the meaning of the endings **-eer** and **-ation**

- Recognize words ending with **-eer** and **-ation**

- Identify words with **-eer** and **-ation**

Material and Supplies:

- Teacher's Guide and Student Workbook

- White board or chart paper

- Phonics flashcards

- Reader: "The Grain of Wheat"

Teaching Tips:

Lesson Introduction. Explain to the student that in this unit he/she will be studying two word endings: **-eer** and **-ation**. Write the word **mountaineer** on the board. Ask the student what he/she thinks the word means. You may want to break down the word for the student to **mountain** and **-eer.** The student knows what a mountain is. When the ending **-eer** is added, it means a person who climbs mountains. The ending **-eer** means a person who does something. The second ending the student will study is **-ation**. The ending **-ation** means something which has been done. Write the word **visitation** on the board. Once again, break the word down to its parts. The word means that a visit has been done.

You may want to have the student make flashcards of words ending with **-eer** and **-ation**. The student can study these throughout the unit.

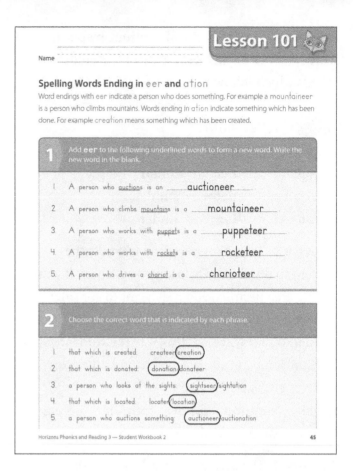

Activity 1. The student should turn to the activity sheet for this lesson. Read through the definition at the top of the sheet. The first activity asks the student to form words ending with **-eer**. An underlined word in the definition indicates the base word. You may want to do one as an example with your student. The answers to the activity are: **auctioneer, mountaineer, puppeteer, rocketeer, charioteer.**

Activity 2. The second activity continues with the student choosing the correct words ending with **-eer** and **-ation.** The student will read the definition and determine the correct spelling and formation of the word for each phrase. The answers to the activity are: **creation, donation, sightseer, location, auctioneer, celebration, imagination, mountaineer.**

Activity 3. The final activity asks the student to apply what he/she has learned to complete sentences using the correct **-eer** or **-ation** words. The student should read each sentence with the word he/she chose to make sure it is correct before filling in the blank. If the student doesn't know the answer to the sentence, he should move on and go back to it later. Sometimes when there are fewer choices the answer will become clear. The answers to this activity are: **imagination, punctuation, graduation, pioneer, career, station, decorations, location, nation, engineer.**

Reading Activity.

1. Before the student reads the selection, begin with a discussion about work. Ask the student if he/she believes that hard work is rewarded. Follow up by asking if he/she has ever been rewarded for working hard. Talk about the types of rewards he/she has received. **(This may include positive encouragement, a food treat, or a monetary reward.)** Ask the student if he/she has ever been rewarded even though he/she didn't work. Tell the student that the selection is going to be about working and not working.

2. Have the student turn to the selection, "The Grain of Wheat." After the student has read the selection, discuss it with the student. What steps did the little red hen take to make the bread she ate at the end of the story? **(She planted seed, harvested wheat, had wheat milled into flour, and made the bread.)** Who did she ask to help her? **(The duck and goose.)** Why didn't they help? **(They said it was too much work.)** When were they willing to help? **(They were willing to help when it was time**

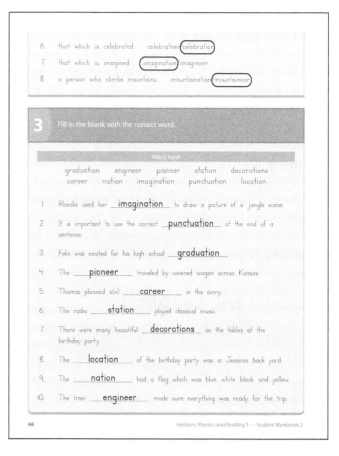

to eat.) Why didn't she give them food? **(They hadn't helped her do the work.)** What lesson does this story have? **(The need for hard work to accomplish a task. The story also talks about the reward of hard work.)**

Lesson 102

Regular Past Tense Verbs

Overview:

- Practice making regular verbs past tense by adding **-d** or **-ed**

- Recognize words which are regular past tense verbs

- Identify regular verbs and their past tenses

Material and Supplies:

- Teacher's Guide and Student Workbook

- White board or chart paper

- Phonics flashcards

- Reader: "Jack and the Beanstalk: The Beans are Planted"

Teaching Tips:

Review for Mastery. Discuss and review any work from the previous lesson that was assigned as homework. Check for completion of the activities and orally quiz the student for comprehension. Review any reading that was assigned, discussing the characters, setting, plot, theme, language, sequence, etc.

Strengthen fluency and phonemic awareness by reviewing words and sentences from the previous lessons. Build vocabulary skills by using some of the words in sentences.

You may want to create flashcards of words which contain regular past tense patterns. The student can study these throughout the unit.

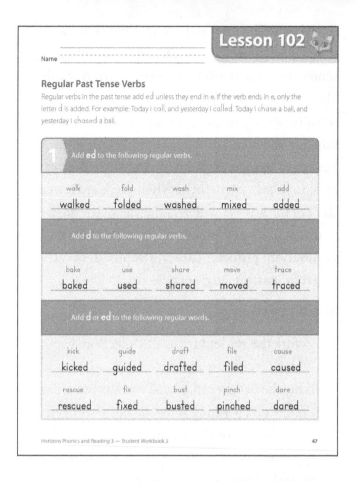

Lesson Introduction. Tell the student that starting with this lesson he/she will be studying regular and irregular verb patterns. Write the sentence **I call my dog.** on the board. Ask the student to identify the word which is the verb or indicates the action in the sentence. The student should identify the word **call**. Ask the student to restate the sentence as if it happened yesterday. For example: **Yesterday I _____ my dog.** What would the verb **call** be in that sentence? Explain that the word would change to **called**. Explain that when an action takes place in the past the verb becomes past tense. Many verbs become past tense by adding either **-d** or **-ed**. Verbs ending with **e** like **bake** become past tense by adding the letter **-d**. Write the following words on the board: **look, chew, hike,** and **hire**. Have the student make these words past tense by adding either **-ed** or **-d**: **looked, chewed, hiked,** and **hired**.

Activity 1. The student should turn to the activity sheet which accompanies this lesson. Read through the materials at the top of the sheet. In the first activity, the student will be asked to form past tense verbs by adding **-ed** to the given words. The correct answers are: **walked, folded, washed, mixed, added**. As an added activity have the student create sentences using the present and past tense verbs.

Continue the activity by having the student work with regular verbs that end in **e**. These regular verbs will only add the letter **-d** in order to correctly form past tense verbs. The correct answers are: **baked, used, shared, moved, traced**. As an added activity have the student create sentences using the present and past tense verbs.

The student will continue working with regular verbs which either add **-d** or **-ed** to become past tense. Whereas in the first two activities the words adding **-d** or **-ed** were separated, in this activity they will be combined. Remind the student to look carefully at the word endings when completing this activity. The answers are: **kicked, guided, drafted, filed, caused, rescued, fixed, busted, pinched, dared**.

Activity 2. The final activity asks the student to read sentences where the underlined word needs to be changed to the past tense. After the student has correctly formed the past tense verb, have him/her read the corrected sentence aloud. The changed verbs are: **visited, practiced, damaged, talked, used, baked, gathered, melted, shared, scratched**.

Reading Activity.

1. Have the student turn to the selection, "Jack and the Beanstalk." Ask the student if he/she is familiar with the story. If the student is familiar with the story, tell the student to look for parts of this story that may be different than other versions of the story he/she has heard.

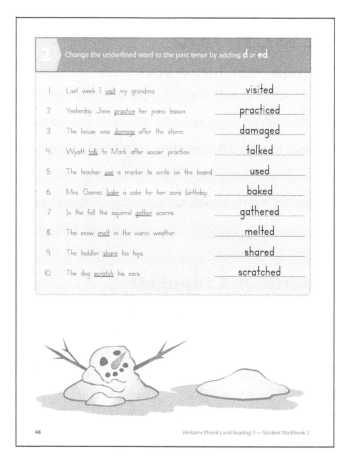

2. Direct the student in reading the first part of the selection, "The Beans are Planted." You may choose to read it together or have the student read it silently. After reading the selection, discuss it with the student. What was the problem in the story? (**Jack and his mother had no food or money.**) How did they try to solve their problem? (**They planned to sell their cow.**) How did the author describe Jack? (**He was described as lazy and good-natured.**) What did Jack get for selling the cow? (**He received some strange beans.**) What did his mother do with the beans? (**She threw them out of the window.**) What surprise did Jack have waiting for him in the morning? (**A fully grown beanstalk.**) What plans did he make? (**He wanted to climb the beanstalk.**)

3. Ask the student to predict what will happen next. Remind the student that there are various interpretations of the story.

Lesson 103
Regular Past Tense Verbs

Overview:

- Learn the rules for forming regular past tense verbs

- Identify words which are regular past tense verbs

- Create regular verbs by adding **-d**, **-ed**, or **-ied**

Material and Supplies:

- Teacher's Guide and Student Workbook

- White board or chart paper

- Phonics flashcards

- Reader: "Jack and the Beanstalk: Jack Captures a Hen"

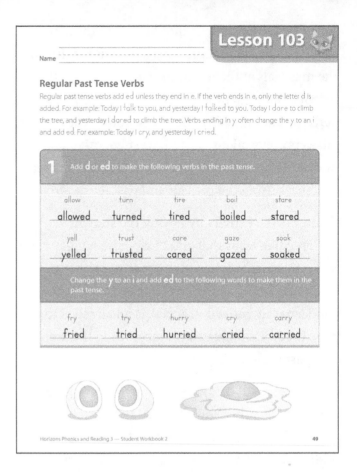

Teaching Tips:

Review for Mastery. Discuss and review any work from the previous lesson that was assigned as homework. Check for completion of the activities and orally quiz the student for comprehension. Review any reading that was assigned, discussing the characters, setting, plot, theme, language, sequence, etc.

Strengthen fluency and phonemic awareness by reviewing words and sentences from the previous lessons. Build vocabulary skills by using some of the words in sentences.

You may want to create flashcards of words which have regular past tense verb endings. The student can study these throughout the unit.

Lesson Introduction. Review the regular past tense verbs the student studied in the previous lesson. The student should remember that the letter **-d** or **-ed** is added to regular verbs to form the past tense. Write the words **trace, pedal, wait,**

and **force** on the board. Have the student form these into past tense verbs. The answers are: **traced, pedaled, waited** and **forced**. As an added activity, have the student write sentences using these verbs in the past tense.

Explain to the student that verbs ending in **-y** change the **y** to an **i** before adding **ed**. Write the words **cry** and **carry** on the board. Have the student form these into past tense verbs based on the rule of changing the **y** to an **i** and adding **-ed**. The correct forms of the words are **cried** and **carried**.

Activity 1. The student should turn to the activity sheet which accompanies this lesson. Read through the definition at the top of the page. The first activity asks the student to form past tense verbs from the list. The list is a mixture of words to which **-d** or **-ed** will need to be added. The answers are: **allowed, turned, tired, boiled, stared, yelled, trusted, cared, gazed, soaked.**

The next activity on the sheet asks the student to take verbs ending in **y** and make them past tense. The correct words are: **fried**, **tried**, **hurried**, **cried**, **carried**.

Activity 2. The lesson continues with the student choosing the correctly formed regular verb in each line. The student will need to recognize those words that become past tense by adding **-d**, **-ed**, or changing the **y** to **i** and adding **-ed**. The correct answers are: **added**, **marked**, **dressed**, **shoveled**, **jumped**, **married**, **bumped**, **fried**.

Activity 3. The final activity asks the student to read sentences and choose the correctly formed verbs to complete them. After the student has correctly answered the sentences, have the student read each aloud. The answers are: **named**, **buried**, **completed**, **allowed**, **performed**, **worried**, **cheered**, **decorated**, **married**, **passed**.

Reading Activity.

1. Remind the student of the predictions he/she made in the previous lesson. Discuss as well the events in the first section of the selection, "Jack and the Beanstalk."

2. The student should turn to the second part of the story, "Jack Captures a Hen." Direct the student in how you would like to read the selection, either silently or together. After reading the selection, discuss it together. Describe Jack's view at the top of the beanstalk. **(He saw nothing. There were no trees, plants, homes, or people.)** What was his mood at the top? **(He was lonely, hungry, and wanted to return to his mother.)** Describe the giant's wife. **(She was worried and afraid. She did help Jack hide from her husband.)** Why do you think she helped Jack? (Answers may include: **She didn't want to see the boy hurt or**

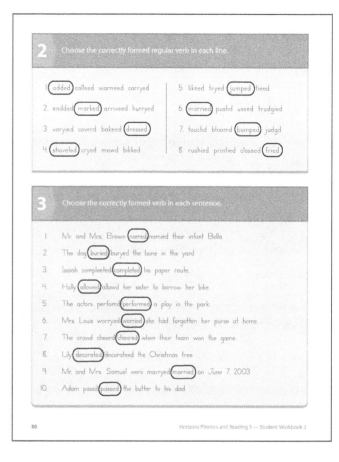

she was a kind woman.) Describe the giant's hen. **(When commanded, the hen would lay a golden egg.)** Why do you think Jack stole the hen? **(He wanted to find a way to get money for him and his mother.)** Do you think Jack will be satisfied and stay away from the beanstalk? **(Allow for individual answers.)**

3. Tell the student that some of the regular verbs in this section of the reading are **walk**, **hope**, **arrive**, **ask**, and **play**. Have the student make these verbs past tense. The answers are: **walked**, **hoped**, **arrived**, **asked**, **played**.

Lesson 104
Irregular Past Tense Verbs

Overview:

- Recognize words which form their past tenses irregularly

- Identify words which are irregular past tense verbs

- Use words which are irregular past tense verbs in sentences

Material and Supplies:

- Teacher's Guide and Student Workbook

- White board or chart paper

- Phonics flashcards

- Reader: "Jack and the Beanstalk: The Giant's Moneybags"

Teaching Tips:

Review for Mastery. Discuss and review any work from the previous lesson that was assigned as homework. Check for completion of the activities and orally quiz the student for comprehension. Review any reading that was assigned, discussing the characters, setting, plot, theme, language, sequence, etc.

Strengthen fluency and phonemic awareness by reviewing words and sentences from the previous lessons. Build vocabulary skills by using some of the words in sentences.

You may want to create flashcards of words which are irregular past tense verbs. The student can study these throughout the unit.

Lesson Introduction. In the previous lessons, the student has learned about verbs which form their past tenses regularly. Have the student share

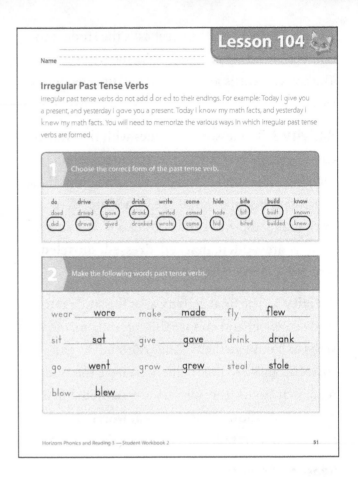

with you how these regular past tenses are formed. The student should recall that they are formed by adding **-d** or **-ed**. Verbs ending with **-y** become past tense by changing the **y** to an **i** and adding **-ed**.

Tell the student that in this lesson the student will learn about irregular past tense verbs. These are words the student will need to memorize. Write the following sentence on the board: **Yesterday I _____ my bike to the store.** Write the verbs **ride** and **drive** on the board. Ask the student what form of each word would be correct to fill in the blank. The sentence would read: **Yesterday I rode/drove my bike to the store.** The student should recognize that neither of these verbs end in **-d** or **-ed**. **Drive** and **rode** are examples of irregular verbs.

Activity 1. The student should turn to the activity sheet which accompanies this lesson. Read through the instructions at the top of the activity sheet. The student should look at the first activity. The student will be asked to choose between two possible past tense verbs. The students must choose the correct word. The answers to the activities are: **did, drove, gave, drank, wrote, came, hid, bit, built, knew**.

Activity 2. The next activity asks the student to write the correct past tense verb for each word. The student may find it helpful to think of a sentence as he/she works through the activity. The correct answers are: **wore, made, flew, sat, gave, drank, went, grew, stole, blew**. As an added activity you may want to have the student write a sentence for each word.

Activity 3. The student should look at the final activity on the sheet. Ask the student to read each sentence and then underline the irregular verb which is incorrect in each. After the student has underlined the incorrect verb form, he/she should write its correct form behind the sentence. The correct answers are:

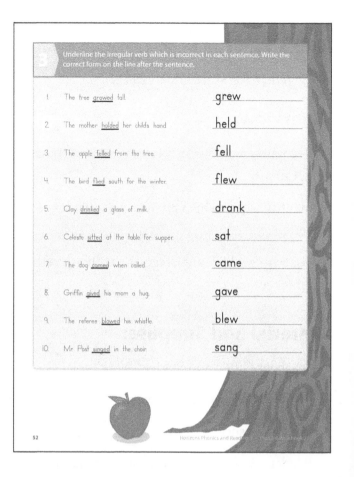

1. The tree **growed** tall. **grew**
2. The mother **holded** her child's hand. **held**
3. The apple **felled** from the tree. **fell**
4. The bird **flied** south for the winter. **flew**
5. Clay **drinked** a glass of milk. **drank**
6. Celeste **sitted** at the table for supper. **sat**
7. The dog **comed** when called. **came**
8. Griffin **gived** his mom a hug. **gave**
9. The referee **blowed** his whistle. **blew**
10. Mr. Post **singed** in the choir. **sang**

Reading Activity.

1. The student should continue reading the selection, "Jack and the Beanstalk." In this lesson the student should read the section entitled, "The Giant's Moneybags."

2. After the student has read the selection, discuss it with the student. Why did Jack want to climb the stalk again? (**He wanted to see if more valuables could be found in the giant's home.**) How did he plan to get past the giant's wife? (**He changed the color of his skin as a disguise.**) How did

the giant's wife treat him this time? (**She didn't recognize him. She told him the story of his last visit, but she said a different boy had come and taken the giant's hen.**) Where did he hide this time? (**He hid in the closet.**) How did the giant treat his wife? (**He was mean and demanding.**) What did the giant do with the money? (**He counted it.**) Why did Jack think he should take the giant's money? (**He knew that he and his mother could use the money. He may have thought the giant didn't deserve the funds.**)

3. Tell the student that the following irregular verbs were used in this section: **tell, lay, give,** and **see**. Ask the student what the past tense verbs would be. The answers are: **told, laid, gave, saw**.

Lesson 105

Irregular Past Tense Verbs

Overview:

- Recognize words which form their past tenses irregularly

- Identify words which are irregular past tense verbs

- Use words which are irregular past tense verbs in sentences

Material and Supplies:

- Teacher's Guide and Student Workbook

- White board or chart paper

- Phonics flashcards

- Reader: "Jack and the Beanstalk: The Harp"

Teaching Tips:

Review for Mastery. Discuss and review any work from the previous lesson that was assigned as homework. Check for completion of the activities and orally quiz the student for comprehension. Review any reading that was assigned, discussing the characters, setting, plot, theme, language, sequence, etc.

Strengthen fluency and phonemic awareness by reviewing words and sentences from the previous lessons. Build vocabulary skills by using some of the words in sentences.

You may want to create flashcards of words which are irregular past tense verbs. The student can study these throughout the unit.

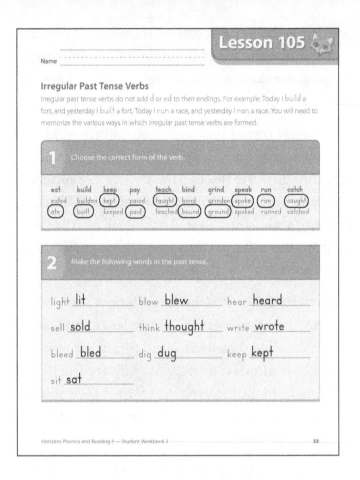

Lesson Introduction. This lesson will continue the study of irregular past tense verbs. Ask the student to write a sentence on the board that uses an irregular past tense verb. An example might be: **I hit a homerun.** Continue by asking the student how irregular and regular past tense verbs differ. The student should recall that regular past tense verbs add **-d** or **-ed**. Irregular verbs are not formed this way.

Activity 1. The student should turn to the activity sheet which accompanies this lesson. Have the student read the description at the top of the page. The student should then look at the first activity on the sheet. The student will be asked to choose the correct past tense form of each verb listed. The correct answers are: **ate, built, kept, paid, taught, bound, ground, spoke, ran, caught**.

Activity 2. The lesson continues with the student making present tense verbs past tense. All of the verbs listed are in the present tense. The answers are: **lit, blew, heard, sold, thought, wrote, bled, dug, kept, sat**. After the student has listed the words, you may want to have him/her write a sentence using each of the past tenses.

Activity 3. The student should look at the final activity on the sheet. Ask the student to read each sentence and then underline the irregular verbs. The correct answers are as follows:

1. The basketball team **won** the game.
2. The child **sat** in the high chair.
3. Mrs. Silva **sent** a letter to her brother.
4. Jack **took** a picture of a beautiful sunset.
5. The Stock family **spent** last week moving into a new home.
6. Jon **ran** home from the library.
7. Mrs. Dixon **lit** the candle.
8. Kayla **kept** a large stuffed animal in her room.
9. Anna **ate** an apple for an afternoon snack.
10. Mr. Kinsley **kept** a picture of his children in his billfold.

Reading Activity.

1. The student will finish reading the selection, "Jack and the Beanstalk." In this lesson the student will read the section entitled, "The Harp."

2. After the student has read the selection, ask him/her to discuss it with you. Why do you think Jack didn't return to the beanstalk for three years? (Answers may include: **The last time he went, he came home to a sick mother. He wasn't ready to meet the giant again or he felt he had enough money.**) When Jack returned up the beanstalk, what did he take from the giant? (**He took the giant's magic harp.**) Why was he almost caught by the giant during this trip? (**The harp began to call for**

his master.) How did the author make the scene of Jack stealing the harp exciting? (**There was a great deal of action with Jack and the giant running and the harp playing. The chaos of the scene created excitement.**) Ask the student if the story had a good ending? (**Allow for individual responses.**)

3. The following irregular verbs can be found in this section of the story: **come, see, hear,** and **think**. Ask the student to put them in the past tense. (The answers are: **came, saw, heard, thought.**)

Lesson 106

Review: Verb Tenses

Overview:

- Recall how regular past tense verbs are formed
- Remember that some past tense verbs are irregular
- Identify words which are regular and irregular past tense verbs

Material and Supplies:

- Teacher's Guide and Student Workbook
- White board or chart paper
- Phonics flashcards
- Reader: "Jack and the Beanstalk"

Teaching Tips:

Review for Mastery. Discuss and review any work from the previous lesson that was assigned as homework. Check for completion of the activities and orally quiz the student for comprehension. Review any reading that was assigned, discussing the characters, setting, plot, theme, language, sequence, etc.

Strengthen fluency and phonemic awareness by reviewing words and sentences from the previous lessons. Build vocabulary skills by using some of the words in sentences. Review the regular and irregular past tense verb flashcards that the student created for previous lessons.

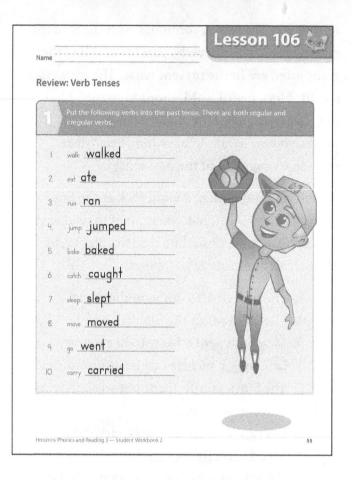

Lesson Introduction. Tell the student that in this lesson he/she will review both regular and irregular verbs. Ask the student to give you an example of a word which is a regular verb. Examples include: **walk, chew,** and **bike**. Continue by asking the student to give you examples of irregular verbs. Answers include: **eat** and **bring**.

Activity 1. Have the student turn to the activity sheet which accompanies this lesson. In the first activity the student will need to put verbs into the past tense. Some of the verbs will be regular and some will be irregular. The answers to the activity are: **walked, ate, ran, jumped, baked, caught, slept, moved, went, carried**.

Activity 2. The student should look at the next activity. Here the student must choose the correct form of the past tense verb. One will be written as a regular verb and the other as irregular. The student will need to determine the correct one. The answers are: **waited, sang, pinched, took, fell, doubled, rinsed, screamed, bled, ground.**

Activity 3. The final activity asks the student to apply his/her understanding of past tense verbs in sentences. Ask the student to read each sentence aloud, paying special attention to the underlined word. The student will need to change these underlined words to past tense verbs. Once the student has changed the verbs, he/she should reread the sentences. The answers are: **visited, barked, began, moved, built, used, planted, kept, blew, sent.**

Reading Activity.

1. The student will spend this lesson reviewing the entire story of "Jack and the Beanstalk."

2. Use the following questions to begin a discussion of the selection. How did the character Jack change from the beginning to the end of the lesson? (**At the beginning of the lesson he was lazy and seemed unmotivated. Once he began climbing the beanstalk he seemed to gain confidence and motivation.**) How did Jack's relationship with his mother change? (**His mother found Jack a burden at the beginning of the story. By the end of the story, he started taking care of his mother. He was concerned when she was sick.**) What three objects did Jack take from the giant and what was the significance of each? (**He took a hen, money, and a harp. The hen laid golden eggs. The golden eggs would give Jack and his mom all they needed. There were two bags of**

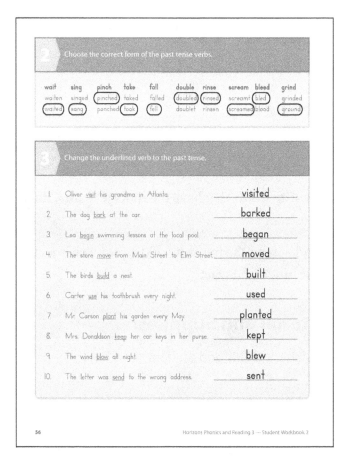

money. One was filled with gold coins and one with silver. Jack thought that the money would make his mother's life better. The harp played beautiful music and talked. Jack thought that he would rather have the harp than the hen or bags of money.**) What did Jack do with these objects? (**He used them as ways to provide for his mother.**) What lessons do you think can be learned from this story? (Answers may include: **The need to care for a parent. The story also encourages adventure over laziness.**)

3. As an added activity the student could write another ending or chapter of the story. Have the student use some past tense verbs. You could also have the student draw one of the scenes of the story.

Lesson 107

Root Words: ject, duc, duct, tract

Overview:

- Review words that have the roots **ject**, **duc**, **duct**, and **tract**

- Identify words that have the roots **ject**, **duc**, **duct**, and **tract**

- Understand the meaning of the root words **ject**, **duc**, **duct**, and **tract**

Material and Supplies:

- Teacher's Guide and Student Workbook

- White board or chart paper

- Phonics flashcards

- Reader: "Song from the Suds"

Teaching Tips:

Review for Mastery. Discuss and review any work from the previous lesson that was assigned as homework. Check for completion of the activities and orally quiz the student for comprehension. Review any reading that was assigned, discussing the characters, setting, plot, theme, language, sequence, etc.

Strengthen fluency and phonemic awareness by reviewing words and sentences from the previous lessons. Build vocabulary skills by using some of the words in sentences.

Create flashcards of words which contain the root words **ject**, **duc**, **duct**, and **tract**. The student can study these throughout the unit.

Lesson Introduction. Write the following words on the board: **reject**, **attract**, and **reduce**. Ask the student what the words mean and to use each in a sentence. To **reject** something means to remove or

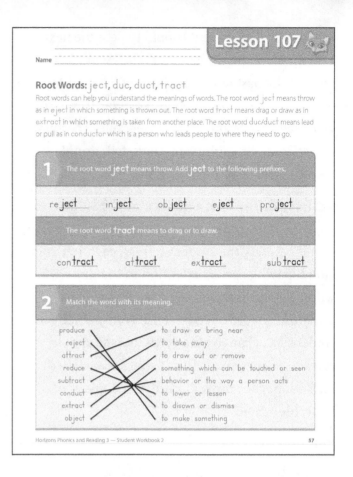

throw out something: **I rejected my teacher's offer for help. Attract** means to draw toward something: **The magnet was attracted to the metal. Reduce** means to lower or lessen: **The family worked to reduce the amount of garbage it threw away.**

Underline the root word in each of the words on the board: **reject, attract,** and **reduce.** Explain to the student that by understanding root words, he/she will be able to define more words. For example, the root word **ject** means to throw, **tract** means to drag or draw, and **duc/duct** means to lead or pull. Discuss how the meaning of these root words applies to the three words **reject, attract,** and **reduce** that you wrote on the board.

Activity 1. The student should turn to the activity sheet which accompanies this lesson. Have the student read the definition of the root words at the top of the page. After reading the definitions, the student should complete the first activity which focuses on the root word **ject**. The student will add the root word **ject** to the prefixes. The answers to the activity are: **reject, inject, object, eject, project.**

The next part of the activity asks the student to focus on the root word **tract**. Again the student should add the word **tract** to the prefixes. The answers are: **contract, attract, extract, subtract.**

Activity 2. The student should continue with the activity sheet. The student will match the words with the root words **ject, duc, duct,** and **tract** with their definitions. As an added activity have the student write sentences using the root words. The answers are:

produce	to make something
reject	to disown or dismiss
attract	to draw or bring near
reduce	to lower or lessen
subtract	to take away
conduct	behavior or the way a person acts
extract	to draw out or remove
object	something which can be touched or seen

Activity 3. The final activity asks the student to fill in the blanks with the correct words with the root words **ject, duc, duct,** and **tract**. If possible, have the student read each sentence with the correct answer before writing the answer in the blank. The correct answers to the activity are: **conduct, product, produce, introduction, reduce, producer, education, conductor.**

Reading Activity.

1. Direct the student in reading the poem, "Song from the Suds." It may be helpful if you read the poem first while the student follows along. Have the student read the poem to you a second time. Have the student read it silently a third time.

2. After reading the poem, ask the student the following questions. What is the speaker doing in this poem? (**Washing clothes and cleaning**

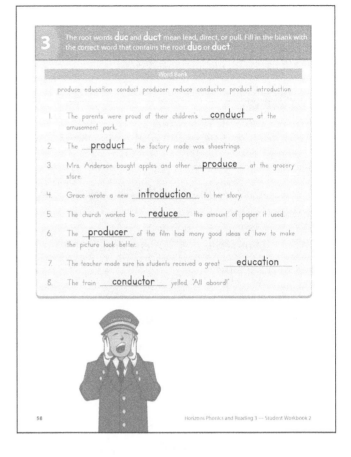

the house. You may want to explain that there weren't automatic washers and dryers at the time this poem was written.) What is the speaker's process for cleaning clothes? (**The author washes, rinses, and hangs the clothes out to dry.**) What images of cleaning does the author use in the poem? (**She speaks of washing laundry, hanging clothes out to dry, and sweeping.**) What does she compare to washing clothes? (**She compares it to the washing away of sins.**) What do you think the author meant when she wrote, "The busy mind has no time to think of sorrow, or care, or gloom?" (Answers may include: **When busy, a person doesn't have time to think about his/her own problems and concerns. Instead, the person is forced to focus on the work that needs to be done.**) What does this daily work bring to the author? (**The daily work brings health, strength, and hope.**)

Lesson 108

Root Words: spect, scribe

Overview:

- Learn the meaning of the root words **spect** and **scribe**

- Identify words containing the roots **spect** and **scribe**

- Use words in sentences which contain the roots **spect** and **scribe**

Material and Supplies:

- Teacher's Guide and Student Workbook

- White board or chart paper

- Phonics flashcards

- Reader: "Wilma Rudolph"

Teaching Tips:

Review for Mastery. Discuss and review any work from the previous lesson that was assigned as homework. Check for completion of the activities and orally quiz the student for comprehension. Review any reading that was assigned, discussing the characters, setting, plot, theme, language, sequence, etc.

Strengthen fluency and phonemic awareness by reviewing words and sentences from the previous lessons. Build vocabulary skills by using some of the words in sentences.

You may want to create flashcards of words with the roots **spect** and **scribe**. The student can study these throughout the unit.

Lesson Introduction. Remind the student of what he/she learned in the previous lesson about knowing certain root words so that he/she is better able to determine the meaning of new words. Write the word **spectacle** on the board. Use the word in a sentence. **Allison ordered new spectacles from the eye doctor.** Based on the sentence, what does the

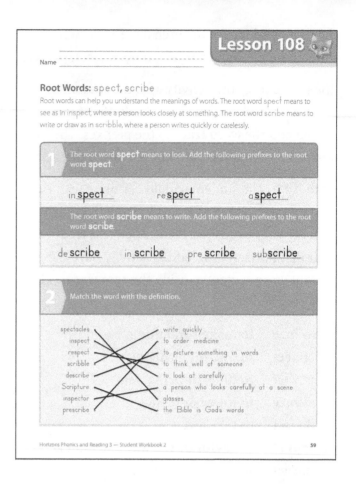

student think the word **spectacle** means? **(glasses)** Underline the root **spect** in the sentence. Explain that the root word **spect** means see.

Next write the word **scribble** on the board. Ask the student to define the word **scribble**. Explain that it means to doodle or write carelessly. Underline the **scrib** root in the word. Explain that the root words **scribe** or **scrib** mean to write. **Spect** and **scribe** will be the two root words discussed in this lesson.

Activity 1. Ask the student to turn to the activity sheet which accompanies this lesson. Read through the directions at the top of the activity sheet. In the first activity the student will focus on the root word **spect**. The student will be asked to add prefixes to the root word **spect** to form words. The answers are: **inspect, respect, aspect**.

The next part of the activity is similar to the first. The student will be adding prefixes to the root word **scribe**. The answers are: **describe, inscribe, prescribe, subscribe**.

Activity 2. Have the student continue with what he/she has learned about the root words to match the word with its definition. Tell the student that if he/she is unsure of a word's meaning to move on in the activity. The student can go back to look at the words of which he/she is uncertain. The answers to the matching activity are as follows:

spectacles	glasses
inspect	to look at carefully
respect	to think well of someone
scribble	write quickly
describe	to picture something in words
Scripture	the Bible is God's words
inspector	a person who looks carefully at a scene
prescribe	to order medicine

Activity 3. The student will apply his/her knowledge of the root words **spect** and **scribe** in this activity. The student will be asked to choose the correct word to complete each sentence. The student may want to read the sentence aloud with what he/she believes to be the correct answer before circling his/her response. The answers to the activity are: **prescribed, Scripture, spectators, scribbled, description, spectacles, inspector, respected.**

Reading Activity.

1. Have the student turn to the reading entitled, "Wilma Rudolph." Before reading, explain to the student that polio was a disease that affected many children and adults. It attacked their muscles, sometimes causing people to become unable to walk or breath. Today there is a vaccine for polio that keeps people from getting this disease. Also explain to the student that at the time Wilma Rudolph lived, African-Americans and whites were not treated equally. This was especially true in the south where African-Americans could not eat at the same restaurants as whites, go to the same schools, or receive the same medical care. Ask the student to read the selection.

2. After the student has read the selection, discuss it with the student. Why was Wilma Rudolph called the world's fastest woman? **(She won three gold medals at the 1960 Olympics. She won two sprints which were the fastest races.)** Describe Wilma Rudolph's family. **(She was the**

20th of 22 children. Her parents were poor African-Americans living in the southern U.S. Her father worked in the railroad yard as a handyman. Her mother cleaned the homes of white people.) What physical problems did Wilma Rudolph have as a child? **(She was often sick as a child and later contracted polio. Her left leg was affected. She was told that she would be unable to walk.)** How did she overcome her physical problems? **(With the help of her family she did a great deal of physical therapy. Eventually she was able to walk without braces.)** How did the fact that she was African-American make her life more difficult? **(She couldn't get treatment close to home. Her family had few financial resources.)** What athletic accomplishments did she have before the 1960 Olympics? **(She played basketball and was a good high school runner. In the 1956 Olympics she was the youngest American to compete and she won a bronze medal.)** What can people learn from her? (Answers may include: **The value of hard work and the importance of a supportive family.)**

Lesson 109

Root Words: pose, pel, port

Overview:

- Learn the meaning of the roots **pose, pel,** and **port**

- Identify words with the roots **pose, pel,** and **port**

- Use words containing the roots **pose, pel,** and **port** in sentences

Material and Supplies:

- Teacher's Guide and Student Workbook

- White board or chart paper

- Phonics flashcards

- Reader: "The Tree Squirrel"

Teaching Tips:

Review for Mastery. Discuss and review any work from the previous lesson that was assigned as homework. Check for completion of the activities and orally quiz the student for comprehension. Review any reading that was assigned, discussing the characters, setting, plot, theme, language, sequence, etc.

Strengthen fluency and phonemic awareness by reviewing words and sentences from the previous lessons. Build vocabulary skills by using some of the words in sentences.

You may want to create flashcards of words with the roots **pose, pel,** and **port**. The student can study these throughout the unit.

Lesson Introduction. Write the words **position, propeller,** and **airport** on the board. Ask the student to define each word. Answers may include that a position is a place where something is located, a propeller on an airplane helps it move, and an airport is a place where planes come and go. Underline the following roots in each of the words: **pos, pel,** and

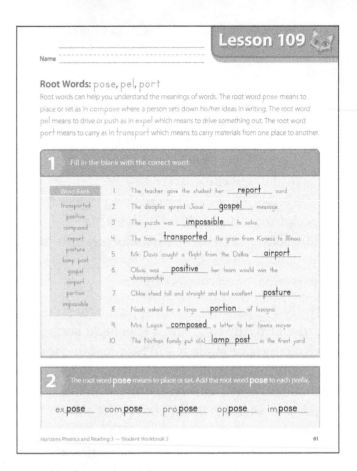

port. Tell the student that these are the root words he/she will be studying in today's lesson.

Explain that the root word **pose** means to place or set. Talk about how the root is evident in the word **position** where an object is put in a certain place. The next root is **pel** meaning to drive or push. A **propeller** causes a plane to move through the air and the connection between the root **pel** and the word is evident. The root **port** means to carry. An **airport** is a place where people are moved from one place to another on a plane. These root words will be the focus of the lesson.

Activity 1. The student should turn to the worksheet which accompanies this lesson. Ask the student to read the definitions at the top of the sheet. For the first activity the student will be asked to fill in sentences with the correct word. The words will be a mixture of ones with the roots **pose, pel,** and **port**. Have the student read the sentence with the correct word before placing the word in the blank. Hearing the word in context may solidify the student's answers. The correct responses are:

report, gospel, impossible, transported, airport, positive, posture, portion, composed, lamp post.

Activity 2. Next the student will be asked to add prefixes to the root word **pose**. As an added activity, you may want to have the student define the words or use them in sentences. The answers to the activity are: **expose, compose, propose, oppose, impose**.

The next section is similar to the first in that the student must add prefixes to a root word. In this case the student will add the prefixes to the root word **pel**. The answers are: **propel, compel, dispel, expel**. As an added activity, you may want to have the student define the words or use them in sentences.

The activity continues with the student adding prefixes to the root word **port**. The correct answers are: **transport, report, import, support, export**. As an added activity, you may want to have the student define the words or use them in sentences.

Activity 3. The final activity is a crossword puzzle. The student will need to answer the clues with words from the Word Bank before completing the puzzle. All the clue words contain the roots **pose, pel,** and **port**. The answers are:

Across:	Down:
1. **positive**	2. **important**
7. **portion**	3. **Gospel**
9. **propeller**	4. **opportunity**
10. **support**	5. **posture**
11. **expel**	6. **chapel**
12. **airport**	8. **oppose**

Reading Activity.

1. The student has read about many interesting and exotic animals. In this reading the student will learn about the common but fascinating tree squirrel. Direct the student in reading the selection, "The Tree Squirrel."

2. After reading the selection, ask the student the following questions. What places in the world do not have tree squirrels? (**The continents**

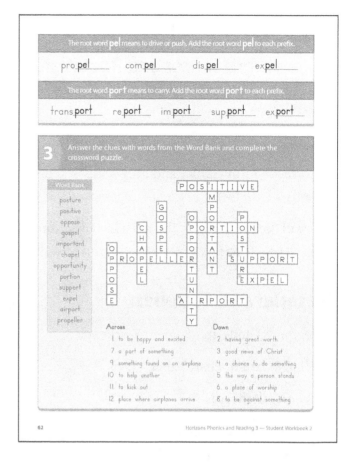

of Antarctica and Australia do not have tree squirrels.) How many varieties of tree squirrels are there? (**Over 300.**) How do tree squirrels communicate? (**They communicate through chirps and also through flicking their tails.**) What is unique about a squirrel's teeth? (**A squirrel only has four teeth and they are continually growing. A squirrel must gnaw in order to keep their teeth the proper length.**) In what ways does a squirrel use its tail? (**It uses its tail as an umbrella, a flag, and a way to balance.**) How have tree squirrels adapted to their environments? (**They'll eat food which people give them. They will live in human structures as well as trees.**) What damage can squirrels cause for their human neighbors? (**They can gnaw through wires, dig up gardens, and make nests in attics.**)

3. Have the student draw a picture of the type(s) of tree squirrels that live in your area. Additionally, the student could spend some time observing tree squirrels and compare their behavior to what they read in the selection.

Lesson 110
Review: Verb Tenses and Root Words

Overview:

- Identify words ending in **-eer** and **-ation**

- Correctly form regular and irregular past tense verbs

- Recall the meanings of the roots **ject, duc, duct, tract, spect, scribe, pose, pel,** and **port**

Material and Supplies:

- Teacher's Guide and Student Workbook

- White board or chart paper

- Phonics flashcards

- Reader: "Come, Little Leaves"

Teaching Tips:

Review for Mastery. Discuss and review any work from the previous lesson that was assigned as homework. Check for completion of the activities and orally quiz the student for comprehension. Review any reading that was assigned, discussing the characters, setting, plot, theme, language, sequence, etc.

Strengthen fluency and phonemic awareness by reviewing words and sentences from the previous lessons. Build vocabulary skills by using some of the words in sentences.

You may want to review flashcards made for words in this unit.

Lesson Introduction. This lesson reviews the material the student learned in the unit. Begin by reviewing words that end in **-eer** and **-ation**. Ask the student to give you examples of a word that ends in one of these letter combinations. Answers include: **mountaineer** and **imagination**. Discuss the meanings of these two endings. For example, a

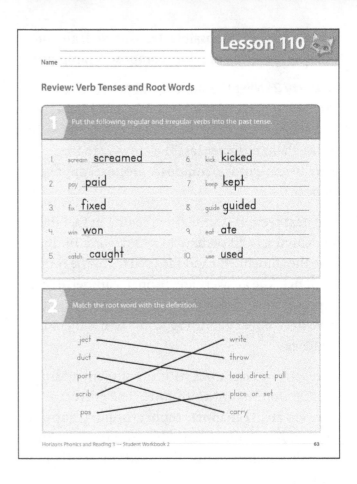

mountaineer is a person who climbs mountains. **Imagination** is that which is imagined.

Continue by talking about regular verbs. Ask the student how most past tense verbs are formed. The student should recall that most past tense verbs end in **-d** or **-ed**. Ask the student to give you examples of regular past tense verbs. Examples may include: **walked** and **baked**. Remind the student of irregular past tense verbs and how many of these needed to be memorized. Again, ask for some examples. These may include: **brought, told,** and **sat**.

The unit concluded with lessons on root words. The root words studied in these lessons were: **ject, duc, duct, tract, spect, scribe, pose, pel,** and **port**. Have the student give you an example of a word formed from each of these roots. Examples include: **inject, reduce, product, tractor, spectator, scribble, propose, expel,** and **airport**. As an added activity, you may want to have the student define the root words.

Activity 1. The student should turn to the activity sheet which accompanies this lesson. The review sheet is arranged in the same way as the test. In the test different examples will be used but the format will remain the same. The student will begin by putting verbs into the past tense. There are combinations of regular and irregular verbs. The answers are: **screamed, paid, fixed, won, caught, kicked, kept, guided, ate, used**.

Activity 2. The lesson continues with the student matching some of the root words learned in the unit with their definitions. The student may find it helpful to think of a word with that root as he/she matches the definition. The answers to the activity are the following:

ject	throw
duct	lead, direct, pull
port	carry
scrib	write
pos	place or set

Activity 3. The student continues with an activity where he/she must circle the correct word for each given definition. The words will be formed using the roots learned in the unit. There are also words formed with the endings **-ation** and **-eer**. The answers to the activity are: **mountaineer, location, spectacles, tractor, expel, celebration, portion, oppose, introduction, subtracting, impossible, auctioneer**.

Activity 4. Finally the student will be asked to circle the word which correctly completes each sentence. Words will test the student's understanding of past tense verbs as well as root words. The answers for the activity are: **drank, rejected, scribe, attracted, arrived, won, flew, positive, describing, prescription**.

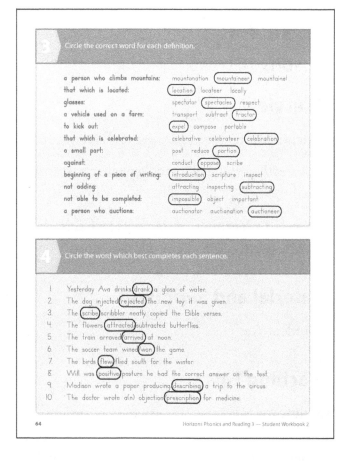

Reading Activity.

1. The student should turn to the poem "Come, Little Leaves."

2. Direct the student in reading this poem for pleasure.

Test 11

Lessons 101-110

Overview:

- Identify words ending in **-eer** and **-ation**

- Correctly form regular and irregular past tense verbs

- Recall the meanings of the roots **ject, duc, duct, tract, spect, scribe, pose, pel,** and **port**

Material and Supplies:

- Student Test

Teaching Tips:

Review for Mastery. Discuss and review any work from the previous lesson that was assigned as homework. Check for completion of the activities and orally quiz the student for comprehension. Review any reading that was assigned, discussing the characters, setting, plot, theme, language, sequence, etc.

Lesson Introduction. This lesson tests the material the student learned in the unit. Before the test you may want to ask the student if he/she has any final questions. There may be questions from the review the student will want to ask. Remind the student that the final test follows the same format as the review.

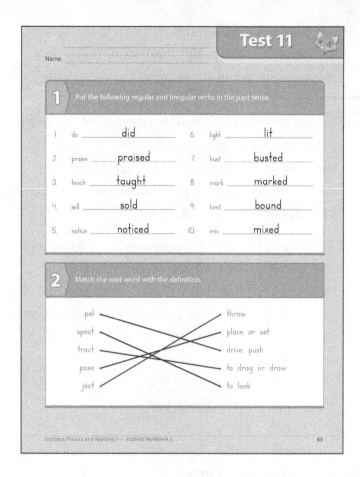

Activity 1. The student should turn to the test. The test is arranged in the same way as the review sheet. In the test different examples will be used but the format will remain the same. The student will begin by putting verbs into the past tense. There are combinations of regular and irregular verbs. The answers are: **did, praised, taught, sold, noticed, lit, busted, marked, bound, mixed**.

Activity 2. The lesson continues with the student matching some of the root words learned in the unit with their definitions. The student may find it helpful to think of a word with that root as he/she matches the definition. The answers to the activity are:

pel	drive, push
spect	to look
tract	to drag or draw
pose	place or set
ject	throw

Activity 3. The student continues with an activity where he/she must circle the correct word for each given definition. The words will be formed using the roots learned in the unit. There are also words formed with the endings -**ation** and -**eer**. The answers to the activity are: **reduce, transport, creation, puppeteer, portion, oppose, possessive, donation, introduction, important, positive, engineer**.

Activity 4. Finally, the student will be asked to circle the word which correctly completes each sentence. This activity will test the student's understanding of past tense verbs as well as root words. The answers for the activity are: **tractor, melted, report, chased, ate, sent, rejected, dug, folded, built**.

Lesson 111

Prefixes: un, re, pre

Overview:

- Understand the meaning of the prefixes **un-**, **re-**, and **pre-**

- Recognize words beginning with **un-**, **re-**, and **pre-**

- Use words with **un-**, **re-**, and **pre-** in sentences

Material and Supplies:

- Teacher's Guide and Student Workbook

- White board or chart paper

- Phonics flashcards

- Reader: "Twinkle, Twinkle, Little Star"

Teaching Tips:

Lesson Introduction. Explain to the student that in this unit he/she will be studying prefixes. Write the word **unhappy** on the board. Ask the student to tell you something that makes him/her happy. Now ask the student to tell you what the word unhappy means. The student should recognize that the prefix **un-** before the word changes the meaning of the word. Write the word **unable** on the board. Ask the student what he/she thinks the prefix **un-** means. Knowing the words **unhappy** and **unable**, the student should recognize that the prefix **un-** means **not**. Write the words **redo** and **return** on the board. Ask the student what the prefix **re-** means. The student should recognize that **re-** means **back** or **again**. Next write the words **preheat** and **preorder** on the board. Have the student explain what the prefix **pre-** means. The prefix **pre-** means **before**. Tell the student that in this lesson he/she will study the prefixes **un-**, **re-**, and **pre-**.

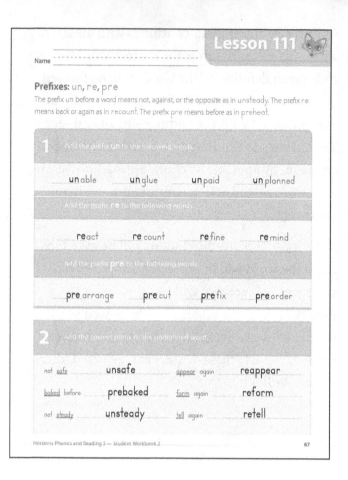

You may want to create flashcards of words with the prefixes **un-**, **re-**, and **pre-**. The student can study these throughout the unit.

Activity 1. The student should turn to the activity sheet for this lesson. Read through the definition at the top of the sheet. The first activity asks the student to add the prefixes **un-**, **re-**, and **pre-** to the words listed. As an added activity you could ask the student to say sentences using the words formed with the prefixes. The answers to the activity are: **unable, unglue, unpaid, unplanned, react, recount, refine, remind, prearrange, precut, prefix, preorder**.

Activity 2. The second activity continues with the student studying prefixes. In this activity the student will need to form words based on the given clues. You may want to complete the first one with the student. The answers to the activity are: **unsafe, reappear, prebaked, reform, unsteady, retell, unzipped, unhappy, redial, preheat**.

Activity 3. The final activity asks the student to apply what he/she has learned to complete sentences using words with prefixes. After the student has completed the activity, ask the student to read each sentence aloud. This will help the student both understand the words formed with prefixes as well as recognize whether or not the activity has been completed correctly. The answers to the activity are: **prepared, unclean, previews, removed, unclear, unwell, returned, unload, resource, preferred**.

Reading Activity.

1. Ask the student turn to the selection, "Twinkle, Twinkle, Little Star." The student may be familiar with the first verse of the poem. If so, explain that the poem has many other verses but only a few are included in the poem listed in the reading.

2. Read the poem to your student. Next ask the student to read the poem to you. After the student has read the selection, discuss the poem. What does the author say the star looks like? **(It looks like a diamond in the sky. The author also talks about the star as an eye which never closes.)** When does the star appear? **(It appears after the sun has set and the grass is wet with dew.)** What does the star do for people? **(It guides travelers.)** Ask the student if he/she has ever heard this poem before? **(The student may have heard the first verse only.)** Explain to the student that the first verse of this poem is famous. The poem in the book is only one version of the remaining verses. There are many variations.

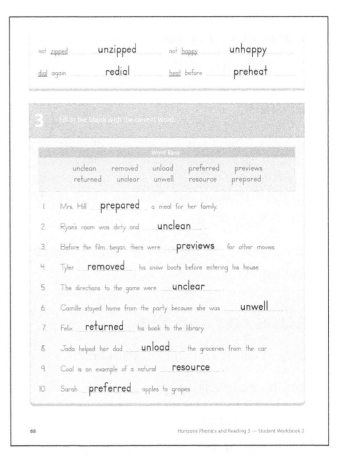

3. Discuss the way in which the poem is written. What words does the poet repeat? **(The poet repeats "Twinkle, twinkle, little star.")** Why do you think the poet repeats that line? (Answers may include: **It reminds the reader of the poem's theme. It also has a nice and memorable rhythm.**) How many syllables are in each line? **(7)** What lines rhyme? **(The first two and the last two lines in each stanza rhyme.)** You may want to mention that the poem is arranged in four-line stanzas.

4. As an added activity, write a new verse for the poem with your student.

Lesson 112

Prefixes: in, im, il, ir

Overview:

- Know the meaning of the prefixes **in-**, **im-**, **il-**, and **ir-**

- Recognize when to place the prefix **in-**, **im-**, **il-**, or **ir-** before a word

- Use words with the prefixes **in-**, **im-**, **il-**, and **ir-** in sentences

Material and Supplies:

- Teacher's Guide and Student Workbook

- White board or chart paper

- Phonics flashcards

- Reader: "The Rabbit and the Wolf"

Teaching Tips:

Review for Mastery. Discuss and review any work from the previous lesson that was assigned as homework. Check for completion of the activities and orally quiz the student for comprehension. Review any reading that was assigned, discussing the characters, setting, plot, theme, language, sequence, etc.

Strengthen fluency and phonemic awareness by reviewing words and sentences from the previous lessons. Build vocabulary skills by using some of the words in sentences.

You may want to create flashcards of words which use the prefixes **in-**, **im-**, **il-**, and **ir-**. The student can study these throughout the unit.

Lesson Introduction. Tell the student that he/she will continue learning about prefixes in this lesson. Write the prefixes **in-**, **im-**, **il-**, and **ir-** on the board. Tell the student that all the prefixes mean **not**.

However, the spelling of the root word determines which prefix will be used. Tell the student you are going to write words using each of the prefixes on the board and you want the student to determine the rules for which prefix to use. The words to write on the board are: **indoor**, **incapable**, **inside**, **immobile**, **impressive**, **illegal**, and **irresponsible**. The student should recognize that most words use **in-**. Words beginning with **m** or **p** add **im-**. Words beginning with **l** add the prefix **il-** and those beginning with **r** use the prefix **ir-**.

Activity 1. The student should turn to the worksheet for this lesson. Read through the definition for **in-**, **im-**, **il-**, and **ir-** words at the top of the page. The student should look at the first activity which asks him/her to put the correct prefix in front of each root. The correct answers are: **immobile**, **immovable**, **impatient**, **impossible**, **illegal**, **illogical**, **irregular**, **irreplaceable**, **irresponsible**, **incapable**, **inactive**, **inhuman**, **infinite**.

Activity 2. Continue the activity by having the student choose the correct prefix for each word. Even if the student doesn't know the definition for the word, he/she should follow the rules for adding prefixes. The correct answers are: **injustice, illiteracy, invalid, irrational, immature, irremovable, inconstant, insanity, illegible, impart.**

Activity 3. The student will continue the lesson by choosing the correct word to fill in the blank in each sentence. After the student has completed the activity, he/she should read each sentence to make sure it is correct. The answers for the activity are: **impossible, incredible, irregular, incomplete, indirect, imperfect, infrequent, irreplaceable.**

Reading Activity.

1. Have the student turn to the selection, "The Rabbit and the Wolf." This is an example of a fable. Tell the student that as he/she reads the selection he/she should look for what lesson is being taught.

2. Read through the selection with the student. This might be a good story in which to have the student read the lines of one animal while the teacher reads the line for the other animal. You may want to read the narrative portions for the student.

3. After reading the selection, discuss it with the student. What caused the problems between the rabbit and the wolf? (**The rabbit liked to tease the wolf. The wolf was tired of the rabbit's tricks.**) How did the wolf decide to teach the rabbit a lesson? (**The wolf planned on cutting off the rabbit's ears, which would be a rather extreme way to teach a lesson.**) What plans did the rabbit make to avoid this punishment? (**The rabbit planned to trick the wolf yet again. This**

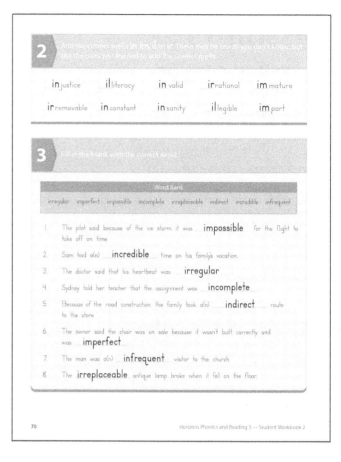

time the rabbit would pretend to teach the wolf a new dance.) How did the rabbit use the dance to escape? (**The rabbit kept dancing in a larger circle which brought him closer to the woods. The rabbit also made sure the wolf was very dizzy when he planned his escape.**)

4. Fables like this often have a lesson for the reader. What do you think the lesson of this story may be? (Answers may include: **You shouldn't trick others. You should be prepared in all situations. Find creative ways to solve your problems.**)

Lesson 113

Prefixes: co, com, con

Overview:

- Learn the rules for forming words with the prefixes **co-**, **com-**, and **con-**

- Identify words which contain the prefixes **co-**, **com-**, and **con-**

- Use words with the prefixes **co-**, **com-**, and **con-** in sentences

Material and Supplies:

- Teacher's Guide and Student Workbook

- White board or chart paper

- Phonics flashcards

- Reader: "The Year's at the Spring"

Teaching Tips:

Review for Mastery. Discuss and review any work from the previous lesson that was assigned as homework. Check for completion of the activities and orally quiz the student for comprehension. Review any reading that was assigned, discussing the characters, setting, plot, theme, language, sequence, etc.

Strengthen fluency and phonemic awareness by reviewing words and sentences from the previous lessons. Build vocabulary skills by using some of the words in sentences.

You may want to create flashcards of words which have the prefixes **co-**, **com-**, and **con-**. The student can study these throughout the unit.

Lesson Introduction. Explain that in this lesson the student will continue the study of prefixes. The prefixes **co-**, **com-**, and **con-** will be studied in this lesson. Write the words **coauthor** and

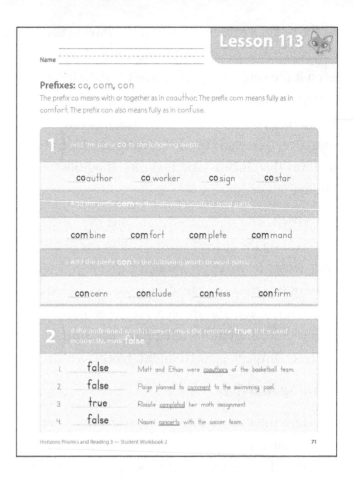

costar on the board. Ask the student what he/she thinks the prefix **co-** means. Help the student to arrive at the definition of **together**. Next write the words **comfort** and **concern** on the board. Ask the student to define these words or use them in sentences. For example: **Mrs. Harris was concerned about the comfort of her children.** Tell the student that the prefixes **com-** and **con-** before a word or word part mean **fully**.

Activity 1. The student should turn to the activity sheet which accompanies this lesson. Read through the definition at the top of the page. The first activity asks the student to add the prefixes **co-**, **com-**, and **con-** to words or word parts to create words. As an added activity, ask the student to write or say sentences with the words. The correct words are: **coauthor, coworker, cosign, costar, combine, comfort, complete, command, concern, conclude, confess, confirm.**

Activity 2. The next activity asks the student to look at sentences in which words with the prefixes **co-**, **com-**, and **con-** are used. The student will need to look at the context in which the word is used to determine whether or not the sentence makes sense. The correct responses are: **false, false, true, false, false, true, true, false, true, false.**

Activity 3. The lesson continues with the student completing a word search using words beginning with **co-**, **com-**, and **con-**. Because the first two letters of all the words are the same, the word search may be a bit tricky. **See image for answers.**

Reading Activity.

1. The selection for this lesson is "The Year's at the Spring." Ask the student to list some of the things he/she sees in the spring. Depending on where you live, these answers will vary. Do talk about the fact that spring is often a time of new birth and animals emerging from hibernation. Tell the student that in the poem, the student is going to read how the author reflects on spring.

2. Read the poem to the student while he/she follows along. Explain any difficult of unusual words in the poem for the student. After you have read the poem ask the student to read the poem to you.

3. Discuss the poem with your student. What does the poet say that spring is like? (**The poet says that the sunrise is at seven, there is dew on the hill, the birds are out, and the snail is as well.**) What do you think the poem means when he says that God is in His heaven? (**The poet may be saying that God is in charge of all things or that God rules over His creation from heaven.**) Why do you think the poet ends with the words, "All's right with the world!"? (Answers may include: **The world is the way God intended it to be or the author loves the spring season.**)

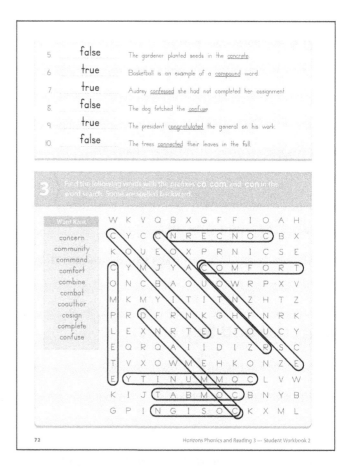

4. Discuss the way in which the poem is written. What lines in the poem rhyme? (**The rhyme scheme of the poem is abcdabcd.**) How many syllables are in each line? (**The lines all have five syllables.**)

Lesson 114

Prefixes: ex, non, dis

Overview:

- Recognize words with the prefixes **ex-**, **non-**, and **dis-**

- Identify words which are formed with the prefixes **ex-**, **non-**, and **dis-**

- Use words with the prefixes **ex-**, **non-**, and **dis-** in sentences

Material and Supplies:

- Teacher's Guide and Student Workbook

- White board or chart paper

- Phonics flashcards

- Reader: "Beauty and the Beast: Beauty and Her Sisters"

Teaching Tips:

Review for Mastery. Discuss and review any work from the previous lesson that was assigned as homework. Check for completion of the activities and orally quiz the student for comprehension. Review any reading that was assigned, discussing the characters, setting, plot, theme, language, sequence, etc.

Strengthen fluency and phonemic awareness by reviewing words and sentences from the previous lessons. Build vocabulary skills by using some of the words in sentences.

You may want to create flashcards of words which contain the prefixes **ex-**, **non-**, and **dis-**. The student can study these throughout the unit.

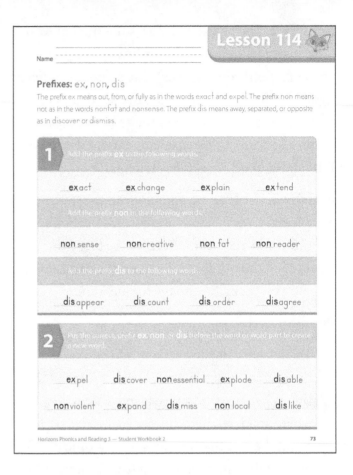

Lesson Introduction. In the previous lessons, the student has learned about prefixes. This lesson will continue the study of prefixes. Tell the student that one of the easier prefixes to remember is **non-** which has the word "no" in it. As the student might imagine, the prefix means **no** or **not**. Examples of words with **non-** include: **nonfat** and **nonstudent**. The next two prefixes have multiple meanings: **ex-** and **dis-**. The prefix **ex-** means **out, from**, or **fully** as in the words **exact** or **exchange**. Point out that the prefix **ex-** in **exact** means **fully** while in the word **exchange** it means **from**. The prefix **dis-** means **away, separated**, or **opposite** as in the words **disappear** or **disorder**. In the word **disappear** the prefix means **away** or **opposite** and in the word **disorder** the prefix means the **opposite**.

Activity 1. The student should turn to the activity sheet which accompanies this lesson. Read through the instructions at the top of the activity sheet. The student should look at the first activity. The student will be asked to put the prefixes **ex**, **non**, and **dis** in front of the words or word parts. The answers to the activity are: **exact, exchange, explain, extend, nonsense, noncreative, nonfat, nonreader, disappear, discount, disorder, disagree.**

Activity 2. In the next section, the student will need to decide which of the three prefixes to put in front of the words or word parts. You may want to have a piece of scratch paper available so the student can practice writing the word before filling in the blank in the activity. This will help the student in determining the correct prefix. The answers to the activity are: **expel, discover, nonessential, explode, disable, nonviolent, expand, dismiss, nonlocal, dislike.**

Activity 3. The final activity asks the student to use words with the prefixes **ex-, non-,** and **dis-** in sentences. The student will need to read each sentence and determine which word correctly completes it. The correct answers are: **exercise, discussed, nonschool, disagreed, excellent, disliked, explained, exactly, discovered, nonsense.**

Reading Activity.

1. Ask the student to turn to the selection, "Beauty and the Beast: Beauty and Her Sisters." This lesson and the next four will be spent reading and discussing this selection.

2. Direct the student in reading the selection. You may want to read it with the student or have him/her read it silently.

3. After the student has read the selection, discuss it with him/her. What is the setting of the story? **(The story begins in the city in a fine house and then moves to a small house in the country.)** Who are the main characters?

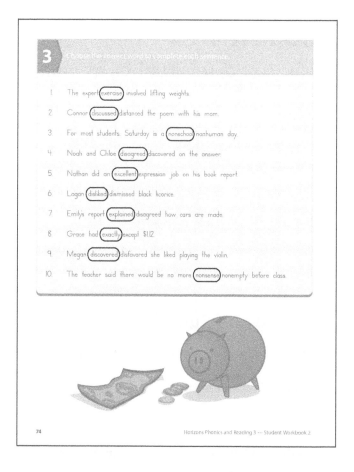

(The merchant and his three daughters.) How was Beauty different than her sisters? **(She was more than pretty. She was kind and helpful. She worked hard. She cared more about her father than herself.)** What happened to the older sisters when the family became poor? **(They were unable to marry the men they had wanted. They became lazy and did nothing to help their father's situation.)** Why did Beauty ask her father to bring home a rose? **(She didn't want to appear better than her sisters by asking for nothing.)** What did the father find when he reached his ship? **(He could not get the cargo that was his. He returned from his trip poorer than when he had started.)**

4. Ask the student to predict what will happen next. If the student is familiar with another retelling of the story, remind him/her that this story does not have to follow a movie or other version.

Lesson 115

Prefixes: mid, semi, uni, bi, tri, multi

Overview:

- Recognize words which are formed with the prefixes **mid-**, **semi-**, **uni-**, **bi-**, **tri-**, and **multi-**

- Identify words which begin with the prefixes **mid-**, **semi-**, **uni-**, **bi-**, **tri-**, and **multi-**

- Use words with the prefixes **mid-**, **semi-**, **uni-**, **bi-**, **tri-**, and **multi-** in sentences

Material and Supplies:

- Teacher's Guide and Student Workbook

- White board or chart paper

- Phonics flashcards

- Reader: "Beauty and the Beast: The Beast at Home"

Teaching Tips:

Review for Mastery. Discuss and review any work from the previous lesson that was assigned as homework. Check for completion of the activities and orally quiz the student for comprehension. Review any reading that was assigned, discussing the characters, setting, plot, theme, language, sequence, etc.

Strengthen fluency and phonemic awareness by reviewing words and sentences from the previous lessons. Build vocabulary skills by using some of the words in sentences.

You may want to create flashcards of words which contain the prefixes **mid, semi, uni, bi, tri,** and **multi**. The student can study these throughout the unit.

Lesson Introduction. This lesson will continue the study of prefixes. In this lesson the prefixes all stand for numbers or measurements. Write the words

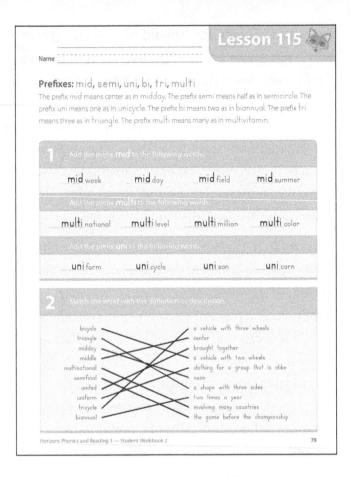

Name

Prefixes: mid, semi, uni, bi, tri, multi
The prefix mid means center as in midday. The prefix semi means half as in semicircle. The prefix uni means one as in unicycle. The prefix bi means two as in biannual. The prefix tri means three as in triangle. The prefix multi means many as in multivitamin.

1 Add the prefix **mid** to the following words.

mid week   mid day   mid field   mid summer

Add the prefix **multi** to the following words.

multi national   multi level   multi million   multi color

Add the prefix **uni** to the following words.

uni form   uni cycle   uni son   uni corn

2 Match the word with the definition or description.

bicycle	a vehicle with three wheels
triangle	center
midday	brought together
middle	a vehicle with two wheels
multinational	clothing for a group that is alike
semifinal	noon
united	a shape with three sides
uniform	two times a year
tricycle	involving many countries
biannual	the game before the championship

Horizons Phonics and Reading 3 — Student Workbook 2   75

bicycle, **tricycle**, and **unicycle** on the board. Ask the student how many wheels each of these cycles has. The student should recognize that the prefix **bi-** means **two**, **tri-** means **three**, and **uni-** means **one**. Next, write on the board **midday** and **multiday**. Ask the student what the prefixes in each of these words means. **Midday** would indicate the **middle** of the day and the word **middle** has the prefix **mid-** in it. The prefix **multi-** means **many,** so a **multiday** sale would be a sale that lasts for **many days**. Finally, draw a **semicircle** on the board. Ask the student to name the object. The student may indicate it is a half circle or an arc. Discuss how the word **semi-** means **half**.

Activity 1. The student should turn to the activity sheet which accompanies this lesson. Have the student read the description at the top of the page. The student should look at the first activity on the sheet. The student will be asked to write the prefixes **mid-**, **multi-**, and **uni-** in front of words or word parts. The correct answers are: **midweek, midday, midfield, midsummer, multinational,**

multilevel, multimillion, multicolor, uniform, unicycle, unison, unicorn.

Activity 2. The lesson continues with the student matching words with prefixes with their definitions. The student should draw a line between each word and its definition. The correct responses are as follows:

bicycle	a vehicle with two wheels
triangle	a shape with three sides
midday	noon
middle	center
multinational	involving many countries
semifinal	the game before the championship
united	brought together
uniform	clothing for a group that is alike
tricycle	a vehicle with three wheels
biannual	two times a year

Activity 3. The student should look at the final activity on the activity sheet. The student will be asked to fill in the blank with the correct word from the Word Bank. The student may want to read the sentence aloud before writing in the correct word. Sometimes hearing the word used in context will help the student determine whether or not he/she has chosen the correct word. The correct responses are: **binoculars, bicycle, uniforms, semifinals, midday, midnight, multilevel, unicorn, united, semicircle.**

Reading Activity.

1. The student will continue reading the selection, "Beauty and the Beast." In this lesson the student will read the section entitled, "The Beast at Home."

2. Direct the student in reading this selection. You may want to take turns reading the paragraphs.

3. Discuss the selection with the student by using the following questions. Describe the merchant's first view of the Beast's home. (**The merchant was afraid he was going to die in the forest. He saw a well-lit castle which seemed to welcome him.**) What did the merchant note was unusual about the palace? (**His horse immediately had food. A**

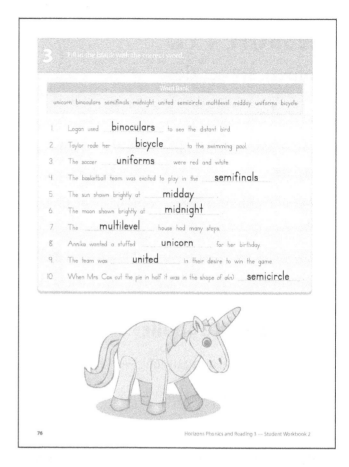

beautiful table was set but no one appeared to live in the palace. After he went to bed, he woke up and found that his clothes had been cleaned.) Why did the Beast appear to the merchant? (**He was angry that the merchant would steal a rose.**) Why do you think that picking a rose angered the Beast so deeply? (**He claimed that he loved the rose more than anything else. He also had provided the merchant with many things, and it seemed as if he was ungrateful when he picked the rose.**) What did the Beast say would happen as a result of the merchant's actions? (**He said that either the merchant would die or that someone else would need to come and die in the place of the merchant.**) What orders did the Beast give the merchant before he left? (**He told him to pack a chest with whatever he wanted and leave. The merchant had three months in which to return.**)

4. Ask the student what he/she thinks the merchant put in the chest. Have the student predict what he/she thinks will happen next.

Lesson 116

Prefixes: ab, ad, de

Overview:

- Understand the meaning of the prefixes **ab-**, **ad-**, and **de-**

- Remember how to form words with the prefixes **ab-**, **ad-**, and **de-**

- Use words with the prefixes **ab-**, **ad-**, and **de-** in sentences

Material and Supplies:

- Teacher's Guide and Student Workbook

- White board or chart paper

- Phonics flashcards

- Reader: "Beauty and the Beast: Beauty Goes to the Beast"

Teaching Tips:

Review for Mastery. Discuss and review any work from the previous lesson that was assigned as homework. Check for completion of the activities and orally quiz the student for comprehension. Review any reading that was assigned, discussing the characters, setting, plot, theme, language, sequence, etc.

Strengthen fluency and phonemic awareness by reviewing words and sentences from the previous lessons. Build vocabulary skills by using some of the words in sentences.

Create flashcards of words using the prefixes **ab-**, **ad-**, and **de-**. The student can study these throughout the unit.

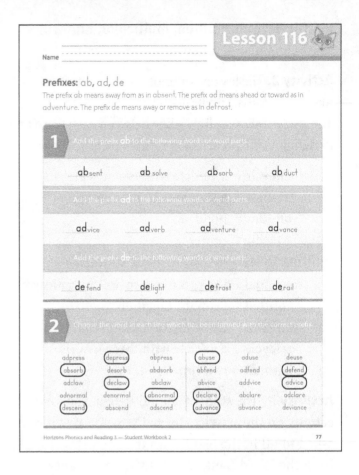

Lesson Introduction. Tell the student that in this lesson he/she will continue the study of prefixes. In this lesson the student will study the prefixes **ab-**, **ad-**, and **de-**. The prefixes **ab-** and **de-** both mean **away** and the prefix **ad-** means **toward**. Write the words **absent** and **defrost** on the board. Ask the student to define these words, keeping in mind that the prefixes mean **away.** Next, write the word **adventure** on the board. Remind the student the prefix **ad-** means **toward.** Have the student define this word. As an added activity, have the student say sentences using the words **absent, defrost,** and **adventure.**

Activity 1. Have the student turn to the activity sheet which accompanies this lesson. Read through the definitions at the top of the page. The first activity is similar to those the student has done in the previous lessons. The student will be asked to add the prefixes **ab-**, **ad-**, and **de-** to words or word parts. The correct answers to the activity are: **absent, absolve, absorb, abduct, advice, adverb, adventure, advance, defend, delight, defrost, derail.**

Activity 2. The student will continue by applying what he/she learned in the previous activity in this lesson. The student will need to choose the correctly written word with a prefix from a list of three. If possible ask the student to say the words aloud. Hearing the words may help the student recognize those which are formed correctly and those which are not. The correct answers to the activity are: **depress, absorb, declaw, abnormal, descend, abuse, defend, advice, declare, advance.**

Activity 3. The final activity continues the application aspect of this lesson. The student will need to choose the correct word to complete each sentence. Again, reading the sentence may help the student understand which word correctly fits the sentence. The correct answers are: **admired, absorbed, defended, defrosted, advice, advanced, admitted, demanded.**

Reading Activity.

1. The student will continue reading the selection, "Beauty and the Beast." Ask the student to read the section entitled, "Beauty Goes to the Beast."

2. After the student has read the selection, lead him/her in a discussion of the material read. What did the merchant do when he came home? (**He gave Beauty a rose and he told his family what had happened.**) How did the oldest sisters react to the merchant's words? (**They blamed Beauty for everything. They claimed her selfishness in asking for a rose brought all this trouble.**) Why didn't the merchant let his family know about the gold in the chest? (**He didn't want to return to town life.**) Why do you think he didn't want to go back to town? (**Allow for individual answers.**) How did the sisters show their true feelings for Beauty? (**They rubbed their eyes with onions**

so that they could pretend to cry.**) How did the Beast greet Beauty and her father? (**He greeted them with a beautiful supper which was followed by a harsh greeting.**) Describe Beauty's room. (**It was filled with all of the things she liked and enjoyed.**) How was Beauty able to see her father? (**She could see him through a magic mirror.**) What questions did the Beast ask Beauty at dinner? (**He asked if he were ugly and if she would marry him.**) Discuss the appropriateness of these questions. (**They were rather blunt and uncomfortable questions for a first meeting.**)

3. Have the student predict what will happen next.

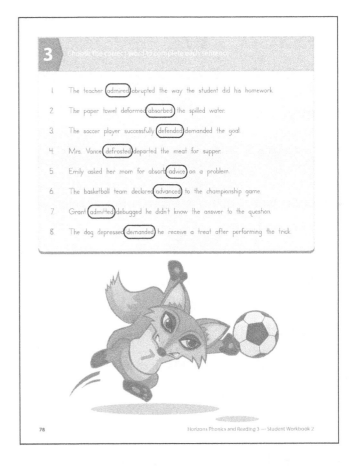

Lesson 117

Prefixes: over, super, sub

Overview:

- Understand the meaning of the prefixes **over-**, **super-**, and **sub-**

- Identify words that contain the prefixes **over-**, **super-**, and **sub-**

- Use words with the prefixes **over-**, **super-**, and **sub-** in sentences

Material and Supplies:

- Teacher's Guide and Student Workbook

- White board or chart paper

- Phonics flashcards

- Reader: "Beauty and the Beast: The Charm is Broken"

Teaching Tips:

Review for Mastery. Discuss and review any work from the previous lesson that was assigned as homework. Check for completion of the activities and orally quiz the student for comprehension. Review any reading that was assigned, discussing the characters, setting, plot, theme, language, sequence, etc.

Strengthen fluency and phonemic awareness by reviewing words and sentences from the previous lessons. Build vocabulary skills by using some of the words in sentences.

Create flashcards of words which contain the prefixes **over-**, **super-**, and **sub-**. The student can study these throughout the unit.

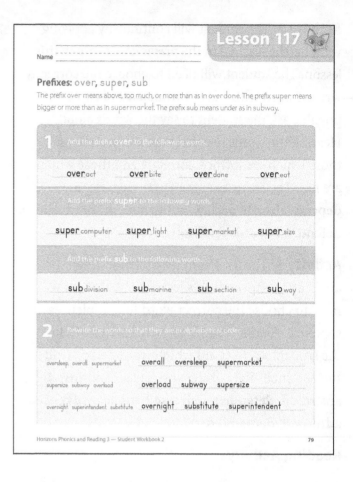

Lesson Introduction. Write the words **overeat, supersize,** and **subway** on the board. Ask the student what each word means. Now have the student break each word apart and determine the meaning of the prefix. The student should recognize that a person who overeats, eats too much. The prefix **over-** means **more than** or **too much**. The word supersize describes something which is larger than normal. So the prefix **super-** means **bigger** or **more than**. Finally, subway is a type of transportation that goes underground. **Sub-** would mean **below** or **underneath**.

Activity 1. Turn to the activity sheet which accompanies this lesson. The student should read the definitions for the prefixes at the top of the page. The student should look at the first activity where he/she needs to add prefixes to words or word parts. The correct responses are: **overact, overbite, overdone, overeat, supercomputer, superlight, supermarket, supersize, subdivision, submarine, subsection, subway.**

Activity 2. The next activity asks the student to put words with the prefixes **over-**, **super-**, and **sub-** in alphabetical order. The student should remember that when the prefixes are the same, the student will need to alphabetize by the letters which follow. The answers are as follows:

> **overall, oversleep, supermarket**
> **overload, subway, supersize**
> **overnight, substitute, superintendent**
> **overcooked, overpower, subzero**
> **subdivision, subtract, supercomputer**

Activity 3. The final activity asks the student to add the prefixes **over-**, **super-**, and **sub-** to words or word parts to make them fit the sentences. You may want to do the first one together so the student knows what he/she must do. The correct answers are: **substitute, overcooked, supermarket, overnight, subtract, overjoyed, subzero, subway, overslept, superstore**.

Reading Activity.

1. The student will finish reading the selection, "Beauty and the Beast." Have the student read the last section of the selection entitled, "The Charm is Broken."

2. After the student has read the selection, discuss it with him/her. Use the following questions to begin your discussion. How long did Beauty live with the Beast before she returned home? **(3 months)** Why did she return home? **(Her father became ill and the Beast said she could go to visit him.)** Why did the Beast let Beauty go home? **(He cared for her and wanted what was best for her. He knew that she loved her father.)** Describe the husbands Beauty's sisters married. **(The student should recognize that the husbands were just as miserable as their wives. The one husband was only interested in his own looks. The other husband said mean and cruel things to others.)** Why didn't Beauty return to the Beast after a week? **(Her sisters appeared to**

appreciate and need her. She enjoyed feeling that she was needed and loved.)** Why did the sisters really want Beauty to remain at home? **(They wanted Beauty to be destroyed by the Beast. Their hatred of her was so strong that they wanted the Beast to become angry and kill her.)** What happened when Beauty returned to the Beast? **(She found him very ill.)** What happened so that the Beast changed from his ugly form into a handsome prince? **(Beauty told him that she loved him and would marry him.)** How did Beauty's life change when the Beast turned into a prince? **(In many ways her life did not change. He remained kind and caring toward Beauty. The area around the castle changed into a thriving kingdom with happy residents.)**

3. Tell the student that in the next lesson you will discuss the overall themes of the selection.

---

subzero overcooked overpower   overcooked   overpower   subzero

supercomputer subtract subdivision   subdivision   subtract   supercomputer

3 Add the prefix over, super, or sub in the blank to complete the word.

1. The students had a(n) ___ **sub** stitute teacher in Sunday school.

2. Mrs. Darling ___ **over** cooked the chicken dish she prepared for supper and it was burned.

3. Mr. Taggart went to the ___ **super** market for fresh lettuce.

4. Emma stayed ___ **over** night at her cousins house.

5. Nate needed to ___ **sub** tract 37 from 99.

6. Ashley was ___ **over** joyed with her birthday presents.

7. The ___ **sub** zero temperatures made it dangerous to play outside.

8. Mr. Perez took the ___ **sub** way to work every day.

9. Mrs. McDougall ___ **over** slept in the morning and was late for work.

10. Mrs. Sutton went to the ___ **super** store to buy groceries, clothes, and a coffee maker.

Horizons Phonics and Reading 3 — Student Workbook 2

Lesson 118

Prefixes: mis, pro, under

Overview:

- Learn the meaning of the prefixes **mis-**, **pro-**, and **under-**

- Identify words containing the prefixes **mis-**, **pro-**, and **under-**

- Use words in sentences which contain the prefixes **mis-**, **pro-**, and **under-**

Material and Supplies:

- Teacher's Guide and Student Workbook

- White board or chart paper

- Phonics flashcards

- Reader: "Beauty and the Beast"

Teaching Tips:

Review for Mastery. Discuss and review any work from the previous lesson that was assigned as homework. Check for completion of the activities and orally quiz the student for comprehension. Review any reading that was assigned, discussing the characters, setting, plot, theme, language, sequence, etc.

Strengthen fluency and phonemic awareness by reviewing words and sentences from the previous lessons. Build vocabulary skills by using some of the words in sentences.

You may want to create flashcards of words with the prefixes **mis-**, **pro-**, and **under-**. The student can study these throughout the unit.

Lesson Introduction. This student will continue the study of prefixes. Write the following words on the board: **misspell**, **protect**, and **undersea**. Ask the student to identify the prefix in each word. The student should identify the prefixes **mis-**, **pro-**, and **under-**. Have the student try to determine the

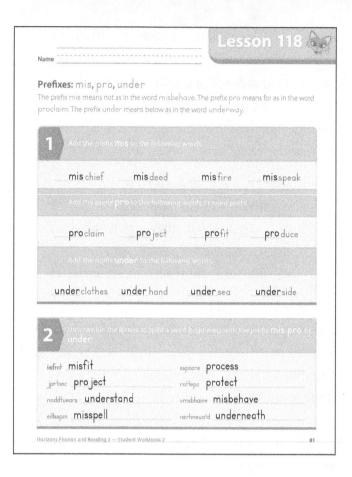

meaning of the prefixes. With guidance, the student should learn that the prefix **mis-** means **not**, the prefix **pro-** means **for**, and the prefix **under-** means **below**. Ask the student to think of other words which have these prefixes. Examples may include: **miswrite, misspeak, provide, produce, underwater,** and **underclothes**.

Activity 1. Ask the student to turn to the activity sheet which accompanies this lesson. Read through the definitions of the prefixes at the top of the page. The first activity will continue the pattern which was begun in earlier activities. The student will add one of the prefixes for this lesson to words or word parts. The answers to the activity are: **mischief, misdeed, misfire, misspeak, proclaim, project, profit, produce, underclothes, underhand, undersea, underside**.

Activity 2. The lesson continues with the student unscrambling letters to spell words with prefixes. The student may find it helpful to first determine the prefix of the word before unscrambling the rest of the letters. By eliminating the letters which are prefixes, the activity will go more smoothly.

The answers to the activity are: **misfit, process, project, protect, understand, misbehave, misspell, underneath.**

Activity 3. The final activity for this activity sheet asks the student to use the words with prefixes in sentences. A Word Bank is provided to help the student with this activity. The student may find it helpful to read the sentences aloud with the word to make sure it is correct. The answers to the sentences are: **mismatched, misspelled, underneath, understanding, program, process, underwent, misbehaved, underwater, mispronounced.**

Reading Activity.

1. The student should turn to the selection, "Beauty and the Beast."

2. Tell the student that in this lesson you will look at some of the overall themes of the selection. Use some of the following questions to lead your discussion. What were the settings of the selection? (**The settings included the merchant's home in town, the merchant's home in the country, and the Beast's castle.**) Ask the student to briefly describe each of the settings. (**When the merchant and his family lived in town, they had all the possessions they wanted or needed. The sisters were spoiled in the town setting, but Beauty was happy as long as she was with her family. The house in the country was poor and lacked the material possessions of the one in the city. The sisters were miserable in the country house, but Beauty remained happy and polite. The Beast's home was beautiful but there was no happiness present.**) Discuss the main characters and their traits with the student. (**Characters which should be discussed include Beauty, Beast, the merchant, and the sisters.**) This selection contains some lessons that people can learn about jealousy, kindness, selfishness, and judging others by their appearance. Ask the student what he/she learned about jealousy in this selection. (Answers may include: **The sisters' jealousy of Beauty resulted in them putting their interests**

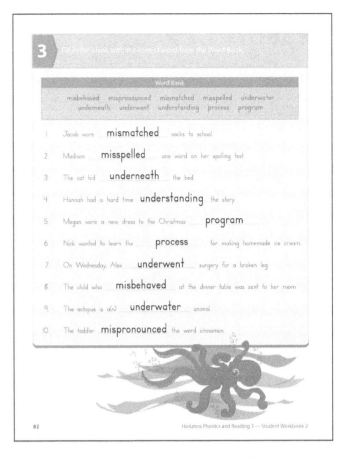

above hers. **The sisters ended up hurting only themselves through their mean and jealous behavior.**) How was kindness shown and rewarded in the selection? (**The Beast's kindness and care for Beauty resulted in her loving him. Similarly, Beauty showed kindness to all people, even those who were mean to her. This resulted in her finding happiness and joy in her life with the Beast.**) Compare and contrast characters which were selfish with those who were selfless. (**Allow for individual responses.**) Discuss how people in the selection judged by appearance. (**The main character in which this was seen is the Beast. However, Beauty was also judged by her appearance.**)

3. There are a number of ways in which you could conclude your study of this selection. The student could write an acrostic poem using the word Beauty or Beast. The student could also write another chapter in the story of Beauty and the Beast. Finally, the student could compare and contrast this telling of the story of "Beauty and the Beast" with others they may have seen or read.

Lesson 119

Prefix Combinations

Overview:

- Form words with multiple prefixes
- Recognize words formed with multiple prefixes
- Identify the meaning of words with multiple prefixes

Material and Supplies:

- Teacher's Guide and Student Workbook
- White board or chart paper
- Phonics flashcards
- Reader: "Clara Barton"

Teaching Tips:

Review for Mastery. Discuss and review any work from the previous lesson that was assigned as homework. Check for completion of the activities and orally quiz the student for comprehension. Review any reading that was assigned, discussing the characters, setting, plot, theme, language, sequence, etc.

Strengthen fluency and phonemic awareness by reviewing words and sentences from the previous lessons. Build vocabulary skills by using some of the words in sentences.

You may want to create flashcards of words with multiple prefixes. The student can study these throughout the unit.

Lesson Introduction. Explain to the student that up until now, he/she has only looked at single prefixes for a word. However, many times more than one prefix may be used at the beginning of a word. Write the words **unimproved, unhappy,**

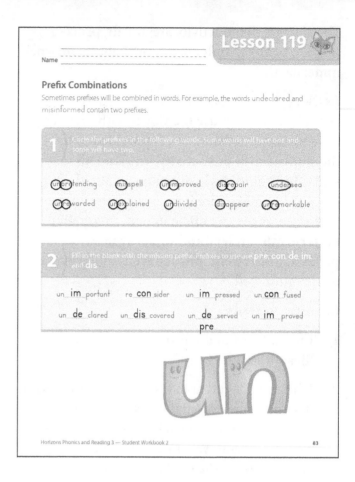

and **unrecovered**. Ask the student which of the three words has/have more than one prefix. The words **unimproved** and **unrecovered** both have multiple prefixes. Discuss the meaning of each of the prefixes in the words. Use these to help define the words. Tell the student that in this lesson he/she will be asked to use words with multiple prefixes.

Activity 1. The student should turn to the worksheet which accompanies this lesson. Ask the student to read the definition at the top of the page. In the first activity, the student will need to circle the prefixes in the words listed. Some of these words will have single prefixes and others will have multiple prefixes. The answers to the activity are: **unpretending (un, pre), misspell (mis), unimproved (un, im), disrepair (dis, re), undersea (under), unrewarded (un, re), unexplained (un, ex), undivided (un), disappear (dis), unremarkable (un, re).**

Activity 2. The lesson continues with the student adding a second prefix to words. The prefixes the student may choose from are **pre-**, **con-**, **de-**, **im-**, and **dis-**. You may want to do the first example together before having the student complete the activity. The answers are: **unimportant, reconsider, unimpressed, unconfused, undeclared, undiscovered, undeserved/unpreserved, unimproved.**

Activity 3. The final activity asks the student to choose a word to complete each sentence. Two choices are provided for each sentence. Have the student read the completed sentences aloud to make sure the sentence makes sense. The answers for the activity are: **unprepared, reconstruct, unimproved, undiscovered, unimportant, unrewarded, mispronounced, unimaginable.**

Reading Activity.

1. The student should read the selection, "Clara Barton."

2. Discuss the selection with the student. Use the following questions to begin your discussion. During what war did Clara Barton work as a nurse? (**She worked as a nurse during the Civil War.**) How did where she worked as a nurse change throughout the war? (**She started working far from the field of battle and continued to move closer to the battlefront.**) What did ambulances look like at the time of the Civil War? (**They were pulled by horses and probably uncomfortable.**) Why was it difficult to know who had died or lived in the Civil War? (**There were no good records. People also didn't have good communication like we do today.**) How did Clara Barton get involved with the Red Cross? (**She went to Europe and worked with the International Red Cross in war zones and natural disasters**

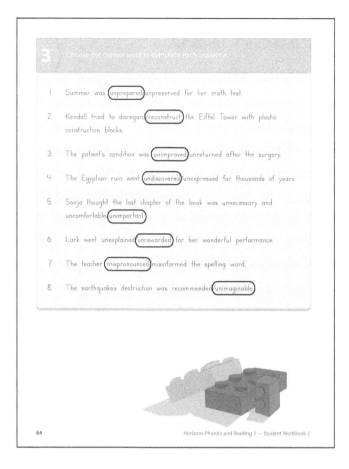

in Europe.) What is the purpose of the American Red Cross which Clara Barton founded? (**The Red Cross provides emergency response to people in disasters whether human or natural.**)

3. Have the student research places where the American Red Cross is at work today.

Lesson 120

Review: Prefixes

Overview:

- Identify words with prefixes
- Correctly form words with prefixes
- Recall the meanings of the prefixes in this unit

Material and Supplies:

- Teacher's Guide and Student Workbook
- White board or chart paper
- Phonics flashcards
- Reader: "The Crow and the Pitcher"

Teaching Tips:

Review for Mastery. Discuss and review any work from the previous lesson that was assigned as homework. Check for completion of the activities and orally quiz the student for comprehension. Review any reading that was assigned, discussing the characters, setting, plot, theme, language, sequence, etc.

Strengthen fluency and phonemic awareness by reviewing words and sentences from the previous lessons. Build vocabulary skills by using some of the words in sentences.

You may want to review flashcards made for prefixes in this unit.

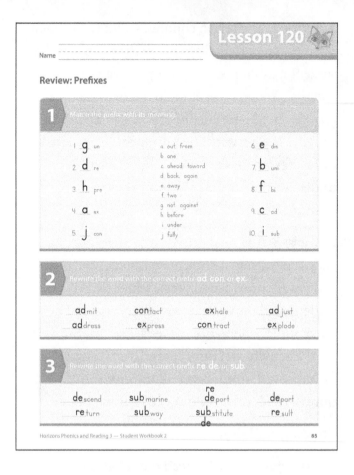

Lesson Introduction. This lesson reviews the material the student learned in the unit. The student will complete activities which review the use of singular and multiple prefixes. You may want to see if the student can remember the various prefixes he/she learned in this unit. The prefixes studied were: **un-, re-, pre-, in-, im-, il-, ir-, co-, com-, con-, ex-, non-, dis-, mid-, semi-, uni-, bi-, tri-, multi-, ab-, ad-, de-, over-, super-, sub-, mis-, pro-,** and **under-.**

Write all of the prefixes on the board. Ask the student to think of words made from these prefixes. These can be words with singular or multiple prefixes. Examples include: **unprepared, return, inside, immobile, illegal, irregular, coexist, complete, contact, explain, nonsense, disappointment, middle, semiannual, uniform, bicycle, triangle, multinational, absent, admit, defend, overuse, superpower, subway, misspell, protect,** and **underway.**

Activity 1. The student should turn to the activity sheet which accompanies this lesson. The review sheet is arranged in the same way as the test. In the test different examples will be used but the format will remain the same. The student will begin by matching prefixes with their meanings. The answers are: 1.—**g**, 2.—**d**, 3.—**h**, 4.—**a**, 5.—**j**, 6.—**e**, 7.—**b**, 8.—**f**, 9.—**c**, 10.—**i**.

Activity 2. The next activity asks the student to rewrite the word or word part with the correct prefix. The prefixes the student will be asked to use are **ad-**, **con-**, or **ex-**. The student may want to have a piece of scratch paper available to practice the words before writing them on the activity sheet. The correct answers are: **admit, contact, exhale, adjust, address, express, contract, explode**.

Activity 3. The activity sheet continues with a similar activity which uses different prefixes. The prefixes used in this activity are **re-**, **de-**, and **sub-**. The correct answers are: **descend, submarine, deport/report, depart, return, subway, destitute/substitute, result**.

Activity 4. The next activity involves the student determining which word is spelled correctly in each line. The student will need to look carefully at the spelling of the prefixes as well as how they are added to the words. The correct answers are: **reheat, undergo, impact, unicycle, biannual, supermarket, excellent, midnight, displace, irregular**.

Activity 5. The final activity asks the student to use words with prefixes in context. The student will need to fill in the blank with the correct word for each sentence. A student may find it helpful to read each sentence aloud to hear if the choice is correct. The answers for the activity are: **illegible, continent, example, reheated, invisible, unwrap, biweekly, reusable, immobile, unicycle**.

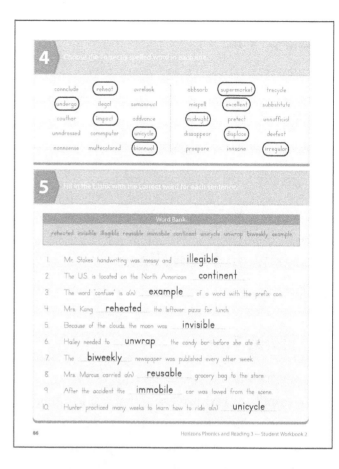

Reading Activity.

1. The student should turn to the selection, "The Crow and the Pitcher."

2. Direct the student in reading this fable for pleasure.

Test 12

Lessons 111-120

Overview:

- Identify words with prefixes
- Correctly form words with prefixes
- Recall the meanings of the prefixes

Material and Supplies:

- Student Test

Teaching Tips:

Review for Mastery. Discuss and review any work from the previous lesson that was assigned as homework. Check for completion of the activities and orally quiz the student for comprehension. Review any reading that was assigned, discussing the characters, setting, plot, theme, language, sequence, etc.

Lesson Introduction. This lesson tests the material the student learned in the unit. Before the test you may want to ask the student if he/she has any final questions. There may be questions the student will want to review. Remind the student that the final test follows the same format as the review.

Activity 1. The student should turn to the test. The test is arranged in the same way as the review sheet. In the test different examples will be used but the format will remain the same. The student will begin by matching prefixes with their meanings. The answers are: 1.—**e**, 2.—**j**, 3.—**b**, 4.—**h**, 5.—**a**, 6.—**c**, 7.—**i**, 8.—**g**, 9.—**d**, 10.—**f.**

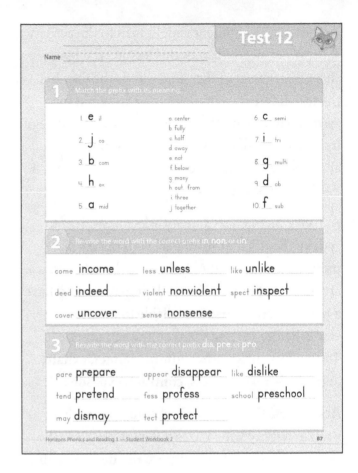

Activity 2. The next activity asks the student to rewrite the word or word part with the correct prefix. The prefixes the student will be asked to use are **in-**, **non-**, or **un-**. The student may want to have a piece of scratch paper available to practice the words before writing them on the activity sheet. The correct answers are: **income, unless, unlike, indeed, nonviolent, inspect, uncover, nonsense**.

Activity 3. The activity sheet continues with a similar activity which uses different prefixes. The prefixes used in this activity are **dis-**, **pre-**, and **sub-**. The correct answers are: **prepare, disappear, dislike, pretend, profess, preschool, dismay, protect**.

Activity 4. The next activity involves the student determining which word is spelled correctly in each line. The student will need to look carefully at the spelling of the prefixes as well as how they are added to the words. The correct answers are: **disrepair, prearrange, unclear, advise, triangle, overdone, absent, confess, subway, unlikely.**

Activity 5. The final activity asks the student to use words with prefixes in context. The student will need to fill in the blank with the correct word for each sentence. The student may find it helpful to read each sentence aloud to hear if the choice is correct. The answers for the activity are: **impossible, confused, untidy, disliked, impatient, reviewed, misspelled, supermarket, repeat, uniforms.**

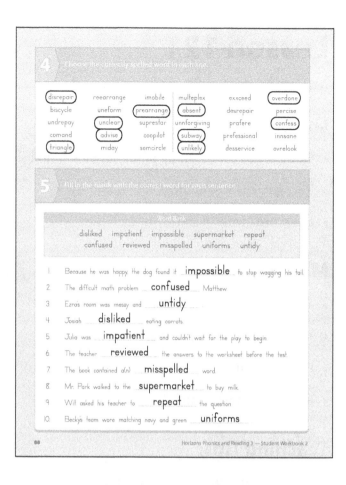

Lesson 121

Suffixes: y and ly

Overview:

- Understand the meaning of the suffixes -**y** and -**ly**

- Recognize words ending with -**y** and -**ly**

- Use words with -**y** and -**ly** in sentences

Material and Supplies:

- Teacher's Guide and Student Workbook

- White board or chart paper

- Phonics flashcards

- Reader: "Foreign Lands"

Teaching Tips:

Lesson Introduction. Explain to the student that in this unit he/she will be studying suffixes. The first suffixes studied will be the very common -**y** and -**ly** endings. These suffixes are often added to the end of words to make them adjectives or adverbs. These are words which describe other words. Write the following sentence on the board: **The dog eagerly waved his tail hoping for a healthy treat.** Ask the student which words in the sentence end in -**y** and -**ly** (**eagerly** and **healthy**). Point out that these two words describe how the dog was wagging his tail and what kind of treat he was wanting. Explain that the suffixes -**y** and -**ly** mean **like** or **how**. Ask the student to think of words which are formed by adding -**y** and -**ly**. Make sure these are not words such as **very** which end in -**y**. Words listed may include: **quickly**, **eagerly**, **hairy**, and **smelly**. Explain that some words change the **y** to an **i** before adding the -**ly** ending. An example is the word **happy**, which becomes **happily**.

You may want to create flashcards of words with the suffixes -**y** and -**ly**. The student can study these throughout the unit.

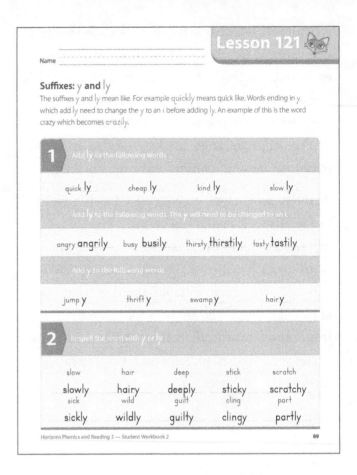

Activity 1. The student should turn to the activity sheet for this lesson. Read through the definition at the top of the sheet. The first activity asks the student to add the endings -**y** and -**ly** to words. The endings are divided in this first activity to help ensure the student's success. The first group adds the suffix -**ly** to words. The second adds -**ly** to words ending in -**y**. The final group adds the suffix -**y** to words. The answers for this activity are: **quickly, cheaply, kindly, slowly, angrily, busily, thirstily, tastily, jumpy, thrifty, swampy, hairy**.

Activity 2. The second activity continues with the student working with words adding the suffixes **-y** and **-ly**. In this activity, the student will need to choose whether or not to add **-y** or **-ly** to the given words. The student may want to have a piece of scratch paper available to write the word both with **-y** and **-ly** and then determine which one is correct. The correct answers are: **slowly, hairy, deeply, sticky, scratchy, sickly, wildly, guilty, clingy, partly**.

Activity 3. The final activity asks the student to use words ending with **-y** and **-ly** correctly in sentences. The student will need to choose the word which best completes each sentence. If possible, have the student read each sentence aloud with the correct word. This will help the student hear if the sentence sounds correct. The answers to the activity are: **sleepy, partly, smelly, sickly, slowly, sticky, itchy, messy, hardly, hilly**.

Reading Activity.

1. The reading selection for this lesson is the poem, "Foreign Lands." Have the student turn in the book to this selection.

2. Read the poem to the student as he/she follows along in the book. After reading it to the student, have him/her read it to you. After reading the poem, lead a discussion of it using the following questions. Where does the author go to look at foreign lands? (**The author climbs the cherry tree.**) What lands are visible? (**The author sees the garden next door, a river, and area roads.**) What does the author say the river is like? (**The river is like a mirror for the sky.**) What does the author think he/she will see from a higher tree? (**The author will see a river flowing into the sea and a magical kingdom.**) What does the author say the magical kingdom will be like? (**The children will eat supper early. They will also have toys that come to life.**)

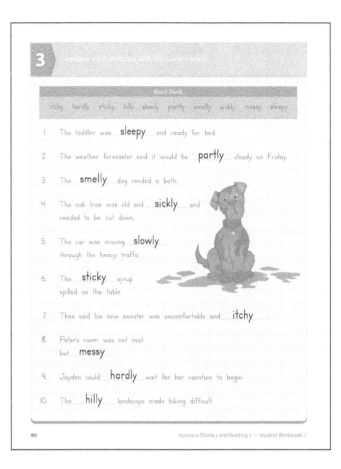

3. Have the student personally reflect on the poem using the following questions. Ask the student if he/she climbed a tall tree in his neighborhood, what would he/she see? (**Answers will vary.**) Ask the student if he/she could bring one of his/her toys to life, which would it be? Why? (**Allow for individual answers.**)

4. Discuss the way in which the poem was written. What is the rhyme scheme of the poem? (**aabb**) Ask the student to give you an example of these rhymes. (Examples include: **tree and see, hand and land.**) How many syllables are in each line? (**There are 7 or 8 syllables in each line.**)

Lesson 122

Suffixes: er, ous, ness

Overview:

- Know the meaning of the suffixes **-er**, **-ous**, and **-ness**

- Recognize when to add the suffixes **-er**, **-ous**, and **-ness** to words

- Use words with the suffixes **-er**, **-ous**, and **-ness**

Material and Supplies:

- Teacher's Guide and Student Workbook

- White board or chart paper

- Phonics flashcards

- Reader: "A Child's Prayer"

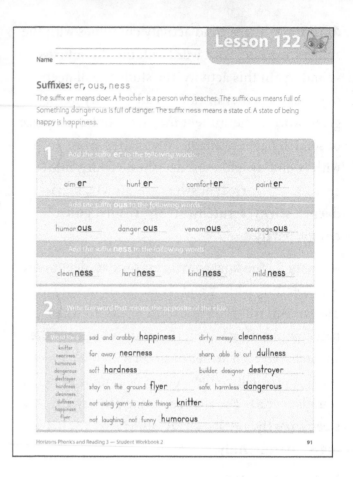

Teaching Tips:

Review for Mastery. Discuss and review any work from the previous lesson that was assigned as homework. Check for completion of the activities and orally quiz the student for comprehension. Review any reading that was assigned, discussing the characters, setting, plot, theme, language, sequence, etc.

Strengthen fluency and phonemic awareness by reviewing words and sentences from the previous lessons. Build vocabulary skills by using some of the words in sentences.

You may want to create flashcards of words which use suffixes found in this lesson and the previous one. The student can study these throughout the unit.

Lesson Introduction. Tell the student that he/she will continue the study of suffixes in this lesson. In this lesson the student will look at three suffixes: **-er**, **-ous**, and **-ness**. The suffix **-er** means **doer** as in hiker, which is a person who hikes. See if the student can think of other examples. Words include:

climber, teacher, and buyer. The suffix **-ous** means **full of** as in **courageous, full of courage**. Ask the student to think of other words with the suffix **-ous**. Answers may include: **marvelous, joyous,** or **dangerous**. The final suffix studied in this lesson is **-ness**. This suffix means **state of** as in **kindness**, which is a state of being kind. See if the student can think of words ending in the suffix **-ness**. Examples may include: **kindness, hardness,** and **happiness**.

Activity 1. The student should turn to the worksheet for this lesson. Read through the definitions at the top of the page. The first activity has the student add suffixes to words. The first group of words adds the suffix **-er**. The answers to this group are: **aimer, hunter, comforter, painter**.

The suffix **-ous** will be added to the words in the next section. The correct answers are: **humorous, dangerous, venomous, courageous**.

The final group adds the suffix **-ness**. The correct responses for this section are: **cleanness, hardness, kindness, mildness**.

Activity 2. Continue the activity by having the student choose the word which means the opposite of the words or phrases given in the activity. You may want to do the first one together. The answers to the activity are: **happiness, cleanness, nearness, dullness, hardness, destroyer, flyer, dangerous, knitter, humorous.**

Activity 3. The student will continue the lesson by choosing the word which best completes each sentence. This activity will give the student an opportunity to practice what he/she learned about words ending in the suffixes **-er, -ous,** and **-ness.** The answers are: **painter, curious, curliness, venomous, dullness, precious, keeper, taster.**

Reading Activity.

1. Ask the student to turn to the selection, "A Child's Prayer."

2. Have the student read the poem silently. After reading the poem through once, have the student read the poem to you. Discuss the poem with the student. What are the four images the author used in the child's prayer? **(The images are light, flower, song, and staff.)** Why does the child want to be a light? **(The child wants to glow in the world. The student may infer that the child wants to be a light that shows God's love to others.)** Why does the child want his/her life to be a flower? **(Flowers spread joy where they are found. A flower doesn't need to be large or grand in order to be noticed.)** Why do you think the child wants to be a song? **(A song encourages others when they are sad or in need.)** Why do you think the child would like to be a staff? **(If the student is not familiar with a staff, explain that a staff can be thought of as a cane. A staff can be used to help those in need of support.)**

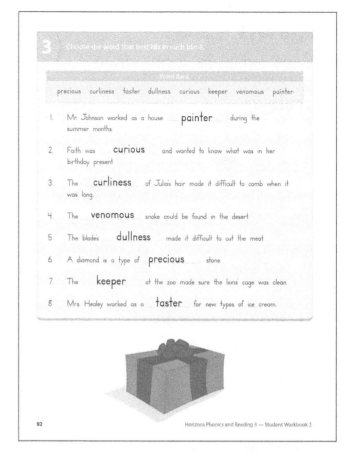

3. Continue by discussing the way in which the poem was written. What is the format of the poem? **(The poem is written in four-line stanzas. The number of syllables in the lines are 8/6/8/6. The poetic rhyme scheme is abab.)**

4. Conclude by asking the student if he/she were to write another stanza, what image would he/she use? (Examples may include: **tree, bird, rope.**) Have the student write another stanza for the poem.

Lesson 123

Suffixes: ful, able, ment, ance

Overview:

- Learn the rules for forming words with the suffixes -**ful**, -**able**, -**ment**, and -**ance**

- Identify words which contain the suffixes -**ful**, -**able**, -**ment**, and -**ance**

- Use words with the suffixes -**ful**, -**able**, -**ment**, and -**ance** in sentences

Material and Supplies:

- Teacher's Guide and Student Workbook

- White board or chart paper

- Phonics flashcards

- Reader: "The Little Hero—A Story of Holland"

Teaching Tips:

Review for Mastery. Discuss and review any work from the previous lesson that was assigned as homework. Check for completion of the activities and orally quiz the student for comprehension. Review any reading that was assigned, discussing the characters, setting, plot, theme, language, sequence, etc.

Strengthen fluency and phonemic awareness by reviewing words and sentences from the previous lessons. Build vocabulary skills by using some of the words in sentences.

You may want to create flashcards of words which use these suffixes. The student can study these throughout the unit.

Lesson Introduction. Explain that in this lesson the student will continue the study of suffixes. Write the suffixes -**ful**, -**able**, -**ment**, and -**ance** on the board. Ask the student if he/she can think

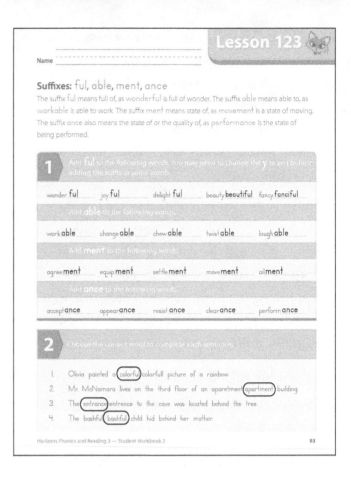

of any words that end with these suffixes. If the student is having trouble, write an example on the board. Words with these suffixes include: **faithful, understandable, assignment,** and **acceptance.** Ask the student if he/she can think of what the suffixes add to the meaning of these words. Since the student has been working with suffixes in some previous lessons, he/she may be able to decipher the meaning of some of the suffixes. The suffix -**ful** means **full of,** -**able** means **able to,** -**ment** means **state of,** and -**ance** means the **state of** or **quality of.**

Activity 1. The student should turn to the activity sheet which accompanies this lesson. Read through the definition at the top of the page. The first activity asks the student to add the suffixes to the end of words or word parts. The first group is composed of words adding the suffix -**ful**. Check to make sure the student spelled these words correctly since some will need to change spelling. The answers for this group are: **wonderful, joyful, delightful, beautiful, fanciful.**

The next group will add the suffix -able. The answers to this group are: **workable, changeable, chewable, twistable, laughable**.

The third group of words will add the ending -ment. These words are: **agreement, equipment, settlement, movement, ailment**.

The final group will add the ending -ance. The correct answers for this last group are: **acceptance, appearance, resistance, clearance, performance**.

Activity 2. The next activity asks the student to look at sentences which include words with the suffixes studied in this lesson. The student is given a choice of two spellings of each word in a sentence. The student needs to choose which spelling is correct. The correctly spelled answers are: **colorful, apartment, entrance, bashful, careful, chewable, usable, Testament, clearance, adorable**.

Activity 3. The lesson continues with the student reading verses from the hymn, "My God, How Wonderful Thou Art." Read through the hymn and discuss the words before having the student complete the activity. The student will need to underline those words which include one of the suffixes studied in this lesson. The answers are: **wonderful, beautiful, wonderful, beautiful, sinful**. As an added activity, have the student circle other words which contain suffixes. These bonus words are: **endless, boundless, glorious, purity, earthly**.

Reading Activity.

1. Ask the student to turn to the selection, "The Little Hero—A Story of Holland." You may want the student to read the selection alone or you could take turns reading paragraphs.

2. After the selection has been read, discuss it with the student. What was the setting of this selection? **(The story is set a long time ago in Holland.)** Why was the job of the boy's father so important? **(He made sure the gates to protect**

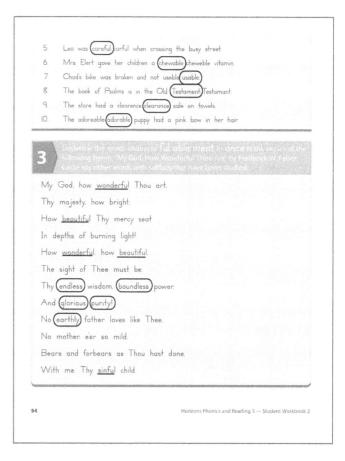

the land from water were opened and shut when necessary. His job kept the land from being flooded and people from being killed.) What do you know about the boy's character? **(He was kind and helped the blind man. He was obedient to his father. He was observant in knowing the dyke was in danger of breaking. He was also a problem-solver.)** Why did the boy put his finger in the hole in the dyke? **(He wanted to stop the dyke from overflowing and flooding the country. He understood the importance of his father's work.)** What was the result of the boy's action? **(The area was saved and no people were killed. The land was also protected.)** Do you think this boy should be seen as a hero as the author stated? Why or why not? **(Allow for individual answers.)**

3. Ask the student to identify three words in the selection which contain one of the suffixes studied in this lesson. Words include: **importance, painful, carefully**.

Lesson 124

Suffixes: ion, ist, ish

Overview:

- Recognize words with the suffixes -**ion**, -**ist**, and -**ish**

- Identify words which are formed with the suffixes -**ion**, -**ist**, and -**ish**

- Use words with the suffixes -**ion**, -**ist**, and -**ish** in sentences

Material and Supplies:

- Teacher's Guide and Student Workbook

- White board or chart paper

- Phonics flashcards

- Reader: "The Ladybug"

Teaching Tips:

Review for Mastery. Discuss and review any work from the previous lesson that was assigned as homework. Check for completion of the activities and orally quiz the student for comprehension. Review any reading that was assigned, discussing the characters, setting, plot, theme, language, sequence, etc.

Strengthen fluency and phonemic awareness by reviewing words and sentences from the previous lessons. Build vocabulary skills by using some of the words in sentences.

You may want to create flashcards of words which contain the suffixes -**ion**, -**ist**, and -**ish**. The student can study these throughout the unit.

Lesson Introduction. In the previous lesson, the student learned about the suffixes -**ful**, -**able**, -**ment**, and -**ance**. This lesson continues with the study of suffixes. Write the following sentences

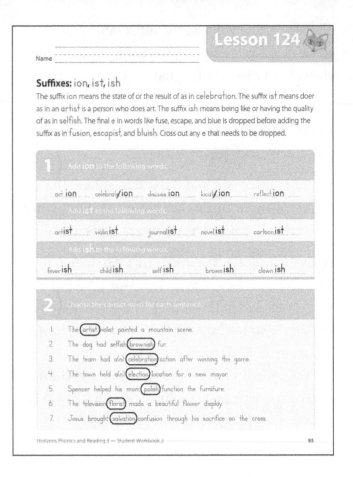

on the board: **She plays the violin. The violinist played in the concert.** Ask the student to describe the difference between the words **violin** and **violinist**. A violin is a musical instrument that can be played. A violinist is a person who plays the violin. Explain that when the ending -**ist** is added to a word, it means **a person who does something**. The suffix -**ion** means **the state of** or **result of**. Write the word **locate** on the board. See if the student can write sentences using **locate** and **location**. Examples would be as follows: **I need to locate my backpack. The location of my backpack is in my bedroom.** Finally, tell the student the last suffix that will be studied in this lesson is -**ish**, which means **like** or **having the quality of**. Write the words **brown** and **brownish** on the board. See if the student can write sentences using both **brown** and **brownish**. For example: **The brown car was parked by the house. A brownish squirrel crossed the street.** Tell the student that the activities in this lesson will help him/her understand how to use words with the suffixes -**ion**, -**ist**, and -**ish**.

Activity 1. The student should turn to the activity sheet which accompanies this lesson. Read through the instructions at the top of the sheet. The student should look at the first activity. Like previous lessons, the student will be asked to add the suffixes to words. The first group adds the suffix **-ion**. The answers to this section are: **action**, **celebration**, **discussion**, **location**, **reflection**.

The suffix **-ist** will be added to the next group of words. The answers to this section are: **artist**, **violinist**, **journalist**, **novelist**, **cartoonist**.

The final group adds the suffix **-ish**. The answers to this section are: **feverish**, **childish**, **selfish**, **brownish**, **clownish**.

Activity 2. In the next section, the student will need to choose the correct word for each sentence. The student will have two choices. You may want to have the student speak each sentence aloud to hear how the word sounds in context. The correct answers are: **artist, brownish, celebration, election, polish, florist, salvation, feverish, location, caution.**

Activity 3. The final activity asks the student to find words with **-ion, -ist,** and **-ish** in a word search. **See image for answers.**

Reading Activity.

1. Ask the student to turn to the selection, "The Ladybug." Tell the student that this reading will focus on a common animal. In the selection the student will learn how important and complex even the most common animal has been created.

2. After reading the selection, discuss it with the student. How many different species of ladybugs are there? (**There are over 5,000 species of ladybugs with at least 400 different species in the U.S.**) How do the appearances of the species of ladybug differ? (**The color of the ladybug can be red, yellow, or orange.**

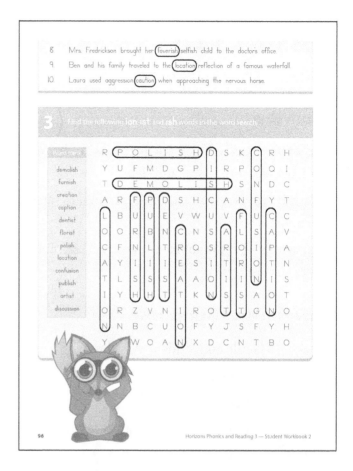

Some ladybugs do not have spots.) Why are ladybugs an important part of gardens and yards? (**Ladybugs eat many garden pests.**) How does the ladybug naturally defend itself from predators? (**The ladybug's bright color is one way in which the beetle defends itself. Ladybugs also have a bad odor and taste which deter other animals from eating them.**) What do the ladybugs do during the winter months? (**The ladybugs hibernate.**) Can you think of other animals that do this? (**The student might think of bears.**)

3. As an added activity, have the student draw a picture of a ladybug in its habitat.

Lesson 125

Suffixes: en, ern, ism, ive

Overview:

- Recognize words which are formed with the suffixes **-en**, **-ern**, **-ism**, and **-ive**
- Identify words which end with the suffixes **-en**, **-ern**, **-ism**, and **-ive**
- Use words with the suffixes **-en**, **-ern**, **-ism**, and **-ive** in sentences

Material and Supplies:

- Teacher's Guide and Student Workbook
- White board or chart paper
- Phonics flashcards
- Reader: "The Husband Who Was to Mind the House"

Teaching Tips:

Review for Mastery. Discuss and review any work from the previous lesson that was assigned as homework. Check for completion of the activities and orally quiz the student for comprehension. Review any reading that was assigned, discussing the characters, setting, plot, theme, language, sequence, etc.

Strengthen fluency and phonemic awareness by reviewing words and sentences from the previous lessons. Build vocabulary skills by using some of the words in sentences.

You may want to create flashcards of words which contain the suffixes **-en**, **-ern**, **-ism**, and **-ive**. The student can study these throughout the unit.

Lesson Introduction. This lesson will continue the study of suffixes. Write the four suffixes **-en**, **-ern**, **-ism**, and **-ive** on the board. Explain that these will be the focus of the lesson. Tell the student that the meaning of the suffix **-ism** is helpful in understanding words which end in it. The suffix means **belief in** or

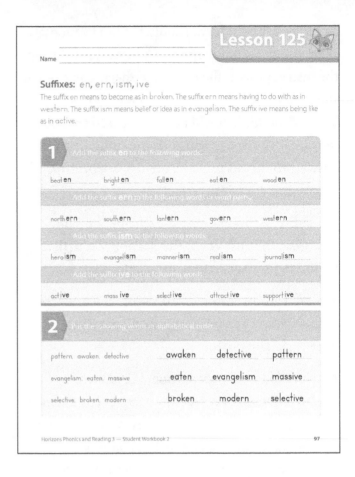

idea. Examples include: **heroism** or **evangelism**. The suffix **-ive** is also helpful in understanding longer words. It means **being like** as in **active** and **massive**. The suffix **-en** means **to become** as in **broken**. The suffix **-ern** means **having to do with** as in **northern**. This lesson will help students practice using words with these suffixes.

Activity 1. The student should turn to the activity sheet which accompanies this lesson. Have the student read the description at the top of the page. The student should look at the first activity. The student will be asked to form words with the four suffixes studied in this lesson. The first group of words adds the suffix **-en**. The correct responses for this section are: **beaten, brighten, fallen, eaten, wooden.**

The next grouping adds the ending **-ern**. The answers to this section are: **northern, southern, lantern, govern, western.**

The third section adds the endings **-ism**. The answers to this section are: **heroism, evangelism, mannerism, realism, journalism.**

The final group adds the suffix -ive. The correct answers for this group are: **active, massive, selective, attractive, supportive.**

Activity 2. The lesson continues with the student putting words with the suffixes **-en, -ern, -ism,** and **-ive** in alphabetical order. The correct answers for this section are:

awaken, detective, pattern
eaten, evangelism, massive
broken, modern, selective
autism, govern, wooden
active, awaken, detective
possessive, waken, wooden
eastern, fallen, heroism
lantern, pattern, selective

Activity 3. The student should look at the final activity. The student will be asked to read sentences and underline the words with the suffix endings **-en, -ern, -ism,** and **-ive** studied in this lesson. Sentences have at least one word with a suffix and some of the sentences have two. The answers to the activity are as follows:

1. **beaten, broken**
2. **evangelism**
3. **concern, wooden**
4. **massive, northern**
5. **heroism**
6. **massive, decorative**
7. **broken, fallen**
8. **detective, motive**
9. **brighten**
10. **lantern, southern**

Reading Activity.

1. Direct the student to the selection for today's lesson, "The Husband Who Was to Mind the House." This is a selection that the student can read independently.

2. After reading the selection, discuss it with the student. Describe the setting of the story. (**The story takes place sometime in the past on a farm.**) Describe the husband. (**He thought he could do everything better than others. He was**

filled with pride. He discovered how well his wife could manage a difficult job.**) Why do you think the wife agreed to change places with her husband? (Answers may include: **She knew the challenges of her job and maybe thought to teach her husband a lesson.**) What problems did the husband have with his wife's housework? (**He had a hard time doing the many tasks she did at the same time. He never did get the butter churned. The cow ended up dangling from the roof and he didn't have dinner ready for his wife.**) What do you think the husband will say to his wife at the end of the day? (**Answers may vary.**) What have you learned from this selection? (Answers may include: **The importance and difficulty of many different types of work. People need to appreciate the work that other people do.**)

3. As an added activity, have the student write a thank you note to someone whose work he/she appreciates.

Lesson 126
Suffixes: less, dom, hood, teen

Overview:

- Understand the meaning of the suffixes -**less,** -**dom**, -**hood**, and -**teen**

- Remember how to form words with the suffixes -**less**, -**dom**, -**hood**, and -**teen**

- Use words with the suffixes -**less**, -**dom**, -**hood**, and -**teen** in sentences

Material and Supplies:

- Teacher's Guide and Student Workbook

- White board or chart paper

- Phonics flashcards

- Reader: "Over in the Meadow"

Teaching Tips:

Review for Mastery. Discuss and review any work from the previous lesson that was assigned as homework. Check for completion of the activities and orally quiz the student for comprehension. Review any reading that was assigned, discussing the characters, setting, plot, theme, language, sequence, etc.

Strengthen fluency and phonemic awareness by reviewing words and sentences from the previous lessons. Build vocabulary skills by using some of the words in sentences.

Create flashcards of words ending with the suffixes -**less**, -**dom**, -**hood**, and -**teen**. The student can study these throughout the unit.

Lesson Introduction. Tell the student that in this lesson he/she will continue the study of suffixes. The ones in the lesson are -**less**, -**dom**, -**hood**, and -**teen**. Start with the suffix -**teen**. Write the words **six** and **sixteen** on the board. Ask the student what the word sixteen means. The student

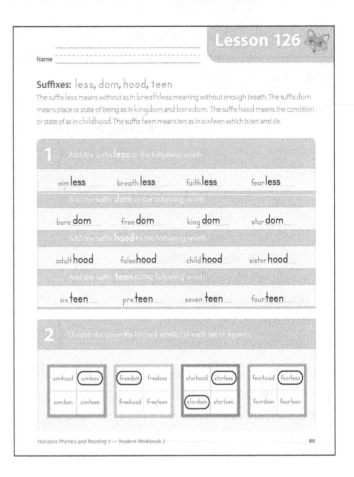

should recognize the word means six and ten. The suffix -**teen** means **ten**. Write the words **breath** and **breathless** on the board. Ask the student how the word with the suffix differs from the first. The student should identify that **breathless** means **without** as in without breath. The suffixes -**dom** and -**hood** both refer to **a place** or **a state of being**. Examples of words with these suffixes include: **kingdom** and **neighborhood**. See if the student can think of other words with these suffix endings. Examples may include: **fifteen, homeless, freedom**, and **childhood**.

Activity 1. Have the student turn to the activity sheet which accompanies this lesson. Read through the definitions at the top of the page. The student will be asked to add suffixes to words which are provided. The student will add these suffixes in groups of the same suffix. This will help ensure the student's success and understanding of the suffixes. The answers to the activity are: **aimless, breathless, faithless, fearless, boredom, freedom, kingdom, stardom, adulthood, falsehood, childhood, sisterhood, sixteen, preteen, seventeen, fourteen.**

Activity 2. The student will continue by looking at four squares of words and choose the word(s) that contain a suffix studied in this lesson. Each square will have at least one correct word. The answers to the activity are: **aimless, freedom, starless, stardom, fearless, fourteen, tasteless, wisdom, adulthood**.

Activity 3. The final activity continues the study of suffixes. The student will need to decipher the clues to determine the correct words to place in the crossword puzzle. A Word Bank is provided to assist the student in the activity. The answers are:

Across:	Down:
4. **sixteen**	1. **hairless**
6. **falsehood**	2. **preteen**
7. **nineteen**	3. **neighborhood**
8. **seldom**	5. **homeless**
9. **fearless**	6. **freedom**

Reading Activity.

1. Ask the student to turn to the selection, "Over in the Meadow." Your student may be familiar with the song, "Over in the Meadow." Before it was a song however, it was poem. There are a number of ways you can read this poem. One is to take turns reading the stanzas. Another is to have the student play the role of the baby animal and repeat the words the mother animal says.

2. Begin by asking the student the format of the poem. (**The poem is written in eight line stanzas. Each line has five or six syllables. The 2nd, 4th, 6th, and 8th lines rhyme.**)

3. Discuss the content of the poem with the student. How is the location of the meadow described in each stanza? (Descriptions include: **sand, sun, blue, stream, hole in tree, reeds on the shore, beehive, nest, even grass, mossy gate, clear pool, den, summer, and digging by people.**) What creatures live in the meadow? (Animals living in the meadow include: **a toad, fish, bluebird, muskrat, honeybee, crow, cricket, lizard, frog, spider, firefly, and ant.**) What types of things do the mothers tell their children to do? (**They tell them to do things which are natural to the animals like the**

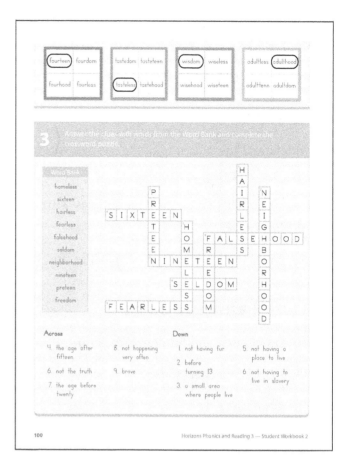

fish swimming, the bird singing, and the bee buzzing.**) What types of things are repeated in each stanza? (**The author repeats the animal's name, the number used, and the item the mother tells the child to do. The second and last lines were repeated.**) What do you think the author's purpose was in writing the poem? (**The poem is a counting poem, a poem about animals, and the skills each animal has. The poem is also about the beauty of the meadow.**)

4. As an added activity, listen to a rendition of the song, "Over in the Meadow." There are many versions available online. The words may differ from those in the poem. Another idea would be to ask the student to write one more stanza following the pattern of the poem.

Lesson 127

Suffixes: ship, like, age

Overview:

- Understand the meaning of the suffixes -**ship**, -**like**, and -**age**

- Identify words that contain the suffixes -**ship**, -**like**, and -**age**

- Use words with the suffixes -**ship**, -**like**, and -**age**

Material and Supplies:

- Teacher's Guide and Student Workbook

- White board or chart paper

- Phonics flashcards

- Reader: "John Philip Sousa"

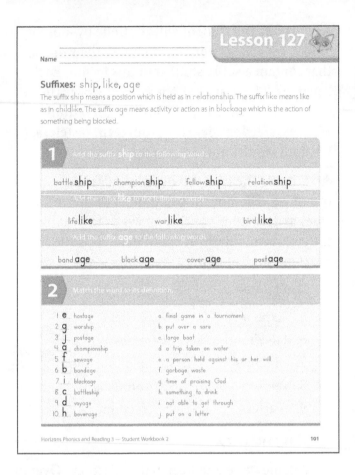

Teaching Tips:

Review for Mastery. Discuss and review any work from the previous lesson that was assigned as homework. Check for completion of the activities and orally quiz the student for comprehension. Review any reading that was assigned, discussing the characters, setting, plot, theme, language, sequence, etc.

Strengthen fluency and phonemic awareness by reviewing words and sentences from the previous lessons. Build vocabulary skills by using some of the words in sentences.

Create flashcards of words which contain the suffixes -**ship**, -**like**, and -**age**. The student can study these throughout the unit.

Lesson Introduction. This lesson continues the study of suffixes. Write the following sentence on the board. **The newspaper contained coverage of the sportsmanlike play of the championship game.** Ask the student which words in the sentence contain suffixes. The words **coverage**, **sportsmanlike**, and **championship** all contain suffixes. Ask the student what suffixes are in the words: -**age**, -**like**, and -**ship**. The suffix -**age** means **activity or action** so coverage would include a description of the action. In the word sportsmanlike the suffix -**like** would mean that the play was **like** what a sportsman would play. The suffix -**ship** indicates a position so the championship would mean that the winner **held the position** of the champion. In this lesson the suffixes -**ship**, -**age**, and -**like** will be studied.

Activity 1. Turn to the activity sheet which accompanies this lesson. The student should read the definitions for the suffixes. Like other activity sheets in this unit, the student will add the suffixes to words to create new words. The answers for the activity are: **battleship, championship, fellowship, relationship, lifelike, warlike, birdlike, bandage, blockage, coverage, postage.**

Activity 2. The next activity asks the student to match words with suffixes to their definitions. The answers to this activity are: 1.—**e**, 2.—**g**, 3.—**j**, 4.—**a**, 5.—**f**, 6.—**b**, 7.—**i**, 8.—**c**, 9.—**d**, 10.—**h**.

Activity 3. The final activity asks the student to identify words which are correctly or incorrectly used in sentences. Each sentence contains an underlined word with a suffix studied in the lesson. The student will need to determine if these words are used correctly or not. The answers are: **I, C, C, I, C, C, I, C**.

Reading Activity.

1. Before the student reads the material on John Philip Sousa, play one of his marches. Many of his marches can be accessed online. Two marches to consider having the student listen to are, "Stars and Stripes Forever" and "Semper Fidelis."

2. After listening to one of Sousa's marches, have the student read the selection, "John Philip Sousa."

3. Discuss the selection with your student. What was Sousa's musical background? (**His father played in the U.S. Marine Band. As a child he played violin. He started with the Marine Band as an apprentice at the age of 13.**) What was John Philip Sousa's relationship with the band? (**He played in it, conducted it, and wrote music for the group.**) What type of music was Sousa known for writing? (**He was known for writing marches.**) What instrument did Sousa help create? (**He helped create the sousaphone.**) Have the student describe this instrument. (**The instrument is like a tuba. The player has the instrument wrapped around his shoulder making it easier to hold. The bell goes up and over the player making the sound easier to hear.**)

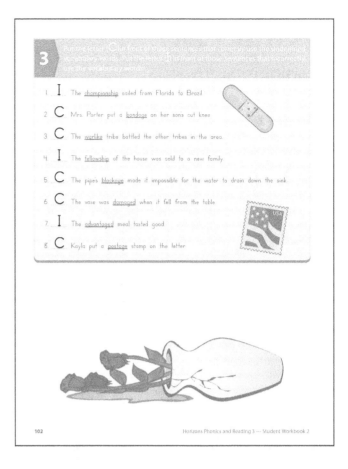

4. As an added activity, have the student find or draw a picture of a sousaphone.

Lesson 128
Combining Suffixes

Overview:

- Discover words with multiple suffixes
- Form words with multiple suffixes
- Identify words with multiple suffixes

Material and Supplies:

- Teacher's Guide and Student Workbook
- White board or chart paper
- Phonics flashcards
- Reader: "The Armadillo"

Teaching Tips:

Review for Mastery. Discuss and review any work from the previous lesson that was assigned as homework. Check for completion of the activities and orally quiz the student for comprehension. Review any reading that was assigned, discussing the characters, setting, plot, theme, language, sequence, etc.

Strengthen fluency and phonemic awareness by reviewing words and sentences from the previous lessons. Build vocabulary skills by using some of the words in sentences.

You may want to create flashcards of words with multiple suffixes. The student can study these throughout the unit.

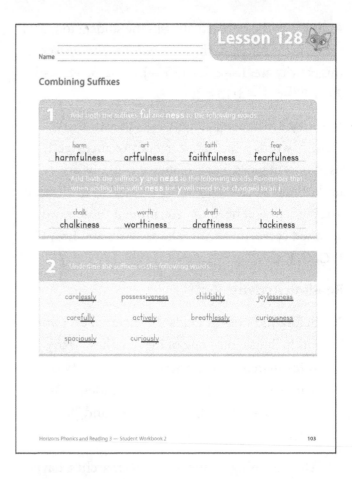

Lesson Introduction. The student will continue the study of suffixes. However in this lesson, the student will look at words which contain multiple suffixes. Write the following words on the board: **chalkiness**, **childishly**, and **spaciousness**. Ask the student to underline the suffixes in the words. The student should identify two suffixes in each word. You may need to explain that in the word chalkiness, a **y** was added and then changed to an **i** before the suffix **-ness** was added. Explain to the student that just like multiple prefixes can be added to words, so too can multiple suffixes.

Activity 1. Ask the student to turn to the activity sheet which accompanies this lesson. The first section directs the student in how he/she is to add multiple suffixes to words. You may want to do the first example in each section with the student so he/she knows how to proceed. The correct answers are: **harmfulness, artfulness, faithfulness, fearfulness, chalkiness, worthiness, draftiness, tackiness.**

Activity 2. The lesson continues with the student underlining suffixes in a group of words. None of the words will contain the **y** ending turned to an **i**. The correct answers are: **care<u>lessly</u>, possess<u>iveness</u>, child<u>ishly</u>, joy<u>lessness</u>, care<u>fully</u>, act<u>ively</u>, breath<u>lessly</u>, curi<u>ousness</u>, spac<u>iously</u>, curi<u>ously</u>**.

Activity 3. The final activity asks the student to locate words with multiple suffixes in sentences. The student should underline the words with multiple suffixes. Two sentences do not have multiple suffixes. The words with multiple suffixes found in the activity are: **carefully, draftiness, possessiveness, faithfulness, breathlessly, fearfulness**.

Reading Activity.

1. The student should turn to the selection, "The Armadillo." This short selection can be read independently by the student.

2. Lead the student in a discussion of the selection. What does the name armadillo mean? (**Armadillo means little armored one in Spanish.**) Describe the armadillo's physical characterics. (**One of its most interesting characteristics is its shell made of rings of bone.**) Where do armadillos live? (**They mainly live in South America. Over time they have moved to Central America and the southern U.S. Armadillos can only live in warm climates.**) What animals are relatives of the armadillo? (**The sloth and anteater are relatives.**) What physical limitations does an armadillo have? (**It has short legs so it can't run. Its underside is not armored. When threatened some armadillos jump straight into the air.**) What do armadillos eat? (**They eat insects and plants.**) What problems do armadillos face? (**Their habitat is shrinking despite the fact they don't have natural predators.**)

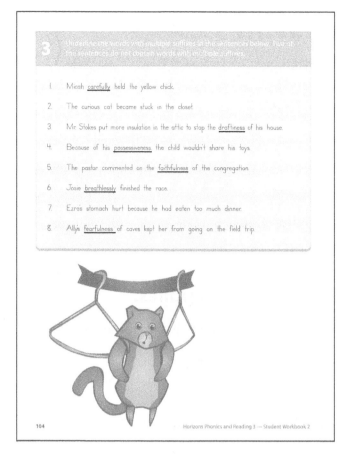

3 Underline the words with multiple suffixes in the sentences below. Two of the sentences do not contain words with multiple suffixes.

1. Micah <u>carefully</u> held the yellow chick.

2. The curious cat became stuck in the closet.

3. Mr. Stokes put more insulation in the attic to stop the <u>draftiness</u> of his house.

4. Because of his <u>possessiveness</u>, the child wouldn't share his toys.

5. The pastor commented on the <u>faithfulness</u> of the congregation.

6. Josie <u>breathlessly</u> finished the race.

7. Ezra's stomach hurt because he had eaten too much dinner.

8. Ally's <u>fearfulness</u> of caves kept her from going on the field trip.

104   Horizons Phonics and Reading 3 — Student Workbook 2

Lesson 129
Combining Prefixes and Suffixes

Overview:

- Form words with multiple prefixes and suffixes

- Recognize words formed with multiple prefixes and suffixes

- Identify the meaning of words with multiple prefixes and suffixes

Material and Supplies:

- Teacher's Guide and Student Workbook

- White board or chart paper

- Phonics flashcards

- Reader: "The Camel and the Pig"

Teaching Tips:

Review for Mastery. Discuss and review any work from the previous lesson that was assigned as homework. Check for completion of the activities and orally quiz the student for comprehension. Review any reading that was assigned, discussing the characters, setting, plot, theme, language, sequence, etc.

Strengthen fluency and phonemic awareness by reviewing words and sentences from the previous lessons. Build vocabulary skills by using some of the words in sentences.

You may want to create flashcards of words with multiple prefixes and suffixes. The student can study these throughout the unit.

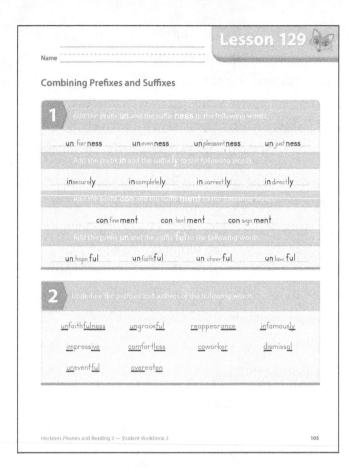

Lesson Introduction. Explain to the student that words are not limited to having either prefixes or suffixes. Some words have both a prefix and a suffix. Some words even have multiple prefixes and suffixes. Write the following words on the board: **uncomfortable**, **reappearance**, and **unhopeful**. Ask the student to identify the prefixes and suffixes in each word. The prefixes used are **un-** and **re-**. The suffixes used are **-able, -ance,** and **-ful**. Tell the student that in this lesson he/she will need to add both prefixes and suffixes to words.

Activity 1. The student should turn to the worksheet which accompanies this lesson. In the first activity the student will form words with suffixes and prefixes. The words, suffixes, and prefixes are grouped so that the student will be able to successfully form words. The answers are: **unfairness, unevenness, unpleasantness, unjustness, insecurely, incompletely, incorrectly, indirectly, confinement, contentment, consignment, unhopeful, unfaithful, uncheerful, unlawful.**

Activity 2. The lesson continues with the student underlining the prefixes and suffixes in the words listed. The answers to the activity are: **<u>un</u>faith<u>fulness</u>, <u>un</u>grace<u>ful</u>, <u>re</u>appear<u>ance</u>, <u>in</u>famous<u>ly</u>, <u>im</u>press<u>ive</u>, <u>com</u>fort<u>less</u>, <u>co</u>work<u>er</u>, <u>dis</u>missa<u>l</u>, <u>un</u>event<u>ful</u>, <u>over</u>eaten.**

Activity 3. The final activity asks the student to choose the correct word to complete each sentence. Have the student read each sentence after choosing the correct word. The answers to the sentences are: **ungraceful, incorrectly, reappearance, coworkers, dismissal, impressive, uneventful, injustice.**

Reading Activity.

1. The student should read the selection, "The Camel and the Pig" You may want to take turns reading the parts of the camel and the pig with the student.

2. Discuss the selection with the student. How are each of the animals initially described? **(The camel is tall with a hump on its back. The pig is short with a twisty tail.)** What did each animal want to prove to the other? **(Each wanted to prove that it's the best created animal.)** How was each animal to prove its ability? **(The camel found a garden with a low**

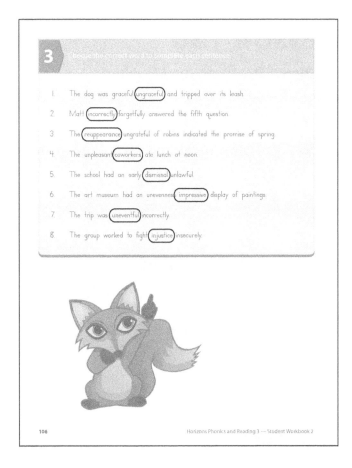

wall. The pig couldn't get in but the camel was able to eat from over the top of the wall. The pig found a garden with a low gate but a high wall. The pig could enter through the gate and eat all it wanted.)** What did the two animals decide? **(Both tall and short are good.)** What do you think was the meaning of this fable? (Answers may include: **People need to be happy with the way God created them. He gave each person abilities and strengths.)**

3. As an added activity, have the student draw a scene from the selection.

Lesson 130

Review: Prefixes and Suffixes

Overview:

- Identify words with suffixes

- Correctly form words with suffixes

- Recall the meanings of the suffixes in this unit

Material and Supplies:

- Teacher's Guide and Student Workbook

- White board or chart paper

- Phonics flashcards

- Reader: "The Bundle of Sticks"

Teaching Tips:

Review for Mastery. Discuss and review any work from the previous lesson that was assigned as homework. Check for completion of the activities and orally quiz the student for comprehension. Review any reading that was assigned, discussing the characters, setting, plot, theme, language, sequence, etc.

Strengthen fluency and phonemic awareness by reviewing words and sentences from the previous lessons. Build vocabulary skills by using some of the words in sentences.

You may want to review flashcards made for words in this unit.

Lesson Introduction. This lesson reviews the material the student learned in the unit. The student will complete activities which review the use of singular and multiple suffixes. You may want to see if the student can remember the various suffixes he/she learned in this unit. The suffixes studied were: **-ly, -y, -er, -ous, -ness, -ment, -ance,**

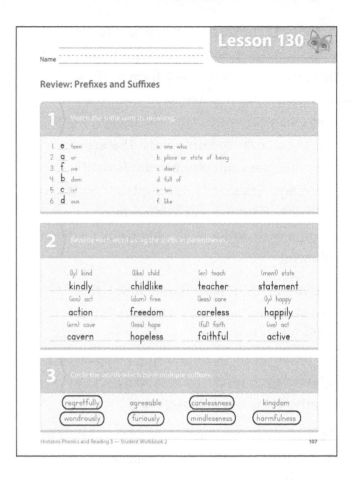

-**ful**, -**able**, -**ion**, -**ist**, -**ish**, -**en**, -**ern**, -**ive**, -**ism**, -**less**, -**dom**, -**hood**, -**teen**, -**ship**, -**like**, and -**age**. See if the student can think of words containing these suffixes. Examples include: **quickly, messy, runner, nervous, happiness, contentment, appearance, careful, replaceable, action, artist, blackish, broken, cavern, active, evangelism, homeless, kingdom, neighborhood, sixteen, leadership, childlike,** and **blockage.**

Remind the student that he/she also learned that words can contain multiple suffixes. See if the student can remember words with multiple suffixes. Examples include: **faithfully** and **carelessness.** Next see if the student can think of words with both a prefix and a suffix. Examples include: **unhelpful** and **removable.**

Explain that in this review lesson the student will review what has been learned in the unit. The unit test will be formatted like the review sheet.

Activity 1. The student should turn to the activity sheet which accompanies this lesson. The review sheet is arranged in the same way as the test. In the test different examples will be used but the format will remain the same. The student will begin by matching suffixes with their meanings. The answers to the activity are: 1.—**e**, 2.—**a**, 3.—**f**, 4.—**b**, 5.—**c**, 6.—**d**.

Activity 2. The next activity asks the student to rewrite each word using the suffix that is provided. The answers are: **kindly, childlike, teacher, statement, action, freedom, careless, happily, cavern, hopeless, faithful, active**.

Activity 3. The activity sheet continues with the student circling words with multiple suffixes. Emphasize that prefixes are not a factor in this activity. Instead, the student needs to focus on multiple suffixes. The answers are: **regretfully, carelessness, wondrously, furiously, mindlessness, harmfulness**.

Activity 4. The next activity involves the student looking for words containing both a suffix and a prefix. The word must have both in order to be circled. The correct answers are: **uncomfortable, restatement, prevention, remarkable, disappointment, excitement**.

Activity 5. The final activity asks the student to choose the best word to complete each sentence. A Word Bank is provided to assist the student with this activity. The answers are: **likeable, poorly, dangerous, wonderful, celebration, violinist, fallen, breathless, championship, disliked**.

Reading Activity.

1. The student should turn to the selection, "The Bundle of Sticks."

2. Direct the student in reading this selection for pleasure.

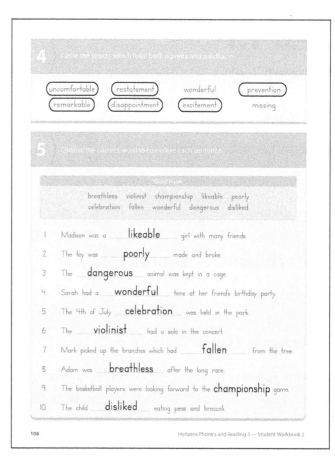

Test 13

Lessons 121-130

Overview:

- Identify words with suffixes
- Correctly form words with suffixes
- Recall the meanings of the words with suffixes

Material and Supplies:

- Student Test

Teaching Tips:

Review for Mastery. Discuss and review any work from the previous lesson that was assigned as homework. Check for completion of the activities and orally quiz the student for comprehension. Review any reading that was assigned, discussing the characters, setting, plot, theme, language, sequence, etc.

Lesson Introduction. This lesson tests the material the student learned in the unit. Before the test you may want to ask the student if he/she has any final questions. There may be questions the student will want to review. Remind the student that the final test follows the same format as the review.

Activity 1. The student should turn to the test. The test is arranged in the same way as the review sheet. In the test different examples will be used but the format will remain the same. The student will begin by matching suffixes with their meanings. The answers to the question are: 1.—**d**, 2.—**a**, 3.—**f**, 4.—**b**, 5.—**c**, 6.—**e**.

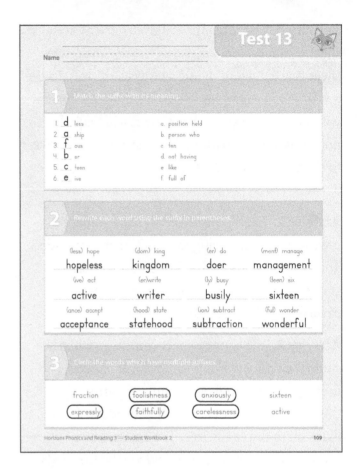

Activity 2. The next test activity asks the student to rewrite each word using the suffix that is provided. The answers are: **hopeless, kingdom, doer, management, active, writer, busily, sixteen, acceptance, statehood, subtraction, wonderful.**

Activity 3. The test continues with the student circling words with multiple suffixes. Emphasize that prefixes are not a factor in this activity. Instead the student needs to focus on multiple suffixes. The answers are: **foolishness, anxiously, expressly, faithfully, carelessness.**

Activity 4. The next test activity involves the student looking for words containing both a suffix and a prefix. The word must have both in order to be circled. The correct answers are: **inactive, unlikely, incapable, replaceable, understatement, regretfully**.

Activity 5. The final activity asks the student to choose the best word to complete each sentence. A Word Bank is provided to assist the student with this activity. The answers are: **knitter, dullness, performance, reflection, dentist, massive, thirteen, fearful, coworkers, prevention**.

Lesson 131

Words with Double Consonants: bb, dd, ff, ll, and mm

Overview:

- Understand the meaning of words with the double consonants **bb**, **dd**, **ff**, **ll**, and **mm**

- Recognize words with double consonants

- Use words with double consonants

Material and Supplies:

- Teacher's Guide and Student Workbook

- White board or chart paper

- Phonics flashcards

- Reader: "The Pony Express"

Teaching Tips:

Lesson Introduction. Explain to the student that in this unit he/she will be studying words with double consonants, comparisons, and inflected endings. The unit will begin with words with double consonants. The double consonants explored will be **bb**, **dd**, **ff**, **ll**, and **mm**. Write the words **bubbling, puddle, waffle, million,** and **comma** on the board. Ask the student what the five words have in common. Help the student to recognize that all the words have double consonants. The student will study double consonants in this lesson.

You may want to create flashcards of words with the double consonants **bb**, **dd**, **ff**, **ll**, and **mm**. The student can study these throughout the unit.

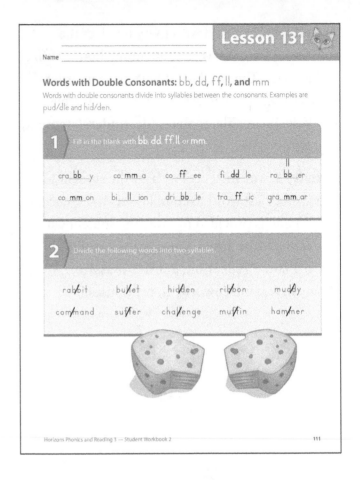

Activity 1. The student should turn to the activity sheet for this lesson. The first activity asks the student to place double consonants in words. The student may want to have a piece of scratch paper on which to practice the words before writing the answers on the sheet. The answers to the activity are: **crabby, comma, coffee, fiddle, robber/roller, common, billion, dribble, traffic, grammar**.

Activity 2. The second activity continues by having the student divide words with double consonants into syllables. The correct word divisions are: **rab/bit, bul/let, hid/den, rib/bon, mud/dy, com/mand, suf/fer, chal/lenge, muf/fin, ham/mer**.

Activity 3. The final activity asks the student to use words with double consonants in sentences. A Word Bank is provided for the student. The answers to the sentences are: **bubble, coffee, traffic, fiddle, cuddle, muffin, muddy, balloon, chilly, stubborn**.

Reading Activity.

1. The student should turn to the selection, "The Pony Express." Direct the student in reading the selection. Explain any words the student may have difficulty understanding.

2. Discuss the selection with the student. Use some of the following questions to assist your discussion. Why was the Pony Express started? **(It was started to bring mail quickly from the east to west coasts of the United States.)** What dangers did the riders from the Pony Express face? **(They faced dangers such as bad weather, Indian attacks, and dark nights.)** What types of riders were needed to carry the mail? **(The riders needed to weigh less than 125 pounds, be brave, and be good horsemen.)** How was the route organized for maximum speed? **(The stations were placed about 10 miles apart so that the horse could gallop at maximum speed. Horses were quickly exchanged so that there was not a lot of wasted time.)** Why did the Pony Express end? **(When the telegraph connected the two coasts, there was no longer any need for the Pony Express. Information could be received more quickly by telegraph.)**

3. Conclude by discussing some of the current methods of communication people use. Discuss how quickly people can communicate with others around the world today.

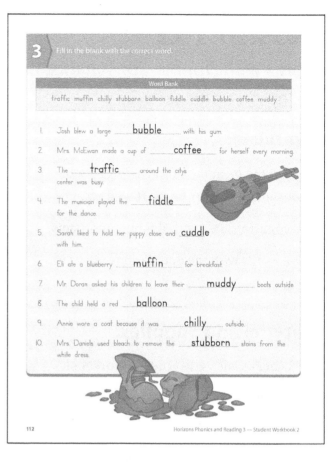

Lesson 132

Words with Double Consonants: nn, pp, rr, ss, tt, and zz

Overview:

- Know the meaning of words with double consonants **nn**, **pp**, **rr**, **ss**, **tt**, and **zz**

- Recognize words with double consonants

- Use words with the double consonants in sentences

Material and Supplies:

- Teacher's Guide and Student Workbook

- White board or chart paper

- Phonics flashcards

- Reader: "Whatever Brawls Disturb the Street"

Teaching Tips:

Review for Mastery. Discuss and review any work from the previous lesson that was assigned as homework. Check for completion of the activities and orally quiz the student for comprehension. Review any reading that was assigned, discussing the characters, setting, plot, theme, language, sequence, etc.

Strengthen fluency and phonemic awareness by reviewing words and sentences from the previous lessons. Build vocabulary skills by using some of the words in sentences.

You may want to create flashcards of words with double consonants. The student can study these throughout the unit.

Lesson Introduction. Tell the student that he/she will continue the study of words with double consonants in this lesson. Ask the student to recall words with double consonants that were studied in

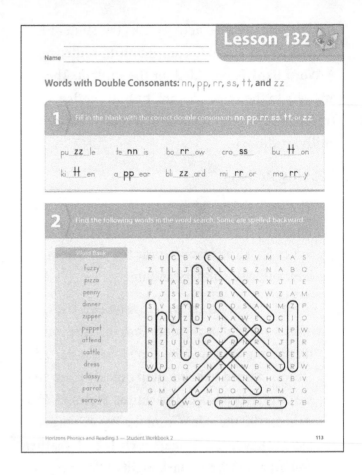

the previous lesson. Examples include the words: **hammer, challenge,** and **command**. Explain that in this lesson the student will look at words with the double consonants: **nn, pp, rr, ss, tt,** and **zz**. See if the student can think of any words with these double letter combinations. Examples include: **bunny, puppy, carry, hassle, cattle,** and **puzzle**. Have the student divide the words listed into syllables. The student should note that the words are divided between the double consonants.

Activity 1. The student should turn to the worksheet for this lesson. Explain that the student will continue the study of words with double consonants. The first activity will ask the student to fill in the blank with double consonants that complete the word. You may want to have a piece of scratch paper available so that the student can practice writing the word correctly before writing on the activity sheet. The correct responses are: **puzzle, tennis, borrow, cross, button, kitten, appear, blizzard, mirror, marry.**

Activity 2. Continue by having the student complete a word search where he/she finds words with double consonants. **See image for answers.**

Activity 3. The student will continue the lesson by completing sentences using words with double consonants. If possible have the student say the sentences to make sure the words are used correctly. The correct responses are: **mirror, lettuce, battery, narrow, puzzle, apples, correct, letter, button, cherry.**

Reading Activity.

1. Before reading the poem, "Whatever Brawls Disturb the Street," ask the student to recall the Bible story of Cain and Abel found in Genesis 4:2b-16. You may want to read the story to the student. Who were the parents of Cain and Abel? **(Adam and Eve)** Which brother was older? **(Cain)** What work did the two men do? **(Cain worked the land and Abel took care of the animals.)** Why was there a conflict between the two brothers? **(Abel's offerings were acceptable to God and Cain's were not.)** What did Cain do as a result? **(He took his brother out to a field and killed him.)** What was Cain's punishment? **(He was condemned to roam the earth and could no longer live with his family.)**

2. Have the student turn to the poem, "Whatever Brawls Disturb the Street." Since some of the language is challenging, read the poem to the student while he/she follows along. Next have the student read the poem with you.

3. After reading the poem, discuss it with the student. How does the poet say life outside the home should differ from life within it? **(Life inside the home should be peaceful and free from conflict.)** What example from nature should siblings learn from? **(Birds in their nests live peacefully.)** How did the author say fights with siblings can escalate? **(They can escalate**

from words, to clubs, to swords, and murder.) What did the author say was the alternative to fighting? **(The alternative is letting anger cool before going to bed at night.)** What prayer did the author give? **(He prayed that God would remove childish rage and fights so that brothers and sisters could learn to love.)** How did this poem address what was told in the story of Cain and Abel? **(The poem spoke of how brothers need to get along and care for each other. In this way, what happened to Cain and Abel would not happen in other families.)**

4. Continue by discussing the way in which the poem is written. What is the rhyme scheme of the poem? **(The poem is written in four-line stanzas. Each stanza has an abab rhyme scheme. The lines follow the pattern of 8686 syllables.)**

Lesson 133

Double Consonant Endings: ll, dd, ff, and ss

Overview:

- Identify words which contain the double consonant ending -**ll**, -**dd**, -**ff**, and -**ss**

- Use words with the double consonant endings in sentences

- Write words with double consonant endings

Material and Supplies:

- Teacher's Guide and Student Workbook

- White board or chart paper

- Phonics flashcards

- Reader: "Book of Nonsense"

Teaching Tips:

Review for Mastery. Discuss and review any work from the previous lesson that was assigned as homework. Check for completion of the activities and orally quiz the student for comprehension. Review any reading that was assigned, discussing the characters, setting, plot, theme, language, sequence, etc.

Strengthen fluency and phonemic awareness by reviewing words and sentences from the previous lessons. Build vocabulary skills by using some of the words in sentences.

You may want to create flashcards of words which have double consonants. The student can study these throughout the unit.

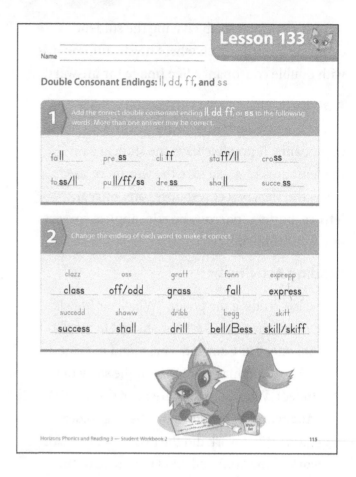

Lesson Introduction. Explain that in this lesson the student will continue the study of double consonants. In this case, the double consonants will all appear at the end of words. Write the double consonants **ll**, **dd**, **ff**, and **ss** on the board. Write the letters **ma** and **o** on the board. Ask the student what words can be made from the double consonants and these beginning word letters. The answers include: **mall**, **mass**, **odd**, and **off**. Tell the student that in this lesson words with double consonant endings will be explored.

Activity 1. The student should turn to the activity sheet which accompanies this lesson. The first activity asks the student to add the correct double consonant ending to the letters to form words. The student may want to practice on scratch paper first. Afterward the student can write in the correct letters on the activity sheet. The correct responses are: **fall, press, cliff, staff/stall, cross, toss/toll, pull/puff/puss, dress, shall, success.**

Activity 2. The next activity asks the student to change the last two letters in each word to make a correct word. Again, it may be helpful to have the student practice this on a piece of scratch paper before writing on the activity sheet. Some of the responses have more than one correct answer. The correct answers are: **class, off/odd, grass, fall, express, success, shall, drill, bell/Bess, skill/skiff.**

Activity 3. The lesson continues with the student completing a crossword puzzle. You may want to point out that the word **puzzle** contains a double consonant. A Word Bank is provided to assist the student in the puzzle. The answers to the clues are:

Across:	Down:
3. **ball**	1. **cliff**
5. **princess**	2. **sniff**
6. **off**	3. **business**
8. **shell**	4. **sell**
	7. **bull**

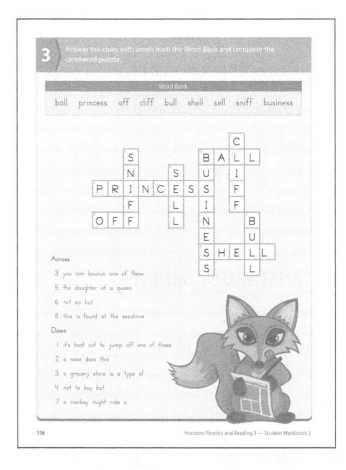

Reading Activity.

1. The selection for this lesson is, "Book of Nonsense" by Edward Lear. Have the student read the poems to you. Help with any words the student may have trouble pronouncing.

2. Tell the student that the three poems he/she read are all examples of limericks. All limericks follow the same rhyming pattern and number of syllables in a line. What is the rhyming pattern of a limerick? **(aabba)** How many syllables are in the lines of a limerick? **(They are not always exactly the same but they are generally 88668.)** What do you learn in the first line of each limerick? **(The limerick tells you about the main character and a special feature about the character that will be the theme of the poem.)** What does the last line of a limerick tell the reader? **(The last line repeats a key part of the first line.)** What happens in between the first and last lines of the limerick? **(A problem occurs with the main feature**
described in the first line. The main character speaks some dialogue as well.)** What is the tone of limerick? **(The tone of a limerick is humorous and funny. Something entertaining happens in the poem to make the reader laugh.)** All of the limericks in this section were written by Edward Lear, who was known for his ability to write limericks.

3. As an added activity, have the student write his/her own limerick.

Lesson 134

Regular Comparisons: er, est

Overview:

- Recognize words ending with **-er** and **-est**

- Identify words which form regular comparisons

- Use words with the regular comparisons in sentences

Material and Supplies:

- Teacher's Guide and Student Workbook

- White board or chart paper

- Phonics flashcards

- Reader: "The Morgan Horse"

Teaching Tips:

Review for Mastery. Discuss and review any work from the previous lesson that was assigned as homework. Check for completion of the activities and orally quiz the student for comprehension. Review any reading that was assigned, discussing the characters, setting, plot, theme, language, sequence, etc.

Strengthen fluency and phonemic awareness by reviewing words and sentences from the previous lessons. Build vocabulary skills by using some of the words in sentences.

You may want to create flashcards of words with **-er** and **-est** comparison endings. The student can study these throughout the unit.

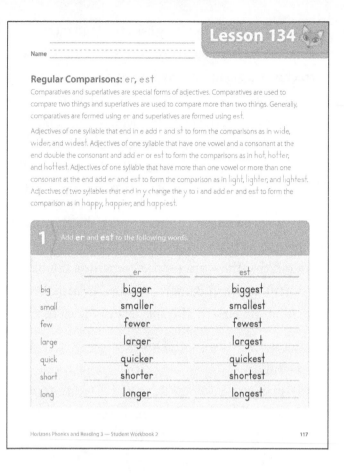

Lesson Introduction. The student will transition from the study of double consonants to looking at words of comparison with **-er** and **-est** endings. Draw pictures of three squares on the board. Make each one larger than the previous one. Under one of the squares write the word **big**. Ask the student, if the first square is big how would he/she describe the next one? The student should recognize that the next square is **bigger**. Go on to do the comparison of the final square which is the **biggest**. Next write the word **small** under the largest square. Have the student describe the previous squares as **smaller** and **smallest**. Underline the endings **-er** and **-est** in the words. Explain to the student that when two items are compared the ending **-er** is added. When three or more items are compared the ending **-est** is added. This lesson will explore words with these types of comparisons.

Activity 1. The student should turn to the activity sheet which accompanies this lesson. Read through the explanations at the top of the sheet. The student should look at the first activity. The student will be asked to add the suffixes **-er** and **-est** to the word endings. The answers to this activity are as follows:

	er	est
big	**bigger**	**biggest**
small	**smaller**	**smallest**
few	**fewer**	**fewest**
large	**larger**	**largest**
quick	**quicker**	**quickest**
short	**shorter**	**shortest**
long	**longer**	**longest**
tall	**taller**	**tallest**
sad	**sadder**	**saddest**
silly	**sillier**	**silliest**

Activity 2. In the next section, the student will need to decide which word is spelled correctly in each box. All of the words have comparison endings. The correct answers are: **shorter, toughest, sweeter, oldest, loudest, thicker, softest, fastest, highest, nicest.**

Activity 3. The final activity asks the student to use words with comparisons in sentences. The student will need to pay close attention to the context of the sentence in order to determine which word of comparison is to be used. The correct responses are: **louder, softer, higher, tallest, wettest, easier, faster, deepest, largest, smaller.**

Reading Activity.

1. The student should turn to the selection, "The Morgan Horse." Before reading the selection, have the student recall the selection he/she read about the Pony Express.

2. After reading the selection, discuss it with the student. Why was this type of horse chosen for the Pony Express? (**The horse had great endurance, adapted to different riders easily,** and was strong.) Why was this horse valued during the Civil War? (**The horse had great endurance and was easygoing. Additionally, it could pull heavy loads.**) What are the origins of the Morgan horse? (**All the Morgan horses descend from Figure. This was a horse bought by Justin Morgan at the time of the Revolutionary War. The Morgan horse was named after him.**) How did the Morgan differ from other types of horses? (**The Morgan was smaller, easily adapted to riders, and lived longer.**)

3. Ask the student to research another breed of horse and compare it with the Morgan. Some other breeds the student could research include the American Quarter Horse, Clydesdale, Mustang, and Thoroughbred.

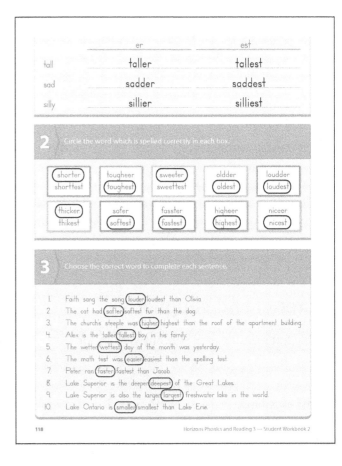

Lesson 135

Irregular Comparisons

Overview:

- Recognize comparisons which are formed irregularly
- Identify words which are examples of irregular comparisons
- Use irregular comparisons in sentences

Material and Supplies:

- Teacher's Guide and Student Workbook
- White board or chart paper
- Phonics flashcards
- Reader: "Lazy Jack"

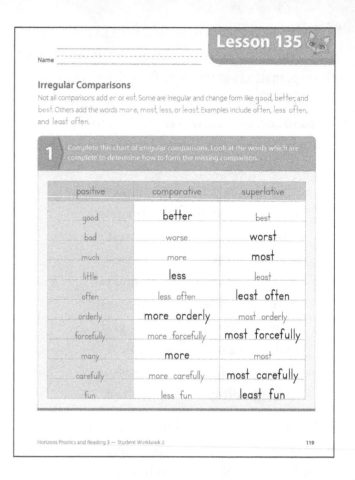

Teaching Tips:

Review for Mastery. Discuss and review any work from the previous lesson that was assigned as homework. Check for completion of the activities and orally quiz the student for comprehension. Review any reading that was assigned, discussing the characters, setting, plot, theme, language, sequence, etc.

Strengthen fluency and phonemic awareness by reviewing words and sentences from the previous lessons. Build vocabulary skills by using some of the words in sentences.

You may want to create flashcards of words with irregular comparisons. The student can study these throughout the unit.

Lesson Introduction. This lesson will continue the study of words of comparison. In this lesson, however, the student will focus on irregular comparisons. Draw three pictures of circles on the board. In the first picture draw three or four

circles. In the next drawing add more circles and in the last picture put the most. Under the first picture write the word **many.** Ask the student how he/she would describe the next pictures building on the word **many.** The student should recognize that the word **many** does not become **manyer** or **manyest.** Instead, the form changes to **many, more,** and **most.** Explain that **many** is an example of an irregular comparison. In this lesson, the student will focus on words which form their comparisons irregularly.

Activity 1. The student should turn to the activity sheet which accompanies this lesson. Have the student read the description at the top of the page. The student should look at the first activity on the sheet. The student will be asked to fill in a chart of irregular comparisons. The student should look at the words which are complete to determine how to form the missing comparison. The answers to the activity are: **better, worst, most, less, least often, more orderly, most forcefully, more, most carefully, least fun.**

Activity 2. The lesson continues with the student filling in the blank with the correct form of a given comparison. If possible, have the student read the sentence aloud so that he/she can hear if the sentence is correct. The answers to this activity are: **better, more, best, more carefully, most orderly, worst, most delicious, favorite, more colorful, more challenging**.

Note: Although **more favorite** and **most favorite** are grammatically correct, the preferred comparative and superlative form is **favorite**. If something is your favorite it is already the one that you like the most.

Activity 3. The student should look at the final activity on the sheet. The student will be asked to determine if the correct comparison is being used in each sentence. Again, it may be helpful for the student to read the sentence aloud before determining the correct answer. The answers to the activity are: **I, I, C, C, C, I, C, C, I, I**.

Reading Activity.

1. The student will read the selection, "Lazy Jack." This is a selection you could read together. Have the student read the narration and the role of Lazy Jack. The teacher can read the role of the mother.

2. Use the following questions to assist the student in discussing the selection. Why was Jack called "Lazy Jack?" **(While his mother worked, he either sat in the sun or by the fireplace.)** What kinds of jobs did Lazy Jack find? **(He worked for a number of farmers, a baker, a butcher, and a cattle-keeper.)** What types of rewards did he receive for his work?

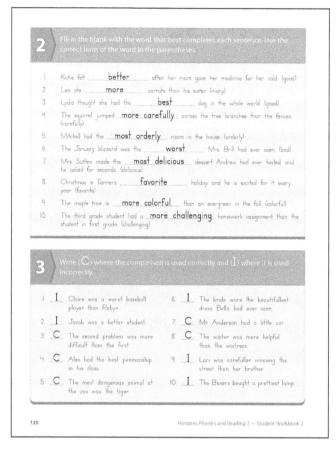

(He received a penny, milk, cheese, cat, roast, and donkey.) Why did none of these items reach his mother safely? **(Jack had no common sense. He didn't care for them or carry them properly.)** How did Jack end up wealthy and living in a large house? **(He made the daughter of a rich man laugh when he was carrying the donkey on his shoulders.)** What advice would you have given Lazy Jack if you had been his mother? (Answers may include: **He should carry everything in a bag, which would have worked for everything but the donkey. The mother could have also said that she would go and pick up what he had earned.)**

Lesson 136
Inflected Endings: ed, ing

Overview:

- Understand the use of inflected endings
- Remember how to form words with inflected endings
- Use words with inflected endings in sentences

Material and Supplies:

- Teacher's Guide and Student Workbook
- White board or chart paper
- Phonics flashcards
- Reader: "How Doth the Little Busy Bee"

Teaching Tips:

Review for Mastery. Discuss and review any work from the previous lesson that was assigned as homework. Check for completion of the activities and orally quiz the student for comprehension. Review any reading that was assigned, discussing the characters, setting, plot, theme, language, sequence, etc.

Strengthen fluency and phonemic awareness by reviewing words and sentences from the previous lessons. Build vocabulary skills by using some of the words in sentences.

Create flashcards of words with inflected endings. The student can study these throughout the unit.

Lesson Introduction. Write the following sentences on the board: **Today I walk. Yesterday I walked. I am walking right now.** Have the student underline the verb or the action in each of the sentences. The student should underline the words **walk, walked,** and **(am) walking.** Ask the student for the root word of the action word or verb. The root is **walk.** What endings have been added to

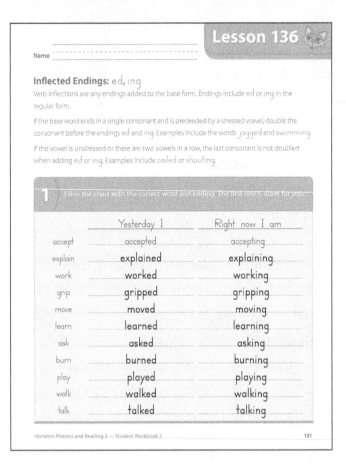

the word? **(-ed, -ing)** Explain that these are called inflected endings. Inflected endings are added to a verb to change their tense or the time in which the action of the sentence takes place.

Activity 1. Have the student turn to the activity sheet which accompanies this lesson. Read through the definitions at the top of the page. The first activity asks the student to fill in the chart with the words with the correct inflected endings. The answers to the activity are as follows:

explain	**explained**	**explaining**
work	**worked**	**working**
grip	**gripped**	**gripping**
move	**moved**	**moving**
learn	**learned**	**learning**
ask	**asked**	**asking**
burn	**burned**	**burning**
play	**played**	**playing**
walk	**walked**	**walking**
talk	**talked**	**talking**

Activity 2. The student will continue by applying what he/she knows about inflected endings. The student will need to add an inflected ending to words based on the sentences which are given. It may be helpful to have the student read each sentence aloud before determining the correct answer. The answers to the activity are: **asked, collecting, stuffed, squeaked, marching, mixing, greeted, jumped, closed, waved.**

Activity 3. The final activity continues with the student looking at sentences with inflected endings. The student will need to determine if the verb in the sentence is correct or incorrect. The student will need to look at what time the action in the sentence is taking place. The correct answers are: **C, C, C, I, C, I, C, I, C, C.**

Reading Activity.

1. Ask the student to read the selection entitled, "How Doth the Little Busy Bee." You may want to read it to the student first. The student can then read it with you a second time.

2. Begin by asking the student some questions about the way in which the poem was written. What was the rhyme scheme of the poem? **(The poem was written in four line stanzas. The rhyme scheme was abab. The stanzas were made of 8686 syllable lines.)**

3. Continue by discussing the themes found in the poem. What did the author ask at the beginning of the poem? **(The author wanted to know how the bee was able to work all day and keep getting better at its job.)** What did the bee do? **(The bee gathered honey, built a hive, and stored honey.)** What lesson did the author say could be learned from the bee? **(Lessons included the need for work and to do the best at whatever was tried.)** What happened when people were not busy? **(They found mischief or troublesome things to do instead of doing that which was good and helpful.)**

Lesson 137

Inflected Endings: ed, ing, s

Overview:

- Understand how inflected endings change verb meanings
- Identify words with inflected endings
- Use words with inflected endings in sentences

Material and Supplies:

- Teacher's Guide and Student Workbook
- White board or chart paper
- Phonics flashcards
- Reader: "A True Story about a Girl"

Teaching Tips:

Review for Mastery. Discuss and review any work from the previous lesson that was assigned as homework. Check for completion of the activities and orally quiz the student for comprehension. Review any reading that was assigned, discussing the characters, setting, plot, theme, language, sequence, etc.

Strengthen fluency and phonemic awareness by reviewing words and sentences from the previous lessons. Build vocabulary skills by using some of the words in sentences.

Create flashcards of words which contain inflected endings. The student can study these throughout the unit.

Lesson Introduction. Tell the student that this lesson will continue the study of inflected endings. In addition to the endings **-ed** and **-ing** the student

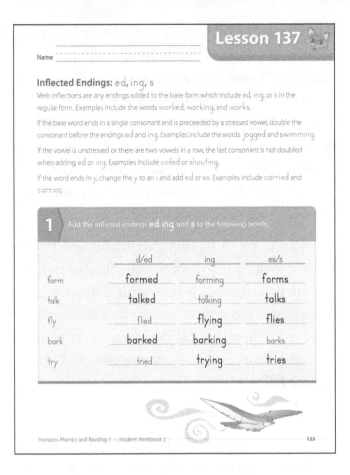

studied in the previous lesson, the student will look at words which add the inflected ending **-s**.

Write the following sentences on the board: **He jumped yesterday. He is jumping today. He _____ right now.** Ask the student what form of jump would fill in the blank. The student should recognize that the word **jumps** is needed in the blank. If the sentence was **They _____ right now.** the word **jump** without an ending would be used. Adding **-s** to a verb generally indicates that the subject is single.

Activity 1. Turn to the activity sheet which accompanies this lesson. The student should read the definitions for the inflected endings at the top of the page. The student should look at the first activity and fill in the blanks with the correct form of the verb. The correct responses are as follows:

	d/ed	ing	es/s
form	**formed**	forming	**forms**
talk	**talked**	talking	**talks**
fly	flied	**flying**	**flies**
bark	**barked**	**barking**	barks
try	tried	**trying**	**tries**

Activity 2. The next activity asks the student to determine if the verb used in each sentence is correct or incorrect. The word is underlined so the student can focus on how it is used in the sentence. It may be helpful to have the student read the sentences aloud to hear how the words are used. The answers to the activity are: **C, C, I, I, C, I, C, C, C, I.**

Activity 3. The final activity asks the student to choose the correct word for each sentence. Two choices are given and the student will need to fill in the blank with the correct one. If in doubt, the student can read the sentence aloud to hear how the word sounds in context. The correct responses are: **applauded, asks, builds, walked, knows, playing, draws, shines, rides, read.**

Reading Activity.

1. Have the student read the selection entitled, "A True Story about a Girl."

2. Ask the student the following questions about the selection. Describe Louisa's childhood. (**The student can comment on her life with her sisters. Her family was poor, yet they had fun and enjoyed being together.**) What types of things did Louisa and her sisters do to entertain themselves? (**The girls would create and put on plays together.**) What types of things do you do to entertain yourself? (**Answers will vary.**)

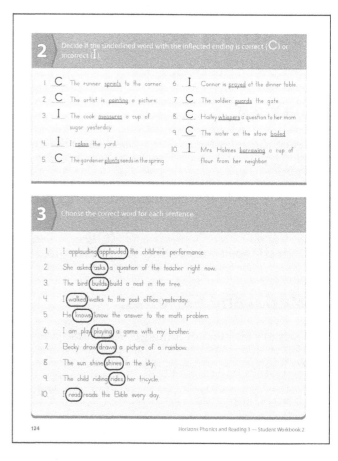

What problems did Louisa and her family face? (**The family was poor and the mother had to work very hard.**) What was Louisa's goal in life? (**She wanted to earn money so her mother did not have to work so hard.**) How did she go about accomplishing this goal? (**She did sewing for other people, she taught girls, and she wrote.**) What was the famous book written by Louisa and what was it about? (**She wrote a book entitled *Little Women* and she took some of the ideas from her life growing up with her sisters.**) Why do you think the author wrote this selection about Louisa? (**She may have wanted to teach people something about the life of a famous author. She may also have wanted to encourage people to show love and respect for their parents.**)

Lesson 138

Inflected Endings: s, es

Overview:

- Learn the rules for adding -**s** and -**es** to the ends of words

- Identify words with the inflected endings -**s** and -**es**

- Correctly spell words with -**s** and -**es** endings

Material and Supplies:

- Teacher's Guide and Student Workbook

- White board or chart paper

- Phonics flashcards

- Reader: "Block City"

Teaching Tips:

Review for Mastery. Discuss and review any work from the previous lesson that was assigned as homework. Check for completion of the activities and orally quiz the student for comprehension. Review any reading that was assigned, discussing the characters, setting, plot, theme, language, sequence, etc.

Strengthen fluency and phonemic awareness by reviewing words and sentences from the previous lessons. Build vocabulary skills by using some of the words in sentences.

You may want to create flashcards of words with -**s** and -**es** inflected endings. The student can study these throughout the unit.

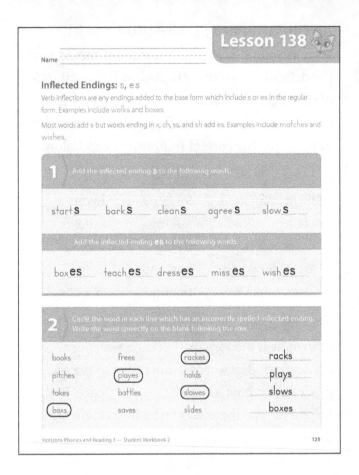

Lesson Introduction. The student will continue the study of inflected endings. In this lesson the focus will be on words ending in -**s** and -**es.** The student will learn the rules for adding -**s** and -**es** to verb forms.

Begin by asking the student to recall the inflected endings that have been presented up to this point in the unit. Those endings are -**ed**, -**ing**, and -**s.** Explain that while most words add -**s** to the ending, some words add -**es.** Words endings in -**x**, -**ch**, -**ss**, and -**sh**, add -**es.** Write the following sentence on the board: **My mom wash windows.** Ask the student what ending should be added to the verb or the action of the sentence. The word **wash** should be changed to **washes.**

This lesson will explore other verbs which add the endings -**s** or -**es.**

Activity 1. Ask the student to turn to the activity sheet which accompanies this lesson. Read through the definitions of inflected endings at the top of the page. The first activity will ask the student to add the endings **-s** or **-es** to words. The words will be separated so that the student will not need to choose which of the endings to add. The answers to the activity are: **starts, barks, cleans, agrees, slows, boxes, teaches, dresses, misses, wishes.**

Activity 2. The lesson continues with the student choosing the word which is misspelled in each row. The student may want to refer to the rules at the top of the activity sheet while completing the activity. All of the words will be adding either **-s** or **-es**. Additionally, the student will need to rewrite the incorrectly spelled word. The correct responses are: **racks, plays, slows, boxes, catches, paints, cooks, washes, rushes, pushes.**

Activity 3. The final activity for this activity sheet asks the student to find words ending in **-s** and **-es** in a word search. **See image for answers.**

Reading Activity.

1. The student should turn to the selection, "Block City." Before reading the poem, write the word "kirk" on the board. Explain that in German the word kirk means church. The word kirk will appear in the poem.

2. Discuss the way in which the poem was written. What is the poetic structure? (**The poem was written in four line stanzas. The rhyme scheme is aabb. The lines consist of ten syllables.**)

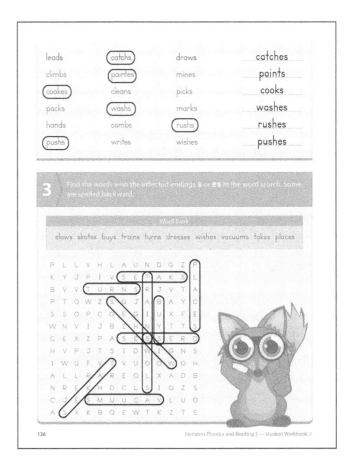

3. Discuss the poem with your student. Why is the child happy being at home? (**The child is happy for the comfort of the house. The child is happy to be out of the rain and not traveling.**) What did the child build with the blocks? (**The child built palaces, docks, and an entire city by the sea.**) How did the author describe the palace? (**He described the pillars, walls, tower, and steps.**)

4. Continue the poem by discussing what the student has built out of wooden or plastic construction blocks. What words would you use to describe the things you have built? (**Allow for individual answers.**)

Lesson 139

Review: Inflected Endings

Overview:

- Form words with inflected endings
- Recognize words with inflected endings
- Identify verb forms with inflected endings

Material and Supplies:

- Teacher's Guide and Student Workbook
- White board or chart paper
- Phonics flashcards
- Reader: "The Larks in the Cornfield"

Teaching Tips:

Review for Mastery. Discuss and review any work from the previous lesson that was assigned as homework. Check for completion of the activities and orally quiz the student for comprehension. Review any reading that was assigned, discussing the characters, setting, plot, theme, language, sequence, etc.

Strengthen fluency and phonemic awareness by reviewing words and sentences from the previous lessons. Build vocabulary skills by using some of the words in sentences.

You may want to review the flashcards with inflected endings.

Lesson Introduction. Explain to the student that in this lesson he/she will be reviewing words with inflected endings. Ask the student to recall the inflected endings that are added to verbs or action words in sentences. The student should remember the inflected endings **-ing**, **-ed**, and **-s**.

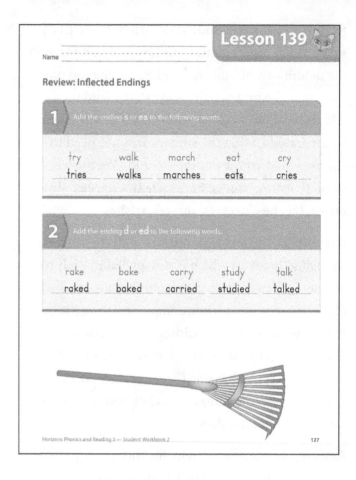

Write the following sentence on the board: **She _____ the windows.** Ask the student what action words or verbs could be put in the blank. Answers may include: **wash, fix,** and **clean.** Tell the student the person in the sentence is doing the action right now. Ask the student what inflected ending would need to be added to the verb in order to make it fit the sentence. The answers would be: **washes, fixes,** and **cleans.** Now imagine that the person did the action yesterday. What verb forms would be used? The correct responses are: **washed, fixed,** and **cleaned.** Insert the word **is** before the sentence blank. What verbs would be used? (**washing, fixing,** and **cleaning**)

Activity 1. The student should turn to the worksheet which accompanies this lesson. In the first activity the student will add the endings **-s** and **-es** to words. The student will need to determine which ending needs to be added and what to do with words ending in **-y.** The correct answers are: **tries, walks, marches, eats, cries.**

Activity 2. The second activity is similar to the first. In this activity the student will need to add the endings **-d** or **-ed**. Again, some words may need to change the **-y** ending to **i** before adding the inflected ending. The correct responses are: **raked, baked, carried, studied, talked.**

Activity 3. The next activity asks the student to circle the verb or action word which rhymes with the word in bold type. If possible, allow the student to say the words aloud. This will enable the student to hear the word endings and which ones rhyme. The correct responses are: **cries, striving, lies, carried, clinked, traced, trying, rowing.**

Activity 4. The student will need to read sentences in the last activity and determine the correct word to complete each. The sentences will take place during differing time periods. The student will need to read carefully to determine the correct word. The correct words to use are: **raked, studied, walks, friendliest, carried, bakes, trying, marches.**

Reading Activity.

1. The student should read the selection, "The Larks in the Cornfield."

2. Discuss the selection with the student. What problem did the mother lark and her babies face? (**The birds were living in the field and it was time to harvest the crop. Once the harvesting began they would have to be moved or face danger.**) What conversations of the father and son did the mother lark ignore? (**She didn't pay attention when the farmer**

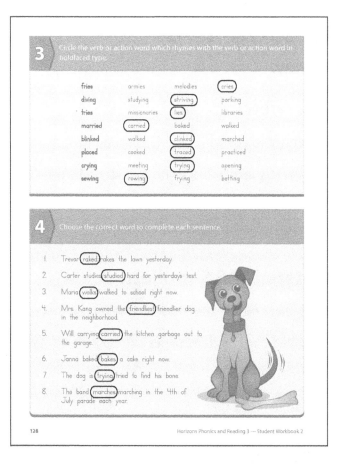

said he was going to ask his neighbors and family for help.) When did she decide the babies needed to be moved? (**When the farmer said he was going to hire workers, she knew the babies would need to leave.**) What do you think was the point of the story? (**When people do their own work, it actually gets done. When people wait for others to do their work, nothing happens.**) Do you agree with this idea? Why or why not? (**Allow for individual answers. Discuss how Christians are called to do their own work but also to care for the needs of others.**)

Lesson 140

Review

Overview:

- Identify words with double consonants
- Correctly form words with regular and irregular comparisons
- Form verbs with inflected endings

Material and Supplies:

- Teacher's Guide and Student Workbook
- White board or chart paper
- Phonics flashcards
- Reader: "God Loves Me"

Teaching Tips:

Review for Mastery. Discuss and review any work from the previous lesson that was assigned as homework. Check for completion of the activities and orally quiz the student for comprehension. Review any reading that was assigned, discussing the characters, setting, plot, theme, language, sequence, etc.

Strengthen fluency and phonemic awareness by reviewing words and sentences from the previous lessons. Build vocabulary skills by using some of the words in sentences.

You may want to review flashcards made for words in this unit.

Lesson Introduction. This lesson reviews the material the student learned in the unit. The student will complete activities which review words with double consonants. See if the student can recall any words with double consonants. Responses may include: **hidden, coffee,** and **wall.** The student also studied words which formed regular and irregular comparisons. Have three

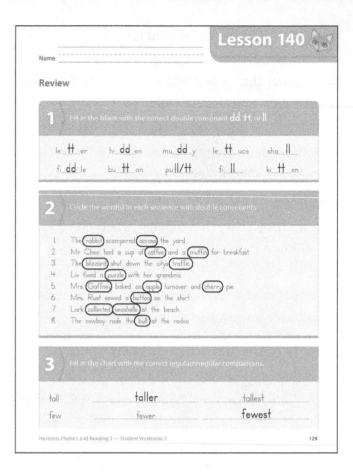

objects of differing sizes in front of class. Ask the student to think of different ways in which the items can be compared. Examples may include: **size** or **weight,** such as, the first object is heavier than the first or the final object is the heaviest of the three. Finally, review the use of words with inflected endings. Ask the student to recall what makes for an inflected ending. Inflected endings include: **-s, -es, -d, -ed,** and **-ing.** Ask the student to list some action words or verbs for you. Write these on the board. The student should then add inflected endings to them.

Activity 1. The student should turn to the activity sheet which accompanies this lesson. The review sheet is arranged in the same way as the test. In the test different examples will be used but the format will remain the same. The student will begin by filling in the blank with the correct double consonant. The student will have the choices of **dd, tt,** or **ll.** The student may want to write out the words first to make sure he/she has chosen the correct double letters. The answers are: **letter, hidden, muddy, lettuce, shall, fiddle, button, pull/putt, fill, kitten**.

Activity 2. The next activity asks the student to circle the words/words in each sentence which contain double consonants. Emphasize that some sentences may have more than one. The correct responses are: **rabbit, across, coffee, muffin, blizzard, traffic, puzzle, Gaffney, apple, cherry, button, collected, seashells, bull**.

Activity 3. The activity sheet continues with the student filling in the chart with regular and irregular comparisons. The student will need to determine which part of the comparison is missing and fill in the blanks. The correct answers are as follows:

tall	**taller**	tallest
few	fewer	**fewest**
happy	**happier**	happiest
bad	**worse**	worst
often	more often	**most often**
many	more	**most**
forcefully	less forcefully	**least forcefully**
soft	**softer**	softest
deep	**deeper**	deepest
short	shorter	**shortest**

Activity 4. The final activity asks the student to complete a chart where the inflected endings **d/ed**, **ing**, and **es/s** are added to the words. Remind the student that words ending in **-y** may or may not need to change the **-y** to an **i** before adding the ending. The answers are as follows:

	d/ed	ing	es/s
trip	**tripped**	**tripping**	**trips**
bake	**baked**	**baking**	**bakes**
fry	**fried**	**frying**	**fries**
color	**colored**	**coloring**	**colors**
show	**showed**	**showing**	**shows**
reach	**reached**	**reaching**	**reaches**
cross	**crossed**	**crossing**	**crosses**
sew	**sewed**	**sewing**	**sews**

happy	happier	happiest
bad	worse	worst
often	more often	most often
many	more	most
forcefully	less forcefully	least forcefully
soft	softer	softest
deep	deeper	deepest
short	shorter	shortest

4 Add the inflected endings **d/ed**, **ing**, and **es/s** to the following words.

	d/ed	ing	es/s
trip	tripped	tripping	trips
bake	baked	baking	bakes
fry	fried	frying	fries
color	colored	coloring	colors
show	showed	showing	shows
reach	reached	reaching	reaches
cross	crossed	crossing	crosses
sew	sewed	sewing	sews

130   Horizons Phonics and Reading 3 — Student Workbook 2

Reading Activity.

1. The student should turn to the selection, "God Loves Me."

2. Direct the student in reading this poem for pleasure.

Test 14

Lessons 131-140

Overview:

- Identify words with double consonants
- Correctly form words with regular and irregular comparisons
- Form verbs with inflected endings

Material and Supplies:

- Student Test

Teaching Tips:

Review for Mastery. Discuss and review any work from the previous lesson that was assigned as homework. Check for completion of the activities and orally quiz the student for comprehension. Review any reading that was assigned, discussing the characters, setting, plot, theme, language, sequence, etc.

Lesson Introduction. This lesson tests the material the student learned in the unit. Before the test you may want to ask the student if he/she has any final questions. There may be questions the student will want to review. Remind the student that the final test follows the same format as the review, discussing the characters, setting, plot, theme, language, sequence, etc.

Activity 1. The student should turn to the test. The test is arranged in the same way as the review sheet. In the test different examples will be used but the format will remain the same. The student will begin by filling in the blanks with the correct double consonants. The student will have the choices of **mm**, **rr**, or **ss**. The student may want to write out the words first to make sure he/she has chosen the correct double letters. The correct answers are:

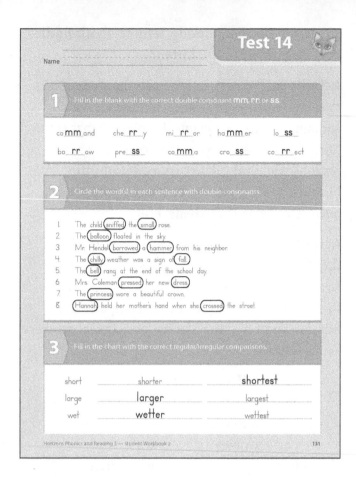

command, **cherry**, **mirror**, **hammer**, **loss**, **borrow**, **press**, **comma**, **cross**, **correct**.

Activity 2. The next activity asks the student to circle the words/words in each sentence which contain double consonants. Emphasize that some sentences may have more than one. The correct responses are: **sniffed**, **small**, **balloon**, **borrowed**, **hammer**, **chilly**, **fall**, **bell**, **pressed**, **dress**, **princess**, **Hannah**, **crossed**.

Activity 3. The test continues with the student completing a chart with comparisons. The correct answers are as follows:

short	shorter	**shortest**
large	**larger**	largest
wet	**wetter**	wettest
good	**better**	best
careful	more careful	**most careful**
favorite	**less favorite**	least favorite
much	more	**most**
sad	sadder	**saddest**
fun	**more fun**	most fun
quick	quicker	**quickest**

Activity 4. The final activity asks the student to complete a chart where the inflected endings **d/ed**, **ing**, and **es/s** are added to the words. The correct responses are as follows:

	d/ed	ing	es/s
burn	**burned**	**burning**	**burns**
talk	**talked**	**talking**	**talks**
move	**moved**	**moving**	**moves**
chirp	**chirped**	**chirping**	**chirps**
cry	**cried**	**crying**	**cries**
wish	**wished**	**wishing**	**wishes**
cook	**cooked**	**cooking**	**cooks**
miss	**missed**	**missing**	**misses**

good	better	best
careful	more careful	most careful
favorite	less favorite	least favorite
much	more	most
sad	sadder	saddest
fun	more fun	most fun
quick	quicker	quickest

4 Add the inflected endings **ed/d**, **ing**, and **es/s** to the following words.

	d/ed	ing	es/s
burn	burned	burning	burns
talk	talked	talking	talks
move	moved	moving	moves
chirp	chirped	chirping	chirps
cry	cried	crying	cries
wish	wished	wishing	wishes
cook	cooked	cooking	cooks
miss	missed	missing	misses

132   Horizons Phonics and Reading 3 — Student Workbook 2

Lesson 141

Compound Words

Overview:

- Understand the meaning of compound words
- Recognize words which are compounds
- Form compound words

Material and Supplies:

- Teacher's Guide and Student Workbook
- White board or chart paper
- Phonics flashcards
- Reader: "The Boy That Never Tells a Lie"

Teaching Tips:

Lesson Introduction. Explain to the student that at the beginning of this unit he/she will be studying compound words. The student will learn about three types of compound words. The first are words which, when combined, form one word. The second are compound words which are hyphenated. The third are open compound words that are spelled as unconnected words.

Write the words **ball, foot,** and **basket** on the board. The student should recognize that all three are singular words. Next, write the words **football** and **basketball** on the board. Explain that when two words are put together to form a new word, the new word is called a compound word.

You may want to have the student create flashcards of compound words. The student can study these throughout the unit.

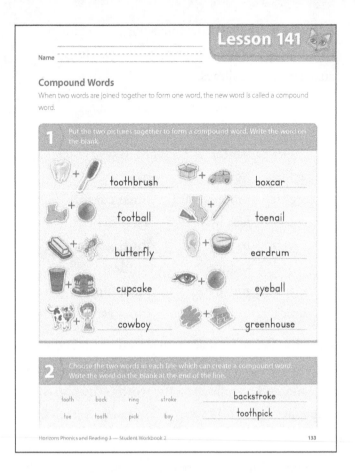

Activity 1. The student should turn to the activity sheet for this lesson. The first activity asks the student to look at combinations of pictures and form compound words. The student should identify each picture and then put the words together to form a compound. The answers to this activity are: **toothbrush, football, butterfly, cupcake, cowboy, boxcar, toenail, eardrum, eyeball, greenhouse.**

Activity 2. The second activity continues by having the student forming more compound words. Each line in the activity has four words. The correct answers are: **backstroke, toothpick, tablecloth, earring, eyelid, fishbowl, grasshopper, brainstorm, headband, haircut.**

Activity 3. The final activity asks the student to choose the correct word to complete each sentence. If possible have the student read the completed sentence aloud to make sure he/she has chosen the correct answer. The answers to the activity are: **earache, toothpaste, eyeglasses, grapefruit, headlight, goldfish, homework, honeybee, racetrack, popcorn.**

Reading Activity.

1. The student should turn to the selection, "The Boy That Never Tells a Lie." Direct the student in reading the selection. You may want to read the poem to the student first. Read the poem a second time with the student reading every other line or stanza. Explain any words the student may have difficulty understanding.

2. Discuss the selection with the student. Use some of the following questions to assist your discussion. Ask the student to describe the boy in the poem? **(He had curly hair and looked nice. Most importantly he never told a lie.)** How did people speak about the boy? **(They spoke of him as never telling a lie, being honest, and they loved him.)** What do you think the author wanted to say in his poem? **(The author wanted children to learn the importance and benefits of telling the truth.)**

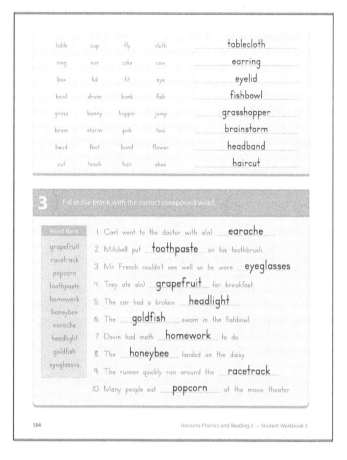

3. Discuss with the student the benefits of telling the truth and the consequences of telling lies. You may want to develop your discussion by asking the student to find passages in the Bible which speak about telling the truth and telling lies.

4. Discuss the rhyme scheme with the student. **(The poem was written in four-line stanzas of eight syllables per line. The rhyme scheme is abcb.)**

Lesson 142

Compound Words

Overview:

- Know the meaning of compound words

- Recognize compound words

- Use words which are compounds in sentences

Material and Supplies:

- Teacher's Guide and Student Workbook

- White board or chart paper

- Phonics flashcards

- Reader: "The Little Turtle"

Teaching Tips:

Review for Mastery. Discuss and review any work from the previous lesson that was assigned as homework. Check for completion of the activities and orally quiz the student for comprehension. Review any reading that was assigned, discussing the characters, setting, plot, theme, language, sequence, etc.

Strengthen fluency and phonemic awareness by reviewing words and sentences from the previous lessons. Build vocabulary skills by using some of the words in sentences.

You may want to create flashcards of compound words. The student can study these throughout the unit.

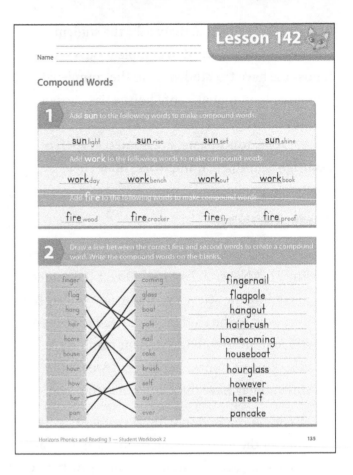

Lesson Introduction. Tell the student that he/she will continue the study of compound words. Ask the student to give you an example of a compound word. Write these examples on the board. Check to make sure the student is giving you words which are compounds and not two separate words. Examples may include: **everything**, **butterfly**, and **basketball**.

Activity 1. The student should turn to the worksheet for this lesson. Explain that the student will continue the study of compound words. The student will be asked to create compound words with three key words: **sun**, **work**, and **fire**. Through this activity the student will see the number of words which can be formed into compounds. The answers to the activity are: **sunlight, sunrise, sunset, sunshine, workday, workbench, workout, workbook, firewood, firecracker, firefly, fireproof.**

Activity 2. Continue by looking at the next activity. The student will see two columns of words. The student will need to combine words from the first column with those in the second. The student may want to have a piece of scratch paper available to write the new words to make sure each is formed correctly. The answers to the activity are: **fingernail, flagpole, hangout, hairbrush, homecoming, houseboat, hourglass, however, herself, pancake.**

Activity 3. The student will continue the lesson by finding compound words in sentences. The student should read through each sentence at least twice before identifying the compound words. The answers to the activity are: **pickup, railroad, pillowcase, bedroom, thunderstorm, rainbow, pineapple, breakfast, butterfly, cornstalk, championship, basketball, clothesline, courthouse, crossroads, highways, bobcat, daybreak, dustpan, bathroom.**

Reading Activity.

1. Direct the student to read the selection, "The Little Turtle."

2. With the student, talk about the way in which the poem was written. (**The poem is written in stanzas of lines with syllables of 7575. The poem also has an abab rhyme scheme.**)

3. Begin by discussing the tone of the poem. Is it serious? Frightening? Fun? (**The student should recognize that the poem is light-hearted and fun.**) How can the student tell that the poem is fun? (**The primary example is the**

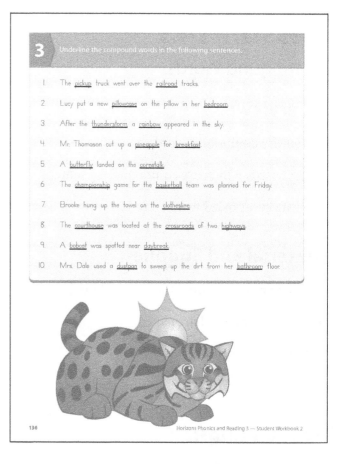

last line where the author states that the turtle was not able to catch him.) Where did the turtle live and play? (**The turtle lived in a box, and he played in the puddle and among the rocks.**) What repetition did the author use in the poem to create the light tone? (**The author wrote who the turtle snapped at and caught.**) What were the four items the turtle snapped at? (**He snapped at a flea, a mosquito, a minnow, and the writer.**)

Lesson 143

Compound Words

Overview:

- Identify compound words

- Use words which are compounds in sentences

- Write compound words

Material and Supplies:

- Teacher's Guide and Student Workbook

- White board or chart paper

- Phonics flashcards

- Reader: "The Three Questions: Part I"

Teaching Tips:

Review for Mastery. Discuss and review any work from the previous lesson that was assigned as homework. Check for completion of the activities and orally quiz the student for comprehension. Review any reading that was assigned, discussing the characters, setting, plot, theme, language, sequence, etc.

Strengthen fluency and phonemic awareness by reviewing words and sentences from the previous lessons. Build vocabulary skills by using some of the words in sentences.

You may want to create flashcards of words which are compounds. The student can study these throughout the unit.

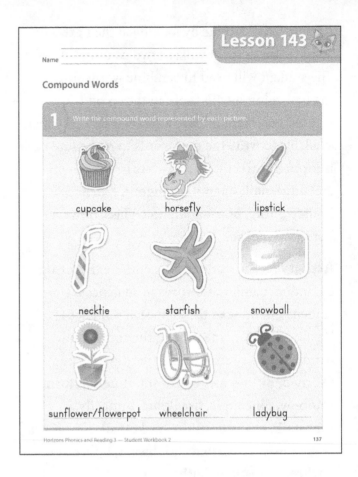

Lesson Introduction. Explain that in this lesson the student will continue the study of compound words. Ask the student to think of their home and compound words which can be used to describe it. Answers may include: **bedroom**, **tablecloth**, and **teapot**.

Activity 1. The student should turn to the activity sheet which accompanies this lesson. The first activity asks the student to identify pictures of compound words. The words pictured are: **cupcake, horsefly, lipstick, necktie, starfish, snowball, sunflower/flowerpot, wheelchair, ladybug**.

Activity 2. The next activity asks the student to circle the word in each line which is a compound. The compounds in the activity are: **inchworm, tablespoon, quarterback, oversize, yardstick, lifeguard, notebook, watermelon, roommate, rowboat.**

Activity 3. The lesson continues with the student completing a word search. Before beginning the word search, ask the student to divide each of the words into its two parts. For example: **down/town** and **drive/way.** This will help the student visualize that compound words are two separate words joined together to create a new meaning. **See image for answers.**

Reading Activity.

1. The selection for this lesson is, "The Three Questions: Part I." Direct the student in reading the selection. You may want to read one paragraph while the student reads the next. The student will read the first part of the selection in this lesson. The reading will be completed in the next lesson.

2. After reading the selection, discuss it with the student. What were the three questions the king wanted answered? (**He wanted to know when he should begin things, who were the right people to listen to, and what was the most important thing to do.**) Where did he first go to get advice? (**He asked people throughout his kingdom to give him advice.**) What kind of advice did they give? (**They gave him all kinds of different advice. He received no good answers.**) Why did he go to the hermit? (**He hoped the hermit would have some good advice for him.**) Why did he dress in poor clothing when he went to see the hermit? (**The hermit saw people who were poor. The king did not want to identify himself.**) What advice did the hermit give him? (**The hermit did not give him any advice.**)

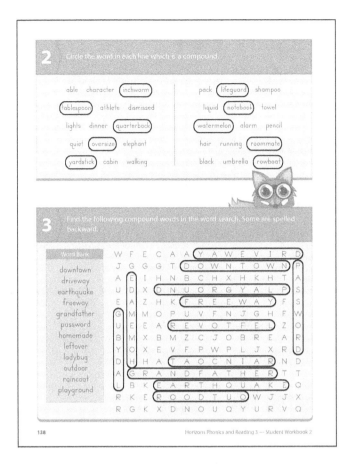

What interactions did the hermit have with the king? (**The hermit had the king dig for him.**) How did the king treat the injured man? (**The king treated the man's wounds, gave him water, and carried him into the hermit's hut.**)

3. Ask the student to predict what will happen next. The student should focus on predicting what will happen to the king, hermit, and wounded man. Additionally, ask the student to think about how the man may have become wounded.

Lesson 144
Hyphenated and Open Compound Words

Overview:

- Recognize words which are hyphenated compound words
- Recognize words which are open compound words
- Identify words which are hyphenated compounds
- Identify words which are open compound words
- Use hyphenated compound words in sentences

Material and Supplies:

- Teacher's Guide and Student Workbook
- White board or chart paper
- Phonics flashcards
- Reader: "The Three Questions: Part II"

Teaching Tips:

Review for Mastery. Discuss and review any work from the previous lesson that was assigned as homework. Check for completion of the activities and orally quiz the student for comprehension. Review any reading that was assigned, discussing the characters, setting, plot, theme, language, sequence, etc.

Strengthen fluency and phonemic awareness by reviewing words and sentences from the previous lessons. Build vocabulary skills by using some of the words in sentences.

You may want to create flashcards of compound words. The student can study these throughout the unit.

Lesson Introduction. The student will continue the study of compound words. In this lesson the student will look at compound words with

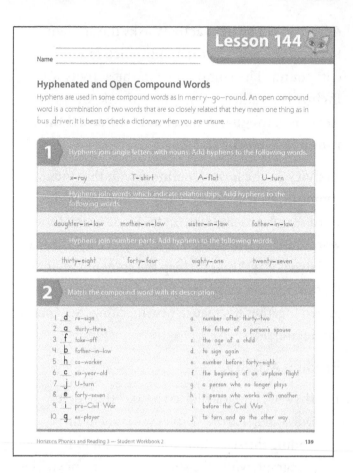

hyphens. Write the word **mother-in-law** on the board. Ask the student to identify the - in the word. The student should recognize that these dashes are called **hyphens**. Some compound words do not join two words without a space. Instead they use hyphens. Words which show relationships like **in-law** use hyphens. Ask the student for another example of this type of hyphenated word. The student may give the examples of **sister-in-law** or **brother-in-law**. Hyphens are used to join words with a single letter and then a word, such as **T-shirt** and **U-turn**. Hyphens are also used to join numbers such as **thirty-eight** and **twenty-seven**. Sometimes it's difficult to know if a word needs a hyphen. In this case, it's best to consult a dictionary.

Activity 1. The student should turn to the activity sheet which accompanies this lesson. In the first activity, the student will be asked to identify different types of hyphenated words. The words are grouped by type. The first type are words which are single letters followed by a word. The answers to this activity are: **x-ray, T-shirt, A-flat, U-turn.**

The next group of words indicates relationships which include: **daughter-in-law, mother-in-law, sister-in-law, father-in-law.**

Number parts are the final group of words. The correct answers to this activity are: **thirty-eight, forty-four, eighty-one, twenty-seven.**

Activity 2. In the next section, the student will need to match the hyphenated compound word with its meaning. The answers are: 1.—**d**, 2.—**a**, 3.—**f**, 4.—**b**, 5.—**h**, 6.—**c**, 7.—**j**, 8.—**e**, 9.—**i**, 10.—**g**.

Activity 3. This activity asks the student to identify hyphenated compound words in sentences. Ask the student to read each of the sentences aloud and then identify the hyphenated compound word(s) in each. The answers to the activity are: **U-turn, one-way, three-year-old, jack-of-all-trades, well-trained, brother-in-law, mid-July, re-cover, back-to-back, T-shirts, seven-year-old, x-ray, pre-Revolutionary.**

Activity 4. The final activity asks the student to form open compound words. Each word in the left column can be matched with a word in the right column to form an open compound word. Open compound words are spelled as unconnected words as in **candy cane, grand jury, middle class,** or **peanut butter.** The answers to the activity are: **ice cream, first aid, middle class, sea salt, park bench, full moon, credit card, post office, French fries**

Reading Activity.

1. Review the predictions the student made after reading the first half of the selection. Remind the student that the selection ended with the king helping the wounded man.

2. The student should turn to the selection, "The Three Questions: Part II." Direct the student in reading the selection.

3. After the student has read the rest of the selection, discuss it using the following questions. Why was the man injured when he approached the king and hermit? (**He had been attacked by the king's guards. The man planned to harm the king and the king's guards kept him from accomplishing his goal.**) Why was the wounded man angry with

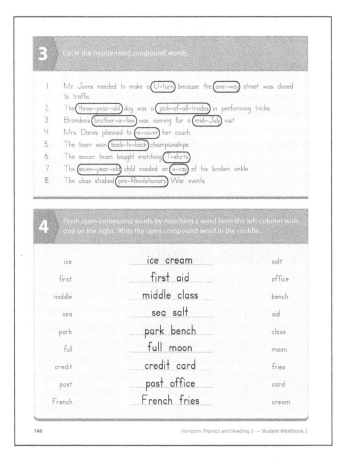

the king? (**The king had taken his brother's property.**) How did the wounded man plan to repay the king for saving his life? (**He said that he and his sons would serve the king.**) What was the king's response? (**The king said he would return the land to the man's brother.**) What did the hermit say was the answer to the three questions the king asked? (**The hermit explained how each interaction the king had while staying at the hermit's house was important. The hermit told the king that who he was with and what he did at each moment had significance.**)

4. Extend the discussion of the selection by applying it to the student's life. Who are some people that the student has interacted with in the last day or week? (**The student may recall parents, siblings, store clerks, or librarians.**) Discuss the significance of these interactions. Explain that sometimes being polite and respectful can be helpful to a person. Friendliness and care for the feelings and needs of others is also important.

Lesson 145
Clipped Words

Overview:

- Recognize clipped words
- Identify words which are clipped
- Use clipped words in sentences

Material and Supplies:

- Teacher's Guide and Student Workbook
- White board or chart paper
- Phonics flashcards
- Reader: "The Good Samaritan"

Teaching Tips:

Review for Mastery. Discuss and review any work from the previous lesson that was assigned as homework. Check for completion of the activities and orally quiz the student for comprehension. Review any reading that was assigned, discussing the characters, setting, plot, theme, language, sequence, etc.

Strengthen fluency and phonemic awareness by reviewing words and sentences from the previous lessons. Build vocabulary skills by using some of the words in sentences.

You may want to create flashcards of clipped words. The student can study these throughout the unit.

Lesson Introduction. The student will move from the study of compound words, which are two joined words, to clipped words, which are shortened words. Begin the lesson by giving the student examples of people they know who have shortened versions of their full names. Examples may include: **grandma** for **grandmother** or **Bella** for **Isabella**. Tell students that names aren't the only type of words shortened.

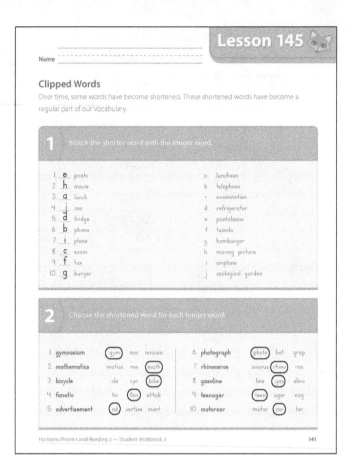

Some common words that people use every day have been shortened from their longer version. For example, when a person says he is wearing **pants**, he is actually saying he is wearing **pantaloons**.

Activity 1. The student should turn to the activity sheet which accompanies this lesson. Have the student read the description at the top of the page. The student should look at the first activity on the sheet. In this activity the student will be asked to match the shortened version of a word with its longer version. The correct answers to the activity are: 1.—**e**, 2.—**h**, 3.—**a**, 4.—**j**, 5.—**d**, 6.—**b**, 7.—**i**, 8.—**c**, 9.—**f**, 10.—**g**.

Activity 2. The lesson continues with the student choosing the correct common shortening of words from a longer word. You may want to read each longer word and then have the student circle the correct choice of the shortened word. The answers are: **gym**, **math**, **bike**, **fan**, **ad**, **photo**, **rhino**, **gas**, **teen**, **car**.

Activity 3. The student should look at the final activity on the sheet. In this activity the student will be asked to create sentences using the clipped words **zoo**, **plane**, **math**, **bike** and **car**. Sentence examples are provided in the image.

Reading Activity.

1. The student will read the selection, "The Good Samaritan." The story of the Good Samaritan may be familiar to your student. Have the student read the selection silently.

2. After reading the selection, discuss it with your student. Tell the student that you want him/her to think about the previous selection of "The Three Questions" while discussing "The Good Samaritan." What were the three questions the king wanted answered in the previous selection? **(He wanted to know when he should begin things, who were the right people to listen to, and what was the most important thing to do.)** Ask the student which person in the parable began things at the right time? **(The Samaritan did what needed to be done at the right time. He cared for the wounded man as soon as he saw him.)** Which of the characters listened to the right person? **(The first two men were worried what others might think of them or about their station in life. The third man did what he knew was right in the eyes of God. He helped the man.)** What was the most important thing to do in this parable? **(The Samaritan did what was most important which was to help his neighbor. You may want to point out how the Samaritan also made sure the injured man would be cared for in the future.)**

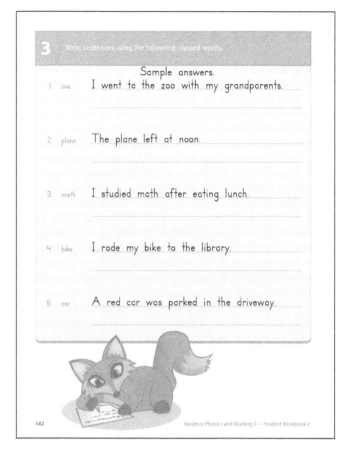

3. Have the student apply the parable of the Good Samaritan to their own lives. What types of things do they do to show their love and concern for others? You may want to have the student do something concrete to help another person, such as bring cookies, pick up sticks, or some other form of help.

Lesson 146

Articles: a/an

Overview:

- Understand when the article **a** or **an** should be used before a word

- Recognize the correct use of the articles **a** and **an**

- Use the articles **a** and **an** correctly

Material and Supplies:

- Teacher's Guide and Student Workbook

- White board or chart paper

- Phonics flashcards

- Reader: "The African Elephant"

Teaching Tips:

Review for Mastery. Discuss and review any work from the previous lesson that was assigned as homework. Check for completion of the activities and orally quiz the student for comprehension. Review any reading that was assigned, discussing the characters, setting, plot, theme, language, sequence, etc.

Strengthen fluency and phonemic awareness by reviewing words and sentences from the previous lessons. Build vocabulary skills by using some of the words in sentences.

Use the flashcards the student has created in this unit and ask him/her to correctly put the article **a** or **an** before each. The student can study these throughout the unit.

Lesson Introduction. Ask the student to give you a list of types of birds. Examples may include: **robin**, **eagle**, **owl**, and **parrot**. Write these names on the board. Next write on the board the words **a** and **an**. Explain that these words are articles and appear before nouns in sentences. (They can appear before any of the birds written on the board, but **a** and **an** can only precede some.) Tell students that the article **an** is only used before words beginning with vowel sounds. Have the student write the article **an** before the bird names with beginning vowel sounds. Examples include **an eagle** or **an owl**.

Continue by telling the student that sometimes a combination of a consonant and vowel can make a vowel sound. Examples of these types of words include **honor** and **hour**. It will be important for the student to listen carefully to the sound at the beginning of words in this activity and not look at the first letter alone.

Activity 1. Have the student turn to the activity sheet which accompanies this lesson. Read through the definitions at the top of the page. The first activity asks the student to place the articles **a** or **an** before words. If possible, have the student say each word before determining the correct article. The answers to the activity are: **a, an, a, an, a, a, a, an, an, a.**

Activity 2. The next activity asks the student to determine if the article placed in front of each word is correct or incorrect. Again, it will be helpful if the student can read the word aloud while completing the activity. The correct responses are: **I, C, C, C, C, C, I, C, I, C.**

Activity 3. The final activity continues with adding the article **a** or **an** before words in sentences. Like the previous activity, it will be helpful if the student can read the words aloud before determining which article to use. The answers to the activity are as follows:

1. **A** butterfly landed on **a** flower.
2. **A** party was held at **a** swimming pool.
3. **An** alligator floated in **a** swamp.
4. **An** hour before bedtime, Devin liked to read **a** book.
5. **A** muffin is **a** good food to eat at breakfast.
6. Carle flew **a** kite in the wind.
7. **A** concert was being held in **a** park.
8. Emily wanted **a** new dress for Easter.
9. **An** eagle landed on **a** nest.
10. Mrs. Riley lost **an** earring.

Reading Activity.

1. Ask the student to read the selection entitled, "The African Elephant."

2. After the student has read the selection, use the following questions to lead a discussion. What is one way you can tell an African elephant from an Asian elephant? (**The shape of the**

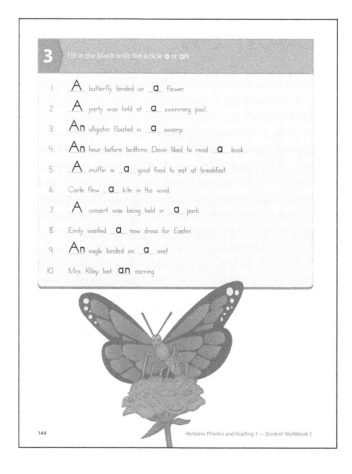

ears of an African elephant is in the shape of Africa. A female African elephant has tusks.) Why is an elephant's trunk important? (**The trunk is used to smell, gather water, and grasp objects.**) Why don't elephant's sleep much? (**Elephants spend much of their time looking for food. Elephants require a great deal of food each day.**) How does an elephant use its tusks? (**It uses the tusks to dig for water and roots.**) Why do people hunt elephants? (**People often hunt elephants for their tusks which are made of ivory.**) What is one interesting fact you have learned about elephants? (**Allow for individual answers.**)

3. This is a selection that has many examples of the use of articles **a** and **an**. Have the student locate three examples where **a** and **an** were used. Have the student explain why each article was used at each place.

Lesson 147
Commonly Confused Words

Overview:

- Understand the differences among words which are commonly confused

- Identify words which are commonly confused

- Use words which are commonly confused correctly

Material and Supplies:

- Teacher's Guide and Student Workbook

- White board or chart paper

- Phonics flashcards

- Reader: "Let Dogs Delight to Bark and Bite"

Teaching Tips:

Review for Mastery. Discuss and review any work from the previous lesson that was assigned as homework. Check for completion of the activities and orally quiz the student for comprehension. Review any reading that was assigned, discussing the characters, setting, plot, theme, language, sequence, etc.

Strengthen fluency and phonemic awareness by reviewing words and sentences from the previous lessons. Build vocabulary skills by using some of the words in sentences.

Create flashcards of words which are commonly confused. The student can study these throughout the unit.

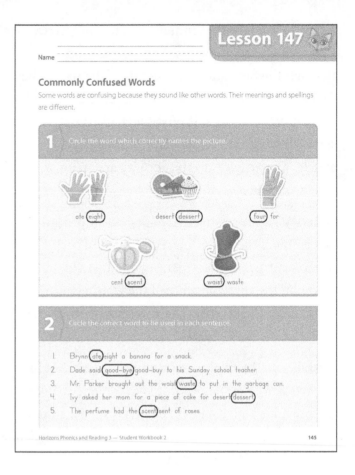

Lesson Introduction. Write the following sentence on the board: **I eight ate carrots.** Ask the student if there is anything wrong with the sentence. The student should recognize that the two words **eight** and **ate** should trade places. Tell the student that this lesson will begin a study of words which are commonly confused. Some are words which sound alike but are spelled differently. Others are words that people often misuse. You may wish to discuss with the student words that he/she may sometimes confuse.

Activity 1. Turn to the activity sheet which accompanies this lesson. The student will look at a picture. Two different words will be used to identify it. The student will need to determine the correct word. The answers are: **eight, dessert, four, scent, waist.**

Activity 2. The lesson continues with the student identifying the correct word to complete each sentence. After the student has finished the activity, have the student read the sentence aloud. The correct responses are: **ate, good-bye, waste, dessert, scent, four, hole, desert, buy, whole**.

Activity 3. Next the student will need to find commonly confused words in a word search. As an added activity, ask the student to say or write a sentence using each of the words he/she will need to find in the word search. **See image for answers.**

Reading Activity.

1. Have the student read the selection entitled, "Let Dogs Delight to Bark and Bite." You may want to read the poem to the student first and then have the student read the poem back to you.

2. Begin by asking the student how the poem was written. (**The poem was written in four-line stanzas. It follows an abab rhyming format. The lines are syllables of 8686.**)

3. Discuss the poem with the student. What qualities did the author say were different between animals and children? (**Animals fight and growl at each other but children should not.**) Who should children try to behave like? (**They should try to behave like Jesus.**) What specific qualities or actions should children follow? (**They should follow Christ's example of being kind, gentle in soul, and growing in favor with God and man.**) What relationship does God have with His children? (**He sees the children as His own.**) Why do you think the author wrote the poem? (**He wanted to encourage children to act and be more like Christ. The author may have also known children who were fighting and wanted to write about the problems of this behavior.**)

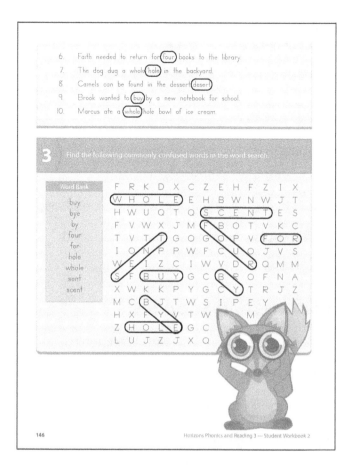

Lesson 148
Commonly Confused Words

Overview:

- Understand the differences among words which are commonly confused
- Identify words which are commonly confused
- Use words which are commonly confused correctly

Material and Supplies:

- Teacher's Guide and Student Workbook
- White board or chart paper
- Phonics flashcards
- Reader: "Theodore Roosevelt"

Teaching Tips:

Review for Mastery. Discuss and review any work from the previous lesson that was assigned as homework. Check for completion of the activities and orally quiz the student for comprehension. Review any reading that was assigned, discussing the characters, setting, plot, theme, language, sequence, etc.

Strengthen fluency and phonemic awareness by reviewing words and sentences from the previous lessons. Build vocabulary skills by using some of the words in sentences.

You may want to create flashcards of words which are commonly confused. The student can study these throughout the unit.

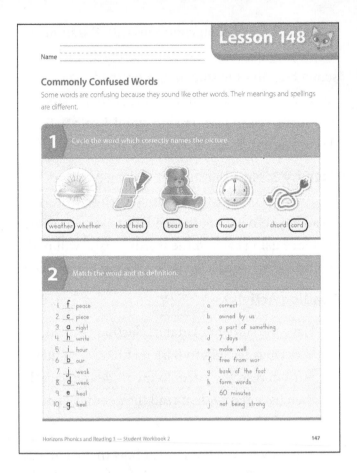

Lesson Introduction. The student will continue the study of commonly confused words. Write the following sentence on the board: **She did not right the write answer on her paper.** Ask the student what is wrong with this sentence. The student should recognize that the words **right** and **write** need to trade places in order for the sentence to make sense. Tell the student in this lesson the study of commonly confused words will continue.

Activity 1. Ask the student to turn to the activity sheet which accompanies this lesson. Read through the description at the top of the sheet. The student will be presented with a picture and two possible answers. The student will need to choose the word that correctly goes with the picture. The answers to the activity are: **weather, heel, bear, hour, cord.**

Activity 2. The lesson continues with a matching activity. The student will need to match the word with its meaning. The answers to the matching activity are: 1.—**f**, 2.—**c**, 3.—**a**, 4.—**h**, 5.—**i**, 6.—**b**, 7.—**j**, 8.—**d**, 9.—**e**, 10.—**g**.

Activity 3. The final activity for this sheet asks the student to choose the correct word in each sentence. Two choices will be given and the student needs to decide which one is correct. The answers are: **weather, whether, wear, new, heels, knew, their, new, There, hour, piece, heal, one, week, write**.

Reading Activity.

1. The student should turn to the selection, "Theodore Roosevelt" Direct the student in reading the selection.

2. Discuss the selection with the student. Describe Theodore Roosevelt's childhood. (**He was sickly and spent most of his time indoors. He was taught at home. He learned a great deal about the outdoors.**) What happened to make Theodore Roosevelt president of the U.S.? (**He was serving as vice president when President McKinley was assassinated.**) What was Theodore Roosevelt famous for saying? (**Speak softly and carry a big stick.**) What did this saying mean? (**He meant that the U.S. needed to keep world peace. The U.S. also needed the weapons to back up their desire for peace.**) Why did Theodore Roosevelt and

others work to see the Panama Canal built? (**The Panama Canal would shorten the amount of time it took to travel between the Pacific and the Atlantic Oceans. People traveling from New York to California would no longer need to travel around South America.**) What did you learn about Theodore Roosevelt's love of nature? (Examples include: **He had a ranch in the Badlands. He went on an African safari. He worked to add land to the U.S. National Park System.**)

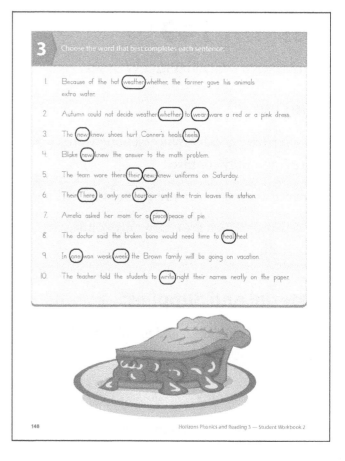

Lesson 149
Commonly Confused Words

Overview:

- Understand the differences among words which are commonly confused

- Identify words which are commonly confused

- Use words which are commonly confused correctly

Material and Supplies:

- Teacher's Guide and Student Workbook

- White board or chart paper

- Phonics flashcards

- Reader: "The Man and the Lion"

Teaching Tips:

Review for Mastery. Discuss and review any work from the previous lesson that was assigned as homework. Check for completion of the activities and orally quiz the student for comprehension. Review any reading that was assigned, discussing the characters, setting, plot, theme, language, sequence, etc.

Strengthen fluency and phonemic awareness by reviewing words and sentences from the previous lessons. Build vocabulary skills by using some of the words in sentences.

You may want to create flashcards with commonly confused words. The student can study these throughout the unit.

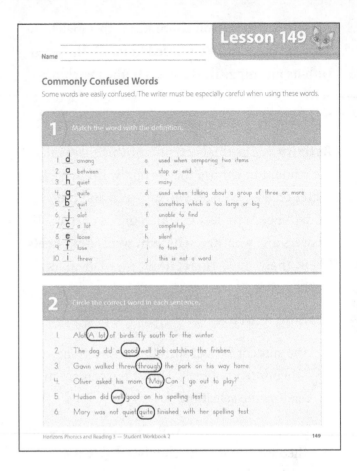

Lesson Introduction. Explain to the student that in this lesson the study of commonly confused words will continue. Write the following sentence on the board: **The dog sat among the tree and the fence.** Ask the student to identify the problem with the sentence. Help the student to recognize that the word **among** is misused. The word **among** should be replaced with **between**.

Activity 1. The student should turn to the worksheet which accompanies this lesson. Ask the student to read the definition at the top of the page. In the first activity the student will match words with their definitions. The student will need to determine the meanings of words commonly confused. The answers are: 1.—**d**, 2.—**a**, 3.—**h**, 4.—**g**, 5.—**b**, 6.—**j**, 7.—**c**, 8.—**e**, 9.—**f**, 10.—**i**.

Activity 2. The second activity is similar to the first. In this activity the student will need to choose the correct word to complete each sentence. Two words which are commonly confused are provided. The student will need determine through the context of the sentence which word is correct. The correct responses are: **A lot, good, through, May, well, quite, threw, filling, between, past.**

Activity 3. The last activity asks the student to use words from the Word Bank to complete sentences. After the student has completed the activity, have him/her read the sentences to you. The correct answers for the activity are: **May, quiet, it's, among, passed, can, its, past, between, quite.**

Reading Activity.

1. The student should read the selection, "The Man and the Lion."

2. Discuss the selection with the student. What discussion were the man and lion having? **(The two were discussing if a lion or a person was stronger.)** What conclusion did the man reach? **(The man said that people were stronger because they were smarter than lions.)** How did the man prove his point? **(He showed the lion a sculpture of a man defeating a lion.)** What did the lion think of this explanation? **(He pointed out that the sculpture was built by a person. A person would, of course, make the lion look defeated.)** Ask the student what type of statue a lion might make of a person and a lion? **(The student should recognize that the lion would have a different perspective where he would be the victor.)**

3. Discuss with the student other times in which people or groups might have different opinions or views of events. For example, discuss how the perspectives of a winning and losing team may differ. You could even challenge the student to write an article or story from two different perspectives.

Lesson 150

Review

Overview:

- Identify compound words
- Correctly hyphenate compound words
- Recognize clipped words
- Use the articles **a** and **an** correctly
- Understand the differences among commonly confused words

Material and Supplies:

- Teacher's Guide and Student Workbook
- White board or chart paper
- Phonics flashcards
- Reader: "The Cats Have Come To Tea"

Teaching Tips:

Review for Mastery. Discuss and review any work from the previous lesson that was assigned as homework. Check for completion of the activities and orally quiz the student for comprehension. Review any reading that was assigned, discussing the characters, setting, plot, theme, language, sequence, etc.

Strengthen fluency and phonemic awareness by reviewing words and sentences from the previous lessons. Build vocabulary skills by using some of the words in sentences.

You may want to review flashcards made for words in this unit.

Lesson Introduction. This lesson reviews the material the student learned in the unit. The student

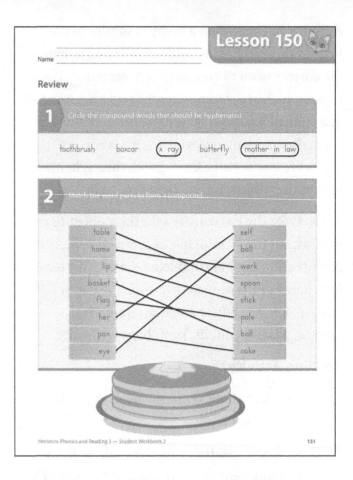

will complete activities which review compound words, clipped words, the articles **a** and **an,** and commonly confused words. Ask the student to give you an example of compound words with and without hyphens. Examples include **basketball,** **three-year-old, A-frame, light year,** and **butterfly.** Write the examples on the board. Next ask the student to give you examples of clipped words. These include **zoo** and **pants.** Again, write the examples on the board. Next ask the student to write the prefix **a** or **an** before the appropriate words on the board. Examples may include: **a basketball, a butterfly,** and **a zoo.** If no words appear requiring **an,** have the student give you an example of when the article might be used. Examples include: **an hour** or **an opera.** Ask the student to name some commonly confused words. The list may include: **ate, eight, among,** and **between.** Ask the student to use these words in sentences. The student could do this in either written or verbal form.

Activity 1. The student should turn to the activity sheet which accompanies this lesson. The review sheet is arranged in the same way as the test. In the test different examples will be used but the format will remain the same. The student will begin by determining in which compound words hyphens should be used. The answers are: **x-ray**, **mother-in-law**.

Activity 2. The review of compounds continues in the next section. The student will match words in order to create compounds. The answers to the activity are: **tablespoon**, **homework**, **lipstick**, **basketball**, **flagpole**, **herself**, **pancake**, **eyeball**.

Activity 3. The activity sheet continues with the student writing the clipped word for each longer word. The answers to the activity are: **pants**, **movie**, **zoo**, **phone**, **lunch**.

Activity 4. The next section asks the student to place the article **a** or **an** before the listed words. The answers to this section are: **a mouse, an honor, a beach, an owl, a hammer**.

Activity 5. The review finishes with the student looking at commonly confused words. The student will need to determine which word correctly completes each sentence. The student will need to pay careful attention to the context of the sentence in order to determine the correct word. The answers to the activity are: **eight, well, quiet, through, scent, dessert, among, ate**.

Reading Activity.

1. The student should turn to the selection, "The Cats Have Come To Tea."

2. Direct the student in reading this selection for pleasure.

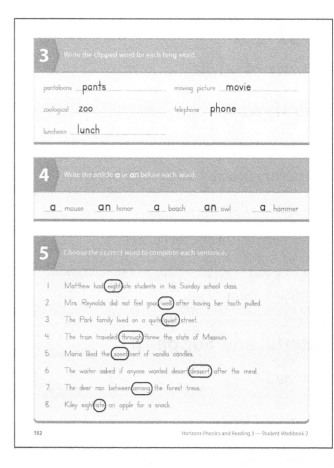

Test 15

Lessons 141-150

Overview:

- Identify compound words
- Correctly hyphenate compound words
- Recognize clipped words
- Use the articles **a** and **an** correctly
- Understand the differences among commonly confused words

Material and Supplies:

- Student Test

Teaching Tips:

Review for Mastery. Discuss and review any work from the previous lesson that was assigned as homework. Check for completion of the activities and orally quiz the student for comprehension. Review any reading that was assigned, discussing the characters, setting, plot, theme, language, sequence, etc.

Lesson Introduction. This lesson tests the material the student learned in the unit. Before the test you may want to ask the student if he/she has any final questions. There may be questions the student will want to review. Remind the student that the final test follows the same format as the review.

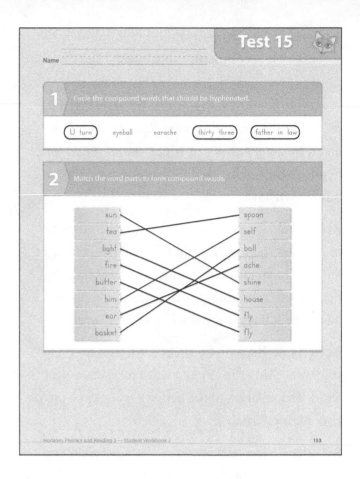

Activity 1. The student should turn to the test. The test is arranged in the same way as the review sheet. In the test different examples will be used but the format will remain the same. The student will begin by determining in which compound words hyphens should be used. The answers are: **U-turn, thirty-three, father-in-law**.

Activity 2. The testing of compounds continues in the next section. The student will match words in order to create compounds. The answers to the activity are: **sunshine, teaspoon, lighthouse, firefly, butterfly, himself, earache, basketball**.

Activity 3. The test continues with the student writing the clipped word for each longer word. The answers to the activity are: **fridge**, **bike**, **math**, **exam**, **tux**.

Activity 4. The next activity asks the student to place the article **a** or **an** before the listed words. The answers to this section are: **a meadow**, **a number**, **an actor**, **an olive**, **a purse**.

Activity 5. The test finishes with the student looking at commonly confused words. The student will need to determine which word correctly completes each sentence. The student will need to pay careful attention to the context of the sentence in order to determine the correct word. The answers to the activity are: **quite**, **desert**, **scent**, **filling**, **ate**, **good**, **passed**, **between**.

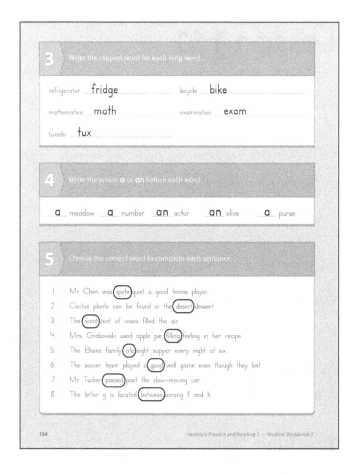

Lesson 151

Palindromes

Overview:

- Understand the meaning of palindromes
- Recognize words which are palindromes
- Use palindromes in sentences

Material and Supplies:

- Teacher's Guide and Student Workbook
- White board or chart paper
- Phonics flashcards
- Reader: "The Loom of Time"

Teaching Tips:

Lesson Introduction. Write the words **eye, bib,** and **civic** on the board. Tell the student you do not want them to focus on the meanings of the words. Instead, you want the student to focus on how the words are spelled. See if the student can find what is common among the words. Explain to the student that a **palindrome** is a word that is spelled the same forward and backward. Look at the words listed on the board. **Eye, bib,** and **civic** can be spelled the same forward and backward.

You may want to have the student create flashcards of words which are palindromes. The student can study these throughout the unit.

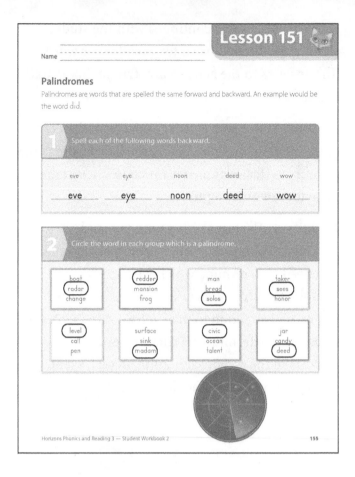

Activity 1. The student should turn to the activity sheet for this lesson. The first activity asks the student to spell the words backward. The student should recognize that the words will be the same. This will reiterate the fact that palindromes are spelled the same forward and backward. The answers to the activity are: **eve, eye, noon, deed, wow.**

Activity 2. The second activity continues by having the student identify the word in each box which is a palindrome. There will be only one palindrome per box. The correct responses are: **radar, redder, solos, sees, level, madam, civic, deed.**

Activity 3. The final activity asks the student to use words which are palindromes in sentences. A Word Bank is provided to assist the student in filling in the blanks. The answers to the activity are: **solos, kayak, radar, noon, sees, pop, eye, bib.**

Reading Activity.

1. The student should turn to the selection, "The Loom of Time." Before reading the poem, find a video of a person weaving with a loom. Explain that the poem will be about weaving.

2. Direct the student in reading the poem. After reading the poem, discuss it with the student. To what does the author compare the life of a person? **(The author compares life to a tapestry made on a loom.)** What types of thread does the weaver use? **(The weaver weaves threads of gold, silver, light, and dark colors.)** Who sees and doesn't see the pattern the weaver is making? **(The weaver knows the pattern but the person whose life is being woven does not.)** What is the meaning of the poem? **(The poem speaks of how God plans and cares for the lives of His people. God knows how the life of a person will unfold.)** How was the weaver's work described? **(It is done with skill and care. The weaver knows what the pattern will look like and when dark or light threads are needed.)** When is the pattern revealed? **(It is revealed when the weaving is finished or when a person's life is complete.)** Continue the discussion by talking about how God is at work in the life of the student.

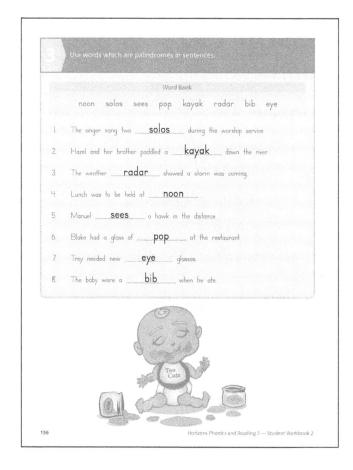

3. Ask the student what poetic form is used in the selection. **(The poem was written in four-line stanzas. The rhyme scheme for the first stanza is abab and the rest are abcb. The lines are syllables from 6 to 10.)**

Lesson 152

French Words

Overview:

- Know the meaning of words which have their origin in the French language

- Recognize that the English language has borrowed words from other languages

- Use words taken from French in sentences

Material and Supplies:

- Teacher's Guide and Student Workbook

- White board or chart paper

- European map

- Phonics flashcards

- Reader: "The Adventures of the Little Field Mouse"

Teaching Tips:

Review for Mastery. Discuss and review any work from the previous lesson that was assigned as homework. Check for completion of the activities and orally quiz the student for comprehension. Review any reading that was assigned, discussing the characters, setting, plot, theme, language, sequence, etc.

Strengthen fluency and phonemic awareness by reviewing words and sentences from the previous lessons. Build vocabulary skills by using some of the words in sentences.

You may want to create flashcards of words borrowed from the French language. The student can study these throughout the unit.

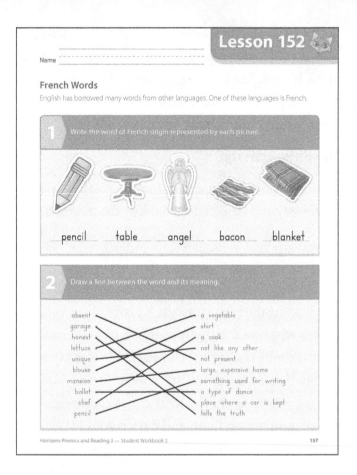

Lesson Introduction. Tell the student that over the years the English language has borrowed words from other languages. Sometimes these words have remained the same as in their original language and other times they have changed.

Show the student a map of Europe. Identify England for the student. Explain that this is where the English language had its start. Next, identify the country of France. Show the student the close distance between England and France. Explain that throughout history England and France often fought each other for the same land. While we normally do not speak about the benefits of war, one of the positive results was that the English took many French words into their language. Examples of some common words which have their origins in the French language include: **pencil**, **table**, and **calendar**.

Activity 1. The student should turn to the worksheet for this lesson. Explain that the student will need to identify the pictures at the top of the page. The words identified all have their origins in French. The words pictured are: **pencil**, **table**, **angel**, **bacon**, **blanket**.

Activity 2. Continue the activity by having the student match the word with its meaning. The student should draw a line from the word to its definition. The answers to the activity are as follows:

absent	not present
garage	place where a car is kept
honest	tells the truth
lettuce	a vegetable
unique	not like any other
blouse	shirt
mansion	large, expensive home
ballet	a type of dance
chef	a cook
pencil	something used for writing

Activity 3. The student will continue the lesson by answering the clues to finish the crossword puzzle. You may want to go over the answers before the student completes the crossword puzzle. A Word Bank is provided to assist the student. The answers to the clues are:

Across:
2. **embrace**
4. **calendar**
7. **jail**
9. **hotel**
10. **tailor**

Down:
1. **jewel**
3. **bandage**
4. **chapel**
5. **absent**
6. **prayer**
8. **addition**

Reading Activity.

1. Direct the student in reading the selection, "The Adventures of the Little Field Mouse."

2. Lead a discussion of the selection. What did the little mouse chase? (**He chased an acorn.**) Where did his chasing lead? (**It led him to the** house of a little man under the tree.) What was the little man like? (**He made the field mouse work for him. He would not let him leave the house.**) Why was the field mouse able to finally leave the house? (**The door did not close when the little man locked it.**) Where did the mouse find the acorn? (**It was hidden near the fireplace.**) What did the mouse find within the acorn? (**He found a beautiful necklace.**) What did he do with this necklace? (**He gave it to his sister.**) How would you describe the behavior of the mouse? (**He was curious, which got him into trouble. He was clever, which allowed him to notice when the door was not locked. He was generous when he gave his sister the necklace.**) Do you think the little man knew about the necklace? (**Answers will vary. Have the student explain his/her answer.**)

3. You may want to direct the student in drawing a picture of one of the scenes from the selection.

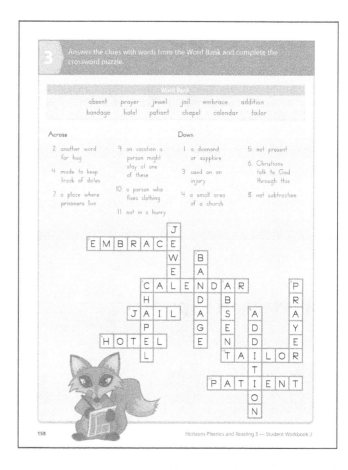

Lesson 153
Dutch Words

Overview:

- Identify words which come from the Dutch language
- Use words which come from Dutch in sentences
- Know the meaning of words which come from the Dutch language

Material and Supplies:

- Teacher's Guide and Student Workbook
- White board or chart paper
- European map
- Phonics flashcards
- Reader: "My Bed is a Boat"

Teaching Tips:

Review for Mastery. Discuss and review any work from the previous lesson that was assigned as homework. Check for completion of the activities and orally quiz the student for comprehension. Review any reading that was assigned, discussing the characters, setting, plot, theme, language, sequence, etc.

Strengthen fluency and phonemic awareness by reviewing words and sentences from the previous lessons. Build vocabulary skills by using some of the words in sentences.

You may want to create flashcards of words which come from the Dutch language. The student can study these throughout the unit.

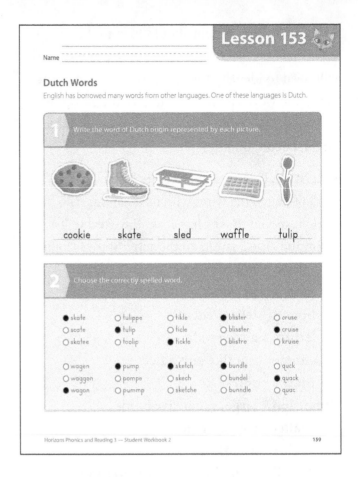

Lesson Introduction. Explain that in this lesson the student will continue the study of words borrowed from other languages. Take out the map of Europe. Have the student identify England. Ask the student to identify the country of the Netherlands. Tell students that although the Netherlands is a small country, it had a big influence on other nations because of its ships. Not only did these ships bring goods back and forth to other countries, they also brought the Dutch language to other places. Some of the words borrowed from the Dutch language include: **skate**, **cruise**, and **boss**.

Activity 1. The student should turn to the activity sheet which accompanies this lesson. The first activity asks the student to identify pictures of words which come from the Dutch language. The answers to the activity are: **cookie, skate, sled, waffle, tulip.**

Activity 2. The next activity asks the student to continue their study of words from the Dutch language. The student will see a word in each line spelled three different ways. The student will need to determine the correctly spelled word. The answers to the activity are: **skate, tulip, tickle, blister, cruise, wagon, pump, sketch, bundle, quack.**

Activity 3. The lesson continues with the student completing sentences with words from the Word Bank. After completing the sentences, you may want to have the student read them aloud. The correct answers are: **blinking, caboose, quack, waffles, boss, pickles, snack, blister, wagon, smack.**

Reading Activity.

1. The selection for this lesson is, "My Bed is a Boat." Ask the student to read the poem to you.

2. What is the format of the poem? (**The poem is composed of four-line stanzas. The rhyme scheme is abab. The lines are syllables of 8888.**)

3. Discuss the selection with your student. With what did the author compare his bed? (**A boat.**) How did the author carry these comparisons throughout the poem? (**He spoke of a sailor's coat, sailing away, the shore, and a pier.**) What happened as the boy sailed from shore? (**He fell asleep and dreamed.**) What did the child take on his voyage? (**He sometimes took cake or a toy.**) If you were to compare your bed to

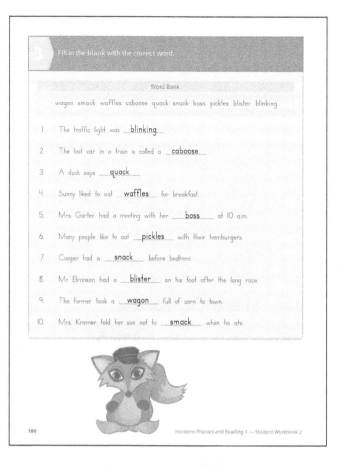

something what would it be? (Answers could include: **a race car, a horse, a castle.**) As an added activity, have the student draw a picture of his/her bed in this new form.

4. Have the student think of other things that could be compared with a bed. Examples may include car, tree, or cloud. Have the student write a poem using one of these comparisons.

Lesson 154

Greek Words

Overview:

- Recognize words that come from the Greek language
- Identify words which have Greek origins
- Use words which come from the Greek language in sentences

Material and Supplies:

- Teacher's Guide and Student Workbook
- White board or chart paper
- European map
- Phonics flashcards
- Reader: "The Ransom of Red Chief: Part I"

Teaching Tips:

Review for Mastery. Discuss and review any work from the previous lesson that was assigned as homework. Check for completion of the activities and orally quiz the student for comprehension. Review any reading that was assigned, discussing the characters, setting, plot, theme, language, sequence, etc.

Strengthen fluency and phonemic awareness by reviewing words and sentences from the previous lessons. Build vocabulary skills by using some of the words in sentences.

You may want to create flashcards of words that come from the Greek language. The student can study these throughout the unit.

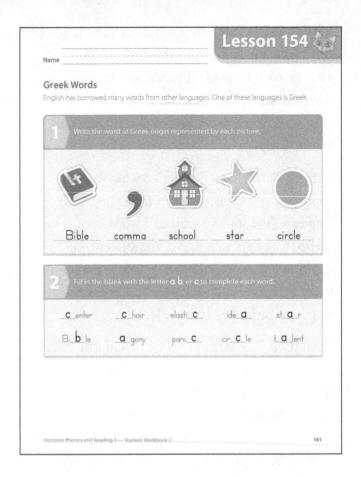

Lesson Introduction. The student will continue the study of words borrowed from other languages. Take out the map of Europe. Locate England and Greece. Explain to the student that many words in English have Greek roots or parts. In this lesson the student will look at words which have been borrowed from the Greek language. Examples include: **Bible**, **athlete**, and **star**.

Activity 1. The student should turn to the activity sheet which accompanies this lesson. Read through the information at the top of the activity sheet. The student will be asked to identify the pictures in the first activity. The answers to the activity are: **Bible**, **comma**, **school**, **star**, **circle**.

Activity 2. In the next section, the student will need to add the letter **a**, **b**, or **c** to the words listed. The student may want to have a piece of scratch paper to practice each word before filling in the blank on the activity sheet. The answers to the activity are: **center, choir, elastic, idea, star, Bible, agony, panic, circle, talent.**

Activity 3. The final activity asks the student to complete each sentence with the correct word from the Word Bank. After the student has correctly finished the activity, you may want to read the sentences aloud. The correct responses are: **choir, cost, athlete, rhyme, circus, theater, hero, history, stomach, center.**

Reading Activity.

1. The student should turn to the selection, "The Ransom of Red Chief: Part I." Explain to the student that this selection will be divided into three parts. The student will read the first part in this lesson.

2. You may want to begin by reading the selection to the student. The characters do not use proper grammar and this may at first seem awkward to the student. Once you have read a few paragraphs, have the student join you in reading the selection.

3. Direct the student in reading the selection on their own, or you may want to take turns reading the dialogue. You may want to have the student read it silently. After reading the selection, discuss it with the student. Who is telling or narrating the story? (**The leader of the pair of kidnappers.**) Who is his partner? (**Bill Driscoll**) Where were they when they decided to kidnap the boy? (**Summit, Alabama**) Why did they choose Summit for

the kidnapping? (**The town did not have many reporters or police officers. They felt they could quickly get their ransom and move on to their next scheme.**) Who did they choose to kidnap? (**They chose to kidnap a child of a well-known and wealthy citizen. They hoped to get a large ransom for him.**) What type of person was the little boy they kidnapped? (**He was a fighter. Bill ended up with bites and scratches. He had red hair and pretended to be an Indian chief.**) How did the boy react to being kidnapped? (**He thought it was a wonderful game. He loved camping and hanging out with the men.**)

4. Ask the student to predict what might happen next in the story.

Lesson 155

German Words

Overview:

- Recognize words which come from the German language

- Identify the meaning of words which come from the German language

- Use words which come from the German language in sentences

Material and Supplies:

- Teacher's Guide and Student Workbook

- White board or chart paper

- European map

- Phonics flashcards

- Reader: "The Ransom of Red Chief: Part II"

Teaching Tips:

Review for Mastery. Discuss and review any work from the previous lesson that was assigned as homework. Check for completion of the activities and orally quiz the student for comprehension. Review any reading that was assigned, discussing the characters, setting, plot, theme, language, sequence, etc.

Strengthen fluency and phonemic awareness by reviewing words and sentences from the previous lessons. Build vocabulary skills by using some of the words in sentences.

You may want to create flashcards of words which come from the German language. The student can study these throughout the unit.

Lesson Introduction. This lesson will continue the study of words borrowed from other languages. Again take out the map of Europe. Have the student identify the countries of England and Germany. Tell the student that many of the German words used in English have to do with food. These include: **noodle, hamburger,** and **pretzel**. In this lesson the student will study these and other words which come from the German language.

Activity 1. The student should turn to the activity sheet which accompanies this lesson. Like the other lessons on borrowed words, this one begins with the student identifying pictures of words which come from German. The answers to the activity are: **hamburger, pretzel, poodle, clock, clown**.

Activity 2. The next activity has the student identifying words which rhyme with the first word in each line. The first word in the line comes from the German language. The rhyming words do not necessarily come from the German language. The correct answers to the activity are: **quake, pickle, collar, pocket, bring, poodle, loop, pole**.

Activity 3. The student should look at the final activity on the sheet. The student will be asked to choose a word which best completes each sentence. Both word choices come from German. You may want to have the student read each sentence aloud in order to hear how the word is used. The answers to the activity are: **brake, muffin, waltz, rocket, icebergs, kindergarten, tackled, sling, dollar, clock**.

Reading Activity.

1. The student will continue reading the selection, "The Ransom of Red Chief: Part II."

2. Have the student recall the events and characters in the first section of the reading. Review as well the predictions the student made.

3. Direct the student in reading the second part of "The Ransom of Red Chief." You may want to take turns reading the dialogue with the student.

4. Use the following questions to lead a discussion of the selection. What do you learn is the name of the narrator? **(Sam)** Why was Bill yelling when he woke up? **(Their captive was trying to scalp him.)** How did Bill change after his near scalping? **(He quit sleeping and he wasn't as excited about the plan. He was nervous and afraid.)** What do you learn about the characters through the way they speak? **(You learn that the two men who are doing the kidnapping are not educated. They use incorrect grammar and also the word ain't. The boy is enthusiastic and excited. He likes to talk and has lengthy speeches.)** What

surprised Sam when he looked down on the village? **(No one seemed to be looking for the boy.)** What demands did the kidnappers make of Mr. Dorset? How was this different from their original plan? **(They asked for a $1500 ransom. They had originally planned to ask for $2000. They were eager to get the boy off of their hands.)** What game did Bill and Red Chief play while Sam delivered the letter? **(Bill acted as the horse while the boy rode on his back for a long distance. Red Chief decided he wanted to play the character Black Scout for the day.)**

5. Ask the student to predict what will happen next. Do you think the ransom will be received?

Lesson 156

Latin Words

Overview:

- Understand words which come from Latin

- Remember the meaning of words which come from Latin

- Use words which come from Latin in sentences

Material and Supplies:

- Teacher's Guide and Student Workbook

- White board or chart paper

- European map

- Phonics flashcards

- Reader: "The Ransom of Red Chief: Part III"

Teaching Tips:

Review for Mastery. Discuss and review any work from the previous lesson that was assigned as homework. Check for completion of the activities and orally quiz the student for comprehension. Review any reading that was assigned, discussing the characters, setting, plot, theme, language, sequence, etc.

Strengthen fluency and phonemic awareness by reviewing words and sentences from the previous lessons. Build vocabulary skills by using some of the words in sentences.

Create flashcards of words which come from Latin. The student can study these throughout the unit.

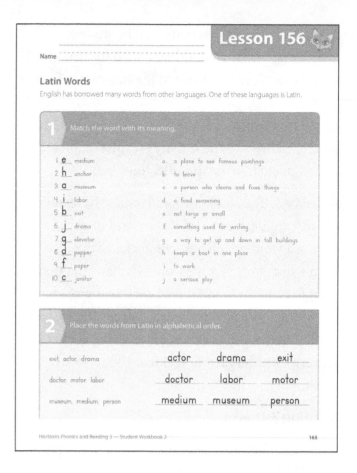

Lesson Introduction. Take out the map of Europe. Ask the student to identify the country of England. Next ask the student to identify the country of Latin. The student will soon notice that there is not a country named Latin. Explain that Latin is the name of a language that was used by people who once lived in what is now Italy. Latin was a very important language in history and many of our English words have their origins in Latin. While the Latin language is still studied today, it is no longer spoken. The words in this lesson will have their origins in Latin.

Activity 1. Have the student turn to the activity sheet which accompanies this lesson. The student will begin the lesson by matching words with their meanings. All of the words are ones borrowed from Latin. The answers to the activity are: 1.—**e**, 2.— **h**, 3.— **a**, 4.— **i**, 5.— **b**, 6.— **j**, 7.— **g**, 8.— **d**, 9.— **f**, 10.—**c**.

Activity 2. The second activity asks the student to put the words from Latin in alphabetical order. The answers are as follows:

> actor, drama, exit
> doctor, labor, motor
> medium, museum, person
> echo, elevator, focus
> favor, janitor, junior
> anchor, honor, object
> horizon, paper, pepper
> area, city, gradual

Activity 3. The final activity asks the student to write sentences with words which come from Latin. Examples of sentences including the words follow:

1. **Mr. Randall took exit 57 off of the interstate.**
2. **The doctor put a cast on the boy's broken leg.**
3. **Carmen took the elevator to the seventeenth floor.**
4. **The third grade student took a trip to the local museum.**
5. **The cook seasoned the meat with salt and pepper.**

Reading Activity.

1. Have the student summarize the characters and events up to this point in the selection, "The Ransom of Red Chief." Recall the predictions made in the previous lesson.

2. Ask the student to read the rest of the selection, "The Ransom of Red Chief: Part III." After reading the selection, discuss it with the student. What happened to Bill the day he spent with the boy? (**He was ridden like a horse, fed sand, and kicked.**) What did the note from the boy's father say? (**He said that they needed to pay $250 for him to take the boy back.**) What was Bill's reaction to the note? (**He thought they were getting a good deal!**) How did they manage to get the boy home? (**They told him**

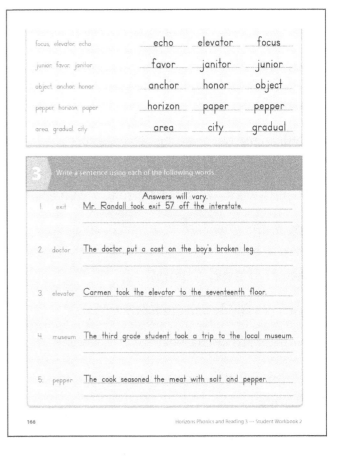

his dad had bought a gun and moccasins.) What did the kidnappers do after returning the boy? (**They left town quickly.**)

3. Continue by discussing the selection in its entirety. What is the tone or mood of the selection? (**The selection is humorous. The men think they are going to make money by taking this boy from his family. Instead, they are forced to pay money.**) How did the author make sure that you understood the lightheartedness of the selection? (**He used clever phrases and interesting dialogue. The author made it clear that the boy thought this was a great adventure and the kidnappers were miserable.**)

4. As an added activity, have the student detail another event that happened between Bill and the boy. The student could also write a description of how the boy would describe his time with Sam and Bill to his father.

Lesson 157

Spanish Words

Overview:

- Understand the meaning of words borrowed from the Spanish language

- Identify words which are borrowed from Spanish

- Use words which are borrowed from Spanish

Material and Supplies:

- Teacher's Guide and Student Workbook

- White board or chart paper

- European map

- Phonics flashcards

- Reader: "Make Me a Picture of the Sun"

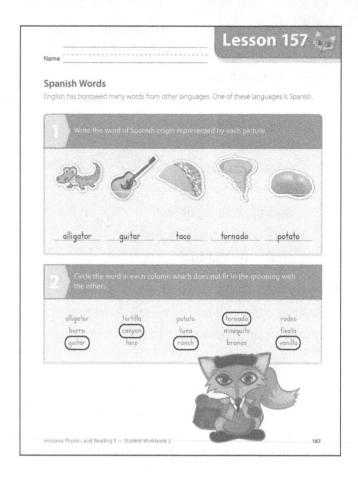

Teaching Tips:

Review for Mastery. Discuss and review any work from the previous lesson that was assigned as homework. Check for completion of the activities and orally quiz the student for comprehension. Review any reading that was assigned, discussing the characters, setting, plot, theme, language, sequence, etc.

Strengthen fluency and phonemic awareness by reviewing words and sentences from the previous lessons. Build vocabulary skills by using some of the words in sentences.

Create flashcards of words which are borrowed from Spanish. The student can study these throughout the unit.

Lesson Introduction. Tell the student that this lesson will continue the study of words borrowed from other languages.

Once again take out the European map. Ask the student to identify the countries of England and Spain. Explain that the Spanish had a large empire and seafaring influence much like England. In fact, Spain and England fought wars which again brought the two languages into contact. Spain was also influential in settling North and South America. Some of the words used to identify items in the Americas were taken from Spanish. Examples include: **alligator** and **llama**. Other words brought into English were: **ranch**, **rodeo**, and **salsa**.

Activity 1. Turn to the activity sheet which accompanies this lesson. The student will need to identify pictures of words which come from the Spanish language. The words pictured are: **alligator, guitar, taco, tornado, potato.**

Activity 2. The next activity has words grouped in trios. All the words in the trio are borrowed from Spanish. In each grouping, two of the words have something in common. They may be animals, foods, or something else. The student will need to identify the word which does not belong in each grouping. You may want to do the first one with the student to make sure the activity is understood. The answers to the activity are: **guitar, canyon, ranch, tornado, vanilla.**

Activity 3. The final activity asks the student to find words borrowed from Spanish in a word search. **See image for answers.**

Reading Activity.

1. Have the student read the selection entitled, "Make Me a Picture of the Sun."

2. Ask the student to read the poem silently and then read it to you. Use the following questions to discuss the poem with the student. What pictures does the author want to hang in the room? **(She would like a picture of the sun and a robin.)** Why does she want these pictures? **(She wants to pretend that it's summer. She wants the days to be warm and the robins to be singing.)** What seasons does she want to skip? **(She wants to skip the winter frost and the russet-colored leaves of fall.)** Continue discussing the poem with the student by asking what his/her favorite season is. Have the student explain any seasons he/she might want to skip.

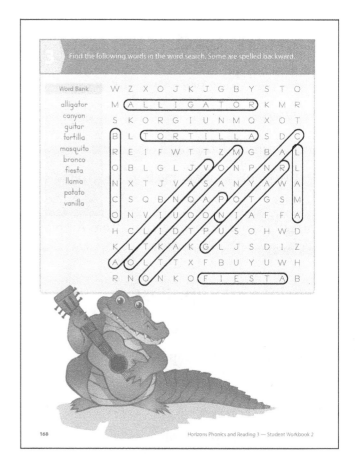

3. Discuss the way in which the poem was written. **(The poem is written in three stanzas. The first two stanzas have four lines and the last stanza has six lines. There tend to be either eight or six syllables in a line.)** While some of the end lines rhyme or nearly rhyme, this is not a focused pattern. The words have a sing-song quality to them.

Lesson 158

Arabic Words

Overview:

- Learn words which come from Arabic
- Identify words which come from the Arabic language
- Correctly use words which come from Arabic in sentences

Material and Supplies:

- Teacher's Guide and Student Workbook
- White board or chart paper
- World map
- Phonics flashcards
- Reader: "Ostriches"

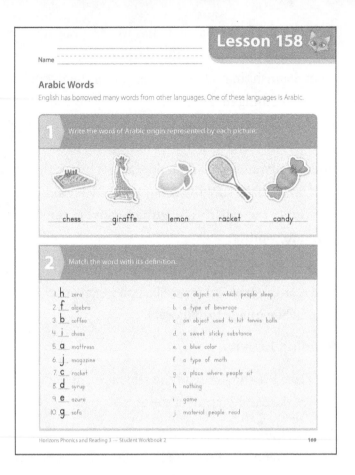

Teaching Tips:

Review for Mastery. Discuss and review any work from the previous lesson that was assigned as homework. Check for completion of the activities and orally quiz the student for comprehension. Review any reading that was assigned, discussing the characters, setting, plot, theme, language, sequence, etc.

Strengthen fluency and phonemic awareness by reviewing words and sentences from the previous lessons. Build vocabulary skills by using some of the words in sentences.

You may want to create flashcards of words which come from Arabic. The student can study these throughout the unit.

Lesson Introduction. The student will continue the study of borrowed words. Take out a map of the world. Tell the student that until this lesson, the borrowed words studied have all come from Europe. In this lesson the student will learn about words which were borrowed from Arabic. On a map, point out the Arabian Peninsula. Explain that

the people of this area, along with the surrounding areas, spoke Arabic. The people from Europe traded with those from the Middle East. The trading of goods also resulted in the trading of words. Examples of words borrowed from Arabic include: **coffee**, **chess**, and **zero**.

Activity 1. Ask the student to turn to the activity sheet which accompanies this lesson. The first activity asks the student to identify the pictured words. Be prepared to help the student spell some of the words. At this point in the lesson, the correct spelling is less important than identifying words which come from Arabic. The correct answers are: **chess**, **giraffe**, **lemon**, **racket**, **candy**.

Activity 2. The lesson continues with the student matching words from Arabic with their definitions. You may want to read through the words on the list with the student to make sure each is correctly pronounced. Tell the student to match the words they know well first and then go on to match those they may not know as well. The answers to the activity are 1.—**h**, 2.—**f**, 3.—**b**, 4.—**i**, 5.—**a**, 6.—**j**, 7.—**c**, 8.—**d**, 9.—**e**, 10.—**g**.

Activity 3. The final activity for this sheet asks the student to identify the word which is used incorrectly in each sentence. The incorrectly used word is borrowed from Arabic. Next the student will use a word from the Word Bank which correctly completes the sentence. These words are also borrowed from Arabic. If time permits, have the student read the corrected sentences aloud. The correct responses to this activity are as follows:

1. Toby opened a <u>giraffe</u> of peanut butter. **jar**
2. Mr. Lee enjoyed a cup of <u>sofa</u> in the morning. **coffee**
3. Mrs. James wrote a <u>gerbil</u> for the cost of her son's piano lesson. **check**
4. The <u>sugar</u> bush has purple blossoms in the spring. **lilac**
5. The family flew to Africa to go on a <u>mattress</u>. **safari**
6. Lilly wanted a <u>jar</u> for a pet. **gerbil**
7. The actor wore a <u>giraffe</u> on stage to hide his identity. **mask**
8. Miss Cameron needed a cup of <u>algebra</u> for the recipe. **sugar**
9. Johnny put maple <u>cotton</u> on his pancakes. **syrup**
10. The answer to the math problem was <u>candy</u>. **zero**

Reading Activity.

1. Before reading the selection, ask the student what he/she knows about ostriches. Write the student's responses on the board.

2. Direct the student in reading the selection, "Ostriches." After reading the selection, discuss it with the student. How are ostriches different from other birds? (**Ostriches do not fly and they are the fastest-running birds on land.**) How do people use the feathers from the ostrich? (**People use them in hats, clothing, decorations, and feather dusters.**) How do ostriches protect themselves from predators?

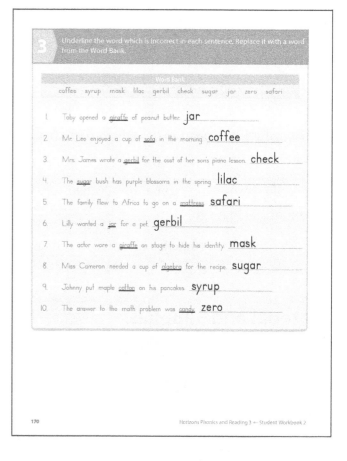

(**Ostriches have excellent eyesight so they can see their predators in the distance. Ostriches are able to outrun many of their predators. Ostriches can also kick hard enough to kill a lion.**) Describe an ostrich egg. (**An ostrich egg is as large as a cantaloupe. It is equal to about 24 chicken eggs. The shell of an ostrich egg is very hard. Eggs from numerous ostriches are all laid in the same nest.**) Ask the student to share one interesting ostrich fact he/she has learned. (**Answers will vary.**)

3. As an added activity, have the student cut out paper the size of an ostrich's egg and the size of a chicken's egg. The student can compare the size of these eggs.

Lesson 159

Native American Words

Overview:

- Know the meaning of words which come from Native American languages

- Identify words which come from Native American languages

- Use words which come from Native American languages in sentences

Material and Supplies:

- Teacher's Guide and Student Workbook

- White board or chart paper

- World map

- Phonics flashcards

- Reader: "The Ostrich"

Teaching Tips:

Review for Mastery. Discuss and review any work from the previous lesson that was assigned as homework. Check for completion of the activities and orally quiz the student for comprehension. Review any reading that was assigned, discussing the characters, setting, plot, theme, language, sequence, etc.

Strengthen fluency and phonemic awareness by reviewing words and sentences from the previous lessons. Build vocabulary skills by using some of the words in sentences.

You may want to create flashcards with words borrowed from Native American languages. The student can study these throughout the unit.

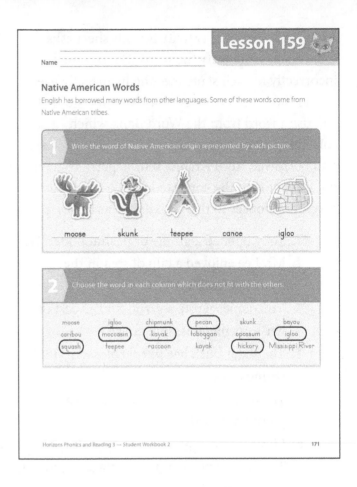

Lesson Introduction. Explain to the student that this lesson will continue the discussion of words taken from other languages. Take out a map of the world. Point to England and then to North America. Explain that when people from England settled in North America, they interacted with Native Americans. In North America, the English encountered animals and foods which were unfamiliar to them. The English borrowed the Native American words to describe these things. There was not one Native American language. Earlier in the unit the student learned that Europeans did not all speak the same language. Instead people from different countries or regions spoke different languages. The same was true in North America. For the purpose of this lesson, the student will look at words which came from various North American tribes.

Many place names also came from Native Americans. Examples include the states of **Illinois**, **Oklahoma**, and **Minnesota**. The **Mississippi** River's name also comes from the Native American language. Other borrowed words include: **canoe**, **raccoon**, and **igloo**.

Activity 1. The student should turn to the worksheet which accompanies this lesson. Ask the student to read the information at the top of the page. In the first activity the student will identify pictures of words which are borrowed from Native American languages. The answers are: **moose**, **skunk**, **teepee**, **canoe**, **igloo**.

Activity 2. The second activity is similar to the first. In this activity the student will need to identify the word in each line which does not fit with the other two. As an added activity, have the student pronounce each of the words aloud. The correct answers to the activity are: **squash**, **moccasin**, **kayak**, **pecan**, **hickory**, **igloo**.

Activity 3. The last activity asks the student to identify the correct word to be placed in each sentence. The student will be given two choices for each sentence and should identify the correct one. Have the student read each sentence to you upon completing the activity. The answers to this activity are: **pecans**, **igloos**, **kayak**, **moose**, **skunk**, **squash**, **toboggan**, **hickory**, **chipmunk**, **moccasins**.

Reading Activity.

1. The student should read the poem "The Ostrich." This is a poem that is fun to read aloud. Have the student read the poem first silently and then have the student read it to you.

2. Discuss the poem with the student. How does the poet view the ostrich? (**The poet thinks that the ostrich is silly and not very smart.**) How does the poet show that she thinks the ostrich is silly and not real smart? (**She describes the ostrich as running around**

without any purpose.) How does the poet's view compare with that of what you know about the ostrich? (**The student may see that an ostrich is more intelligent than what the poet describes.**) Have the student provide some examples of an ostrich's abilities. Ask the student why a poet might write a silly poem about an ostrich. (Answers may include: **An ostrich is a rather funny-looking bird. The author may have been in a silly mood and wanted to play with words.**)

3. Discuss the way in which the poem was written. (**The poem was written in two stanzas of four lines. The rhyme scheme is abcb. The lines are syllables of 8686.**)

Lesson 160

Review

Overview:

- Recognize words which are palindromes
- Identify words which are borrowed from other languages
- Use words borrowed from other languages in sentences

Material and Supplies:

- Teacher's Guide and Student Workbook
- White board or chart paper
- World map
- Phonics flashcards
- Reader: "A Fly and a Flea in a Flue"

Teaching Tips:

Review for Mastery. Discuss and review any work from the previous lesson that was assigned as homework. Check for completion of the activities and orally quiz the student for comprehension. Review any reading that was assigned, discussing the characters, setting, plot, theme, language, sequence, etc.

Strengthen fluency and phonemic awareness by reviewing words and sentences from the previous lessons. Build vocabulary skills by using some of the words in sentences.

You may want to review flashcards made for words in this unit.

Lesson Introduction. This lesson reviews the material the student learned in the unit. The student will complete activities which review palindromes and words borrowed from other

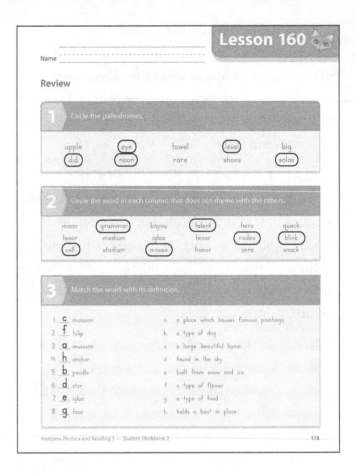

languages. Begin by reviewing words which are palindromes. Ask the student if he/she can remember the meaning of the term palindrome. A palindrome is word that is spelled the same forward and backward. Ask the student to think of words which are palindromes. Examples include: **level**, **dad**, and **solos**.

The student also studied words which came from other languages. Ask the student to recall the countries or regions where words borrowed from have come. The student should remember words coming from France, the Netherlands, Greece, Germany, Italy, Spain, the Middle East, and North America. Ask the student how these borrowed words came into English. The student may recall that the interactions in war, trade, and settlement all brought words from other languages into English. Have the student recall three animal names that have come from other languages. The student may remember the following names: **poodle**, **giraffe**, and **skunk**.

Activity 1. The student should turn to the activity sheet which accompanies this lesson. The review sheet is arranged in the same way as the test. In the test different examples will be used but the format will remain the same. The student will begin by circling words which are palindromes. The palindromes listed in the group are: **eye, level, did, noon, solos.**

Activity 2. The rest of the lesson will review words borrowed from other languages. This activity asks the student to identify the word in each column which does not rhyme with the other two. All of the words listed are those borrowed from other languages. The words which do not rhyme in each column are: **cell, grammar, moose, talent, rodeo, blink.**

Activity 3. The activity sheet continues with the student matching words with their definitions. Remind the student to start with those matches of which he/she is confident. Go on to complete those that may be unfamiliar. The answers to the activity are: 1.—**c**, 2.—**f**, 3.—**a**, 4.—**h**, 5.—**b**, 6.—**d**, 7.—**e**, 8.—**g.**

Activity 4. The final activity asks the student to complete sentences by filling in the blanks with the correct words. A Word Bank is provided to assist the student. This activity asks the student to use the words in context. The correct responses are: **jar, chess, mattress, choir, waffle, garage, stove, athlete.**

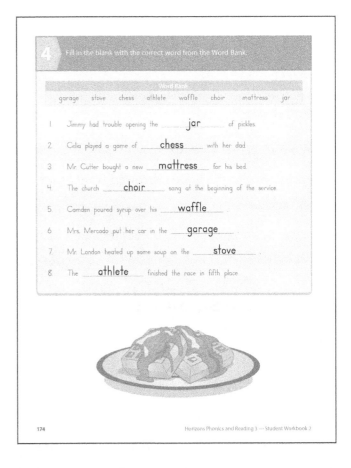

Reading Activity.

1. The student should turn to the selection, "A Fly and a Flea in a Flue."

2. The student should read this poem for fun. It is a tongue twister and should be read aloud. See how fast the student can read the poem.

Test 16

Lessons 151-160

Overview:

- Recognize words which are palindromes
- Identify words which are borrowed from other languages
- Use words borrowed from other languages in sentences

Material and Supplies:

- Student Test

Teaching Tips:

Review for Mastery. Discuss and review any work from the previous lesson that was assigned as homework. Check for completion of the activities and orally quiz the student for comprehension. Review any reading that was assigned.

Lesson Introduction. This lesson tests the material the student learned in the unit. Before the test you may want to ask the student if he/she has any final questions. There may be questions the student will want to review. Remind the student that the final test follows the same format as the review.

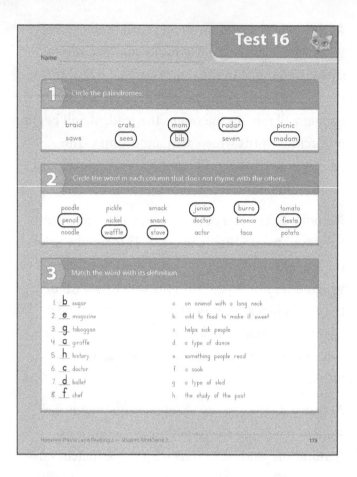

Activity 1. The student should turn to the test. The test is arranged in the same way as the review sheet. In the test different examples will be used but the format will remain the same. The student will begin by circling words which are palindromes. The palindromes listed in the group are: **mom, radar, sees, bib, madam**.

Activity 2. The rest of the test will focus on words borrowed from other languages. This activity asks the student to identify the word in each column which does not rhyme with the other two. All of the words listed are those borrowed from other languages. The words which do not rhyme in each column are: **pencil, waffle, stove, junior, burro, fiesta**.

Activity 3. The test continues with the student matching words with their definitions. The answers to the activity are: 1.—**b**, 2.—**e**, 3.—**g**, 4.—**a**, 5.—**h**, 6.—**c**, 7.—**d**, 8.—**f**.

Activity 4. The final activity asks the student to complete sentences by filling in the blanks with the correct words. A Word Bank is provided to assist the student. This activity asks the student to use the words in context. The correct responses are: **blanket, poodle, pickle, elevator, Bible, giraffe, racket, syrup.**

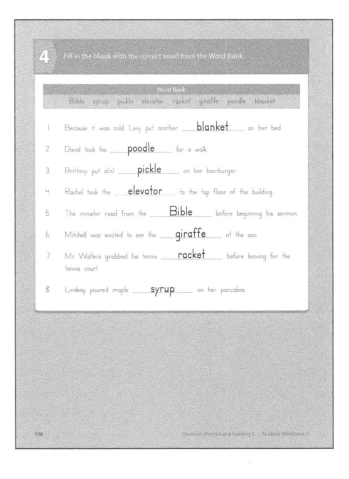